# SARA TEASDALE

## Woman & Poet

# SARA TEASDALE

## Woman & Poet

## WILLIAM DRAKE

◇

Published in San Francisco by
HARPER & ROW PUBLISHERS
New York Hagerstown San Francisco London

*For*
*Elizabeth*
*"It will not change now. . . ."*

SARA TEASDALE: Woman and Poet. Copyright © 1979 by William Drake.

All rights reserved. Printed in the United States of America. No part of this book may be used or reproduced in any manner whatsoever without written permission except in the case of brief quotations embodied in critical articles and reviews. For information address Harper & Row, Publishers, Inc., 10 East 53rd Street, New York, NY 10022. Published simultaneously in Canada by Fitzhenry & Whiteside Limited, Toronto.

**FIRST EDITION**

*Designed by Patricia Girvin Dunbar*

**Library of Congress Cataloging in Publication Data**

Drake, William D.
  Sara Teasdale, woman and poet.

    1. Teasdale, Sara, 1884–1933—Biography.
2. Poets, American—20th century—Biography.
PS3539.E15Z64                    811'.5'2 [B]                    79-1776
ISBN 0-06-250260-3

79  80  81  82  83  10  9  8  7  6  5  4  3  2  1

# Contents

# Preface

Sara Teasdale was one of the most widely read poets in America for over a decade preceding her death in 1933. She shrank from public exposure, however, and withdrew into a privacy that became almost pathological in her last years. Even the memoirs of her friends tended to shield her personality rather than to reveal it.

For nearly half a century after her death, Sara Teasdale's letters and other personal papers were, according to her wish, withheld from publication, so that she remained a shadowy figure, one of the few women poets in our history to escape the close study she deserves. Margaret Carpenter, in *Sara Teasdale: A Biography* (1960), gathered much information about her girlhood and youth in St. Louis from relatives and associates who have since died, and, although unable to quote from the unpublished materials, presented the first full length treatment of her life. Interest in her life and work have continued to grow with the increasing concern for feminine questions; her *Collected Poems* have gone into a new edition and other work has been reprinted. With the passing of Sara Teasdale's generation and virtually everyone associated with her personally, the reasons for refusing publication of her letters are, in the considered judgment of Margaret Conklin, Sara Teasdale's Literary Executor, no longer applicable. Miss Conklin has therefore generously approved my extensive quoting from the previously unpublished materials, so that Sara Teasdale's hidden life can be brought to light for the first time.

Sara Teasdale was remarkably methodical, entering each of her poems in a small notebook as she wrote it, and then dating it carefully and often noting where it was accepted for publication. It is possible, then, to reconstruct the chronology of her work with unusual fullness, to trace her development almost from day to day during her most productive periods, and to link the poems with circumstances of her life. She held concise views on the composition of poetry, which have been gathered here from scattered sources and used to illuminate her own practice.

It is not generally realized that Sara Teasdale was also a talented prose writer who ventured on rare occasions into fiction and criticism. Generous samples of her prose have been included in this study, both because they are little known and because of the particular interest they hold as the work of a poet.

Above all, the attempt has been made to view her life as a whole, to reconstruct the tragic history of a vivid and sensitive personality, with respect and sympathy.

San Francisco, May 1, 1979

# Acknowledgments

I am deeply indebted to the countless persons who assisted me throughout the writing of this book with their insights and ideas, their personal knowledge, their helpful criticism and encouragement, and the supplying of information and documentary materials.

My late wife, Elizabeth, herself a gifted writer, first led me to the subject and opened my eyes to its importance. She gave shape to my thinking, found the right word often when I could not, and left some of her genius lovingly infused in the design of this narrative. If I have succeeded in the portrayal of a woman's inner life, it is thanks to her. Where I falter, it is my own responsibility.

Margaret C. Conklin, Literary Executor for the Estate of Sara Teasdale, has generously given permission to quote from the letters of Sara Teasdale, almost all of which have been restricted and never before published. With the concurrence of the Morgan Guaranty Trust Co. of New York, Trustees of the Estate of Sara Teasdale, Miss Conklin has also granted me permission to quote selected lines and to paraphrase a number of Sara Teasdale's unpublished poems in order to illustrate her psychological and artistic development. This has been judged to remain within the terms of the Teasdale will, which forbids publication of any of her poems in full except those which she had marked for publication.

Margaret Conklin has graciously given me permission for unrestricted use of the manuscripts and notebooks for Sara Teasdale's unfinished biography of Christina Rossetti, and has arranged to have these materials remain sealed in the Wellesley College Library until publication of this book. I thank Miss Conklin also for permission to reprint Sara Teasdale's short story, "The Sentimentalist," which first appeared in *Smart Set*, vol.48 (April 1916), and to quote from Sara Teasdale's manuscript notes on the composition of poetry addressed to a Professor Lewis, 1922.

In addition to discharging her duties as literary executor with integrity and sensitivity, Margaret Conklin has also been of inestimable assistance to me throughout the writing of this book, correcting errors of fact where necessary and offering her own valuable reminiscences, while allowing me full freedom to treat the subject as I chose. I am privileged to count her as a cherished friend.

I am grateful to Margaret Haley Carpenter, author of *Sara Teasdale: A Biography* (New York, 1960), for sharing her collection of Teasdale memorabilia, which I have acknowledged with pleasure in footnotes throughout, and for her own published researches into the family background and youth of Sara Teasdale.

The late John Hall Wheelock granted me a memorable Saturday afternoon on February 15, 1975, talking candidly about his twenty-year close friendship with Sara Teasdale and providing information and psychological insight available from no one else. Mrs. J. H. Wheelock has kindly given me permission to quote from this tape-recorded interview as well as from his letters and other documents.

Mrs. Lisette Marsh and Mrs. Catherine Filsinger Hoopes, nieces of Ernst Filsinger, have graciously allowed me to quote from letters written by their uncle and from letters written by Sara Teasdale to members of the Filsinger family. The late Mrs. Irma Filsinger Wetteroth of St. Louis, Ernst Filsinger's sister, was warmly cooperative in supplying letters, photographs, new clippings, and other material in her possession, as well as her own remarkable insights and memories.

I am indebted to Lynda Marin for her expert close reading of this work in manuscript and her many suggestions for improvements in clarity and grace. I thank Carol Orr for her early encouragement of this study and her penetrating observations and advice. Virginia L. Radley also read portions of the manuscript and shared her valuable responses.

Dr. Dana Atchley, Sara Teasdale's personal physician, obligingly answered questions about her medical history, and Dr. M. E. Aronson, medical examiner for the City of Philadelphia, assisted me in interpreting the autopsy report on her death.

Among the many librarians and archivists who were helpful in locating and providing materials, I wish especially to thank Mrs. Frances H. Stadler of the Missouri Historical Society, St. Louis; Dr. Donald Gallup, Curator, Collection of American Literature, Beinecke Rare Book and Manuscript Library, Yale University; Diana Haskell, Curator of Modern Manuscripts, The Newberry Library, Chicago; and Eleanor L. Nicholes, Special Collections Librarian, Wellesley College.

I wish to thank the following institutions and individuals for permission to quote from manuscripts in their possession:

For a letter of Sara Teasdale to John Gould Fletcher, March 25, 1921, from the John Gould Fletcher Papers, University of Arkansas Library; for letters of Sara Teasdale to Jean and Louis Untermeyer, and to a Mr. Rosse, from the Poetry/Rare Books Collection of the University Libraries, State University of New York at Buffalo; for letters of Sara Teasdale and Ernst Filsinger to Harriet Monroe, from the *Poetry* papers, 1912–1936, the University of Chicago Library; for letters of Sara Teasdale, Ernst Filsinger, and Aline Kilmer to Jessie B. Rittenhouse, the Mills Memorial Library of Rollins College; for letters of Sara Teasdale to Amy Lowell, to John Reed, and to Witter Bynner, the Houghton Library, Harvard University; for letters of Amy Lowell to Sara Teasdale and to Jessie B. Rittenhouse, the Houghton Library, Harvard University, and G. D'Andelot Belin and Brinton P. Roberts, co-trustees under the will of

Amy Lowell; for a letter of Jessie B. Rittenhouse to William Stanley Braithwaite, Houghton Library, Harvard University, and Rollins College, trustee; for letters of Sara Teasdale to John Myers O'Hara, from the O'Hara Papers, The Newberry Library, Chicago; for letters of Sara Teasdale to Marion Cummings, from the Marion Cummings Papers, The Newberry Library, Chicago; for letters of Sara Teasdale and Ernst Filsinger to Eunice Tietjens, from the Eunice Tietjens Papers, The Newberry Library, Chicago.

Further, for letters of Sara Teasdale to Marguerite Wilkinson, the Library of Middlebury College; for a letter of Sara Teasdale to Thomas S. Jones, from the Thomas S. Jones Papers, Rare Book and Manuscript Library, Columbia University; for a letter of Sara Teasdale to William Greet, from the William Greet Papers, Rare Book and Manuscript Library, Columbia University; for two letters of Sara Teasdale to H. L. Mencken, from the H. L. Mencken Papers, Manuscripts and Archives Division, The New York Public Library, Astor, Lenox, and Tilden Foundations; for a letter of Sara Teasdale to Genevieve Taggard, from Miscellaneous Papers, Manuscripts, and Archives Division, The New York Public Library, Astor, Lenox, and Tilden Foundations; for a letter of Sara Teasdale to a Mr. Rosse, from the Henry W. and Albert A. Berg Collection, The New York Public Library, Astor, Lenox, and Tilden Foundations; for a memorandum by John Hall Wheelock, appended to a manuscript copy of Sara Teasdale's *Rivers to the Sea,* and for two letters of Sara Teasdale to Orrick Johns, from the Sara Teasdale Collection (accession no. 8170), Clifton Waller Barrett Library, University of Virginia Library; for a letter of Sara Teasdale to Mrs. Edwin Markham, the Library of Wagner College; and for the manuscripts and notebooks of Sara Teasdale's unfinished biography of Christina Rossetti, from the English Poetry Collection in the Special Collections of the Library of Wellesley College.

I wish to thank the Missouri Historical Society, St. Louis, for their permission to quote from the following manuscripts in their Sara Teasdale Papers: Letters of Sara Teasdale to Ernst B. Filsinger, to Vine Colby, and to Williamina Parrish; Williamina Parrish's "Notes on Sara Teasdale"; a letter of Jonathan Cape to Sara Teasdale; and letters of Williamina Parrish to Mrs. D. L. Parrish.

I thank the Beinecke Rare Book and Manuscript Library of Yale University for permission to quote from the following materials in their Collection of American Literature: The Travel Diary of Sara Teasdale, 1905; the Poetry Notebooks of Sara Teasdale, 1911–1932; and the letters of Vachel Lindsay to Sara Teasdale. I am also grateful to Nicholas Cave Lindsay for permission to quote from his father's letters.

I am indebted to Eleanor Ruggles for permission to use the photograph of Vachel Lindsay, 1913; Mrs. John Hall Wheelock for the photograph of J. H. Wheelock circa 1918; Charles Scribner's Sons for the photograph of J. H. Wheelock circa 1930; Mrs. Lisette Marsh and the late Mrs. Irma Wetteroth for the photographs of Ernst Filsinger; and Margaret C. Conklin for the photographs of Sara Teasdale and of herself.

The poem "Song, I," by John Hall Wheelock, is reprinted by permission of Charles Scribner's Sons from his *Poems New and Old*, copyright 1955.

The poem "I Heard Immanuel Singing," by Vachel Lindsay, is reprinted by permission from *The Collected Poems of Vachel Lindsay*, copyright 1914 by Macmillan Publishing Co., Inc., renewed 1942 by Elizabeth C. Lindsay. The poem "The Chinese Nightingale," by Vachel Lindsay, is reprinted by permission from *The Chinese Nightingale*, copyright 1917 by Macmillan Publishing Co., Inc., renewed 1945 by Elizabeth C. Lindsay. Selections from the Preface to *The Answering Voice*, revised edition, edited by Sara Teasdale, are reprinted by permission of Macmillan Publishing Co., Inc., copyright 1917, 1928 by Sara Teasdale Filsinger, renewed 1945, 1956 by Mamie T. Wheless. Selections from Sara Teasdale's comments on poetry in *New Voices*, revised edition, edited by Marguerite Wilkinson, Macmillan Publishing Co., Inc., 1936, are reprinted by permission of Margaret C. Conklin, Literary Executor for the Estate of Sara Teasdale, and Mrs. Nealy A. Chapin, Trustee for Marguerite Wilkinson.

The poems "The Little Love," "I Lived in My Life as a Dream," "The Strong House," "Shadows," "It Is Not I," "A Man Who Understood Women," and "Sleepless Night," published by Sara Teasdale in magazines but never printed in any of her books, are reprinted by permission of Margaret C. Conklin, Literary Executor for the Estate of Sara Teasdale. Selections from "Fear," "The Blind," "On the Tower," "By the Sea," and "The Princess in the Tower," from *Helen of Troy and Other Poems* (Copyright 1911 by Sara Teasdale), and "The House of Dreams" from *Sonnets to Duse and other Poems* (Copyright 1907 by Sara Teasdale), are reprinted by permission of Margaret C. Conklin, Literary Executor for the Estate of Sara Teasdale.

Lines from "To a Picture of Eleonora Duse in the 'The Dead City' " are reprinted with permission of Macmillan Publishing Co., Inc. from *Collected Poems* by Sara Teasdale, copyright 1907 by Sara Teasdale. Lines from "Testament," "The Star," and "New Year's Dawn-Broadway," are reprinted with permission of Macmillan Publishing Co., Inc. from *Rivers to the Sea* by Sara Teasdale. Copyright 1915 by Macmillan Publishing Co., Inc., renewed 1943 by Mamie T. Wheless. Lines from "The Treasure," "Oh You Are Coming," and "Since There Is No Escape," are reprinted with permission of Macmillan Publishing Co., Inc. from *Flame and Shadow* by Sara Teasdale. Copyright 1920 by Macmillan Publishing Co., Inc., renewed 1948 by Mamie T. Wheless. Lines from "Madeira from the Sea," "Guenevere," and "Pierrot" are reprinted with permission of Macmillan

Sleep," "Even To-Day," "Autumn on the Beaches," "In a Darkening Garden," "To the Sea," "Last Prelude," "To M.," and "Advice to a Girl" are reprinted with permission of Macmillan Publishing Co., Inc. from *Collected Poems* by Sara Teasdale. Copyright 1933 by Macmillan Publishing Co., Inc., renewed 1961 by Morgan Guaranty Trust Co. of New York, Executor.

# Works by Sara Teasdale

*Sonnets to Duse and Other Poems.* Boston: The Poet Lore Company, 1907.

*Helen of Troy and Other Poems.* New York: G. P. Putnam's Sons, 1911. Revised and reissued by The Macmillan Company, New York, 1922.

*Rivers to the Sea.* New York: The Macmillan Company, 1915.

*Love Songs.* New York: The Macmillan Company, 1917. Reissued in revised format, 1975.

*The Answering Voice; One Hundred Love Lyrics by Women,* selected by Sara Teasdale. Boston: Houghton Mifflin Company, 1917. Revised, with fifty recent poems added. New York: The Macmillan Company, 1928.

*Flame and Shadow.* New York: The Macmillan Company, 1920. Revised, London: Jonathan Cape, Ltd., 1924.

*Rainbow Gold; Poems Old and New Selected for Girls and Boys by Sara Teasdale.* Illustrated by Dugald Walker. New York: The Macmillan Company, 1922.

*Dark of the Moon.* New York: The Macmillan Company, 1926.

*Stars To-Night, Verses Old and New for Boys and Girls.* Illustrated by Dorothy Lathrop. New York: The Macmillan Company, 1930.

*A Country House.* With drawings by Herbert F. Roese. Borzoi Chap Books, #4. New York: Alfred A. Knopf, 1932.

*Strange Victory.* New York: The Macmillan Company, 1933.

*The Collected Poems of Sara Teasdale.* New York: The Macmillan Company, 1937. Reissued in new format, 1945; reissued with Introduction by Marya Zaturenska, 1966.

"It is all one, the coming or the going,
If I have kept the last, essential me. . . ."

# CHAPTER ONE

# Sara Teasdale and the Feminine Tradition

S ara Teasdale was born in St. Louis on August 8, 1884, the late and unexpected child of middle-aged parents —a circumstance of timing that shaped the course of her life. While younger parents struggling to advance their own lives and managing several other children might have been more casual, hers were driven to impose on her all the crippling inhibitions that summed up the Victorian middle-class ideal of feminine propriety and refinement. Shy, excruciatingly sensitive, almost an invalid, she was cast in the same mold as Christina Rossetti, Elizabeth Barrett, and Emily Dickinson and, like them, was gifted with a force of character and poetic talent that learned to thrive on pain. Unlike them, however, she was born into a later generation destined to revolt against the Victorian conventions in an explosive quest for freedom. At first shocked and then attracted by the new liberation, she lived in contradictory worlds of feeling. "Puritan and Pagan" or "Spartan and Sybarite," she called her warring selves that were locked in evenly matched combat. No matter who won, she observed, she herself would be the loser. In the end, the conflict cost her her life.

Sara Teasdale's place in American poetry has no parallel. Temperamentally, through the sheltered childhood that held her an unwilling prisoner of the past, she belonged to the tradition of women's poetry that flourished through the middle and late nineteenth century. But, thrown as she was into the conditions of a new age that arrived with shocking suddenness, she responded with courage, turning her girlish lyrics from conventional sentiment to a mature and unflinching exploration of the realities of her emotional life. Nowhere else in our literature has such a transition been recorded so clearly and articulately. She spoke for all women emerging from the humility of subservience into the pride of achievement, recognizing that her art sprang from the conflict of forces that pulled her in opposing directions.

The consciousness of the earlier women poets had never reached that point. "It is remarkable," writes Lionel Stevenson in *The Pre-Raphaelite Poets*, "that the principal women poets of the nineteenth century were all recluses, either from choice or by the compulsion of ill health. Emily Brontë, Christina Rossetti, and Emily Dickinson withdrew further and further from external contacts until their lives ended; Elizabeth Barrett followed the same course up to the age of forty, when she was forcibly emancipated by Browning. It is further noteworthy that all four belonged to closely knit family units fulfilling the needs of affection and intellectual stimulus."[1] Sara Teasdale might have followed that pattern if conditions had not drawn her out of it; and even then she constantly retreated into solitude and chronic illness despite marriage, career, and popular success. The nineteenth-century women poets forced themselves to accept and endure the life that custom had decreed, converting their deprivation into a kind of stoic strength. To Sara Teasdale and the younger poets, this was no longer possible. They left the protection and seclusion of their family home for the arena of life, although vulnerable and unprepared.

The pattern of life imposed on an intelligent girl of the Victorian middle class encouraged her in the creative arts, yet undermined her confidence and rendered her precariously unfit for practical success. Dabbling at music or drawing or verses was expected of a refined and educated young lady, like skill at embroidery, but the creative drive for achievement equal to that of men was an affront not easily tolerated. This is why, when women poets began to appear in abundance, they formed a distinctively feminine school of their own, limited by the conventions that governed middle-class women generally. Nevertheless, women of genius turned those limitations to advantage by expressing the complex pain their situation forced on them, not in the spirit of revolt, but simply in an undisguised and eloquent outcry. The result was, as Sara Teasdale wrote, that "for the first time in the history of English literature, the work of women has compared favorably with that of men."[2] In fact, there had been no comparable outburst of poetic achievement by women since Greece in the seventh century BC.

The chief theme of the feminine school of poetry was love. Byron had spoken for the century: Love was "woman's whole existence." Even the other major themes of religion, death, and beauty were related to that central concern. The feminine lyric cry was woman's supposed need for protective love, her ecstatic desire for submission to an ideal lover whose powerful personality would envelop her own. Trying dutifully to feel this way, however, gifted women found they were restive and at odds with themselves. The suppression of their own personalities contradicted the ambition for authorship, the instinctive desire for self-realization through their art rather than through a man. As a result, sensing themselves deprived of love by virtue of their own uniqueness, they wrote fatalistically of loves lost or unattainable. They learned to sustain themselves on denial, as in Emily Brontë's best poem, "Remembrance":

> Then did I learn how existence could be cherished,
> Strengthened, and fed without the aid of joy.

> Then did I check the tears of useless passion—
> Weaned my young soul from yearning after thine.

The dead love so powerfully evoked was largely imaginary. So, too, in a sense were Emily Dickinson's Reverend Wadsworth and Christina Rossetti's Charles Cayley, whose idealized attractiveness must have been based in part on their unsuitability for marriage. It is not the ecstatic union of lovers that is celebrated by the chief feminine poets, but rather its impossibility.

Their deprivation, squarely faced, could be turned by an act of will into martyrdom. To Emily Dickinson, love renounced was a crucifixion, and whatever merit might be earned in life was extracted "through Calvaries of Love." Both she and Christina Rossetti pictured themselves as secular nuns, their poems a kind of religious offering. Like Emily Brontë, Dickinson, too, could find a wild, triumphant despair in her losses.

The sensual aspect of love had no legitimate outlet in poetry, for any open expression of sensual feeling was absolutely forbidden in decent women. Nevertheless, it can be assumed that women with strong, creative personalities were plagued by emotions they were unprepared to accept or deal with in their art. They found their solution in the ecstatic love of beauty, whose seductive and sensuous appeal could also become a vehicle of exalted suffering, an expression of desire that simultaneously afflicted itself with pain. Christina Rossetti saw the appeal of the beautiful as temptation, portraying her heroine in "Goblin Market" assailed by a swarm of animated gargoyles trying to solicit her with offerings of luscious fruits, but, failing that, pressing them against her tightly closed lips until the juices ran down her face. Edmund Gosse thought "the sensuousness of it seems at first sight to contradict the austerity and voluntary sacrifice generally represented by the attitude of Christina. She is in her poetical capacity no withered nun or colourless anatomy, but full of the sap and glow of human emotion. This prophetess of renunciation is actually a hedonist. . . . She renounced not what it gives her no pain to renounce, but her very blood, her soul, and her senses."[3] Sensuous natural beauty was also intoxicating to Emily Dickinson's supersensitive nerves, threatening to overturn her balance, like exposure to the presence of someone loved. The passion of love, deprived of its rights and its natural object, flowed in other directions, seeking transfiguration. Sara Teasdale, who found the religious self-denial of the nineteenth-century poets repellent, was even more insistent than they on the crucifying agony of sensory beauty:

> Oh burn me with your beauty, then,
> Oh hurt me, tree and flower . . .
> Wound me. . . .4

These renunciations of love for men were morbidly suffused with a powerful attraction to death. The feminine poets habitually imagined themselves as dead, sometimes addressing their hapless lovers from their own graves: Christina Rossetti's "When I am dead, my dearest," and Sara Teasdale's "When I am dead and over me bright April/ Shakes out her rain-drenched hair." Emily Brontë, addressing a dead lover in "Remembrance," "Sternly denied" her soul's "burning wish to hasten/ Down to that tomb already more than mine." Emily Dickinson obsessively rehearsed her own funeral or identified herself with others dying or dead. Elizabeth Barrett Browning, rescued into marriage and wondering how she could possibly be really loved, pictured herself as "A poor, tired, wandering singer, singing through/ The dark, and leaning up a cypress tree." Death and love were ambivalently equated, voicing the fear of losing identity that lurked within the ideal love surrender. Many of Emily Dickinson's poems of giddy crisis, of falling, fainting, or hysteria are enactments of the love swoon, simultaneously desired and dreaded. Elizabeth Barrett Browning, who expressed grateful submissiveness in many of the *Sonnets from the Portuguese,* overtly identified her seizure by love with death in Sonnet 1:

> And a voice said in mastery while I strove—
> "Guess now who holds thee?" —"Death," I said. But, there
> The silver answer rang— "Not Death, but Love."

The fear and denial of love may have the same psychological effect as rejection by a lover, accompanied by a sense of inadequacy and low self-esteem. Perhaps feelings of frustration and worthlessness, and guilt at disobeying the command to give themselves in love, found a release through imagery of self-destruction.

The mysterious physical weakness and chronic ill health that afflicted so many of the women poets probably had their origin in that same mingled sense of inadequacy and self-denial. Illness was another penalty exacted for venturing into independent selfhood. It was widely believed that women could not bear the strain of creative or mental work as men could. Vern L. Bullough writes in *The Subordinate Sex* that "a Dr. Edward H. Clarke in 1873 argued that women could not possibly plan to devote the number of hours to schooling required to become educated and still hope to emerge whole and healthy women. He said their attempts to compete with men would only reduce them to unhealthy invalids and unfit childbearers."[5] Dr. Ralph W. Parsons, in an article entitled "The American Girl versus Higher Education, Considered from a Medical Point of View," in the *New York Medical Journal* in 1907, wrote that woman's "nervous system has been developed at the expense of other bodily organs and structure. The delicate organism and sensitive and highly developed nervous system of our girls was never intended by the creator to undergo the stress and strain of higher education, and the baneful results are becoming more and more apparent as the years go by."[6] The society that permitted women to work in factories or in fields at labor that would exhaust a man, professed alarm at the damage to their physical health that would result from using their minds.

Women who discovered through poetry that there was a life of self-fulfillment other than submission to love found their way barred at every turn. They could not appear to take their careers seriously and commonly deprecated their work publicly as insignificant or incidental, despite the earnest hours spent on it privately. They could not devote themselves to intellectual or artistic achievement without a profound sense of loneliness and inadequacy, for it meant abrogating their womanhood. The choice was intolerable. The most gifted women poets nevertheless renounced domesticity and submissiveness and made that renunciation their theme instead of the pieties they were supposed to celebrate. The great irony in the century that elevated love between men and women into a religion is that its chief poetic cry is thwarted passion, transfiguration through refusal rather than union, anguish and deprivation in place of joy. Women who had the capacity for free and independent artistic achievement, equal to men, were crippled in the restrictions that not only surrounded them but that also were implanted within their minds from childhood, undermining confidence and infusing their best efforts with a sense of guilt. To fight against these restraints made them enemies of themselves. Christian piety could render such a life tolerable through its doctrine of the saving grace of self-denial. But the new age was soon to preach that deprivation was a crime, self-fulfillment was everyone's right —including woman's.

Sara Teasdale's heritage was the divided self—a personality ready for self-fulfillment, rich in outgoing emotion, sensuous, and keenly sensitive, attuned to esthetic rather than moral imperatives, but stricken with a paralyzing obedience to the rigorous proprieties imposed on her in childhood, mainly by her mother. Sara withheld and privately worried her natural impulse of emotion before releasing it, so that she appeared reticent and austere, except to the few with whom she felt free. The shrinking from life just at the point of ebullience was the paradox out of which she produced her poems, balancing passion against restraint, easy flow against containment, apparent simplicity against suggested complexity, desire against despair. Tension was the keynote of her life, although she hid it beneath her gentleness and let it show least when it was most intolerable.

Kate Chopin's portrayal of Edna Pontillier in *The Awakening* seems applicable to Sara Teasdale: "Even as a child she had lived her own small life all within herself. At a very early period she had apprehended instinctively the dual life—that outward existence which conforms, the inward life which questions." Sara accepted joyfully, at first, the necessity that as a woman she should marry and live for her husband, although he was not the man she had really wanted romantically to marry. From the beginning, there were qualifications, for she had no aptitude for cooking or domesticity in general, and her public career was rising spectacularly, requiring attention. As the years passed, she gave up the idea of having children and gradually found that simply being married conflicted with the sense of being a free person in her own right. Her inward life compelled her in a direction that all the amassed weight of her background told her was selfish and wrong. She divorced her husband under conditions of bizarre secrecy to avoid scandal, suffering excruciatingly to injure a man who was devoted to her, who had indulged her as probably no one else would have done. It was impossible to explain to anyone why she had to do this in order to survive and remain true to herself. And so she lived an inviolate, secret, inner life in silent desperation under the surface of agreeability and normality, growing outwardly more calm as she resigned herself to the hopeless and painful contradictions of her life. Her work grew immensely in depth and mastery: she knew the price she was paying for it. But the continual presence of a shadow, a "great black vulture circling the sky," eventually eclipsed her mind; she took her life in January 1933, asking her friends to destroy her letters, prohibiting publication of all her unpublished poems she felt were imperfect, virtually trying to expunge the record of her personal self.

Her plight as a woman and a creative artist have since emerged as one of the critical concerns of our time, and her work can be better understood now than it was at the height of her popularity. "Under the leaf of many a Fable lies the Truth for those who look for it," she quoted at the beginning of a little verse play written in her twenties, inviting the reader to look for more beneath the neat surface of her art than she was willing to expose openly. When applied to all her work, it reveals the inward questioning of her outward existence, on which, in the long run, the value of her achievement will rest.

# CHAPTER TWO

# The House of Dreams

Sara Teasdale's childhood home was a citadel of safety from the world, a haven of comfort, quiet, and order. The house at 3668 Lindell Boulevard in St. Louis was presided over by her patriarchal father, John Warren Teasdale, whose silent dignity, kindness, and lofty sense of integrity always remained a source of consolation for her in stress or panic. He was forty-five when she was born. "Sara adored her father," according to the memoir of her friend Williamina Parrish; "he was really more like a grandfather to her, so great was the difference in their years."[1]

But if the calm, self-secure spirit of her father comforted her, the restless and insatiable force of her mother created tension within the seeming serenity of the household. Mrs. Teasdale, like Sara, had suffered a listless, sickly childhood. But on reaching eighteen she had undergone a metamorphosis and emerged full of driving energy, fiercely domestic, keeping house like a tiny commander of military forces. In contrast to her quiet husband, she talked incessantly and dominated her family through her irritable temperament. At least Sara saw it this way.

Mrs. Teasdale's house had to be perfect, reflecting the best taste and manners of the upper middle class with its pretensions of English aristocratic refinement. She collected Oriental rugs, loved to travel, and kept a maid and a cook. It was inevitable that at forty, with her values fixed, her house in order, and her husband's business doing well, she should view her late-arriving daughter as an object to be brought up in the most exemplary genteel fashion.

Having a child at forty, however, must also have been a shock and an

7

embarrassment. Victorian middle-class morality insisted that sexual relations were limited to producing children, and even the manuals of hy-
giene assumed that couples entering middle age were long past the years
of sexual intercourse. An unplanned pregnancy, fourteen years after her
childbearing years were presumably over, advertised her marital relations
to the world. Given the Teasdales' keen sense of propriety, one can
surmise the shame and resentment she must have felt. She would have
doubled her efforts to rear the child properly, to compensate for this
shadow on her reputation.

Sara was never treated as an unwanted child, an intrusion into the
settled lives of her parents. On the contrary, she was smothered with
anxious care and attention to an irrational degree. Perhaps her aging
parents were foolishly indulgent as grandparents would be, or perhaps
it was Mrs. Teasdale's belief that good breeding proved itself in a girl by
her delicacy and sickliness; there were plenty of models in popular literature of girls whose constitutional weakness was a mark of superiority, and
she herself was supposed to have been on the verge of death throughout
her childhood. If an ordinary cold threatened, Sara was put to bed and
treated as if she were dying of pneumonia. Her health was assumed to be
precarious—although there is no evidence that it actually was—and she
was constantly made to rest and save her strength. An apprehensive
parent creates by contagion a fear-ridden child; and so Sara suffered a
lifelong morbid anxiety about her health, a terror of death, and an obsessive wrapping of herself in layers of clothing and shawls. Jean Starr
Untermeyer wrote that Sara "told me that when she was a very young girl
in her native St. Louis, a physician had warned her she would always be
delicate because she lacked the last protective layer of epidermis."[2] Medi-
cally improbable as this is, it does express the excruciating sense of
vulnerability that haunted her from her earliest memories, voiced in her
early sonnet, "Fear":

> The cold black fear is clutching me to-night
> As long ago when they would take the light
> And leave the little child who would have prayed,
> Frozen and sleepless at the thought of death.[3]

Mrs. Teasdale's inflicting such a paralyzing sense of physical inadequacy on her daughter seems to go far beyond the simple desire for refinement and good breeding. One is inclined to see in it an expression of guilt
and resentment against this offspring whose birth embarrassed her as a
kind of sexual indiscretion, a hostility veiled by a cloud of parental over-
concern. Hence, the irrational anxiety over Sara's health and survival,
which would express both the hidden wish to be free of the child and a
compensatory public demonstration of lavish concern—crippling her, as
it were, with kindness and stifling her with inhibitions and a horror of

sexuality so she would not repeat her mother's error. Whatever the reasons, it is evident that a tangle of negative emotions underlay her mother's overgenerous treatment of her, emotions that had not been roused by her three older children. Eventually, Sara seems dimly to have sensed that beneath the exaggerated display of maternal anxiety was an adversary and to have looked to her father instead for emotional support.

But, like all well-mannered households, that of the Teasdales maintained on the surface its pleasant if somewhat rigid serenity. Sara was a placid, sweet-tempered, obedient child who learned early to suffocate all hostile feelings and be "nice" at all times. The oval face framed by long loose curls that gazes from her childhood photographs strikingly bears the same look she wore in maturity—a gentle willingness to please, the mask of a half-smile, a glint of intelligent and ironic amusement in the eyes. It was a face destined to be interesting rather than beautiful, much to her later chagrin. She bore herself with straight-backed propriety and moved with the sensitive restraint of a child bred indoors who never knew the physical vigor of playing with other children.

If she was the prisoner of good breeding, she was also pampered to a degree that awed her less well-to-do friends. "Sara lived the life of a princess in her tower, as far as I could see," wrote Williamina Parrish, who knew Sara when she still lived in the "fine old white stone-front house" on Lindell Boulevard. "Her family were very indulgent with her, and humored all her whims—quite as a duck family would humor a swan in their midst." She had no household chores, not even an expectation that she would ever learn how to manage a home or support herself by working, as if her life were to be a perpetual childhood. Her family were virtually her whole world, and they were all adults. Her sister Mamie, the only one she ever really liked besides her father, was seventeen when Sara was born and seems to have supplied the kind of uncomplicated maternal warmth lacking in her mother. Her brother George Willard was nineteen, and John Warren, Jr., was fourteen. She viewed both brothers with ironic detachment; at times, outright distaste. There were few other children in her early life, for she was always too "frail" to venture out into the street world, and she did not attend school until she was nine years old. Mamie tutored her at home, teaching her to read and cultivating her fondness for poetry.

In the isolation of her room, which Miss Parrish remembered as "quiet as a tomb," she would sit in "a sort of bay in the west wall with windows that looked north and south," and daydream. She very early learned to comfort herself and drive off insomnia by inventing stories "of what would happen if things were very nice." She wrote to the sonneteer John Myers O'Hara in 1909,

My earliest recollections are of just such story-spinning to myself when

I was a baby. I have always put myself to sleep with it, and I can remember the funny little tales I used to tell myself when I was a wee tot. A good many of them had to do with a lame boy who lived across the street and was about twelve or fifteen years older than I. It was long before I knew how to read, so you see I fell in love very early. I don't know why he had such a fascination for me unless it was that he played several instruments. I used to hear him on summer evenings. They had a beautiful lawn . . . and he used to play out under the trees. Sometimes the sheet-lightning would be shining fitfully—it always used to frighten me—but still he kept playing.[4]

She later tried to develop this memory into a poem, "Summer Nights," never published, in which the music of a mandolin player cannot quell her fear of the lightning as she lies awake in bed in the dark. Alone with the threatening storm, she turns for comfort to the sounds of music. The imagery epitomizes the meaning to her of her art, which grew out of that sheltered, apprehensive childhood when she spent so many hours fantasizing in solitude, converting her anxieties to stories and poems.

Sara, or "Sadie" as she was called until she was grown up, was also a very orderly child, with a surprisingly firm grasp of practical matters when it suited her. One side of her complex character was businesslike and quite unromantic. "Sara was nothing if not practical!" Williamina Parrish recalled. "She said to me once, 'perhaps if Miss Sadie were less methodical and if she could keep her bureau drawers in disorder and her life at loose ends, she would be a better poet.' But I think not. The absolute perfection of every line of hers is the reflection of herself—nothing in disorder or at loose ends. . . . In the scheme of life she had carved out for herself, many people could not possibly fit—she never allowed herself to burn *her* candle at both ends. This was the very essence of her. She could not have changed, no matter what the temptations from the outside. Her life was a fixed and ordered entity, into which other lives had to fit, if they entered hers at all. It never entered her head to fit herself to others."

This nature, so passive and given to daydreaming, so obedient to discipline, so stubbornly practical and orderly, was also sensuous and keenly responsive to physical sensation. Her feelings were vivid, "Sybaritic," as she later called them. She found ascetic self-denial simply unpleasant. Her languorous sickliness was a paralysis of emotional energy, not a lack of it. Everyone believed piously in her poor health, although she once said to Williamina Parrish, "I often wonder if I had been born into a family with no means if I would have had better health." Miss Parrish wondered too—"for in the hours I was with her she did not seem frail or weak, and she burned up energy at break-neck speed in her enthusiasms. What an infectious enthusiasm she had! Though her interest was limited to the things of art and beauty, in that range she was omniverous." Her mother told Sara that her first spoken word was "pretty." She was of the generation of James Joyce, nourished on the estheticism of the nineties, and she remembered her childhood for the intensity of her sensations in response to beauty, associating such experience with words and pictures she loved. One of her favorite poems was Christina Rossetti's "A Christmas Carol," with the lines

> Snow had fallen, snow on snow,
>   Snow on snow,
> In the bleak mid-winter
>   Long ago.

"I think that I liked it better than the other poems read to me partly because snow is mentioned in it," she told a newspaper interviewer in 1922. "I dearly loved snow. Another set of verses that I loved for the same reason, though, perhaps, these verses were not deserving the name of poetry, had some lines that ran, 'Oh, see it blow, the falling snow, in shadows far away.' These words were magical to me. I used to stand at the window during a snowstorm literally enchanted by their music."

When she was nine, in 1893, Sara was finally judged strong enough to start school. But it was only to Mrs. Ellen Dean Lockwood's private school for children one street away. She was apparently precocious, with her quick mind, her store of memorized poems and tales, and her association with adults, but she was shy with other children. Mrs. Lockwood, to her credit, was able to help Sara bridge the painful gap between the isolated, sheltered life she had led in her family and the normal social life of children her age. Sara never forgot Mrs. Lockwood's unfailingly patient attentiveness in drawing her out.

Mrs. Lockwood taught nature study in the poetic manner of the Victorians, which stressed appreciation of beauty along with careful observation and collecting of specimens. This seems to have instilled in Sara a lifelong interest in amateur botanizing and a sharp eye for natural facts, though little of the romantic naturalist carried over into her poetry, where nature simply provides a generalized setting for personal emotion, along with the streets of New York or the formal gardens of Paris. Eunice Tietjens, who spent much of the summer of 1913 with her at her family's summer home in northern Michigan, wrote of their daily walks in the woods or along the shore of Lake Michigan: "I have never known anyone so sensitive to certain aspects of nature as Sara, or more influenced by them. . . . But she always talked concretely, of the wild plants by the stream bank which she knew by name every one." In later years, astronomy assumed the central place in her interest because of the abstractness and sense of fate in its infinite design, but even in 1913 "she used to keep a big chart of the heavens on her bedroom wall on which she had always pricked the position of the planets." She had no theoretical interest in scientific thought, however, except for the idea of evolution, which also appealed to her sense of an orderly destiny. Eunice Tietjens seems to have been responsible for first getting her to read a little book on evolution in that summer of 1913:

> One day while it was still fresh in her mind, on one of our walks we came upon an old jawbone, of a sheep perhaps or a donkey, with the teeth attached. There had been various pictures of dentition in the volume, and Sara pounced upon the bone at once with an intensity of interest that surprised me. . . . Suddenly Sara began to shine with her rare light. Squatting in the dirt in one of the lovely gray gowns she always wore—she was always exquisite in everything that belonged to her—she began to speak of the blaze of hope for mankind that the concept of evolution gives when one first grasps it.

But when she proposed taking the bone home for study—a habit Mrs. Lockwood had taught—Eunice burst out laughing, for "the picture of the none-too-savory jawbone of a modern donkey in Sara's dainty boudoir was too much for me. . . . The light went out of Sara's face, and with a ruefully humorous expression she rose and dusted herself off. Perhaps I did her a wrong. I never heard her speak of evolution again."[5] Despite the rebuff, the sensitive Sara did not lose interest in evolution, however, for in 1918 she wrote her mother-in-law, "I am reading with real delight Darwin's 'Origin of Species'. . . . I have always imagined it to be a dry deep book, far too learned for me, but to my surprise it is immensely entertaining and opens up vast vistas to me."[6] It remained an interest that can be traced in the thought underlying a number of her mature poems.

But more important to Sara than nature study at Mrs. Lockwood's school in the 1890s was reading. She always took her reading very seriously and tended to feel that her background was deficient, periodically launching into a systematic program of filling in the gaps. Perhaps Mrs. Lockwood instilled in her the methodical approach, because sometime before leaving the school at the age of thirteen she had begun to keep a record of her reading, and she later entered in a pocket-sized account book the "titles of only those books that I have read from cover to cover," starting with *Little Women.* The record continued, somewhat sporadically, for thirty years. She listed over a hundred books read during the years with Mrs. Lockwood, most of them standard girls' fiction of the time, like *What Katy Did* and *Polly Oliver's Problem,* but including a few scattered pieces of literary value by Shakespeare, Hawthorne, and Ruskin. Her girlhood reading was as unrelated to the realities of life as the sheltered way she herself lived, although this was characteristic of books written for girls. In her late teens, she read through the major fiction writers of the nineteenth century, with periods of infatuation for Scott and Dickens, even Cooper, and began a systematic reading and rereading of Shakespeare that continued for years. On the whole, the record shows a book-ish girl acquainted with the authors approved and recommended by teachers, mostly the English classics. The iconoclastic modernists, the great European innovators, were to come later, as something of a shock.

The Teasdales were assiduous summer travelers during these child-hood years. Sara wrote on the last page of her reading notebook a list of the family vacation spots from 1887 to 1903. They ranged the country from Wisconsin to New England, the Adirondacks, Colorado, North Carolina, the cities of Chicago, Boston, and Washington, and in 1898 a "Western trip as far as Cal." Sara retained all her life the love of respect-able old-fashioned resort hotels and inns with good food and attentive service. Traveling was as natural to her as staying home, perhaps even preferable, and like many intensely nervous, self-absorbed people she welcomed a trip as a way to shake off depression and regain a saner perspective, until later it became an habitual necessity.

When the five years at Mrs. Lockwood's school came to an end in 1898, Sara was placed in Mary Institute, which her sister Mamie had attended before her. This prestigious girls' school had been founded by T. S. Eliot's grandfather, the Reverend William Greenleaf Eliot, a New En-gland Unitarian minister, and Eliot himself spent the first sixteen years of his life in a house next door to the Institute. Probably it summed up the stifling, feminine-dominated atmosphere that sapped the manhood of the figures in his early poems. Eliot's mother and four sisters had all been students at Mary Institute. When speaking at the school's centenary in 1959, he told of playing in the deserted schoolyard and gymnasium on weekends, but fleeing once when he ventured on the grounds too early and faced a girl looking out a window at him.

But the daily trip by streetcar through the crowded city, often having to stand, proved too much for Sara. Accustomed to a sheltered atmos-phere and long hours of rest, of being taken care of, never having to endure physical inconvenience, she was so jostled and fatigued by the exertion of going to and from school that her parents withdrew her after the first year. She never believed she had strength for even the ordinary stress of daily life. The next year, 1899, she was enrolled in Hosmer Hall, another girls' school of high academic standing, but farther out from the city and requiring less strenuous travel. Occasionally she was driven to school in her father's carriage, an event that must have given her an air of privilege.

Sara was fortunate in her schooling, for probably no city in America outside New England experienced such an idealistic ferment over educa-tion as St. Louis in the latter half of the nineteenth century. The catalyz-ing influence flowed from New England to the community of German intellectuals in St. Louis, some of whom were refugees from the unsuccessful revolution of 1848. Emerson and Alcott were familiar lecturers there, and for a time New England transcendentalism provided a significant base of ideas for the St. Louis group. In contrast to the New Englanders, however, they were chiefly teachers rather than Unitarian ministers, and they thirsted for a program of action that would have a practical impact on society through education. W. T. Harris, a leader of the St. Louis movement, a participant in the Concord School of Philosphy, and editor of the *Journal of Speculative Philosophy,* was an administrator in the public school system and eventually became U.S. Commissioner of Education. Over a dozen others were professional teachers or principals of schools, in positions ranging from kindergarten to college. Another, Henry Conrad Brockmeyer, who labored for years on a translation of Hegel's *Larger Logic,* entered politics and served as governor of Missouri. Others wrote prodigiously in all fields, publishing novels, plays, treatises on philosophical theory, education, the arts, and law. The schools of St. Louis showed the impact of their ideals—their reverence for culture and admiration for high standards of intellectual performance. From the end of the Civil War until 1885 their movement made St Louis, then fourth largest city in America, one of the liveliest, intellectually. The influence emanating from the schools continued to affect the community for years, long after the great heyday of expansion.7

During the postwar boom, St. Louis had competed feverishly with Chicago to become the future capital of mid-America in population, wealth, and power, even dreaming of moving the national capital from the banks of the Potomac to the Mississippi. But the dream had failed by the 1880s, and Sara's generation grew up in the settled atmosphere of a large commercial city whose culture, although vigorous, was growing increasingly conservative.

Hosmer Hall, which Sara attended from 1899 until her graduation in 1903, had been founded in 1884 and liked to recruit its instructors from among the graduates of prestigious women's colleges such as Wellesley. The curriculum stressed preparation for college. Sara applied herself vigorously to French and German, and the entries in her reading notebook show the first listings of titles in those languages. She prided herself on her mastery of German script and did some translations of Heine, whose lyrics were often credited with being her first important poetic influence. Because of the vitality of the local German culture, she may have at first exaggerated its impression on her, for she did not keep up an interest in German language or literature for very long and only once traveled in Germany when abroad. She wrote to her sister-in-law, Irma Filsinger, in 1919, "I think that my love for German lieder may have had some slight influence—but after all, not much. Of course my first ventures were translations from German lyric poets."

If her first serious compositions were translations from German—a language spoken, taught, and published in St. Louis—she had been writing poetry privately before, for she told an interviewer in 1922 that "I wrote my first verses when I was a schoolgirl, and they were very bad, indeed. They were the result of an unhappy affaire du coeur. I was fifteen. One of the bad rhymes, 'dusk' and 'trust,' haunts me to this day." And she once wrote to Louis Untermeyer, "I remember that all my verses at the age of sixteen were parodies and attempts at humor."[8] At any rate, before graduation she was known to teachers and friends as a poet. With her sense of the ridiculousness of solemn public occasions, her self-deprecating irony, and her dread of exposure to the public, she probably felt more pain than pleasure when she was asked to compose a class song. She had declined the invitation to read any of her poems at graduation exercises. But the song was duly written and set to music by a local composer, and performed at graduation ceremonies on the evening of May 28, 1903, amidst "a billow of girls in sheer white," as Williamina Parrish remembered it. Mercifully, those words did not survive to haunt her. Four years after graduating, she did publish locally a "Sonnet Written for the Twenty-First Anniversary of the Hosmer Hall Literary Society," whose description of the students as "wanderers thro' Learning's maze" gives some idea of the poetic style on which she was nourished at school.

Her four years at Hosmer Hall are almost as shadowy as her childhood, for she left her usual impression of shy reticence and ill health, seldom participating in social events and associating with few friends. Her talent for versification was recognized and encouraged by her teachers, her reading tastes matured, and she responded vigorously to the intellectual discipline in language. But she would not have stood out in any conventional group of well-educated middle-class girls in her time. Certainly she could not have entertained any serious ideas about a career as a poet, and it is probable that at eighteen she viewed her life as stretching hazily ahead much as it had been in the past—living at home with her parents, burdened with the belief that ill health kept her from living normally, amusing herself with books and pictures and music, and dreaming indistinctly of lovers and eventual marriage.

The wide-ranging family vacations had stopped in 1901 when Sara's father, now in his sixties, no longer cared to travel. They had bought a summer home in Charlevoix, Michigan, where the rear windows looked out over the changing blue of the lake, with a wooded bluff and a stretch of sandy beach. Mr. Teasdale, a fancier of fine horses who never owned an automobile, shipped his horses to Charlevoix every season and kept a stable and a coachman, silently ignoring Mrs. Teasdale's frequent criticism of the expense. During those summers, Sara predictably found the sort of tranquil hideaway she always managed to create for herself wherever she went. Here, it was a little summer house on stilts looking out over the water, where she could withdraw from the family bustle and find peace to read and write.

The stimulus for her to approach her writing with professional seriousness came soon after graduation from Hosmer Hall, and she dated the real beginning of her artistic maturing from that year. Sometime in the summer of 1903, a friend in her class, Caroline Risque, brought Sara and Williamina Parrish together for the first time at her home, hoping they would become friends. Will, as her friends called her, was five years older than they, quick-witted, humorous, down to earth, with the instincts of an executive. She was probably abrasive at times, but her energy and goodwill seemed to dominate any group of which she was a part. She and her younger sister Grace were amateur photographers and enthusiasts for all the arts, throwing themselves unabashedly into painting, poetry, or acting, as they pleased. Williamina was a relentless critic who saw it her duty to help others develop their talents, and Sara seems to have been drawn to her commanding and energetic personality. Before long, other friends of Caroline Risque and Williamina Parrish joined them in a kind of loose-knit group with a common interest in the arts, and in 1904 they formed a club they called the Potters. Sara's first publishable work was done as a member of this group under Williamina's firm leadership.

The year 1904 was also the year of the great exposition commemorating the Louisiana Purchase, an extravaganza staged in part to prove that St. Louis was not second-rate despite its failure to become the major city of the mid-continent. The keynote of the fair—Universal Knowledge—bespoke the idealistic aspirations of the affluent middle class, so appropriate to the city's thirst for superiority, and there is more than a chance relationship between the occurrence of the exposition and the formation of a girls' club called the Potters in the same year. All the young women in the group were products of that upward cultural movement that had begun in the schools, had spread into women's clubs and societies supporting the arts, and had culminated by the turn of the century in a burgeoning of museums, exhibitions, performances, and quality journalism. It is no accident that Sara Teasdale's generation in St. Louis also produced T. S. Eliot, Marianne Moore, and scores of less well-known but reputable writers and artists.

St. Louis in 1904 was already a metropolis, a sprawling factory city under smoky skies, having little in common with the small-town culture surrounding it that stretched from Sherwood Anderson's Ohio to Willa Cather's Nebraska. The bitter loneliness of the unappreciated small-town intellectual, so often depicted in American fiction, had no counterpart in St. Louis, where the bright children of the business and professional class enjoyed a sense of cultural community, "discussed the new books and plays only a little later than New York and [were] stirred by nearly all the same influences," as Henry F. May writes in *The End of American Innocence.* "The writers who came from St. Louis, either to Chicago or later to the East, ... had no village in them."9 They were products of the urban middle class, representative of the so-called genteel culture earnestly fostered by the schools, societies, and women's clubs.

The Genteel Tradition, so important to understanding the development of American poetry at the turn of the century, defies concise definition and may prove to be only a convenient label for the middle-class cultural aspirations that prevailed between 1865 and 1915—in short, a name for an era rather than a definable tradition. Douglas Stenerson has conveniently summed up the genteel social pattern and its relation to the arts, particularly to women: "The tradition stressed the sanctity of the home, the sacredness of the marriage ties, and strict observance of a rigid code of conduct, especially by women. The proper concerns for most men were business, breadwinning, and politics. Religion, the arts, and cultural activities were primarily the domain of ministers, college professors, and women. In sexual matters, reticence was the rule. The mother was the guardian of her family's morals; the young girl was the exemplar of purity. Ideally, she should be protected from influences which might threaten her innocence or disturb her faith in the family code."10 This was the world of Sara Teasdale and her friends, and its strictures and ideals affected them more profoundly than they did the rebellious and innovative male poets of their generation—Frost, Eliot, and Pound—and partially explains the remarkable flourishing of women poets in that era.

The artistic culture into which the Potters threw themselves with such enthusiasm was suffused with an exalted ethical idealism that strove to lift poetry and the fine arts above the level of mundane reality. The British literary tradition and the classicism of the English Victorians dominated the schools and colleges, feeding the cult of ideal beauty against the realities of industrial strife, political corruption, commercial vulgarity, and the new realism and naturalism in literature. Women, especially, were supposed to be shielded from this unpleasant side of life.

But although the genteel culture has usually been denigrated in favor of the masculine artistic rebellion against it, the culture itself was the seed bed of the values and attitudes of the rebellious young, both men and women. If one considers the worst of it—the trite ideals, the repressive proprieties, the slavish commitment to the past—it was unquestionably ripe for attack. At their most intelligent, however, these same characteristics emerged as a genuine love of the beautiful, a respect for artistic discipline, a cultivation of sensibility, and a creative reassessment of the traditions of the past, values shared by rebels and conservatives alike. The young writers possessed a new cosmopolitan outlook, a sense of belonging to the European mainstream, a view of the earlier American authors as parochial and lacking in both sophistication and self-discipline. The

erratic individualism of the Romantics had given way to an admiration for
dedicated craftsmanship, an ambition to master a wide range of literary
forms and techniques and breathe new life into tired tradition. It was a
time of internationalism and cultural maturing, and without it there
would have been no revolution in the arts in the twentieth century. Above
all, it provided greatly expanded opportunities for women in the arts.

The name "Potters" signifies the central importance the young women
attached to skilled craftsmanship and professional seriousness. Beginning in November 1904, they prepared a magazine called *The Potter's
Wheel,* one elegantly hand-lettered and illustrated copy each month, em-
bodying their interest in all the arts, including decoration in the art
nouveau style. The poems, sketches, and reviews were all contributed by
the members. Their frequent meetings were marked as much by playful
camaraderie as by serious intellectual discussion, and there were personal
tensions beneath the surface of their cooperative venture, but they were
herded along and kept in hand by the breezy and dedicated Williamina
Parrish. Their idols were the famous actresses and singers of the day—
Julia Marlowe, Nazimova, Olga Nethersole, and Mary Garden, who frequently performed in St. Louis. Will and Grace Parrish photographed the
girls in costume, posing in the theatrical roles they admired or as characters in literature.

Sara's reading notebook shows a decided shift in direction under the
influence of the group, away from the conventional school classics to
popular trends of the times. One of their favorite authors was Fiona
MacLeod, pseudonym of the well-known Scottish writer William Sharp,
who later made a deathbed confession of his secret identity. The Potters,
of course, assumed the poet to be a woman. Fiona MacLeod's major
theme was the burden of women's suffering, written in the incantatory
manner of the Celtic twilight, as in this characteristic poem from *The Hills
of Dream,* a volume Sara read in 1904:

THE PRAYER OF WOMEN

Save us from the desire of men's eyes,
And the cruel lust of them.
Save us from the springing of the cruel seed
In that narrow house which is as the grave
For darkness and loneliness ...
That women carry with them with shame, and weariness, and long pain,
Only for the laughter of man's heart,
And for the joy that triumphs therein,
And the sport that is in his heart,
Wherewith he mocketh us,
Wherewith he playeth with us,
Wherewith he trampleth upon us.

The "Rune of the Passion of Woman" states a popular theme common to Sara's own early poetry, more baldly than she stated it herself:

> We who love are those who suffer,
> We who suffer most are those who most do love.

This expiation of masculine guilt for women's sexual suffering, by a man secretly playing the role of a plaintive woman poet, is one of the more interesting psychological involutions of that complex time. In the same season, Sara was also reading *A Doll's House.*

Sara's heavier reading, however, pursued one of the major thematic trends in late Victorian literature, the Arthurian romances. Now swept aside by the torrent of realism, these tales preoccupied the imagination of several generations, even the poets of revolt, and provided the most popular medium for dealing with the all-important questions of men-women relationships. In its evasion of unpleasant realities and its inveterate idealizing, the mind of the time dramatized some of its most sensitive problems through the ennobling imagery of medieval legend. These tales of courtly love were particularly the province of poetry and poetic drama, which had to portray life from the "higher" or ideal point of view, in contrast to the modernity and realism already established in serious fiction. They suited perfectly the genteel temper, too, with their glorification of Anglo-Saxon history and manners.

Intense interest centered on the tragic love stories of Launcelot and Guinevere and Tristan and Iseult, and the quest for the Holy Grail. Countless poets from Tennyson through Arnold, Swinburne, and Symons treated the tales, a vogue that ran well into the twentieth century with major works by Hardy, Masefield, Robinson, and Eliot. Wagner's *Tristan und Isolde* was held by Sara and her friends to be the supreme masterpiece of the century. Maeterlinck's *Pelléas et Mélisande,* another romance in the genre, was set to music by Debussy, Fauré, Sibelius, and Schoenberg. Sara had read *Idylls of the King* twice by 1904 and was into Book I of *The Faerie Queene.* Over the next two years, she read William Morris's "Defence of Guenevere," Swinburne's "Tristram of Lyonesse" (four times), a translation of the libretto of Wagner's *Tristan und Isolde,* and several modern prose retellings of the Tristan story. She was evidently planning a work of her own on themes from these sources.

Probably most influential, however, was her familiarity with Richard Hovey's four poetic dramas, *The Quest of Merlin, The Marriage of Guenevere, The Birth of Galahad,* and *Taliesen,* portions of a vast cycle left unfinished at his death in 1900 at the age of thirty-five. Sara read *The Marriage of Guenevere* for the third time in May 1904 and again "four or five times" the following year as she prepared her own blank verse monologue, "Guenevere," whose publication launched her career nationally in 1907.

Hovey was a perfect example of the transition between worn-out tradition and modernism, the position of poetic art when Sara began to write. As a student at Dartmouth he imitated Wilde, wearing knee breeches and carrying a sunflower, and repudiated his New England background by flirting with high-church Episcopalianism. He lived for a time in France, attended Mallarmé's salon, promoted the Symbolist movement, and translated and published an important edition of Maeterlinck's plays, with which Sara was also familiar. Yet his own Arthurian "dramas in poetry," as he called them, failed to overcome the dead weight of warmed-over Shakespearean rhetoric to which the tradition was addicted and which was so incongruous with his modern psychological handling of character. His Guenevere, on whom Sara modeled her own poem, was the type of vital new woman searching for freedom in love.

Sara also shared the enthusiasms of the other Potters—the plays of Barrie, Maeterlinck, and D'Annunzio, and the poetry of the Celtic revival, of Swinburne and Wilde. She first read Yeats in 1903—*The Wind Among the Reeds*—but was not much impressed. By the 1920s, however, she considered him the greatest living poet and "The Wild Swans at Coole" the finest poem of the twentieth century. Having absorbed the tastes and interests of the group, she was quick to outgrow her dependence on them. A few years after the Potters disbanded, Sara had come to regard most of their enthusiasms as juvenile and out of date, and their own poetic productions heavy and pretentious. "You should see the things they do," she wrote to John Myers O'Hara in 1911. "There is neither form nor comeliness to them. And yet they believe that their 'tremendous ideas' can not be expressed in any better form." At Christmas in 1910, eight of the women put out a collection of old and new poems, "and many of them were so 'tremendous' that the ten books which fell to my share are still waiting in the bottom of my shirt-waist box unopened." But the club's youthful mimicry of the artist's life set her on the course of her own genuine professionalism. She had friends with whom she could talk about poetry, who "kept up," and she could obtain immediate criticism and advice on her work and learn to discipline herself to an audience. These were opportunities denied to Emily Dickinson in the stagnant atmosphere of Amherst and only fortuitously available to Christina Rossetti and Elizabeth Barrett Browning by virtue of family or marriage. Sara, too, had been reared in the old-fashioned inhibitory way, but she was soon caught up in the vigorous professionalism of women in the early 1900s, a freer world where ambition and pride in workmanship could be taken for granted.

Forming a club was the most natural thing for women of common cultural interests to do. From 1868, when the first Women's Club was founded in Boston by Julia Ward Howe, the idea had spread rapidly across the country culminating in the General Federation of Women's

Clubs in 1890. St. Louis, not surprisingly, had a more intellectually pre-stigious group than was the rule, the Wednesday Club, organized in 1887 to study the work of Shelley and then broadening its interests while limiting its highly prized membership to invitation only. The Potters were in fact an informal offshoot of the Wednesday Club, for the suggestion to organize and give themselves a name was made by Celia Harris, a younger member of the Wednesday Club, who supplied her house for the girls' meetings and participated in their activity.

Professionalism among women was especially encouraged by female teachers, who had risen from only a fourth of the national teaching force in 1860 to over 80 percent in 1910. One of the most prominent teachers in the city's public schools, Miss Lillie Rose Ernst, a botanist and member of the Wednesday Club, also lent her patronage to the Potters and attend-ed many of their meetings. Formidable in her starched shirt-waists and gold-rimmed glasses, with hair tightly pulled back, she radiated an air of lofty standards, intensity of purpose, and ceaseless application to hard work. Even one of her hobbies, mountain climbing, was strenuous. Her career carried her eventually into school administration and service in half a dozen civic organizations. The rigor of her professionalism con-cealed great personal warmth, and Sara, although never one of her stu-dents, shyly joined the other girls in adoration and awe. She dedicated a sonnet "To L. R. E.," beginning

> When first I saw you—felt you take my hand,
> I could not speak for happiness.

She was looking, as always, for guidance and care from more mature women who possessed the confidence she lacked.

Sara was not then, and later was even less, given to participation in clubs or organizations. But the schools and women's clubs, the foremost purveyors of the high cultural ideal, rescued her from isolation, taught her the idea of discipline and a respect for cosmopolitanism and held up for models women of character and achievement—actresses, writers, educators, scientists—so that she could strike out on her own.

Henry Adams, a student of world's fairs, visiting the exposition in 1904 saw a different St. Louis from that of the earnest young artists, teachers, and clubwomen. In the ten years since his previous visit, agriculture had been replaced by smoking factory chimneys and "dirty suburbs filled with scrap-iron, scrap-paper, and cinders." It had become the cityscape that haunted Eliot's memory. The population now included masses of central Europeans, "Germans and Slavs," children of the new age of power brought together solely by the needs of industry. "One saw here a third-rate town of half-a million people without history, education, unity, or art, and with little capital—without even an element of natural interest except the river which it studiously ignored—but doing what London, Paris, or New York would have shrunk from attempting. This new social conglomerate, with no tie but its steam-power and not much of that, threw away thirty or forty million dollars on a pageant as ephemeral as a stage flat."[11] Adams' perspective was patrician rather than middle class, and it enabled him to see more clearly the harsh social realities that underlay the genteel lives of families like the Teasdales. An entirely unfamiliar world lay beyond the circumference of Sara's timid, sheltered existence, a world that did not obey the laws of idealism and beauty.

John Warren Teasdale's money, the golden island on which Sara lived, derived from a prosperous wholesale business in dried fruits, beans, and nuts. His entry in *The Book of St. Louisans: A Biographical Dictionary of the Leading Living Men of St. Louis* (1906) reads, "Since 1862 at head of J. W. Teasdale and Co., of which is president. Republican. Baptist; for over fifty years member of the Third Baptist Church." His father had been a Baptist minister, killed in a train accident when John Warren was seventeen. His uncle Thomas Teasdale had been a prominent clergyman too, and thus both had followed the path of their grandfather, a dissenting Baptist who emigrated from Durham in northern England in 1792 to Sussex County, New Jersey. A son emigrated with him, to become a captain in the war with England in 1812, and later a member of the New Jersey legislature and a judge in the Court of Common Pleas. This son, Sara's grandfather, left New Jersey for Fredericksburg, Virginia, where he preached and where Sara's father was born in 1838. The family returned for a while to New Jersey, came west to Illinois in 1850, and finally settled in St. Louis in 1854. Reverend Teasdale was pastor of the Third Baptist Church when he was accidentally killed in the autumn of 1855.

Sara's father and mother met each other at that church, for Mary Elizabeth Willard's family were staunch Baptists too, and among the church's organizers. Her ancestors were somewhat more distinguished than his, however, for she was a direct descendent of Captain Simon Willard, one of the founders of Concord, Massachusetts, in 1635. The prolific Willards boasted two presidents of Harvard, one of whom baptized Benjamin Franklin, and signers of the Declaration of Independence. Mrs. Teasdale's father, George Washington Willard, was an exceptionally vigorous and enterprising man, educated at Amherst, who roamed west, traded for furs with the Indians at the site of present-day Milwaukee, and ended up in Peoria, Illinois, running a large and prosperous fleet of steamboats on the Mississippi, Ohio, and Missouri rivers. His ceaseless activity took him throughout southern Illinois and into Missouri. His wife, Sarah Ann Trevor, brought the Baptist religion into the Willard family, and it was after her that Sarah Trevor Teasdale was named—the "h" being dropped by Sara at the beginning of her career as a poet.

Sara took considerable interest in her family background, although the Willards appealed more to her pride and imagination than the Teasdales.

The strength of ancestry, the strong masculine spirit of captains, judges, and adventurers, supported her when wrestling with her own inadequacy; particularly in her last years, it gave her the sense of a standard to live up to.

More influential than that, though, was the Puritanism in the Willard line, which Sara could invoke as an explanation of her own Victorian inhibitions. Concord stirred her with a sense of family history, of curiosity about her forebears. She and her husband were to spend their honeymoon in Boston in late December 1914, with one wintry afternoon in Concord, sipping tea before the fire at the Colonial Inn, after looking at tombstones. New England was the place where she most often went for peace and healing. If at times she warred against the Puritanism in her nature, she also drew on its strength.

Sara impressed her friends among the Potters as something of an aristocrat. "One could not, or did not, drop in on her casually, as one did with other friends," Williamina Parrish recalled, "for Sara lived the austere life of a nun, each hour having its fixed and set task—hours of rest, hours of work on her poetry, hours when friends were expected, by appointment. I had a fixed day and hour weekly with her, and I was very careful to appear on the exact minute, and to leave on the exact minute she had set as the permitted length of our visit—no such thing with her as lingering on until all subjects had been exhausted. . . . So well do I remember being ushered into the large dim parlor at the left of the front door by the maid, who would go up and announce my arrival quite as though I were visiting royalty." Sara had fed her own imagination on the romantic chivalry of the nineteenth century from Scott to Hovey, and the imagery of queen, princess, and knightly lover lingered in her work for several years, gradually given modern dress before disappearing altogether.

But although Sara may have played the role of fairytale princess in imagination, she did not see herself in reality as very attractive, much to her chagrin. Sara "was a passionate, highly geared woman," according to John Hall Wheelock, her closest friend for most of her adult life, "and she felt, and there was some truth in it, that she was not beautiful. . . . She certainly had a very interesting face, very charming personality, but she was not beautiful."[12] Her large, sensitive eyes were impressive, and her look characteristically expressed intelligence, candor, and kindness, but her face was difficult to photograph without an appearance of length and heaviness in the mouth and chin. Her hair has been described variously as "auburn" and "sandy," but a lock of it, preserved, is a light reddish-brown with glinting highlights of red and gold. "It isn't a very aggressive color," she wrote to John Myers O'Hara in 1908, who was pressing her for detailed information about her appearance—"in fact it looks almost brown sometimes tho' it flames very much in the sunlight; and—I'm afraid there's no denying it—it is surely red." She also told O'Hara that she was five feet four and three-quarters inches tall, "just a little above the average height for a woman," and "Yes, I'm slender." She had small hands and feet, wearing a size five and one-half glove. Wheelock believed that "there was, I think, in Sara's feeling, that she had not been born into as beautiful a body as she was entitled to have. She had a beautiful spirit, and she had this extraordinary talent, but . . . she would have appreciated so much being born as a strikingly beautiful woman like Elinor Wylie. . . . Men would not be drawn to her on the basis of her physical appeal, and that is what she wanted."

The central figures in Sara's youthful literary imagination were all women—strikingly beautiful, but the victims of sexual tragedy because of their appeal to men—Helen, Sappho, Guenevere, Eleonora Duse. "I think that I am far more likely to idealize women than men," she wrote O'Hara. "I should like to know a woman who is all that I should love to be myself. But of a man one does not expect so much, in a way." Men were essential to provide respect, shelter, and defense of beautiful women, but it was the statuesque, self-contained perfection of ideal femininity itself that she worshiped. The portrait is familiar in Victorian literature and art. She loved Poe's "To Helen," quoting the line "How statue-like I see thee stand" as one of her favorites, and she loved the sad, mysterious pre-Raphaelite ladies and pale Maeterlinck princesses. But the feminine image ambiguously had two sides: one, the childlike virgin, and the other the full-bodied woman with sexual allure, as John Hall Wheelock perceived. Among her favorite paintings was Giorgione's sensuous "Venus," and the height of her youthful rapture was seeing the Venus de Milo in the Louvre on her first trip abroad in 1905. She wrote in her travel diary:

> We went down-stairs next, and when we got to the door, I looked to the end of the long, long corridor and way at the end of it, against a dark red curtain, beautifully lighted, stood the most beautiful thing in the world—the Venus de Milo. Oh, I could hardly contain myself, her beauty made me so happy. She is far, far more lovely than any reproduction that I ever saw. The nearer I came to her, the more I loved her. Yes, I really love her—almost as one loves a real person. I can understand how Pygmalion loved Galatea. I cannot express the pleasure one has in being near this glorious woman. You are glad, as was Theophile Gautier, that her arms are gone, because they might hide her body. I have never seen so noble and pure and unconscious a woman as this Venus. The marble is so magnificently carved that it looks like flesh. I have left the loveliest thing until the last. It is her mouth. In no reproduction is it at all like the original. It is so very near a smile, and yet so full of repose. I don't believe that the exact reproduction of it will ever be caught by anyone. The lips are the most beautiful shape—you can tell from them that she is the goddess of love, but it is a spiritual love.[13]

Several years later she wrote to O'Hara, "I made an altar to Aphrodite last winter and . . . I used to repeat the Ode to Aphrodite before it—half in fun, half in earnest. I can confess to you—tho' I'd be afraid to tell most people—that she is more real to me than the virgin."

Her sonnet "Aphrodite," written about that time and published in *The Papyrus* in November 1910, might have been recited before the shrine:

> Mother of Love, oh daughter of the sea,
> Harken and hear! . . .
> A lonely worshiper, the last and least,
> I lift my voice and call upon thy name.

This pagan prayer has a curiously chaste and Christian tone, and the voice is that of a wistful girl more experienced in literature than life. But her private attraction to the goddess of sexual passion not only is sincere but also has a certain small note of stubborn defiance.

Yet, when she wished to be attractive to any particular man, Sara was forced by the strict conventions of her upbringing to turn instinctively the other face of love. Decent Christian men like her father were supposed to find appealing only the virginally innocent, the childlike, women. She once asked Williamina Parrish to take her picture seated on the wide sill of her secluded bedroom window "clad in 'virgin white' and flanked by Easter lilies . . . 'Make Miss Sadie as virginal and chaste and beautiful as you can, for she wants to impress him.' . . . Who this 'him' was, I do not remember." The Puritan in her nature always tended to win out publicly over the pagan sensualist, in spite of her secret worship at the shrine. And she shrank from being photographed with any hint of sensationalism. Miss Parrish confided once in a letter to her mother that she had done a spectacular portrait that Sara thought was "too too," but "she really looks like a person who is Somebody with a capital S. . . . Fancy being *able* to make Sara look so really interesting! It's a stroke of genius."[14] Sara was more complicated than her family or friends realized, a compound of sensual feeling and prudery, of luxuriant fantasy and shrewd common sense, and she was also confused and ridden with secret conflict.

So sweepingly have American mores changed since Sara Teasdale's girlhood that it is difficult to invoke convincingly the atmosphere of ignorance, secrecy, silence, and fear that cloaked the subject of sexual love. She had no knowledge of men or boys other than her father and two brothers, who were in their thirties when she graduated from Hosmer Hall. She had been educated in a girls' school, participated in a girls' club, and never attended social events where boys or young men were present. But there was always someone, Williamina Parrish said, "around whom her poetic fancy was weaving a dream." Just as she seized upon the boy who played a mandolin on summer nights under the sheet lightning and made him a character in her chivalric fantasies, she daydreamed of others she saw from a distance. Until she was twenty-eight, the lovers of whom she wrote poems were almost entirely imaginary, although sometimes, unknown to the reader, they were addressed to women friends. Her mother's effort to stifle her sexual impulse had led only to a consuming interest and habitual fantasizing.

"Her romantic and sensuous nature had need of an outlet," Miss Parrish continued, and during her late adolescence and the several years with the Potters Sara developed crushes on one or another of her girl friends. Intense friendships not only were common in the sexually segregated society of young people but also were deliberately fostered in order to discourage too great an interest in the opposite sex. In this pre-Freudian era, feminine love was regarded as "higher" and more spiritual than love between men and women and was not considered sexual in nature. Sara herself naturally assumed this view. With her deep feelings of personal unattractiveness, she idealized other girls who possessed the traits she admired. One of these was a classmate named Bessie Brey, also an occasional participant in the Potters' club. "This girl was tall and slim with finely chiseled features," Williamina Parrish wrote in her memoir, "but with very little else that answered Sara's spiritual needs. I think, frankly, that the poor girl was bewildered by Sara's outpourings, and responded as best she could, for Sara never took No for an answer when she felt a thing and wanted to share it. Most of Sara's first lyrics were written to this girl, though I do not think the girl knew this." Williamina, or Will, or Willie, never served as a focus for Sara's idealizing imagination. In 1911, several years after the Potters had disbanded, Sara wrote to O'Hara, "You amused me by asking if Will and I were 'sweethearts' still. What a funny notion! No indeed, we are 'friends the merest,' tho' very old and dear ones. I am awfully fond of Will and she of me—but my days of 'crushes' are long over, and if they weren't, Will isn't the sort of woman I would idealize."

The first year and a half with the Potters brought a modest but steady output of poetry. Sara was excruciatingly conscientious, distressed by flaws like imperfect meter, forced rhyme, or false emotion. Will Parrish, her "literary confessor," was the first of many friends to whom she submitted her poems for severe criticism, always listening humbly and trying to apply their advice. If anything, she was too willing to take advice in the beginning. "I am always thankful for criticism and I am very docile even tho' it is severe," she wrote O'Hara in 1910. "There are several people at home who have widely differing views on the subject of poetry, and I find myself changing things to suit one and then changing them back to suit another until I am so confused that I have no idea which is the best critic." Sara "worked awfully hard over those seemingly artless simple poems of hers," John Hall Wheelock remarked, "and she was a very severe critic of other people's work."

The emotions dramatized in her poems arose from deep within herself, but there was never the slightest intention to parade personal feelings in public. A poem was personal in origin, impersonal in execution. Sometimes her readers felt pangs of sympathy for the anguish of her maturer work and wrote to commiserate. "She resented the patronization of these people who felt compassionately for her and wanted to cheer her up," according to Wheelock, "and she wanted them to understand that she didn't need any cheering up, that she had a life of her own." Her poem "The Treasure," written in 1913, begins

> When they see my songs
> They will sigh and say,
> "Poor soul, wistful soul,
> Lonely night and day."

It continues in her notebook with a stanza not used in publication:

> They will never know
> With what patient care
> I have made the songs
> Sorrowful and bare.[15]

The disciplining of personal emotion to art was the first and most important lesson she learned. It suited naturally her reticent personality, which submitted to propriety but cried out for communication.

In 1905, the year Sara turned twenty-one, her activities with the Potters were interrupted by a three-month trip abroad, the first of half a dozen voyages she made to Europe during her life. Mrs. Teasdale's interest in travel had continued unabated, even though her husband, now sixty-six, seldom went with her about the country to her favorite resorts. She combined culture with piety by signing herself and Sara on a tour of the Mediterranean and the Holy Land, along with a contingent of Protestant ministers, reminiscent of Mark Twain's pilgrimage aboard the *Quaker City* fifty years before.

The cold and drafty S.S. *Arabic* sailed from New York on February 2, 1905, and Sara immediately began her travel diary, squeezing as many fine lines of handwriting as possible on to sheets of ship's stationery. The cold chilled her to the bone. "It will be a wonder if I can stand it," she wrote. "Thank fortune for the hot water bottles!" It was an ominous beginning for someone who loved comfort like a cat before a warm fire and who lived in perpetual dread of sore throats. Nevertheless, she was stoically cheerful and let her thoughts roam, characteristically, to friendship and romance. Five days out, she wrote, "I should like to meet a girl whom I often see on deck who reminds me of _____ [sic], but I never get a chance. It is rather hard to meet people for the party is so enormous. There seems *very* little danger of my falling in love with anybody. Didn't I say so before I left? I don't see why I should when—well, I don't see why I should." Unluckily, there seem to have been few young people aboard to respond to her wistful wish for an emotional adventure.

For Mrs. Teasdale, the trip was a fulfillment of her religious convictions —to walk on the soil of the Bible lands that had fired the literalist imagination of generations of Baptists. But for Sara it was an esthetic pilgrimage. The "peacock-blue" sea, "restless, passionate, and powerful," the foam of waves "like lace laid over sea-foam green satin," Madeira rising "from the blue sea like a great mountain of emerald dotted over with pearly white houses," the violet depths of ravines in the hazy hills—"Such a beautiful sight I have seldom seen." The vision later became a poem, "Madeira from the Sea":

> Out of the delicate dream of the distance an emerald emerges
> Veiled in the violet folds of the air of the sea.[16]

The world was an impressionist painting, and she unfailingly recorded the tints and lights and atmospheres as she saw them. It was a quest for beauty. But, in her usual methodical fashion, she studied her Baedecker intensively and jotted down the solid facts that impressed her as well as the vision—thirty-seven chapels in the cathedral at Seville, ninety-seven stained glass windows. A painting of Murillo struck her because "You will hardly be able to see how a Crucifixion could be sensuously beautiful, but it was." She had been educated to worship the beautiful, to be accurate in detail, and to develop critical judgment. Europe provided the grand opportunity, and she seized it with determination.

From Seville, the ship sailed to Greece, "the place of all places on the cruise, except Rome, that I'd most love to see." It was for her the equivalent of her mother's Bible land, the place where the very spirit of perfect beauty had been born. The romantic classicism of Keats—"the most Greek of our poets"—Poe, and later writers had made Athens a shrine for the worshipers of beauty in "the regions which/ Are Holy Land." But to Sara's deep disappointment, the sore throat that had threatened ever since they settled into their frigid stateroom, where the temperature had ranged from 49 to 60 degrees Farenheit, finally forced her to bed. It was the pattern of illness that marked her entire life: emotional excitement followed by the inevitable sore throat, a deep cold, loss of strength, and nervous depression. Illness always seemed to step in and deprive her of what she wanted most. As the ship lay at Piraeus, she wrote, "How can I bear it? to be so near—in the very harbor—only a few miles from the city, which is inland—and yet perhaps go to my grave without laying eyes upon it!" To her further annoyance, her mother insisted on staying at her bedside and refused to leave the ship on a sightseeing trip she might have enjoyed. "God knows best," she told herself. "I should be glad of what I've had. . . . I suppose it is for my own good." The English ship's doctor painted her throat "with some horrible bitter stuff," observing, as she later recounted to O'Hara, "You are a very curious young person, Miss Teasdale," and the next day let her go on deck. "And what a magnificent color scheme I saw before me!" her diary exclaimed. "The deep blue sky against the mountains—many of them entirely covered with snow—and the city at their feet, with the Acropolis like the crown of it all, standing high, high above the city, her glorious Parthenon glistening yellow in the sunshine." She got her wish after all. Two days later, Dr. Craster let her spend three hours ashore, and she went straight to the Acropolis, where "we had two Greeks make a basket of their hands and I was carried to the very top." That night she could hardly sleep for excitement, thinking she had walked where "how many many feet had pressed the same stones before."

Her throat improved, but the next stop, Palestine, proved to be miserable beyond endurance. The weather was dark, cold, and windy, the hotel was unbearable—"Our first night in Jerusalem will always be one of the most terrible in my memory"—and she was appalled at the filth, the beggars, the disease, she saw on the streets. She and her mother both felt desperately homesick for America, but tried to take in the important sights. An afternoon's drive to Bethlehem was "dreary," and the squalid town itself "the most absolutely abject and heartbreaking thing I have ever seen." She naturally thought of the familiar Christmas carol and wrote, "What a strange place for 'the hopes and fears of all the years' to meet in!"

Egypt was equally depressing, and Sara's throat worsened again in the bad weather. Nevertheless, they kept up with the sightseeing excursions arranged for the tour; Sara rode a camel and dutifully recorded her critical reactions to the art and culture of the ancient Egyptians after viewing the ruins of Karnak. Greek ruins were golden and alive, Egypt's the color of dust and smelling of death. "The heaviness and stiffness of Egyptian art would become intolerable if one had to see a great deal of it." All in all, the Near East was oppressive—a land that "God has forgotten about," so much suffering, "so much knowledge of pain and disease and sin."

Italy, after that, was like coming back to life again, although it rained throughout their three days in Rome, and she had to school herself again in patience to drive by the cemetery where Keats and Shelley and Symonds were buried without being able to stop: "Theirs are the first graves that I ever really cared to visit." She had only a minute to look at Michelangelo's ceiling in the Sistine chapel, found it "the very pinnacle of the masculine principle of art," and was whisked on to other tourist attractions. She decided she preferred Gothic to Renaissance in churches, because "Renaissance style is too ornate to be sincerely religious." And then on to France, where at last they parted from the touring group and could go about as they pleased. Up to this point, except for Seville, the tour had been marred by frustration, disappointment, ill health, and bad weather.

But Paris made up for it all. The Louvre was a feast, with the Venus de Milo; Ste. Chapelle was the most beautiful building she had ever seen. She went for the first time to a performance of *Tristan und Isolde,* "one of the most wonderful things that was ever done by anybody." She came out of the performance dazed: "I could hardly walk—I was so weak," she later wrote O'Hara.

The trip ended with two weeks in England, where abruptly her interest shifted from artists to authors, for "things are just as they are in books." She looked up Swinburne's name in the telephone directory and went out to No. 11 Putney Hill, where her idol, now sixty-eight, lived with his supervisory friend Watts-Dunton. "How I longed for the front door to open and S. to come out!" But alas, he didn't, and of course one couldn't knock. She made another pilgrimage, to No. 50 Wimpole Street, feeling "very unworthy to be there" and marveling that she stood on the very stones where the Brownings had walked. She stopped in during evensong at Marylebone Church, where they had been married. Later, after seeing Shakespeare's home at Stratford-on-Avon, she wrote, "I am quite sure that I appreciate Shakespeare as much as most people, but I cannot help admitting that the sight of 50 Wimpole Street, London, moved me more than all the various shrines of Stratford put together." She viewed the Elgin marbles in the British Museum, a lock of Shelley's hair and some of his manuscripts in the Bodleian Library at Oxford, and even a skylark, which she asked the driver on the way to Stratford to show her. And when she heard a nightingale "I was so happy that I could hardly sit still and listen." Sailing home on May 10, 1905 from Liverpool, Mrs. John Warren Teasdale and daughter might have been minor characters in a novel by Henry James—the mother, bustling and efficient, "doing" Europe as a duty, the daughter, proper and silent with her inner thoughts, filled with her own unpredictable future.

Back in St. Louis in mid-May, Sara probably saw her friends only briefly before going on to Charlevoix for the summer. In the two years since graduation, her poetic output had been delicate and painstaking, her most ambitious project a set of sonnets, in the grand style, about Eleonora Duse. Her most typical pieces were childlike lyrics reminiscent of Robert Louis Stevenson, one of the favorite writers of her girlhood, or wistful love songs imitating those of the English poet A. Mary F. Robinson. This competent but timid work hardly seemed to promise a reputation. But later that year William Marion Reedy, editor of *The Mirror*, agreed to publish an article on the Potters by Mrs. Frances Porcher, wife of a St. Louis book dealer and formerly Reedy's assistant. Mrs. Porcher's terribly high-toned article appeared in *The Mirror* on April 6, 1906, to a great flutter of excitement among the Potters. And Reedy, in browsing through copies of *The Potter's Wheel* Mrs. Porcher had lent him, picked out a short prose sketch by Sara Teasdale that he liked, "The Crystal Cup," and published it in *The Mirror* on May 17, 1906.

Reedy, whom Sara called her "literary God-father,"[17] was the Mencken of the Midwest, albeit a less irascible version, a sentimental and desultory genius, lacking intellectual focus, but gifted with a pungent, racy style and a boldness that made him a highly successful editor. He was city editor of *The St. Louis Mirror* when it went bankrupt in 1893 and the owner presented it to him as a gift. Reedy, then thirty-one, lifted the low tone, began discussing serious contemporary literature as well as politics, and within a few years had created a journal of opinion with an international reputation: "He has done more to stimulate the thought of his country through the medium of his own original comment on men and things than anyone else now editing in America," Alexander Harvey wrote.[18] He was an internationalist in both literary and political sentiment, an advocate of honesty and tolerance, without any particular program, and sometimes inconsistent in his opinions. Perhaps his most significant literary contribution, and one that may have directly influenced the young St. Louis poets, including Eliot, was his advocacy of the French decadent writers for their refinement of sensibility and artistic purity, separating the artist's personal life from his work. He also preached the belief in craftsmanship that distinguished modern writing from the supposed romantic self-indulgence of the previous era. "There is no such thing as spontaneous poetry," he wrote to Sara in 1907, "but in reality the great work is produced by great labor and by constant unremitting application of the file."

Reedy's personal reputation was always something for proper St. Louisans to gossip about. He was a huge jowly man with large, dark, sensitive eyes—"Machiavelli must have had to look out upon his world through such gleaming dark eyes as glorify the face of William Marion Reedy," according to Alexander Harvey. He was unable for many years to control his drinking, and even married the madam of a St. Louis whorehouse once after a heavy drinking bout, but left her after three months. He eventually settled down with a third wife into quasi-respectability.

Reedy probably liked the neatly careful language of Sara's sketch, its sophisticated pretense of simplicity, and the sensuousness of its imagery. He substituted a quotation from "Jami" for some lines of Dowson she had used, to give it a currently popular air of oriental exoticism.

THE CRYSTAL CUP

*Under the leaf of many a fable lies*
*The truth for those who look for it.*
*If thou wouldst look behind and find the Fruit,*
*Have thy desire.*
                              —Jami

There was once a man who possessed a wonderful cup of crystal. So cunningly was it fashioned that it seemed sometimes to be the red of the flame, and anon it was blue, or, maybe a green like the sea where it is shallow at the shore.

The man knew that the cup was a priceless treasure, and he longed to fill it with wine. In the hot golden sunshine he went from vineyard to vineyard where the girls were gathering the honey-sweet grapes, and from the warmth of the sun he passed into the chill of gray wine-cellars to taste and see what was good.

One virtue of the cup was this: the greater number of rare wines that were mixed within it, the more valuable the cup became. For the crystal shone more brightly as the wine mounted within it. When at last it was full, the man was happy. He longed to be alone so that he might dream over the beauty of the cup and very slowly drink the wine.

He turned away from the grape gatherers, and, as he turned, he saw a woman coming toward him. She walked beside the stone wall of the vineyard, now in the sun and now in the shadow, for there were tall trees above her. Her hair was mixed with the sun, like gold that the goldsmith had worked over lovingly. When she came quite close to the man, having nothing else to give her, he handed her the crystal cup. She drank the wine without looking into his eyes. Then she set the empty cup down roughly on the stone wall, and passed on. The man's eyes followed her. He turned to take the empty cup because she had held it in her hands. But it was broken into a thousand pieces, each stained faintly by the wine.

And the man went his way empty handed and full of sorrow.

Sara's little fable, like so much of her work, seemed to avoid personal reference while actually revealing a great deal. The beautiful woman in her sketch is not merely the traditional *femme fatale* of Romantic literary tradition, now golden-haired to show her spiritual quality—she is the alter ego of Sara herself; not the plain girl in glasses who was forced to be good rather than alluring, but the mysterious, aloof, feminine goddess whom men worship. Although she accepts the offering of the man's treasure as her just due, she is self-contained and has no need of him, attracting him with her sensuous appeal only to freeze into indifference, dashing to pieces the goblet of Tristan and Isolde in a gesture of virtuous superiority. And so she remains good, an ambivalent Virgin-Aphrodite.

Reedy mailed her a check for the sketch, which sent her reeling with delight. Having tasted success, she determinedly set about repeating it.

She had already gathered her sonnets to Eleonora Duse into the form of a little brown book and was clearly hoping to find a way to publish them. That summer the family vacationed in Colorado, but afterward she sent Reedy some lyrics and he accepted "The Little Love" for publication in *The Mirror* on November 22, 1906. In this, her first published poem, the Little Love offers her all that he has but she rejects it. The Great Love comes along, and she gives him everything but receives only half in return as he leaves her in tears. And so the Little Love comes back, after all, "to ease my heart." The quest for a Great Love, and her dissatisfaction with what she always found, were to be the pattern of her life. Perhaps Reedy sensed the underlying self-realism that was to distinguish her poetry from conventional women's love poetry; perhaps he liked her commitment to a natural unaffected diction, which at that time stood out cleanly against the cluttered verbiage of the popular poets. At any rate, he encouraged her, and he usually did not bother with what he felt was a second-rate talent.

Meanwhile, Will Parrish had taken Sara in hand to help her prepare her little book for publication. Throughout her life, the preparation of a new book was agonizing and slow, with constant shuffling and reshuffling of the order and arrangement of poems, dropping or adding, touching up words or lines, considering the effect of the opening pages, of each poem in relation to the ones before and after it. She always turned to some single person to review all her decisions before she felt satisfied in letting the manuscript go. Will Parrish probably first instructed her in these subtleties.

Sara's interest in the Potters' meetings seemed to be waning, and the other members, too, began to go their separate ways, disbanding after the last issue of *The Potter's Wheel* in October 1907. Sara suffered one of her periods of unidentifiable illness in the winter and spring of 1906–1907, probably signaling a flareup of emotional conflict, although the causes cannot be pinpointed, as they can be later on. There was sometimes tension in her relationship with Will Parrish, who tended to be autocratic in her dealings with Sara. Two years later, Sara wrote a friend about running over to make peace with Will, because "I thought I would make a trial and see if W. really wanted to let me alone. She seemed very glad to see me and quite her old self, but I can tell you that I steered clear of all disturbing subjects."[19] The misunderstanding was doubtless insignificant, but it hints at an occasional clash in their opposing temperaments. The domineering Will revealed her somewhat patronizing attitude in a letter about Sara written to her mother in 1911: "I didn't realize how really nice she was in so many ways. . . . She's a *nice* child."[20] Still Sara turned to her often for advice and help until marrying in 1914, and they both remained loyal to their friendship throughout their lives.

Eleonora Duse was at the pinnacle of her reputation when Sara began writing sonnets about her and hand printing them in *The Potters' Wheel.* The actress had completed her third great American tour in the season of 1902–1903 with an all-D'Annunzio repertoire, even though her much publicized affair with him had just ended. His novel, *Il Fuoco,* published in 1900, candidly depicted their relationship, and Duse's agent was privately advised not to allow her lover to come to America with her, for "His recent book in which the great Italian actress figured as the central character has been thoroughly discussed by the American press with the result that he has gained the contempt of every woman in the land."[21] Not so with the Potters, who adored the novel. Sara named her kitten "Fosca," after the novel's heroine, Foscarina. She and her friends were mad about the plays D'Annunzio had written especially for her, second-rate and static as they were in the theater. Of D'Annunzio himself, a cruel, sensual, self-aggrandizing man, later a strutting Fascist, they really knew nothing at all.

Sara never saw Duse perform and seems not to have cared. Out of the reviews, her idealizing imagination had constructed a woman who embodied all her ideas of the perfect feminine artist of the beautiful. "Eleonora Duse is a great artist, the type of the artist," Arthur Symons, an admiring friend of Duse over many years, wrote, "and it is only by accident that she is an actress . . . she would have been equally great in any other art. . . . She is the artist of the soul, and it is her force of will, her mastery of herself, not her abandonment to it, which make her what she is."[22] Eva LeGallienne wrote that "Her acting was sacrificial; it was as though each time she played she immolated herself upon an altar."[23] Duse's style was new—"natural" and simple, in contrast to the artificial theatricality of Bernhardt, whom she eventually overshadowed. She rejected cheap publicity, lived for her art, refused to discuss herself. Symons said she even perversely hated her art—"It is sorrow, discontent, thwarted desires, that have tortured and exalted her into a kind of martyrdom of artistic mastery, on the other side of which the serenity of a pained but indomitable soul triumphs." Americans swarmed to see the aloof, tragic actress wherever she went or whatever she played in, even though she could not speak English and performed in Italian.

Sara's Duse is another incarnation of Aphrodite, the Venus de Milo, and Sappho, the eternal Greek spirit of beauty and love, transfigured, however, by suffering, as modern feminine life required. Some of the eight sonnets are virtually prayers to an animating soul that lived in ancient Greece and is revived in Duse's person: in her, "vanished Grecian beauty lives again." Her voice carries an undercurrent of the siren's song, "Sappho's hand has lingered in your hand." The best sonnet in the group, "To a Picture of Eleonora Duse in 'The Dead City,' " makes the identification complete:

Carved in the silence by the hand of Pain,
And made more perfect by the gift of Peace . . .
A sister to the noblest that we know,
The Venus carved in Melos long ago.[24]

Sometime in 1907 she submitted the collection of twenty-nine poems, twenty of them short lyrics, to the Poet Lore Company of Boston, which offered to publish the book at her expense. Her parents, always willing to indulge her, paid $290 for the printing of a thousand copies. She fretted over proofs during summer at Charlevoix, and in early September the attractive little volume, *Sonnets to Duse and Other Poems,* illustrated with three photographs of the actress, was in her hands. *Poet Lore* magazine had also accepted "Silence," another sonnet dedicated to Eleonora Duse but not included in the book. Buoyed by the excitement of being a real author at last, however small a figure she cut among her great idols, she generously mailed copies to her friends and others whose attention she wanted to get. From the outset, she showed a remarkable shrewdness in promoting her career—never aggressively so as to offend, always with charm and gratitude, as befit a genteel lady, but with unyielding persistence. One copy went immediately to Arthur Symons—"You know how beautifully he has written about Duse," she told O'Hara—who replied on October 4 that he found her poems "so altogether delightful that I take it as a fine flattery that you should tell me that you like some of the things I have written in verse. Here is an entirely genuine book, full of faint, real beauty."[25] He dashed off a brief notice that appeared in the *Saturday Review* on October 5, praising the lyrics more than the sonnets. She mailed a copy, too, to the actress Julia Marlowe, a friend of Symons, who in return sent her the most recent picture of Duse she could find. And of course she tried to get one into the hands of the great Duse herself, through the American consul in Florence, who wrote that he had delivered the book to her home at 54 Via Robbia on November 30. Duse could not read English, and Sara never received an acknowledgment.

Reedy wrote her that "My only objection to the Sonnets to Duse is that they are too intense an idealization; that is to say, to one who has lived somewhat close to the world of the stage and its people." But he encouraged her to keep writing. Sara herself had already outgrown the book before it was printed. When she sent John Myers O'Hara a copy in March 1908, she said "It is so pitifully a typical 'first book'—so many of the things already sound school-girlish." While preparing the poems for publication in spring, 1907, she embarked on a more ambitious course, a series of blank verse monologues about the legendary destructive loves of famous women, each reflecting in a quiet moment on her tragic career. The first, "Guenevere," was published in Reedy's *Mirror* on May 30,

1907, and was then widely reprinted in newspapers and magazines, doing more to launch her popular reputation than her fragile little book.

Behind the poem was Sara's intensive study of Richard Hovey's *The Marriage of Guenevere* (she used his spelling of the name) with its modern point of view. The April 1907 edition of *The Potter's Wheel* was dedicated to Hovey, and its opening selection was Sara's poem. His Guenevere is the "Lady of the Hills," a free spirit who ranges the out-of-doors, "wild as the sea-mew, restless of restraint," a "temperament that suffers and achieves." The theme of his drama is the submission of this rebellious girl to the conventional marriage bond, with its tragic consequences when she breaks her vow in the name of true love for Launcelot. She is envious of male freedom:

> While they are running on the battlements,
> Playing at war or at the chase, she sits
> Eating her heart out at embroidery frames.

Older women advise her to stop dreaming of a free life and accept the feminine fate, offering shrewd advice on how to control men, even though subjugated. Guenevere allows the "granite walls of circumstance" to close her in, because she has no choice; "As well Arthur as another—I care not. If I must, I must." Among the compensations, however, are the facts that Arthur is a "perfect gentleman," and marriage is better than the inactive, restricted life of a spinster. It was a drama that Sara was to enact in her own life within a few years. The alternative to the conventional prison house of marriage, however, is not the communion of equals that Ibsen advocated, but surrender to a powerful genuine love in the person of Launcelot. Guenevere discovers her true femininity, saying,

> I am so glad I am a woman, love.
> I have quarreled with my sex . . .
>         But now
> I would not be a man for all the world.

So much for her envy of the boys' freedom of play. Hovey's outspoken "new woman" asserts her freedom to love as she chooses without penalty, but it is still her nature to give herself totally to a man.

Sara's debt to Hovey is evident in her conception of the character as a woman who claims her right to love and puzzles over the community's rejection of her because of it:

> The world would run from me, and yet I am
> No different from the queen they used to love.[26]

She also incorporated Hovey's passionate surrender scene in the garden, and her Guenevere's lover, too, "made me a woman." But while Hovey's judgment was poor in choosing a form too grandiose and diffuse for his capacity, Sara turned to the selective and controllable dramatic monologue, reworking her lines until the language was simple, firm, and natural, and the rhythm was effectively sustained throughout. Before long she was, in the mind of the public, the outstanding specialist in love poetry.

With "Guenevere" and *Sonnets to Duse,* the shy, almost invisible, schoolgirl had become a sudden object of curiosity in St. Louis, and the newspapers began to carry stories about her that continued at intervals throughout her life. The St. Louis *Republic* printed a photograph and feature story on September 9, 1907, which must have made her wince: "While American women have compelled the homage of the world for their beauty, womanly worthiness and goodness, the noble sons they rear, and for innumerable other most admirable things, it is quite unfortunately true they have so far shown slight gift of song." "Poetesses are precious," it continued, and should be classed with public assets such as "an eminent baseball player, a splendid police force, an adequate garbage plant, a superb sanitary system." It was the mercantile spirit's sincere tribute to art. And in October a local gossip columnist wrote, "I hear also that Mr. and Mrs. J. W. Teasdale of Lindell Boulevard have bought a lot in Kingsbury Place and intend to build a fifty thousand dollar residence. Mr. Teasdale is an excellent judge of horses and has the finest equipped stables in town. His youngest daughter, Miss Sara Teasdale, is a poetic genius and has written some remarkably beautiful poetry for so young a girl." She was then twenty-three, but even when she was in her thirties and married, the local papers referred to her as a "St. Louis girl." From this time on, she systematically sent her poems to the magazines, undaunted by rejections, and within a year was planning a second book.

At twenty-three, she stood finally on the threshold of life, having conceived of it in terms of literature and fantasy, dealing boldly with the themes of feminine emotion so close to her but without experience to show whether her thoughts were valid. She had been kept a child, deprived of the strength and self-sufficiency to make an independent life for herself, or even to cope with the emotions she summoned up. With the intuitive honesty that she continually brought to her work, she wrote a lyric defining where she now stood in relation to the crippling childhood that had fed on dreams rather than reality. The adult world beckoned her away, but she questioned whether she had the endurance to survive:

THE HOUSE OF DREAMS

I built a little House of Dreams,
  And fenced it all about,
But still I heard the Wind of Truth
  That roared without.

I laid a fire of Memories
  And sat before the glow,
But through the chinks and round the door
  The wind would blow.

I left the House, for all the night
  I heard the Wind of truth;—
I followed where it seemed to lead
  Through all my youth.

But when I sought the House of Dreams,
  To creep within and die,
The Wind of Truth had levelled it,
  And passed it by.[27]

CHAPTER THREE

# *"If I Were Only Beautiful and a Genius"*

**S**ara used her new-found poetic voice to explore the sense of emotional deprivation that was the inescapable fact of her adult life:

> I weave a web of fancies
>   Of tears and darkness spun.
> How shall I sing of sunlight
>   Who never saw the sun?[1]

She was a dutiful and dependent daughter, a princess locked in a tower:

> ... the peasant lovers go by beneath,
>   I hear them laugh and kiss.[2]

But she had only her daydreams. In those twilight years before the literary revolution, "dreams" and longings were the accepted substance of serious poetry, and Sara Teasdale's skillful lyrics, admired by poets and public alike, seemed to breathe genuine emotion into the conventions. But the psychological morbidity implicit in those conventions belied the neat prettiness with which they were stated, and even though she set her troubled feelings to music Sara could apply the tortured meanings literally to herself. As she sat week by week at her desk studying her emotions in order to translate them into poems, she suffered spells of unexplainable illness that grew in intensity until in February 1908 her worried parents sent her on a brief trip to San Antonio, hoping she would improve in the warmer climate. These neurasthenic attacks seemed to have no

more physical cause than an ordinary cold or sore throat, but they reduced her to infantile helplessness.

In the battle with herself, Sara was two people: one, distraught and ill,
sealed behind a wall of reticence; the other, candid, witty, seemingly
transparent, filled with lively good humor. Her friends among the Potters
were aware that she often vanished without warning into a private world,
but none of them shared any intimate knowledge of her problems, except
perhaps, at a later date, Williamina Parrish. The adolescent character of
the group did not provide the help she needed for a more mature understanding of herself, and even before the Potters disbanded in the fall of
1907 Sara had begun to go her own private way. As the only celebrity
among the Potters, she was invited to meet other St. Louisans active in
the cultural life of the city and occasionally even attended teas and social
gatherings. She steeled herself in patience and waited, like an immobile
flower for pollination, for whatever opportunities might come along. If
she was denied the initiative, or the appearance of it, she could always
capitalize on fortuitous events. She even expressed her reliance on them
for survival in a later poem, "Lovely Chance":

> You rise between myself and me
> With a wise persistency;
> I would have broken body and soul,
> But by your grace, still I am whole.[3]

In 1908, two new acquaintances materialized through correspondence
about her work, and she was quick to recognize that each offered an
emotional escape from the stifling confinement of her family. One was
a man, the other a woman. Because of her agonizing shyness, it was
probably easier for her to form new relationships through letter writing,
while she cautiously felt her way at a safe distance.

The man was John Myers O'Hara, a young poet about her own age who
had recently moved from Chicago to New York where he professed to
hate his job as a stockbroker because it was unpoetic—although he
dreamed of becoming rich. He was a personal friend of Jack London and
the California poet George Sterling and hung about the fringes of New
York literary life. In the fall of 1907, he had privately printed a volume
of free translations from Sappho. Sara read some selections in the magazines, excitedly tried to acquire a copy of his book, but couldn't, and so
wrote to O'Hara on February 25, 1908, asking if he would help her
procure one. She had clipped some of his poems, she said, and "put them
in my Dr. Wharton's 'Sappho,' where the richness of your verse makes
the other renditions all the paler." O'Hara, like other poets, had freely
combined the Sapphic fragments into coherent poems that were praised

by Yeats and Symons and went through three editions. They were the best work among the eight volumes of poems and translations he published between 1907 and 1932.

Sara felt she had discovered someone who appreciated the Greek spirit as she did. Sappho, the literary equivalent for her of the Venus de Milo, enjoyed an extraordinary vogue throughout the nineteenth century, when, with the increasing literary interest in women, she answered, as she still does, to whatever type of feminine personality a writer or a movement wished to epitomize. In the Victorian controversy over the propriety of sexual passion in women, "burning Sappho" was at the forefront, a symbol of either spirituality or corruption, depending on the point of view. Sara's image of her derived from the Romantic Hellenism of the nineteenth-century English poets, in which "The Poetess" was gradually elevated to the purest expression of sublime beauty. John Addington Symonds in his *Studies in the Greek Poets* praised her "absolute perfection and inimitable grace," her "heart-devouring passion" and "overwhelming emotion," the "yearnings of an intense soul after beauty."[4] When Sara wrote to O'Hara that she couldn't decide whether "Keats. . .or Shakespeare or Sappho or Swinburne is best of all," she only echoed the popular taste, which placed Sappho alongside Homer, Shakespeare, and Dante in the pantheon of Great Writers. Her name, Sara noted with delight, is inscribed with theirs on the façade of the Boston Public Library.

Against this idealistic cult of beauty was the sensual and "shameless" Sappho of the French decadents, abandoning herself to uncontrolled sexual passion. Daudet's novel *Sapho* (1885) identified her with sexual license and Pierre Louÿs's voluptuous *Les Chansons de Bilitis* (1895), pretending to be translations of newly discovered fragments, portrayed sexual infatuation between women. Sara was ignorant of the decadent version of Sappho's reputation until later, and according to Louis Untermeyer refused for a long time to give it any credence. She glimpsed the "wild" French version of Sappho only through Verlaine and objected to this depiction of her heroine tearing her hair and behaving violently. She preferred Swinburne's English approach, which avoided the overt expression of passion for fear of being misunderstood. O'Hara's version was derived, like Sara's, from the cultists of ideal beauty.

Sara had initiated the correspondence with John O'Hara, an impropriety for a woman, but she excused it on the grounds that they had a mutual acquaintance. And so with a rush of pleasurable excitement she began a weekly exchange of letters, trading poems for criticism, and chattering about authors and art and music. She did not meet him for three years, and they did not even address each other by their first names for two years and a half. And yet, guarded as she was against becoming too openly personal, it became a kind of experimental love affair, a trial of emotion that she could carry on in privacy and safety. Eventually it taught her some disturbing things about both herself and him.

In mid-March, 1908, her illness worse than ever, Sara's parents sent her for an extended rest cure to a sanitorium in Cromwell, Connecticut, in the rolling wooded hills southeast of Hartford, the first time she had been away from her family for more than a brief stay. The regimen at Cromwell was "puritanical," she told O'Hara (although she missed the aptness of the name); "the prevailing philosophy is: 'Ask yourself what you want, and then know for a certainty that is exactly the thing you should not have.' Hence, if you like cold baths, you have hot ones, and if you like to be alone, you are told to be with people, and if you hate meat, you *must* eat it." Her doctor prescribed absolute rest, allowing her to write only twenty minutes a day, and discouraged reading, talking, or exercise. She ate all meals alone in her second-story room and spent hours sitting out on her little porch wrapped in shawls or blankets, where she could watch Venus in the evening sky, her non-Puritan symbol of love. "I don't like people who are always reading sadness into nature," she said with a certain pathos, "it doesn't fill me with 'the thoughts that lie too deep for tears.' It is just joy, joy, joy." But on April 25 the doctor ordered her to stop writing all letters except one a week to her parents and forebade her to receive any. His theory was that she tended to be too easily excited and needed subduing. She was moved to a detached cottage in the orchard where she would be even more isolated. "I can think of you as one who knows and loves all the things I know and love," she said in farewell to O'Hara and then obediently remained silent until the end of July, when she was set free to tour the coast for a month with her nurse as companion. Then she wrote him five times in August, from various inns from Newport to Gloucester.

As soon as the letters resumed, O'Hara began a gradual campaign of insinuating himself into her personal feelings, first by a self-pitying appeal for sympathy and then by flattery. But the practical-minded Sara lectured him: "You believe that nothing remains to us in the end but despair. I admit that the thought of death frightens me unspeakably, and yet, (I can scarcely tell how the two feelings are reconciled) it seems like a priceless gift. . . . I have never been sure whether life is happy or miserable, but it is certainly vastly interesting, and so long as we find it so, it is worth living. . . . People who love beautiful things cannot be bored— there is so much beauty. Being bored must be the worst thing of all, and tho' I am sometimes horribly unhappy and lonely (in all of which I know you know that I take a sort of pleasure) I escape the worst, and so do you, so you ought not to talk about the end of things being despair." True to the ideals of her generation, she enshrined the experience of the beautiful as a religion. To the young, it seemed enough to sustain them, with its odd mixture of Christian uplift and optimism. Yet it might give way without warning to fits of nihilistic despair for which it had no remedy. The almost rigid pattern of Sara's life doubtless supported her through such spells, but she feared pessimism and futility. "*Please* don't talk about 'the disenchantment that comes with years,' " she begged. "I don't think that it has come to you and I hope that it will never come to me. . . . I don't like to think that things are futile. I have never learned that wanting things doesn't bring them." But he continued writing of his "wrecks of mighty dreams," a youthful burnt-out case, and Sara soon stopped taking his complaint seriously. Because he worked in a stockbroker's office, she did not believe he was really eccentric and suspected that his gloominess was only a pose. Besides, it was her belief that men should be stronger than women.

Feminine submissiveness, however, was at odds with ambition and a professional career, and in writing to a male poet she felt compelled to erase any image he might have of her as an aggressive or competitive female. "I don't *want* to be a 'literary woman,' " she told him. "And please don't think of my verses as playing a very great part in my life, as seeming important to me—for my real life is quite apart from them. . . . Maybe it is at bottom a wish that nobody would ever think of me as 'a woman who writes.' I *know* I'm not like most of the 'women who write,' for they love to argue and I don't, and they are never afraid of people, and I always am, and they know all about the subconscious mind and food-values and politics. . . ." Yet she fretted at the lack of vigor in her own work: "As for my own poetry, it is far too weak and plaintive to please me." But she would not like it even if it were stronger—"It is only incidental to my life. Art can never mean to a woman what it does to a man. Love means that." O'Hara, oblivious to the conflict that pulled her in opposite directions, was apparently encouraged by her references to love and so determined to take her as a woman rather than as a poet, for that is what she seemed to ask.

By the time she returned to St. Louis in early September, apparently having recovered from the collapse of her health, they had fallen into a tone of easy familiarity, and O'Hara was beginning to make compliments about her physical appearance, fishing for personal information, and alarming her that he might expect too much in the way of beauty and personality. She shrank from romantic idealization of herself, insisting she was very ordinary in every way, and parried his offer of a "candid confession" without really rejecting it, claiming not to know what he meant by the "cerebral iniquities" he said he had been committing. And so his flirtation progressed, under the serious exchange of literary talk and his constant mawkish appeals for sympathy and for "more intimate" letters. Like the golden-haired lady of "The Crystal Cup," she encouraged him while feigning aloofness.

On September 6, 1908, the St. Louis *Republic* published another illustrated article about her, this time in larger scale: "Reared in luxury, Miss Teasdale withdrew herself in a large measure a few years ago from all but a few close and dear friends, and began devoting herself to her work and her studies. . . . For days at a time she is secluded in her study, surrounded by her books and art treasures." Sara exploded in disgust. "The reporter of the Sunday thing sat down to imagine what a 'poetess' must be like, and lo and behold I find that I am 'sad, strong and reserved.' Ye gods! And that I am accustomed to shut myself for days in my study, and a lot of the most absurd trash." It was another skirmish in the conflict between reality and the preposterous idealization that was imposed on her as a woman poet.

The $50-thousand house in Kingsbury Place was under construction now, fulfilling Mrs. Teasdale's ambition for a grand residence. Many of the houses on the exclusive block were even grander, behind the dignified iron gates and monumental stone façades at the entrance to the divided street with its center strip of lawn and trees. Sara was to have her own study and bath, which she was decorating to please herself, as if she were never to leave home. Every day she went driving, on doctor's orders, in her "own little phaeton" with a monogram on the side she had designed herself. Her horse's name was Lady Clare. She engaged a tutor for French lessons, having gotten deep into Balzac, Gautier, and the French poets in poor translations. One day she went over to Attica, Illinois, to visit her old friend Bessie Brey, now Mrs. Williamson Dunn Vater, wife of a minister, and on the train coming home composed "all but fifteen or twenty lines" of another of the monologues about disastrous love, "Helen of Troy," sending it off to O'Hara for criticism, remarking she had never enjoyed writing any poem so much. Even though the question of being a woman writer troubled her, especially when discussing it with a male writer, she was pushing steadily ahead with her unfolding career, keenly enjoying the pleasure of seeing her words in print. In obedience to custom that decreed that a woman should put nothing above domesticity and her love for a man, she spoke and behaved as she believed she ought to. Nevertheless, her work was the unacknowledged center of her whole existence.

The other friend from a distance who figured importantly in her emotional development came on the horizon about the same time as O'Hara. This was Marion Cummings Stanley, a philosophy instructor at the University of Arizona, who had written to Sara spontaneously in February 1908 after discovering that a student in one of her classes was a mutual acquaintance. She was eight years older than Sara, married, and given to intense enthusiasms and spells of depression that she recognized as virtually an illness. Sara had never known anyone of such high-pitched sensitivity. She was almost a feminine Shelley, wearing her heart on her sleeve, stretching her nerves to the limit, driving herself to exhaustion in the pursuit of elusive ideals. They were soon exchanging letters overflowing with their enthusiasms, and in October 1908 Marion invited Sara to come to Tucson for a winter visit. Mrs. Teasdale reacted with characteristic alarm. Sara, at twenty-four, had never been allowed to travel anywhere without approved supervision, and even in St. Louis, she told O'Hara, "if I am out after dark my mother and father are so dreadfully worried." She consented on condition that Sara be accompanied by Mary, their Irish maid. They rented a house next door to Mrs. Stanley, a few blocks from the university, at what is now the corner of Mountain Avenue and Speedway, and on November 11 Sara was on her way to Tucson with maid and trunks full of linens and other supplies.

Marion turned out to be all she had anticipated, she delightedly told O'Hara: "She is the finest, most charming, most lovable person I have ever known." Marion, with her delicate childlike features, spiritual restlessness, and sweet temper, also wrote creditable poetry and was interested in the same writers that Sara was. They talked excitedly for hours and, in lieu of musical performances, whistled classical music together. Marion tried to launch them on an ambitious reading program in philosophy, psychology, and French, as well as literature, but they managed only a few authors—Hauptmann, Sudermann, D'Annunzio, Dante, and Shakespeare. Her husband, Bruce, who worked for the Southern Pacific Railroad, seems to have shared her intellectual interests, and Sara in her subsequent letters remembered him with cordiality, although he was probably absent from most of their excited discussions. Marion's pronounced independence may already have foreshadowed her separation from Bruce Stanley five years later and their subsequent divorce. But most of the letters exchanged by Sara and Marion were destroyed, and the record of what they may have said about Marion's marriage is silent.

Sara quickly established a routine with her usual afternoon rest and several hours of writing, taking lunch with Marion but dinner alone in her cottage. She found out for the first time how much money it cost to live from day to day—"I was always writing for checks to Papa," she told O'Hara—a discovery that she gradually realized was of immense importance to a woman. Her maid called her "Baby," a name Marion took up with the affectionate protectiveness that Sara seemed to inspire in older women whom she looked up to with admiration. "Marion is a perfect dear," she wrote to O'Hara—"only she is so easy to manage. It's always a dreadful temptation to make people do your way when you can—but somehow I rather like to feel that I can't do a thing without them, and that I am being managed myself." Yet, she fretted from time to time that everyone treated her like a child and sheltered her from adult knowledge and responsibility. "Do you, too, think of me as a child and keep sad things from me for that reason?" she asked O'Hara. "Almost every one treats me so . . . but you know how old I am, and that I have 'put away childish things,' and that I can understand suffering."

But nothing was more indicative of Sara's immaturity than her uncritical and adoring enthusiasm for Marion. One gathers from her correspondence with Marion afterward that for the first time she could talk without inhibition about the private questions that troubled or fascinated her, including her curiosity about sex. She had lived all her life boxed in by silence and restrictions and was at last, at twenty-four, able to break free for a few weeks of impassioned sharing of her intimate concerns. She recognized it as a turning point in her life. They talked about her ill health; Marion, who had grown up in San Jose, California, her parents separated, her mother struggling to make a living, even reduced at times to giving guitar lessons, thought that Sara only intensified her problems by the inactivity and rest prescribed by her parents and doctors. The supposed cure was more harmful than helpful, actually generating the overexcitement and nervous exhaustion she was trying to escape. She needed instead to get out into the world and work, to live a normal life. The key to her cure, she argued, lay within Sara herself. Apparently Marion recommended "mental science," for Sara wrote to O'Hara in December 1908 that she was terribly interested in it, "because I think that there is so real a connection between mind and body that it ought to be a very great help, especially in cases like mine where 'nervous prostration' . . . seems to be the only thing the matter." Her life would be among the "happiest that I have known about" but for her ill health, which "has been so constant and unpleasant that . . . I see no way of getting out of it even in the future. Not that there is anything serious the matter—fortunately there isn't." Marion, in trying to help her overcome the neurasthenic attacks, challenged her to think seriously about their psychological meaning, probably for the first time.

Alone in her room with the turmoil and excitement of her thoughts, she wrote the sonnet, "Fear," and told O'Hara she had been having some bad moods; "In fact I have gone so far as to quite agree with you that the whole thing is useless and death is better than life." But she relied, she said, on her "cheerful disposition and such spells are short-lived, though they are bitter enough while they last."

Marion was older, liberal, and better informed, and wanted to help Sara in her struggle to escape from the chrysalis of her childhood, bringing home to her for the first time the hard lesson of self-sufficiency that was the story of her own life. Sara's poem "Day's Ending (Tuscon)," written in August 1921 after a decade of painful growth, looked back on the encounter with Marion and said, in part:

> It was not long I lived there
> But I became a woman

> Under those vehement stars.
> For it was there I heard
> For the first time my spirit
> Forging an iron rule for me,
> As though with slow cold hammers
> Beating out word by word:
> "Only yourself can heal you,
> Only yourself can lead you,
> The road is heavy going
> And ends where no man knows;
> Take love when love is given,
> But never think to find it
> A sure escape from sorrow
> Or a complete repose."[5]

"Becoming a woman" no longer meant surrendering herself to a man.

In early February 1909, she was on her way home to St. Louis after two and a half months that had changed her life. Marion was "the most thoroughly congenial friend I have ever had," she told O'Hara. But at home on her own, away from her teacher and under the repressive thumb of her mother again, she fell into a miserable fit of depression, complaining that she couldn't even turn it into a poem—"as soon as a thing is nicely arranged in rhyme and meter it ceases to bother one." She asked her mother to read to her, and "she read something about 'Life's Ideals' —very good, but not what I wanted either." She was lonely, writing to Marion every few days and filled with disconsolate restlessness. "My stomach is acting like a fiend," she told her. Marion urged her again not to rely on the doctors, but Sara protested that they "are very cheerful and anxious for me to take exercises and go about like anybody else. You see, blessed, I have been throwing up my meals (forgive me for telling you, but you seemed to think it a mistake for me to be seeing them so much) and eating almost nothing and having hurts by the 10,000 and feeling feverish all the time etc. so it was really best to have them." Reedy wrote to her with advice much like Marion's: "Have you ever tried telling the doctor to hie him to the deuce and just doing all he tells you not to? I was 'given up' once by the M.D.'s, got mad, threw away my medicine, went out and got soaked in a big storm on top of a freight car, caught an awful cold—and there's been nothing doing for the doctors since." But neither succeeded in prying her from her dependence on the doctors.

Sara was sending O'Hara's letters on to Marion to read, for "Mr. Man," as they called him, was beginning to make more insistent advances, and Sara at last had someone to confide in. He sent her a postcard of "Cabanel's Venus," forcing her to complain that "the mood in which the picture is conceived is not altogether a pleasing one to me. Perhaps after all I am somewhat of a Puritan at bottom." Undaunted, O'Hara "gave me a funny

little talk," she wrote Marion, "about not believing in the social conven-
tions of the present day. . . . He will be told as delicately and sweetly as
I can tell it that I have nothing against conventions, and that if I am a
Pagan, I am a Puritanized one—or else the other way around, a Paganized
Puritan." But she softened the admonishment when actually delivering
it to O'Hara: "I've never been able to tell whether I am a Puritanized
Pagan or a Paganized Puritan. Both sides seem pretty strong. A long line
of ministers in my ancestry almost turns the scale" but she is "true to the
old gods too—after my fashion. However, I don't agree with your rather
radical ideas about our social institutions, and I have very little patience
with the Noras (that was the name of the woman in 'The Doll's House,'
wasn't it?) who try to 'realize themselves' at the expense of other people.
But enough of this, because I don't know much about it anyway."

O'Hara did not feel rebuffed and intensified the tempo of his unconventional courtship. She tried to keep the tone of her letters light. But
by April her feelings had put her ill in bed again. She had been reading
*The Master Builder* and *Peer Gynt* but confessed to O'Hara, "I'm afraid that
I don't like it very much"; and Matthew Arnold, whose work she found
depressing: "He makes me so dreadfully unhappy." She had a "trained
nurse," and her parents were talking about sending her back to Cromwell
for another rest cure. The spring, like the one the year before, had been
filled with intense and restless excitement. *Scribner's* had taken her "Hel-
en of Troy." Swinburne, the idol of her generation, had died, and she,
along with everyone else, was writing a poem on his death. Will and Grace
Parrish were off to New York to hear Mary Garden in "Salome," and Will,
she told Marion, was so taken with enthusiasm for Sara's new friend in
Tucson that she "announced that she 'wanted to take you up.' " But Sara
unobtrusively kept them apart, to protect Marion from Will's aggressive
advances. Sara now had a new "literary confessor."

Early in May 1909 she was shipped off to Cromwell again in the hope
of quieting her symptoms. Will Parrish met her in New York, and they
drove out to O'Hara's apartment building on Riverside Drive in early
morning to stare at it and wonder if any of the men emerging on their
way to work would be he. "I wish that there weren't such things as
conventions," she wrote him, "for I would have let you know of my
arrival." But they did not meet. He felt her manners were too stiff. "No,"
she protested, "you mustn't think me too formal—I'm not at all—but it
would have been a rather awkward way to meet for the first time in a
railway station."

O'Hara was determined to break down her defenses, and now that his
letters were becoming unabashedly personal she began to panic. It suddenly occurred to her that he might have imagined the love poems she
had been sending him for criticism were written to him. "I shouldn't send
you such a lot of dreary love songs if you weren't a poet, for otherwise
you would think that they all had to do with me and what Mr. Reedy calls

'an overpopulated heart.' As it is, I'm sure that you realize how purely fanciful most of them are." But she had already undercut this position by insisting that for a woman love came before art. Nevertheless she was caught up in the irresistible appeal of the sexual innuendoes in his letters and poems, and on May 12, sitting in her cottage at Cromwell, cold and lonely, wrapped in blankets and a scarlet bathrobe, she wrote him: "I wish that you were here to read to me. . . . I should like to take an automobile ride to-night and go far, far and very fast—to pass thro' town after town and see the flickering lights and then out again into the free country. The wind has been wild all day and I think that it makes me a little wild too—what a disjointed letter!"

It was an indirect confession of what she wrote to Marion more openly a few days later:

My darling: I am so sick and unhappy. . . . My stomach is a veritable fiend and then there are other things just as bad—my heart for instance. Dearest, I have never felt so utterly ashamed of myself and horrid in my life as I have this spring. You are the only person I would ever speak of it to. . . . I have had the nastiest streak of "Imeros" that ever beset me. What can I do about it? I can't control my thoughts—they go a thousand ways that they ought not to go. When I was with you it wasn't so. I feel like saying: "Paola, give me peace. It is so sweet a thing to live forgetting, to be no more out in the tempest tossed." I'm dreadfully tired of the tempest.

I had a wild communication from J. M. O. the other day—no letter simply two poems—not by him. . . . It was hard for me to write a simply light letter back. And yet I'm not a bit in love with him in the nice way—or at least, very little. This is part of one of the poems:

"Take all of me. I am thine own—heart, soul,
Brain, body, all—all that I am or dream
Is thine forever"—etc.

The emotion O'Hara had succeeded in arousing frightened her, because years of forbidding silence had made her believe it was dangerous and wrong. "Imeros," a more simply physical passion than "eros," was known to her through its traditional association with Sappho, in whose poems the word appears half a dozen times. To fight it, she applied the Puritan theory of doing the opposite of what she desired and busied herself reading the New Testament and the *Paradiso* of Dante, instead of the new free-thinking writers, "really enjoying both—which somewhat astonishes me," as well it might, since only three months before she had written to Marion, "To be very frank, isn't the 'Divine Comedy' boresome? I've read the Inferno twice and Purgaturio once but couldn't keep patience and courage for the Paradiso." But courage and patience were just what she needed now, wrestling with her guilty emotions. The inner battle seesawed back and forth. Since the Puritanical doctor admonished her not to write so much, then writing a letter to O'Hara must be wicked—"But the Greek isn't afraid—she says that what you want to do is best of all—and she's uppermost." And she sent him some forget-me-nots "plucked to-night beneath the moon." He begged for a photograph, but she refused on the grounds that "I'm not at all nice to look at," and besides, "I don't know you well enough." And then O'Hara again overstepped the line of good manners. "I'm afraid I must tell you," she chided him, "that neither the Greek nor the Puritan enjoyed your last letter. I think that your 'Paganism'—tho' they didn't take it in the least seriously, offended both of them a little." Such mild chastisement only seemed to challenge him, and she had to deliver another stern, though gentle, scolding. It was unconventional enough for her to be writing him without knowing him, but "You mustn't make it any more unconventional," or she would have to break it off. She tried to convince him she was really unattractive: She wore glasses, "which I loathe to an unexampled extent," was unromantically practical, and had a sense of humor. And "Please don't say that you hate Christianity. . . . Oh I wish you didn't hate so many things that are good. . . . I wish you knew my father who is one of my ideals and *is* a Christian."

And so it went, allowing herself the unaccustomed freedom of feeling "Greek," only to have the Puritan freeze in fear—in part, a deep fear of her own inadequacy. She wanted him to come to Cromwell for a visit before she left in July 1909 but was frightened at the prospect. They had built up images of each other through letters, she said, and would almost certainly be disappointed.

Whether the doctors at Cromwell Hall helped her or not is uncertain, but she seemed to be recovering. She hammered at brass in the workshop —part of the therapy now was doing handicrafts—and they focused the rays of the sun through a magnifying glass into her sore throat. She continued reading the authors whose harsher realism offended her: Ibsen again, and Hardy, whose "style is horrid—if such a commonplace way of writing can be dignified by the name." She could not align herself with the progressive drift of the times without resistance. In New York on her way home early in July, she again avoided O'Hara. "Did you really think that I'd let you know when I passed thro' New York after you had persuaded me that dreams in some cases are better than realities?"

Another reason for the long stay in Cromwell was that the family's move to the splendid new house in Kingsbury Place would be made during her absence, for the disorder of moving would have upset her too much. She paused long enough in St. Louis to enjoy her new quarters a bit, with their green walls, brown woodwork, and red Persian rug. She had been putting her new book together and dropped in to see Reedy for his advice. He had urged her to get away from Richard Badger, the *Poet*

*Lore* publisher, who was, he said, "no good—a faker and I fear a wolf in the bargain. And any real stuff he may publish is hurt by the frightful amount of bad stuff he prints." Reedy advised her to approach the reputable ones like Harper, Scribner, or Macmillan. He thought Witter Bynner at Small and Maynard in Boston might like it.

And then she was off to Charlevoix, where the case of "imeros" returned in August with greater rigor than ever. Everything converged— she felt a sense of freedom in her summer-house overlooking the lake, Marion was coming for a visit, and O'Hara persisted in his attempted seduction through the mails. "I'm in a very Greek mood," she wrote him, knowing well now what she meant by that. "My Puritan and my Greek have been in constant combat lately and I am rather tired out in consequence. The Greek declares that she is in the ascendant, but I am unhappy and have a cold, so I imagine that the Puritan has the real victory. . . . Oh I wish I could fall asleep and sleep and sleep and sleep." The pressure of imagined love and of the impending visit of Marion, who in her maternal way would give her peace, brought her around to an attack of illness and the fear of death again. "I'm afraid that I'm very unbrave about it," she wrote O'Hara. "Sometimes the thought of having to die becomes literally terrible. There seems to be a means of escape from almost every horrible thing but that. . . . I'm too anxious to live now. Even pain and sorrow are precious—they are living, at any rate." She was also an incurable insomniac, telling stories to herself and even ritualistically repeating her childhood prayers to put herself to sleep—"tho' such a procedure must be distasteful to the Deity"—and had long fallen into the shameless habit of sleeping late every morning to make up for it, sometimes not rising till ten or eleven o'clock.

Marion's visit did quell the unrest, for Sara was able to focus herself, as before, through the personality of her friend. In a poem written the previous winter, she had stated the relationship with Marion with her usual surface simplicity and underlying half-hidden complexity:

> You bound strong sandals on my feet,
>     You gave me bread and wine,
> And sent me under sun and stars,
>     For all the world was mine.
>
> Oh, take the sandals off my feet,
>     You know not what you do;
> For all my world is in your arms,
>     My sun and stars are you.[6]

She printed it in her new book under the heading "Love Songs," a designation that deliberately created a misleading sense while concealing the true one. Marion had opened the door to freedom; but the pupil shrank from the world, preferring to stay in the protective arms of the teacher, for she recognized that the new luster of experience was not in the world itself but in the vision of it caught through her friend. It was a confession of enraptured dependence.

This summer in Charlevoix, Marion played the role assumed three years earlier by Will Parrish—the advisor in putting her new book together. It absorbed most of their time, and by mid-September, when Marion was on her way back to Tucson, the manuscript was ready to be sent on its rounds. It went first to Small and Maynard, who returned it in October. But she indefatigably continued to circulate it.

O'Hara himself had published a volume of poems of his own composition in August 1909, *Songs of the Open,* which Sara praised perfunctorily. She lacked genuine enthusiasm for most of his work except the Sapphic poems. He was already busy on another volume, to be called *Pagan Sonnets,* published the following year. Sara probably read many of these sonnets as he wrote them, for he fired off poems to her in profusion. The "pagan" sonnets seem commonplace and undistinguished today, and the daring assertion of his anti-Christian "Greek" attitude could hardly have been very shocking even then:

> Intuitive, and loving earth, the Greek
>   Discerned the saner wisdom that we seek;
>   Weary of worship for the noumenon,
> We turn from Calvary to Helicon,
> From subtle introspection to the free
>   And soul-uncaring life of Arcady.

Or in "Aqua Religio":

> My soul revolts at that ascetic sign,
>   The cross whose pity stifled pagan glee.

The contrast between Christian gloom and Greek joy was already a commonplace, and O'Hara's supposed wickedness was a faint echo of the decadent poets of the nineties who exploited the pathological side of the cult of beauty. His "The Dream of Caligula" is a sadistic description of the whipping of a nude red-haired young woman, and in "The Baths of Caracalla" he imagines himself to be the water running from the mountain to the city to be warmed and scented, in which a female slave, "nude, immersed in me, will soon be mine!" The note of sensual heavy breathing, the sidelong smirk, was precisely what Sara found offensive in his letters, although she allowed herself to be lured by the promise of unselfconscious freedom of feeling. She did not yet realize that O'Hara was as morbidly inhibited as she was, and his "Greek" spirit existed only on paper.

When Marion left her in September 1909, Sara suffered another relapse into emotional turmoil and stomach disorder, as she had the previous spring after the Tuscon visit. They agreed to write to each other twice a week, an arrangement to which Sara was more faithful than Marion. But within two weeks she was begging for a reassurance of Marion's affection: "You are so far away and have so many people who are fond of you I have to reassure myself quite often on the subject. . .truly, it is indispensible to me." During the next year, she clung to Marion like a child to a mother's skirts, with a determination that must sometimes have taxed Marion's own slender strength. Nothing so reveals the cost in anxiety, fear, and insecurity of Sara's abnormal upbringing as her desperate need for someone to take the place of her mother in supporting her during her struggle to adulthood. And Marion, who suffered a sympathetic personal agony for all the deprivation in the world, pouring her emotions out in cloudy schemes for world peace and human progress, welcomed the opportunity to answer that need.

The Teasdale household in the fall of 1909 after the return from Charlevoix was not a pleasant place, Sara confided to Marion. "The family rubs and annoyances have begun again with renewed vigor now that my mother is on her native heath. The unwelcome members of the family seem to be as firmly fixed here as ever. . . . My stomach is gone to smash again." Sara's older sister Mamie had married, and she and her husband, Joseph Wheless, had moved in for a while. Sara frankly detested him throughout her life, despite her love for Mamie. He compiled and published several reference books on law, and the noise of his typewriter now drove her out of her study to the third floor with her bedclothes and notebooks, where she could also escape the noise of her mother's domestic management "in fortissimo tones" and the slamming of kitchen doors "at the unholy hour of six or six thirty a.m." She had also let Marion talk her into taking some classes at Washington University, something to help her develop, and now had to face actually going through with it. She enrolled in courses in French and ancient philosophy that met on the same days, to minimize travel, but complained volubly about the long streetcar rides and pavements and stairs, and the three and a half hours it took from her day to do it all. Probably she was inviting Marion to release her from the commitment. She eventually dropped the French course but finished the philosophy except for the final examination, taking a grade of incomplete. The experience doubtless accomplished little that Marion had hoped for. Sara's interests had never been academic.

More engrossing were her friends and some of their gatherings, now that she had graduated from the circle of the Potters. She had begun to see an old acquaintance from school days at Hosmer Hall, Zoë Akins, daughter of the postmaster of St. Louis, who was writing poetry and verse plays, acting in a local company, and developing a sophistication that Sara half admired and half ridiculed. Zoë had all the brashness and theatricality that were totally the opposite of her own temperament. Sara was induced to attend a party one evening in September in the rooms of a colorful local personality, a Comtesse de Venturini, where, to Sara's mind, decadence reigned. "The gods, but *she's* a decadent looking creature—small, dark, with a very pale green skin and a brilliant vermillion mouth (evidently painted), eyes painted around with charcoal and wild fuzzy black hair. . .with a *big* black velvet rose in her girdle—all dreadfully Baudelairish." This scene from Toulouse-Lautrec included several other local French people, George Sibley Johns, editor of the *Post-Dispatch,* and Zoë Akins, who, "with a cigarette, legs crossed in a delicately revealing fashion, and her most Frenchy manner. . .quite rivalled Madame la Comtesse." The Countess, she was told, was author of something called *Le Journal Erotique*—"Isn't that a nice title? So wholesome." Zoë willingly recited her poems, but Sara declined to do her own. "I never feel more utterly puritanical than when I am with such people."

Her prudishness was further titillated by Zoë's producing some suppressed poems of Baudelaire, in French, which had been lent to her; "several of the poems are about Sappho and her 'girl friends' as Mr. Man calls them, and Zoë was quite ready with unpleasant details (she and the countess read them together, the countess translating) but I didn't like to hear them so I stopped her. Albeit, I'm going to glance over the book, which proves that I'm no angel after all." One of the poems, she said, depicted Sappho as murdered by a man who discovered she had had sexual relations with women before loving him—"surely one of the strangest, most morbid things I've ever heard!"

A few years later, both Zoë Akins and Sara were in New York, where Zoë achieved the kind of flamboyant success as a playwright she wanted. They were never intimate friends. Sara viewed her with mingled sympathy and pathos—"Poor youngster—there are so many nice things about her and so many 'flimsy' ones," one of them being her constant play for attention. But in St. Louis they found each other stimulating enough to meet occasionally, and they were joined by Orrick Johns, three years younger than they, son of George Sibley Johns. All three were writing poetry, all went on to New York to literary careers. Orrick had lost a leg in a childhood accident and lived in the shadow of his more forceful father. While Zoë had her ambition and Sara the small, clean circumference of her art, Orrick was a bundle of uncertainties in search of a purpose. He was given to cloudy enthusiasms and despondent confusion, chafing to escape from St. Louis. His youthful ideal was Beauty, the religion of the young intellectuals from 1890 to 1914, as he wrote in his autobiography, *Time of Our Lives:* "The famous creed of Louis Dubedat in 'The Doctor's Dilemma' was the perfect echo of our aspiration: 'I believe in Michelangelo, Velasquez and Rembrandt, in the might of design, the mystery of color, the redemption of all things by beauty everlasting, and the message of Art that has made these hands blessed, amen.' How we thrilled to those rolling syllables, and how confidently we looked to that abstract thing Louis called 'beauty' to solve all problems."[7] And, like so many others, he later translated his esthetic idealism to "social consciousness" and finally to communism. He died a suicide.

Orrick remembered Sara Teasdale in St. Louis as having "very little existence outside her poems. She herself said, 'I suppose my work is more truly I than I am myself. . . . I am helpless as a babe at anything but my poor little tunes.' . . . She was solitary, frail, and a devourer of books; modest about her own lyrics, yet confident and assured when her stanzas satisfied her. Her delight was contagious—it was childlike, extraordinary —when she read something of her own or of another's that pleased her."[8] John Hall Wheelock also recalled the intensity of her enthusiasms: "She would suddenly get up from the chair she was in and leap up into the air and clap her hands and cry out, 'Isn't that beautiful! My God, isn't that wonderful!' " Orrick Johns was impressed, too, with the keenness of her critical judgment. "She had very strong dislikes. Confused or decadent or too-clever work brought quick disapproval from her, but she would labor over a beginner's lines, offering suggestions rather than alterations."[9] As to his own poetry, Orrick "has done some striking work, I think," she told O'Hara, "tho' it is morbid usually."

"She was as firm of character as she was frail of body," Orrick Johns remembered. "The family had a surrey and I often drove with her through the park. One day going over a snowbank, the surrey tipped far over, its top scraped the side of a running trolley and the horse reared. I was at the reins and managed to ease down over the bump and stop the horse, but Sara was cooler than I was. We drove without talking, and only after we got home did she say that her heart had been in her mouth."[10] Like many intensely nervous people, she was usually stoically calm in an actual emergency.

Sara was courted, if that is the word for it, by another sonneteer during the fall of 1909 and for several years afterward, this time a local poet named Robert E. Lee Gibson, whom she probably met at one of the social gatherings, and whose attentions she had some difficulty in shunting aside gracefully. Gibson had published a little volume, *Sonnets and Lyrics*, in Louisville in 1901. At forty-six, he was portly and balding, twenty-one years her senior. A good sample of his work is his sonnet "Autobiographical," beginning

> An arch-contriver of sweet phrase, I gain
> An entrance to the wonderlands of song;

To me the happy faculties belong
The shining peaks of Pindus to attain.

Sara dreaded hurting anyone's feelings and agonized over simple social situations in which she might inadvertently appear inconsiderate. John Hall Wheelock recalled that she never found it easy to say goodbye, "because the two difficult times for a shy person are entering a room and leaving it. There are people who have been known to stay all night because they couldn't summon up the courage to leave, it makes them so conspicuous. Sara was like that." Although she recognized a comic element in Gibson's interest in her, she felt obliged to let him call on her but required him to come on Saturday afternoons "because I'm afraid he'll stay late if he comes at night and I'm not just wild to lose my sleep for him." Shortly she was writing Marion, "He seems to have a bad case." But his conversation bored her and his obvious infatuation made her uncomfortable. When *Helen of Troy and Other Poems* was published in the fall of 1911, Gibson wrote in his tiny neat script a cry of smothered adoration: "I cannot trust myself to tell you in sober words how ardently I admire your book! It came this morning and I am all in a fever of excitement over it. It has completely enchanted me. I have never seen a book of poems that I love as I love yours. . . . Everything in the book is so sweet and wholesome."[11] A few days later she told Marion, "You ask about poor R. E. L. G.—he's just the same as ever—just as foolish and slow as he was at first. I let him come to see me the other day for the first time since April. I can't bear him—he is so sort of like a cat." "Poor R. E. L. G." fades from the record after that. He died in 1917 at the age of fifty-four.

Marion's teaching to the contrary, Sara had thought enough about her developing career to conclude now that she would not, like Zoë Akins, try for independence and the masculine kind of success. Money was at the root of a woman's problem. Always having her needs met, even her whims, and never having to think where the money came from, she could not imagine how she could ever support herself. "I am glad that I am a woman," she told O'Hara. "I have sometimes thought that if I ever had to support myself, I should commit suicide. It is so hard for a woman to make even enough to keep soul and body together—and if one is hampered by ill health one might about as well give it up altogether." The actual dimensions of that burden had apparently first dawned on her in Tucson, and at twenty-five she decided what her future had to hold in store for her—a husband who could support her. For reasons of survival, her poetry could not be the central commitment of her life.

Sara had also calculated precisely the amount of income she needed in order to be independent: $150 a month, not including doctors' bills or travel, both of which for her were actual necessities. Cromwell Hall cost $45 a week, and she stayed there months on end, and in St. Louis her parents hired the perennial "trained nurse" to be with her when she had one of her sieges of the grippe. She was probably unaware that her minimal needs far exceeded the salary on which millions of working men supported families with three or four children. "But fortunately, I have never had to put it to the test," she confessed to O'Hara.

If her mode of life seemed extravagant to others, it was not so in the usual ways that Veblen would have branded "conspicuous consumption." Money was needed simply to guarantee the freedom from stress, from exertion, from ugliness—a life of safety, quiet, and attractive surroundings, an extension of her childhood home. She shrewdly calculated the means required for such a life and cared nothing for any amount of wealth beyond it. She did not specify how much of her budget would go for clothing, the one expense in which she might admit to self-indulgence. Her letters often speak of dresses she can't resist buying, and she freely admitted to comforting herself with something new to wear, like the "most gorgeous cream color antique Chinese shawl" she mentioned once to Jean Untermeyer, "that I blew myself to one day, when being extravagant seemed the only cure for a bad case of blues." But the colors and style of her clothing were low-keyed and conservative, of rich, soft, receding greys rather than bright colors that would attract attention. She had to stretch her monthly $20 allowance when living at home to cover all the little luxuries she loved, and in the fall of 1909 was somewhat ashamed of herself for selling some books and pictures to a second-hand dealer for two dollars in order to help pay for some plaster casts for her study, including a fifty-four-inch replica of several slabs of the Parthenon frieze.

December 1909 was cold, and Sara had been fretting to escape both the weather and the family prison for a while with a trip to St. Augustine, Florida, this time without a chaperone. She badly wanted to be alone. There is no record showing how much she wrote during the fall; she had jokingly warned that going to college in obedience to Marion Stanley's advice would cut her productivity, so she may have wanted circumstances more conducive to writing. The two had read Housman's *A Shropshire Lad* together in Charlevoix; it was her only literary enthusiasm of the season, which included Matthew Arnold, Swinburne, and Plato's *Republic*. She had grown so hypercritical, she told O'Hara, that she had experienced nothing so exciting as Housman for a long time. But the hope for a trip alone was soon dashed—her mother decided to go along with her. In the end, Sara seems not to have minded, for it was more important to get to a warm climate, and they were off to "Paradise" on January 14. She was soon sending off new poems, reveling in the warmth, and reading Balzac, who, after first alarming her a year before—"Balzac grips your arm— there is no escape from him. He frightens me"—had now become her favorite novelist. The newly developed taste for Housman and Balzac signaled the intellectual toughening that she had begun to develop after the shock of Marion's analysis.

She was also reading the Old Testament, a sure sign of emotional unrest, for it meant she was applying her Puritan principle of doing what was good for her rather than what she desired. The drift of her emotions is not clear on the surface, but O'Hara figured in them still, judging by the late spring and summer, when his love making by letter reached a crescendo. Her reading, her inexperience, and her fantasizing had prepared her to be the princess swept up in a consuming passion, to lose her own identity in blissful submission to her king. But her practical spirit, and perhaps Marion's advice, asserted itself when love actually hovered as a reality. And, if the year before she had lost control of her thoughts, she had since learned to study the phenomenon with detached curiosity. There was antiromantic honesty, sometimes irony, in her constant reiteration to O'Hara of the commonplace aspect of her life. Being a "Poetess," writing "milk-and-watery love songs," as she called them, she knew that men tended to idealize her according to that same chivalric formula she was beginning to dissect. Whenever O'Hara played the role of poetic lover, she nudged him with the ordinary facts of her life and insisted her poems were of little consequence. "I sometimes wonder if there is *any* hope for me as a poet since I am neat and terribly punctual," she wrote, "and care for clothes." O'Hara, however, preferred the princess to be above such things. "You amuse me," she retorted, "by saying that you would rather think of me 'above the sphere of domesticity.' What a funny notion—only I know that you aren't in earnest." But beneath the pro testations she had obviously begun to think of herself as someone who might seriously be loved.

She was home in St. Louis in April 1910, ill again with the flu. O'Hara sent her a steady stream of sonnets, dashed off on any subject she happened to mention, even the furnishings of her new study. She was better looking than she used to be, she told him. And in May she sent him some pressed pansies—'Je vous envis quelques petites pensees de mon jardin —et de mon coeur." They wrote in French when they wanted to signal serious feeling cloaked in play, and her gesture unleashed a torrent of it from him, "bestowing kisses by mail," she wrote Marion Stanley, "and in French! Since he didn't venture it in English I decided to let the matter pass. . .even though it was a pretty flagrant case and signed 'Jean'!!! Mes levres sont les violettes de son desir et il les presse passionement; d'un long baiser d'ardeur. Well, one couldn't help being somewhat surprised to get a letter written the next day after in which the temperature had fallen from 100 in the shade to a sharp frost—all this change of course without a word from me." She had been probing the genuineness of his passion for months, trying to give him a footing in some sense of what she was really like. The depths of her shyness, of her sense of personal inadequacy, must have been jolted by his incomprehensible shift of mood, just when she had begun to encourage him openly. She had also been "in a very blue mood in regard to my poetry. It seems to me that it is almost utterly worthless. I have never hated it so before." She was taking osteopathic treatments and had been "very miserable for several weeks and am longing to get away for a few days at Saxton's." She needed another escape to be alone and at peace while she thought her way through her problems.

Saxton's Farm had been a favorite place of the Potters for outings, an isolated farmhouse near Sulphur Springs on wooded hills and bluffs overlooking the Mississippi River, where the widowed Mrs. Saxton took in boarders. It was a more convenient place than Cromwell Hall where Sara could smooth her turbulent emotions, and so she spent several days there in late May 1910, the only guest at the time. Walking a path one afternoon along a stream that flowed into the Mississippi and imagining herself in Thessaly, seeing dryads, she suddenly "saw a man in a blue shirt—remembered that I was far from home and started back quickly." It symbolized the intrusion of the problem on her mind into the idyllic Greek region of literary imagination. One night, too, she was terror-stricken when the old ladies who lived at the farmhouse didn't return until long after dark, leaving her alone in the country blackness.

While at Saxton's Farm she wrote a brief "semi-symbolical" blank verse play, "On the Tower," later published in *Helen of Troy*, which explored in the literary terms of Hovey or Maeterlinck the deeper problems on her mind. At the head of it, she prefixed the quotation Reedy had once given her allegory "The Crystal Cup": "Under the leaf of many a Fable lies the truth for those who look for it."

The scene is the "top of a high battlemented tower of a castle," where a Knight has brought a curiously unwilling Lady. She is terrified of the height and fears falling off. She is not his love, she protests, but his "conquered foe," whose gates have been battered down, and now she hands him the key to the highest tower to prove her "homage true." He is exhilarated, wishing he could climb these heights "a thousand times." "I am a woman," she says. "I shall never come/ This way but once." He wants to kiss her, but she is "too tired to kiss." Nevertheless, he lifts her veil and kisses her, "at last your love, your castle's lord." But the virginal white veil blows over the parapet, and there are "Faint cries and laughter from men and women under the tower." She is embarrassed to be seen kissing in front of the people, but "All of them have loved," he says.

The Knight wants to take the keys immediately and go through the

"hundred quiet halls" of her castle, the "hundred chambers," including
her bedroom where she has slept and daydreamed. She puts him off with
a promise. "Some of the halls have long been locked and barred,/ And
some have secret doors and hard to find. . . . We two will search together
for the keys,/ But not to-day." She makes him sit quietly while she sings.
It grows dusk, and he falls asleep:

> All of his vows were sweet to hear,
> Sweet was his kiss to take;
> Why was her breast so quick to fear,
> Why was her heart, to break?
>
> Why was the man so glad to woo?. . .
> Why were the maiden's words so few—

Clouds darken the stars, she "moves to the corner of the parapet and
kneels there" saying the Ave Maria as a page arrives to summon the
knight to a tournament. He wakens, befuddled: "There was a lady on this
tower with me—" But, not seeing her in the dark and apparently forgetting her, he rushes off to his horse and shield. She emerges from the
shadows, hesitates a moment, and then "throws herself over the parapet."[12]

As an allegory of marriage, it depicts a woman unable to provide sexual
love to her husband, a man of easy naturalness in contrast to her fear-
ridden shyness. He plays the masterful chivalric role without difficulty,
but she cannot play the submissive role expected of her. Since she is not
able to hold his interest, he goes off to his masculine games and commitments, forgetting her, just as O'Hara's affections had suddenly turned to
"a sharp frost." The Lady's suicide, which seems so abrupt and un-
motivated in the playlet, is understandable if one fills in her complex
unspoken fears of inadequacy, failure, rejection, and abandonment. Because she cannot tell him she is afraid or unwilling, she is forced to appear
tired and uninterested. Only her songs—as Sara always called her own
poems—are candidly expressive of her conflicting feelings. But he is
asleep and does not hear them.

The dilemma she explored was that of a woman helpless to care for
herself, forced by both convention and practical necessity to marry, but
unable to manage the emotional role imposed on her. The artistic model
for her miniature drama was undoubtedly Maeterlinck. From him and the
French poets, she was learning how to turn the nuances of a simple
description to symbolic suggestion, thereby freeing her from the overt
statement of ideas and allowing her to explore her own intimate thoughts
without immodest public exposure.

By the early summer of 1910, when she wrote "On the Tower," she was
enjoying being analytical and met O'Hara's epistolary love making with
half-joking remarks about her temperament, which never experienced

extremes of emotion because she couldn't help standing aside and watching herself. If the surface of her poems seemed worked to a consummate smoothness, a distillation of tradition rather than a rebellion against it, she nevertheless drew vitality from an honest scrutiny of her own private emotions. An example of this is "Youth and the Pilgrim," written about the same time as "On the Tower" and dealing in ballad form with the idea again of suicide as an escape from love. One recalls her letter to O'Hara the year before when troubled by "imeros": "Oh I wish I could fall asleep and sleep and sleep and sleep." The youth yearns for a "land where love is not," hoping to escape from the oppressive god of Love, and is answered:

> "There is a place where Love is not,
>     But never a ship leaves land
> Can carry you so quickly there
>     As the sharp sword in your hand."[13]

Periodically, when deeply troubled, she experienced a recurrence of her obsessive terror of death, which probably had mingled with it a frightening impulse to resolve her conflicts by destroying herself. Sometimes she answered it with an affirmation of life. But the summer of 1910 was only one of many times when she found relief and peace only in the expectation of death.

With a clearer and more mature mind about her own feelings, she found her attitude toward Marion changing. "She is a very dear person," she told O'Hara, "but she does not loom as large as she did in the beginning." She and Marion remained good friends until they gradually drifted apart four or five years later, but the childlike emotional dependence on Marion, or any other older woman, was over.

In mid-July, she dutifully went off to Charlevoix with her parents, but now, sitting in her little "look-out" above the lake, she found it all boring, and craved to satisfy her restlessness. Life was at a standstill in the slow, sunny summer. For companionship, she talked to her cat and her dog, and for reading—apparently again feeling the need of mental discipline— "I am boring my soul with either the Iliad or the Bible or Marcus Aurelius. They are all so stupid that I get along even more slowly than usual. . . . I can't help wondering why people have read the Iliad for thousands of years. . . . I get so tired of hearing just where each man was wounded with a bronze spear. It would all be very well if the Trojan War were only left out!" Homer, Dante, and Milton, those great masculine literary monuments, were all tedious to her, and she finally stopped caring about them altogether. Marcus Aurelius, however, she decided was "a dear after all."

A spell of illness put her in bed, and an attack of moodiness made her again feel that "After all, sleep is the most satisfactory thing in the world." This produced a poem, "The Quest," never published, which depicts her searching for peace, beseeching the natural elements but receiving no answer, until finally she asks Death, who does not reply but stares at her meaningfully. And this was followed shortly by a lyric about a bee clutching a rose, so richly sexual that she felt obliged to tell O'Hara that her poems had nothing to do with her personal feelings. The trouble with a lyric was that "it always sounds horribly personal." And then another sudden outburst: "I feel very wicked and am wild for some excitement. I think I'll end my letter with my first name, since that is the only dreadful thing I can think of at present." She was wearing a black ribbon in her hair, she said, and a low-necked dress without fear of catching a sore throat. "I am in high spirits, since I happen to have a nice neck." The Greek in her asserted a victory over death and Puritanism for the moment.

Marion came to Charlevoix once more for a visit, and although Sara was lonely in September when she left, there was not the sense of desolation she had felt before. Her father, now in his seventies, was being sued by a neighbor because the stable of which he was so fond was charged with being a nuisance, an ordeal for the old gentleman that although he won the case, distressed Sara immensely. Pushing on through the classics she hadn't read, she discovered Chaucer with apparently more pleasure than Homer or the Bible. But her own work depressed her, as it had all summer. She could not seem to find the clue to what would release her. "How utterly commonplace and childish my songs must seem to you," she told O'Hara, "and to everyone, for that matter; yet, as Leonardo says, 'So hath nature disposed me.' Oh how I should love to make one really fine poem before there is no more *me*. Isn't it *terrible* to think of stopping, of being nothing but a little heap of—oh dear, death is so full of horror. I sometimes think if I ever went mad, it would be from the terror of death."

On through the fall, back in St. Louis, she fretted inwardly, suffered the frustrations of her mother and the household—"she is rather given to managing everything and everybody"—and waited for life somehow to begin. After recovering from the attack of "imeros" in August—possibly because she and Marion had decided not to believe in O'Hara's sincerity —she had taken to teasing him about his flattering and wheedling letters to her. Being a poet herself, she said, she could see through him: "A poet's heart is apt to be like the asbestos wool in a gas grate—it always seems to be on fire but is never burning." She reminded him that although she wrote love poems, "I'm not writing in my heart's blood." When he compared himself fancifully to Villon, she was driven to ridicule: "But poor 'Villon the Vagabond'—who lives in a beautiful apartment on Riverside Drive! What a sad case! I can imagine the 'rags and tatters.' " It was a sensible way to protect herself against the consequences of a dubious involvement.

Amidst the flaming autumn colors, she went off to Saxton's Farm again, which instead of bringing peace seemed empty and lonely. She read Greek mythology to a ten-year-old chore boy, and was disappointed in a Presbyterian minister who came to board while conducting revival meetings in town. "I feel a sort of personal grievance against him for not being better looking." He tried without success—hardly surprising—to interest her in becoming a missionary in China, and she in turn thought of asking him to help her with Chaucer but decided he would be shocked. She had to fall back on her "old Puritan philosophy" and steel herself in patience and cheerful self-denial. There were still friends to see occasionally. But her life had nowhere to go, nothing to fill its need. She was a grown woman, living at home with her parents in the shadow of their old age, waiting for love and fame. "If I were only beautiful and a genius," she sighed, "what fun life would be." Like Baudelaire, she wrote O'Hara, "It seems to me I should always be happy if I were somewhere else."

# CHAPTER FOUR

# "But Oh, the Girls Who Ask for Love . . ."

In mid-December 1910, everything Sara had waited for seemed to happen at once, and her illness and boredom were swiftly dispelled on a flood of excitement. *Helen of Troy,* after having been circulated for over a year in both England and America and rejected by half a dozen publishers, was accepted by Putnam's, who did not require her to bear the expense. Her second book was not a hobby in which her wealthy parents indulged her, but a professional work making its own way. Arriving almost at the same time was an invitation to join the Poetry Society of America and attend their first annual dinner meeting in New York on December 28—a legitimate opportunity, at last, to break free of the stifling atmosphere of her home. She immediately begged her parents for permission to go.

The Poetry Society had been founded two months earlier, in October 1910, the outgrowth of a proposed salon of New York poets who decided instead to form a national organization. Their standards were strictly professional, and to avoid being inundated by amateurs they established membership by invitation only. Sara's name had been put up by Madison Cawein, an immensely popular and facile poet of Louisville, Kentucky, and a friend of Sara's forlorn sonneteer, R. E. L. Gibson. "This was still the period when one had to be apologetic about poetry, when the poet was considered a variant from the normal," Jessie Rittenhouse wrote, one of the founders of the society and for many years its indefatigable secretary. "The Society was the subject of all sorts of good-humored bantering and was the target of many gibes from facetious young reporters who were sent to write up 'The Poets' Union.'"[1] The shrewd Miss Rittenhouse, herself a newspaperwoman as well as a poet, was well suited to deal with the press, quietly minimizing the sensational or the bohemian, and creating around the society an aura of respectability. It was not an organization of which one's aging middle-class parents could disapprove.

Although Sara was now twenty-six and desperately eager to go to New York, she confronted as usual her parents' fearful concern for her health and safety. Her plans were on, then off, and on again, as she missed the dinner meeting of December 28, 1910, and aimed for the society's next regular meeting on February 7, 1911. It was probably only the presence of the resourceful and independent Will Parrish in New York that finally convinced her parents that she could safely go alone. Will Parrish, in fact, told her own mother in St. Louis that Mrs. Teasdale "wrote me asking that I sort of see to it that she is all right, because they were sort of afraid to let her come alone."[2]

She was doubtless in a high state of excitement when her train rolled into New York City at 4:30 in the afternoon of January 18, 1911, delivering her at last from the perpetual childhood and isolation of her home to the glamorous literary life of the great world, where like her own life, its twilight interval was about to come to an abrupt end. Not only were the professional poets organizing, but in another year Harriet Monroe's *Poetry* would be launched, inaugurating the era of little magazines and the most expansive period in the history of American poetry.

Will Parrish had engaged a room for Sara in a boarding house at 53 Irving Place, not far from where she herself was staying, hoping it would be adequate for her aristocratic friend, for, as she told her mother, "To me it is a perfect palace." Williamina, with her photographer's eye, took Sara around Manhattan to see her favorite views when the best light was on them, she reported to O'Hara, "the Metropolitan Tower at dusk . . . the Belvedere in Central Park just as the sun is going down." Within the week, Sara had been to an opera at the Met, had ridden the subway, and been dutifully impressed by her first view of Broadway at night. Somewhat to the discomfort of the frugal Parrish sisters, she insisted on paying fares and treating them to the most expensive seats at the theatre, a style they considered lavish.

And there was to be, at last, a meeting with John Myers O'Hara. Sara must have been privately keyed up at the prospect of encountering face to face her literary lover, the man whose feelings about her she had not been able to define. His letters had been, by turns, respectful, shockingly seductive, coolly distant, and self-pitying. "Pathetically honest," as her friends called her, she took his occasional declarations of love seriously, although cautiously. A week or more passed after her arrival before they finally managed to see each other. It can safely be assumed that she was anxious not to appear too interested and that he also was shy.

It was a sad disappointment. As Sara later reported their meeting to

Marion, he obviously didn't really love her "except in the merest surface way—and I'm not sure even that he does that. Poor old fellow! I wonder what he thinks of me after all." He told her that some lines of his sonnet "The Greek Frieze" in *Smart Set* were written to her. "That was almost the only 'passage of love' that we had, and that was very slight and was over in far less time than it takes to tell it. He is really chivalrous in his attitude toward women—but I think he sees very little of them, for I am convinced . . . that he leads an almost solitary existence. I tried my best to make him see that I wanted to be good friends and nothing more—but I doubt if he understood. He is almost morbidly shy and solitary, and in spite of a very real modesty, he has a queer inconsistent sort of vanity."

The romantic glamor bred by distance quickly evaporated, along with the spells of imeros that had troubled her lonely evenings in Cromwell and Charlevoix. Like her relationship with Marion, this one too had thrived on the needs of her immature years and did not last. For another two or three years, however, she loyally kept up her end of the correspondence, walked the streets of New York with him when she visited there, and listened to his gloomy complaints with patience and sympathy, trying to draw him out of himself. Still, he was a puzzle to be worked out, a man who had roused her by claiming to be in love but who retreated from any actual involvement. During the ensuing months of 1911, she carefully studied both him and herself under the surface of their pleasantry.

The excitement of attending a gathering of the best-known poets in America must have minimized any disappointment she felt in John Myers O'Hara, for this was the magnet that had drawn her to New York. At her first meeting with the Poetry Society, in the gallery of the National Arts Club on Gramercy Square, on Tuesday evening, February 7 at 8:30, she sat shyly and inconspicuously near the wall, feeling provincial, "young and eager, tasting the first intoxication of contact with older poets,"[3] as Jessie Rittenhouse remembered her. It was the practice of the new organization to appoint someone to read aloud the poems submitted anonymously by members for criticism. Witter Bynner, the reader that evening, handsome, well-tailored, and rich-voiced, presented among other poems Sara's dramatic monologue "Helen of Troy" to a very favorable response. "Just back of her," wrote Jessie Rittenhouse in her memoir, "sat Ezra Pound, on his one and only visit to the Society, as he was about to sail for England, being unable longer to 'bear the brunt of America.'" Pound sparkled, exchanging clever gibes across the room with Gelett Burgess "until the audience was in a gale of laughter most of the evening."[4] Although Sara overflowed with delight at that meeting, she did not like Pound, characterizing him later to Louis Untermeyer as a "wobbly blond youth" who displayed "a miserable coarseness every now and then that always crops out when a naturally weak person tries to be 'virile.'"

If she had lain half the day in her bed in St. Louis only six weeks before, too exhausted and depressed even to write, she now threw herself zestfully into the life of New York, determining to stay on another month for the next meeting of the Poetry Society on March 7. She continued seeing the sights with the Parrish sisters, went for occasional walks with John O'Hara, took tea with Witter Bynner and with Willa Cather, called on magazine editors she knew only through correspondence, and saw Isadora Duncan perform one evening in late February; truly "Greek!" she exclaimed to O'Hara. As always, she slept late, went out until lunch, and then worked at her writing and took an afternoon rest.

The exhilaration of being in New York released a flood of new poems, many of them about places she visited. With Williamina Parrish earlier, in the days of the Potters, she developed the idea that poets freely appropriated people, places, or experiences as pegs on which to hang poems— "pegs for Pegasus," in Will's catch-phrase. This knowledge made her suspect the sincerity of O'Hara's outpouring of poems to her and tended to place an ironic distance between herself and her own observed emotions. In the New York poems, the companion on a walk was transformed into a male lover, and the place visited became an appropriate setting for a crucial moment in an imaginary love relationship. In "Coney Island," for example, visited in early March, a love affair has run its course and fails in an effort at revival ("There cannot be . . . a second spring"):

> With foam of icy lace
> The sea creeps up the sand,
> The wind is like a hand
> That strikes us in the face.[5]

Sara notoriously disliked the physical discomfort of cold, windy walks, and this, coupled with the poem's opening line—"Why did you bring me here?"—suggests how she turned a bleak visit to the Coney Island beach with Will Parrish into a dramatic fantasy on a conventional theme.

The poems written during her seven weeks in New York in 1911—"The Metropolitan Tower," "Gramercy Park," "In the Metropolitan Museum," "Coney Island," "Union Square," and "Central Park at Dusk"— have their roots in a literary tradition vigorous throughout the Victorian era: the fascination of place. Places, like people, had distinctive character, and to evoke their names in literature was to arouse a crowd of associations. The mood, or mystique, of locale had nothing to do with regionalism in literature and was in fact its opposite—an appreciation of the foreign, the exotic, the place one visited rather than lived in, like James's Paris or Hemingway's Pamplona. Sara had absorbed the tradition through both reading and actual travel—her travel diary in 1905 falls into a recognizable genre—and she relied heavily throughout her life on her frequent trips away from home for the descriptive imagery of her poems, as even the titles sometimes indicate—"Vignettes Overseas," "In a Cuban Garden," "Nahant," "Fontainebleau." Only one poem deals conspicuously with St. Louis as a locale, and that describes the traveler's homecoming. Despite her indebtedness to the rich tradition of travel literature, however, she rarely showed any interest in merely describing or evoking places in verse for their own sake. Only personal emotion counted as subject for a poem. It was rather that she required the liberating cosmopolitanism of travel, as did other writers of her generation, with its promise of personal emotional escape. She had been a lifelong prisoner in her room, looking wistfully out of windows on imagined worlds of beauty, and New York seemed to provide everything she had been waiting for.

Her sense of liberation in New York is most strikingly evident in the poem "Union Square," which gained her instant notoriety when it appeared in her book eight months later. But it was an eight months fraught with hesitation and doubt as to whether she should publish it at all. She assumed in the poem her characteristic pose of the woman who could not attract a man's love:

> With the man I love who loves me not,
>   I walked in the street-lamps' flare;
> We watched the world go home that night
>   In a flood through Union Square.
>
> I leaned to catch the words he said
>   That were light as a snowflake falling;
> Ah well that he never leaned to hear
>   The words my heart was calling.
>
> And on we walked and on we walked
>   Past the fiery lights of the picture shows—
> Where the girls with thirsty eyes go by
>   On the errand each man knows.
>
> And on we walked and on we walked,
>   At the door at last we said good-bye;
> I knew by his smile he had not heard
>   My heart's unuttered cry.
>
> With the man I love who loves me not
>   I walked in the street-lamps' flare—
> But oh, the girls who ask for love
>   In the lights of Union Square.[6]

Her literary heroines had always been women who unhesitatingly asserted their feminine sexuality regardless of consequences; now for the first time she spoke directly in her own voice. Sara "claimed that her

poems were all based upon personal emotions in her own life," John Hall
Wheelock said, and cited "Union Square" as an example. She had been
taught that men were "aggressive creatures" in love, but in actuality they
seemed to shrink from the "pursuit that men were supposed to be so
famous for. . . . She envied the girls in Union Square who could go up
to a man and take the aggressive step themselves." Believing that men
were free of the inhibitions that imprisoned women, she could not understand their mysterious reluctance to take the initiative a woman waited
for, and she tended to attribute it to shortcomings in herself. The poem
reveals the prurient notion, in which Sara had been reared, that sex was
essentially pornographic. Any woman who dared to assert herself sexually was automatically branded a whore; decent women preserved the virginal image. "Union Square" was an act of boldness, remarkable for any
woman writing in 1911 and doubly so for someone of Sara's genteel
background.

Immediately she was seized with misgivings, and for months afterward
sought the advice of friends on whether she should add the poem to her
forthcoming book. She was especially worried about what men might
think of her. In early April, after returning home to St. Louis where the
conventional family atmosphere enfolded her again, she tried to rewrite
the poem around a different theme:

> And on we walked and on we walked
>  Past the fiery lights of the picture shows
> Where the crowd went in to half forget
>  The grave where each man goes.

It was characteristic of her to turn from love to death as a poetic theme
when troubled, but the revision was poor, and she drew large X's through
the stanzas and wrote "Housman" in the margin.

Fortunately for the fate of "Union Square," she had asked the advice
of Jessie Rittenhouse, with whom she had struck up a friendship just
before leaving New York. Miss Rittenhouse admired the poem and emphatically urged her to publish it. "She thought it exceedingly strong and
beautiful," Sara wrote Marion Stanley, "and while she called the idea
'daring' she seemed to feel that I ought to use it in the book." Marion
seems not to have approved, however, fearing it would hurt Sara's reputation. When *Helen of Troy and Other Poems* appeared in October 1911, the
poem predictably attracted attention. The reviewer in the *New York Times*
on Sunday, December 3 captioned his review "Woman Articulate," and
asked "Has the woman who speaks in that very unusual poem, 'Union
Square,' been always with us but inarticulate?" Sara, in the end, was
pleased to have had the nerve to do it, even though it cast her in the
unwelcome role of New Woman, and she credited Jessie Rittenhouse with
turning the scales: "But for your assuring me that it wasn't so wicked after

all, I should have let it stay in the seclusion of my tiny red note-book."7

At the March 7 meeting of the Poetry Society, she apparently mingled more confidently with the poets, proudly writing to Marion that she had met Edwin Markham, the grand old man of American Poetry and presiding spirit of the Society, who must have reminded her of her white-bearded father. Jessie Rittenhouse invited her to tea with a few other poets at her home, where she often arranged a more intimate group than the public meetings afforded. But Sara's time was running out—she was due to leave on Saturday, March 11—and her landlady had already rented her room to someone else and had no other vacancy. With reluctance, she decided it was best to go home and not try to find another room. The night before she left, she and Miss Rittenhouse nevertheless managed to have dinner together and talked poetry for three hours.

Jessie Rittenhouse was ten years older than Sara, unmarried and now in her mid-thirties, a cheerful, businesslike woman whose metier was organizational work. She always found herself at the center of one society or another, swamped with innumerable details about which she fretted and fussed because they took her away from the composition of her own lyrics, even though she enjoyed it all immensely. There was a touch of Machiavelli in her scheming for the good of the organization, for poets, she felt, had egos that required skillful handling. Born in central New York State, she had been a schoolteacher, freelance writer, newspaper reporter, an activist in prison reform, and editor of an important anthology, *The Younger American Poets* (1904), one of the early symptoms of the coming renaissance. She now wrote for the *New York Times Book Review*, from which vantage point she had become personally acquainted with poets across the country. Later she was to edit a series of popular anthologies, the Little Books of Modern Verse. She felt herself at times a rival of Harriet Monroe for leadership in promoting the new poets, but she was more conservative, and lacked Miss Monroe's even-handed support of the avant-garde along with the traditional, of Ezra Pound as well as Joyce Kilmer. Her own poetry was limited to brief love lyrics and revealed, as Sara discovered, great depths of sentiment usually hidden except to her friends by the clutter and busyness of her interminable affairs.

"She knows *everybody*," Sara wrote to Marion, "and she said that she would have 'taken me under her wing' and I could have met them all if she had known me sooner. . . . She is very gentle but firm in her judgments and is decidedly 'well balanced' mentally. I guess she's about your age." Sara had again found an older woman friend to guide her passage into a still larger world, although this time she did not form such a childish bond of emotional dependence. The three-hour dinner conversation about poetry began a friendship that lasted for the remaining twenty-two years of Sara's life. It was to Jessie Rittenhouse that she fled in emotional collapse in December 1932, a month before her death.

Sara arrived home in St. Louis in mid-March with a case of the grippe, which she believed she had caught from a man opposite her in the Pullman car. She now faced her usual letdown and depression. "Oh, but I'm homesick for New York!" she cried to John O'Hara. Things were not well in the family, either. Her father's misgivings about modern transportation were proving only too valid, for in December one of his horses had been struck by an automobile and probably permanently injured, her brother had been injured in a taxi in Paris when it was struck by a streetcar, and now her parents' phaeton had collided with a trolley car and been dragged nearly seventy-five feet. Ill and depressed, Sara was driven to exasperation by her mother, and at last poured it out to John:

> I am ill and very much in the dumps generally. It seems to me as tho' the whole creation, and myself in particular, were pretty much of a failure. My mother, who is a sort of super-woman, nearly drives me mad. I ought not to say this, but sometimes I feel that I *must* tell somebody. Since her accident she is more terrible than ever. You have no idea how utterly selfish and restless and jealous she is. I keep saying to myself, 'You must not grow like her, you must not grow like her.' I don't know what is to become of her. She is sixty-seven and has as much strength in her little finger as I have in my whole body. She has nothing to do in the world but to worry and fret people. There, do you think me horrible and unnatural to speak so? You must forgive it. If it were not for my father I should—Oh I *will* stop. I have no right to bore you.

Sara's desperation must have been very great for her to write about it at all. It was characteristic of her to open up her troubled feelings only a little way and then to smother them in a sense of guilt and impropriety. If she wrote to anyone else about her mother, none of the letters have survived. But this one passage reveals the sense of worthlessness and failure incurred because of her anger and guilt, a loss of self-esteem that ends in a veiled threat. Her obsessive fear that she could not attract and retain a man's love very likely sprang from this deep-seated sense of personal worthlessness, centered in her relationship with her mother. Like a helpless child, she felt overwhelmed by the aggressive vitality of her mother, whose tyranny was backed up by all the precepts of church and society that the pliant, good-natured child had been taught to respect. One can well understand the paralyzing bouts of unidentifiable illness, for they permitted her rebellious anger to express itself as an acceptable form of overt suffering. The chronic illnesses allowed mother and daughter to care and be cared for, a semblance of a loving relationship that was in fact a sickness itself. The elements of this family tragedy were further compounded by Sara's vital desire to escape, to live, to write, to be famous and fulfilled; while her aging and ailing parents clung to her tightly, fitting out a beautiful private apartment for her in the home, lavishing on her money, attention, and endless worry and fear, all of which intensified her sense of duty and made it harder to repudiate.

On returning from the free and happy life in New York to the gloom of St. Louis, Sara subsided into unproductive silence and finally went off in April 1911 for a few days to an old pre-Civil War plantation near Barnhart, Missouri, where she read some dialogues of Plato and began to feel better. When struggling to regain her balance, she always turned to what she felt was the humbling and impersonal wisdom of the Great Books. During May, still writing little that satisfied her, she whiled away long afternoons in the public library, looking up one subject in an ency-clopedia and being led by it to another, and then to another. So she preoccupied herself as the turbulence of her emotions subsided and could be contained. The glorious spring weather seemed finally to re-store her sense that life was worthwhile.

John O'Hara reopened the game of love, although Sara would no longer risk taking it seriously. "Playing at love isn't a very dangerous game for poets," she told him. "But before one starts on the friendly duel, the weaker party has a right to know how nearly the weapons are to resemble real ones, n'est ce pas?" It was woman's disadvantage that concerned her. "How nice it must be to be a man and to be able to write love letters without anybody's taking them seriously! If a woman does, she is supposed to be *dreadfully* in love—and maybe she isn't at all." He had treated her poems that way, she reminded him—"thinking that my love songs were a sort of tender confession . . . in spite of my elaborate and utterly truthful explanations to the contrary. 'Vous n'avez rien com-pris à ma simplicité' as Verlaine says—tho' maybe, if you haven't under-stood the simplicity, you've understood some of the complexity—of which there is quite a lot." Unfortunately, he did not rise to the invitation to declare whether he "really" loved her.

When he pressed her for poems on overtly sexual themes, encouraged by "Union Square," she dropped the playful pose. "I hate women who dabble in things of that kind, and if the idea at the end of 'Union Square' had not been an accident suggested by the rhyme, I should never have said what I said." This was patently untrue and she knew it, but she was sensitive about the issue the poem raised. "It is all very well for men to say what they please in their work—but unless a woman were a supreme artist—and even if she *were* one—I don't like the idea. Besides that, tho' you seem not to believe me, I have positively no desire to write daring things."

The burst of freedom and assertiveness that produced "Union Square" had doubtless precipitated the emotional crisis with her mother on re-turning from New York, for the poem defied her mother's hysterical fear that she might commit some sexual indiscretion. Perhaps in a dutiful effort to prove herself still on the side of traditional femininity, a posture that would please everyone who found her independence objectionable, she wrote two sonnets so submissive that Will Parrish, she told O'Hara, called one of them " 'The Door-Mat'—her pet phrase for anything unnecessarily humble." In the poem "Crowned," she says love has made her a proud and secret queen; but when her lover decides to take back the crown after all (that is, reject her),

> I shall not weep, nor will a word be said,
> But I shall kneel before you, oh my King.

It is not hard to read beneath the conventional imagery of medieval romance her psychological enactment of the problem that could not be resolved: Pride and self-security come from being loved, but they are not destined for her. Rejection by the lover is inevitable, almost welcomed as something to be stoically endured, a humiliation to be embraced rather than resisted. After her first modest and defeated effort to fly free, she could find some comfort in her old habitual pain, for it was at least familiar and safe.

In this mood, she decided again, she wrote John, "A woman ought not to write. Somehow it is indelicate and unbecoming. She ought to imitate the female birds, who are silent—or, if she sings, no one ought to hear her music until she is dead." Not surprisingly, her more successful poems written in the early summer of 1911 dramatize not stoic submission but death. On June 15, she wrote one of her most popular lyrics, "I Shall Not Care":

> When I am dead and over me bright April
> Shakes out her rain-drenched hair . . .[8]

In the vein of Christina Rossetti's early work, she imagines herself in her grave and at peace, indifferent to the grieving lover who now must suffer because he did not pay attention to her in life. It was one way of assuaging feminine pride. And on July 2 she wrote of yearning for annihilation, a sonnet, "Sea Longing," in which she wishes that

> over me
> The cold insistence of the tide would roll,
> Quenching this burning thing men call the soul.[9]

In the 90° heat of St. Louis in July, she stayed on alone while her parents made their annual retreat to the cooler climate of northern Michigan. The heat was probably easier to bear than the boredom and loneliness of Charlevoix and the inescapable proximity of her mother. She thought fondly of her father, now white-haired and over seventy, described by everyone as "courtly," and she browsed in his extensive library of books on horses, recalling his famous pair of trotters Vendetta and Black Bess who in local history had never been surpassed. She corrected the proofs of her book, *Helen of Troy and Other Poems*, due to come out in October, and read Browning, she told John, "with a queer mixture of admiration and annoyance." His "ugly words and harsh music are almost inexcusable sometimes." On July 18 the heat finally drove her to Charlevoix for relief after all, and Will Parrish mitigated the loneliness by visiting her there in August.

O'Hara's stream of sonnets continued without letup, but unlike Sara he liked to write descriptive pieces about places, like Riverside Drive or the Palisades. Now he proposed that they collaborate on a sonnet series about New York. At first she thought the idea "splendid," with her habitual desire to please, and began to try her hand at it. She quickly realized, however, that it was useless for her to attempt a poem with a physical place as its focus rather than an emotion. It would be "awkward to have them in a little book with yours which are so frankly descriptive." What she meant was something more than that, although she apparently did not feel able to tell him outright. She had confided to Will Parrish in July that O'Hara "is writing New York sonnets to burn (some of them are frankly not good for much else, tho' others are beauties) and they are all to me. . . . He wants me to do a series too, and suggests that we get out a tiny little book of them together, with both our initials on the title page . . . a *very* limited edition of only about a dozen copies. I should feel as tho' we were having a baby! But my sonnets would all be love sonnets and his wouldn't . . . and there I'd be! No thank you. . . . People would say: 'What an exhibition! . . . throwing herself at his head in every line.'"[10] A girl could not ask for love, however envious she might be of those who did.

Nevertheless, during the summer of 1911 she wrote four New York sonnets for the venture—"Broadway," "In a Restaurant," "From the North," and "The Lights of New York"—but quietly tried to let the project drop, after pleading with him that "I'm no good at descriptions." The sonnets are memorable chiefly as an expression of her vivid enthusiasm for New York. One of them, "From the North," written at Charlevoix, is an interesting footnote to American literature for its reversal of traditional male primitivism—she can't sleep amid the quiet of woods and lake, for "I am restless for the subway's roar."

While deftly keeping John O'Hara in his place with baffling quips and misleading simplicities, she coolly went about summing him up in analytical prose, in the form of a short story. Back in St. Louis from Charlevoix in mid-September, ahead of her parents—"it is always a relief for me to leave my mother for a few days"—she briskly set about finishing it. In late September or early October, she sent Marion the draft: "It's only a psychological study—that is, it's not exactly a story. . . . It's a horrid picture of John, and to save his feelings and mine, I suppose, I'll have to use a pen-name if I ever publish it." Marion thought that O'Hara was not a suitable figure for a short story, but Sara liked her sketch nevertheless. She showed it to Jessie Rittenhouse the following February, announcing

she might publish it under the pseudonym "Mary Frances Levering."
Then it lay in her desk until December 16, 1915, when she sent it off to
Mencken for possible use in *Smart Set,* titling it "The Black Hearth." "The
man in the story is a contributor to the Smart Set, by the way. It really
is like him."[12] "The story pleases me a lot," Mencken replied. "I wish you
would do more prose."[13] She was offered $25, which she thought too
little, and the editors insisted on using her name, now well known, rather
than a pseudonym. But she was agreeable, and the story appeared in
*Smart Set* in April 1916 under the ironic title "The Sentimentalist." She
told Mencken, "I have a lot more things in my mind to say in about the
same style."[14] But it was the only fiction she ever wrote.

"The Sentimentalist," which barely filled three double-columned
pages of *Smart Set,* is little more than a sketch in which she took pains to
disguise the surface facts of their relationship while exploring its essential
meaning to her. For the portrait of John Myers O'Hara is actually less
important than the emotional crisis endured by the unnamed central
feminine figure. Here is the story in its entirety:[15]

### THE SENTIMENTALIST

#### by Sara Teasdale

She had taught for seven years in a boarding-school for girls, and
though she was not always patient, half of the pupils adored her. She
watched their worship with an amused reserve that baffled them; and in
spite of her sense of humor they thought her romantic—perhaps because
her parents were dead and because she wrote short stories. The back
numbers of the magazines that held her work were soiled with much
treasuring. They had passed from generation to generation of school
girls, but the delicate intensity of the tales looked to an older audience for
appreciation.

One morning while she was dressing, she noticed three white hairs. She
felt that they had come too soon—she was twenty-eight—and they made
her a little bitter. After that, she saw them every time she arranged her
hair.

It was some months later that she learned of a small fortune, her inheritance from a great-uncle. The news was as a sudden coming of spring to
her. In the girls' eyes she was beautiful that day; life was waiting for her.
She handed in her resignation for the fall term, and at night, when she
met one of the girls in the dark corridor, she kissed her. It was a wonderful
kiss—the girl never forgot it.

By autumn she had arranged her affairs and was settled in a small
apartment in New York. Her short stories brought her friends, and both
the men and the women liked her. She felt more at her ease with the
women—she had known very few men in her life.

It was at the house of one of her new friends that she met a poet whose
work she had always disliked, though it had a certain fascination for her.

His poems were cold and hard, with sudden touches of an almost cruel sensuality that made her think of a glowing coal cast into a bowl of ice. She saw him talking with the hostess before he entered the room. Neither his face nor his manner pleased her, and it seemed to her that in an unusual degree the man and his work were one. She was watching him intently when he turned, and across the intervening space, filled with men and women and the sound of voices, their eyes met. A feeling of resentment that he should have divined her glance made her join hastily in the conversation of those near her. But she was deeply conscious of his presence, which seemed to pervade the room, and to call to her almost audibly. When he was presented to her at last, she felt that love was in her eyes, and she blushed. He enjoyed the blush and sat beside her. They talked of his poetry, and moment by moment she asked herself why she loved him. It was characteristic of her that she immediately acknowledged this love to herself, and characteristic of him that he knew of her love as soon as she felt it. She wanted to like his voice, but she found it monotonous and unsympathetic—the voice of a man who has given little to life, and who has ceased to expect much in return.

Intense women pleased him, and he asked if he might take her home. The hostess whispered, as she helped her on with her cloak, that he had never done such a thing before and that he seldom went any place. She blushed again, and the hostess kissed her. He had already made her like a child, yet she realized that he took her home because she loved him—not because he loved her.

That night she read his latest book of poems through before she went to bed. She did not like them any better than before. They should have been bound in black and scarlet, she thought. When she finished them she looked into the mirror for a long time, trying to see herself with his eyes. She was sorry that her hair was not "red gold." He must like that color since he had used it so much in his poems.

After that he came to see her once a week with chilling regularity, and sometimes took her to dinner or to the theater. The week revolved around the day when he came. Everything in her life existed for the few hours when she was with him. Sometimes he sent her a note or two between his visits. They came often enough to make her always impatient for the postman.

One day in late March they took a long walk together in the park. The branches under the cold sky were feathery with the promise of new leaves. It was dusk and the lights were lit. Standing on the Belvedere overlooking the reservoir, they could trace the walks and roadways by their lamps like bordering chains of amber. He was less somber than usual, for the first warm day had brought back the ghost of his youth and made him gently sentimental. He told her that he was forty-one. He thought that she would be surprised, and was piqued when she said simply, "You are twelve years older than I am." She had thought him as old as that. Nothing that he had ever told her about himself surprised her. He had an uncomfortable feeling that she knew all of his weak points. She was too honest to flatter him, and he never had from her the boundless admiration that he craved. He was silent for a while, but the contrast of her fair skin and dark hair pleased him, as they always did, and he took her hand. Before she could draw it away, he felt a shiver run through her.

She had planned to go to Europe in the summer, but she let the weeks go by without engaging her passage, and ended by leaving the city for only a fortnight at the seashore. The fall and winter that followed were so much like the ones before that she sometimes wondered if the year had not slipped back. She tried to become interested in charity, and he listened with a bored politeness to her talk of Christmas trees and Christmas dinners.

In the spring, just as in the year before, a little wave of sentiment swept over him. He wrote verses to her, and even took the trouble to evolve a sonnet or two. But they never rang true, and the occasional touch of sensuality was so false a note that it hurt her. She knew that there was no passion in him. The battle between them was pitifully unequal, and when the little wave ebbed away again, his visits became evenly spaced as before.

In June she bought a small cottage at Ardeen in the Catskills. She wanted to be away from him—but not so far away as Europe. The voyage was postponed for still another year. With a methodical regularity he wrote to her twice a week, and when the letters came a tremulous happiness made her long to be friends with every living thing that she saw. The rest of the week existed only to bring the letter-days nearer. In spite of his lack of humor, he could talk well, if he were in a good mood, but his letters were uniformly brief and commonplace. They were like his stiff, regular handwriting.

When she came back to the city in September, he was at the station to meet her. She had not expected him, and when she saw him coming toward her in the crowd, a thrill of pain shot through her to the tips of her fingers. He took her hand and felt that it was cold through the thin summer glove. She found him looking at her critically. He was relieved to see that she loved him as much as ever. Her letters had been so light and whimsical that he had wondered if she might not have changed. He put her into a cab to drive home alone. She waited impatiently for her trunk, and when it came she took from it the package of love-letters that she had written to him during the summer. She had never meant to have him read them. It was a little device to make the other letters easier for her. His look when he met her made her want to destroy them, and she put them on the ashes in the grate, and watched them smoke and blacken. It was the first autumn fire.

The monotonous weeks began revolving again around his visits. It was two years since she had met him, and she asked herself if this was the life that had waited for her. He came sometimes wet with rain and sometimes powdered with snow, and when three hours had passed he went out into the rain or into the snow, without a regret at leaving her. At Christmas the usual package of books came. Each one bore the greeting that he had

written in his gifts of the years before. His way of repeating the same
action week after week and year after year was maddening to her. She
wondered what he had been fifteen years before. Had passion been for
him only a subject for art, a thing of his brain?

They walked together in the park when the days grew warmer at last.
She would have been glad to escape the spring, but the seasons are
pitiless and full of memories. One of their walks in the silvery May twilight
brought them again to the Belvedere. In the great buildings that loomed
far away over the trees, windows were lighted here and there. She saw
them—the buildings were full of homes. He was absently watching the
park lights change from amber to white as it grew darker. Neither of them
spoke. When he turned toward her from the long chain of lights, he saw
that she was crying without making a sound. A little wave of tenderness
made him take her in his arms. He kissed her and his face was wet with
her tears. Her mouth was convulsed with weeping. He half regretted that,
and yet it made the sensation more novel. He kissed her again and again.
She grew quiet, and he took off her glove and kissed the palm of her hand.
It was damp against his lips. Suddenly she drew away from him and ran
into the twilight. He hurried after her and took her arm, trying to speak
to her as a lover would speak. But he saw that he failed. She seemed
scarcely able to stand, but she walked on, looking straight before her and
never speaking—not even when he left her at the door.

When she found herself in her room, she sat down on the bed to draw
off her glove. She looked for a second at the palm of her hand, and then
she laid it against her lips. It was a long time that she sat there. After
several hours had passed, the tumult of her thoughts receded, leaving one
voice that had the insistence of a cry. She felt that life was possible to her
only on one condition. At last she got up, turned on the light and found
pencil and paper. She did not know what she was going to write, but after
the first sentence there was no hesitation, and she wrote rapidly: "You
know that I love you. Tomorrow morning I am going to my cottage at
Ardeen on the early train. Come to me there. You need not stay long—
only come to me. You will not have this letter until after I have gone, but
you can take the second train. You will come—for a little while." She put
the paper into the envelope, stamped it, sealed it, and directed it to him.
Then she looked for her hat and jacket to take the letter to the post box.
They were still on. She had not taken them off since she left him.

A boy carried her suit-case from the station at Ardeen to the cottage,
and when they reached it, the cold dead air of the closed house made her
feel faint. She tried to open the window while the boy laid a fire, but she
had to ask him to help her. At her order he went to get some provisions,
and left her alone. She sat down in the chair before the fire. When he came
back, she tried to eat a piece of bread from the loaf that he brought, but
though she had eaten nothing since noon the day before, she could not
swallow a morsel. Everything in the house was exactly as she had left it
except for a delicate coating of dust. In a vase were sprays of withered wild
asters that she had forgotten in the fall. She looked up at the shelf where

the clock had stood idly during all the winter. It had stopped at a ridiculous hour. She wound and set it, and it began to tick. She sat down again. The light fire had gone out. She watched the clock so closely that she could see the minute-hand move with little jerks. She was shivering, and she remembered a shawl that she had left in the cottage. It was in the bedroom. She went to the door and opened it a little way—then suddenly she turned as though she could not enter it, and came back to the black hearth.

Like the swinging of a sword in the air, she heard the whistle of the train that had left the city at ten o'clock. She went to the window, though she knew it would take him twenty minutes to walk from the station. A feeling of terror took her. She could scarcely stand, and she went back to the chair. She put her hands over her eyes so that she would not look towards the window. Her heart was beating madly—the throbs were like blows. She counted the ticks of the clock. They grew louder and louder until she felt that they were deafening her. By their terrible insistence they seemed to be measuring eternity. She felt that she had been counting them forever.

There was a step on the veranda—the heavy, hurried step of a man. She reached the door and opened it. An overgrown boy stood there with a telegram. It read:

"Sorry cannot accept your invitation. Sailing for Europe next week."

There is no hint of what Sara might have imagined the consequences of the rebuff to be, except the ominous note that "life was possible to her on only one condition." The woman is the inhibited type who loves intensely but silently, as her upbringing and inexperience dictate; but when she is finally driven by her cold lover's reticence to take the initiative and offer herself, a desperate act on which she stakes her whole life, he fails to respond. The anguished desire for love, underscored by her fear of the bedroom and her terror at her lover's supposed approach, is subtly tied to the expectation of rejection and humiliation: If she were to gamble and lose, pride dictates that she could not go on living. The story projects her wish for economic independence and freedom to adventure —"her parents were dead"—but undercuts it with irony.

Sara accurately saw that the streak of sensuality in O'Hara—his love letters, his urging her to write "wicked" poems—was both an invitation for her to take the initiative and an expression of his own weakness and inability to do so. Unlike the woman in the story, she could predict the inevitable outcome of the relationship, and so did not let it develop.

Autumn in St. Louis in 1911 seems to have been as dreary for her as ever, and as she gradually sank into listlessness and depression, and New York and her friends receded into the distance, she continued to preoccupy herself with the theme of the poet lover who loves the sound of his

own music more than the woman who is the occasion for it. "By the Sea"
echoes her disappointment in O'Hara:

> He woos me with an easy grace
> That proves him only half sincere;
> A light smile flickers on his face.
>
> To him love-making is an art,
> And as a flutist plays a flute,
> So does he play upon his heart
>
> A music varied to his whim.
> He has no use for love of mine,
> He would not have me answer him.[16]

In "Pierrot," too, she stands, "quite forgotten" while Pierrot "thinks he
plays for me."

> ... Pierrot loves his music,—
> But I love Pierrot.[17]

Her dilemma was to be attracted to men who shared her intellectual and
artistic interests, but who threatened to be too absorbed in themselves
to love anyone else—while men who lacked these qualities were uninter-
esting: "To men with an artistic temperament women are here to be made
love to—not to be loved," she told John. "And the men without an artistic
temperament can only love without making love—which is stupid." But
these poems and her short story seem to idealize John O'Hara somewhat,
attributing his coldness to an absorption in his art rather than to the
neurotic inhibitions that would have caused him to flee from any actual
initiative on her part, to take refuge in his sensual fantasies.

Feeling "sick and miserable" all fall, and probably suffocated by her
mother's constant irritable display of concern for her health, she completed few poems that satisfied her, and she tended to dwell on morbid
subjects. "The Sea Grave" depicts a strange burial ritual—taking the
body of a girl out to the sea at night, "Deep in the waves where she longed
to be." "At Midnight" recounts her insomniac restlessness, "tired of love
that is but hungering," and wishing to be "a quiet lifeless thing." Two
other poems express a yearning to be held like a child in the arms of an
older man. The men referred to in these poems—"Two Friends" and
"Long Ago"—were very likely actual persons. One of the "two friends,"
"a man whom gods have made a god," may be identifiable. A few months
earlier, she had written to John: "No, indeed, you're not a Greek god—I
never knew but one, and I've worshipped him since I was seventeen. In
all that time I've never spoken a hundred words to him. Mortals may not
talk freely to the gods, you know. I wish that I could show him to you.
He is—a real god ... an organist ... a musician of international reputa-

tion and a composer too." Williamina Parrish recalled that Sara maintained a "romantic fancy" for the prominent organist Charles Calloway, whom she could secretly watch passing her house from the window of her room. The persistence of this idealized love for nearly ten years contrasts sharply with the disappointing realities she had been conceiving about male artists.

Although most of her work in the fall of 1911 reflects her troubled thoughts and her inability to resolve them artistically, one poem, "The Inn of Earth," written in early December, foreshadows succinctly the philosophical attitude of her mature years. Coming to the "crowded Inn of Earth," she requests bread and wine but is ignored by the host. She is joined by other souls "from the outer night" who, like her, find the atmosphere jarring.

> "Then give me a bed to sleep," I said,
>   "For midnight comes apace"—
> But the Host went by with averted eye
> And I never saw his face.
>
> "Since there is neither food nor rest,
>   I go where I went before"—
> But the Host went by with averted eye
> And barred the outer door.[18]

The "Inn of Earth" is of course the conscious life between birth and death, and the Host is whatever force or lawgiver sets the terms of living, himself a part of the puzzling life process, unable to satisfy one's demands for an explanation. Finding no enjoyment, no answer to her needs, not even rest, she would go back into the "outer night" where the "souls" are—that is, to take her own life, finding it not worthwhile—but even that is forbidden. Life was only a brief interval in the darkness, and one could do no more than make the most of it. In the summer, she had written "While I May," a celebration of "soul's distress and body's pain," for they were at least living, her own life soon to be

> Buried in a lasting night,
> Even pain denied to me.[19]

And "The Runner," a poem she discarded probably because of its Housmanesque mannerisms, depicts her as a breathless "runner in the sun," striving for the shining trophies "that other men have lost and won." Summoned out of the "dim encircling night," she strives eagerly only to find the race lost in the end to death. Nevertheless, "I love my hour of wind and light." She had given up the view of human purpose and destiny supplied by her Christian background and was searching for something to replace the large emptiness that remained.

The excitement of seeing *Helen of Troy and Other Poems,* her second book, in print in early October 1911 did not relieve her underlying depression, but she was caught up in a whirl that must have hidden it from others. This time she was reviewed in the major national magazines and newspapers with almost uniform praise. Again she sent copies to friends and poets everywhere, including her idol A. E. Housman, who replied from Trinity College, Cambridge, that he had read her poems "with a great deal of pleasure."[20] The book was dedicated to Marion Cummings Stanley, who had been her closest friend when many of the poems were written and who had helped her arrange the manuscript for publication. Marion felt that "sometimes it seems almost as if they were my own—I mean that I had written them, they are so dear and familiar."[21]

It was her last book to be shaped by the eclecticism of the 1890s—the triolets and rondeaus, ballads, blank verse monologues, and verse dramas. Jessie Rittenhouse had already encouraged her to "specialize" in the lyric and abandon the ambitious rhetoric of the receding age.

The six blank verse monologues in *Helen of Troy* are poetic equivalents of the art nouveau style, with the static theatrical pose of their female figures, voluptuous and chaste, richly colored, clean-cut in line yet complicated in design, like stained-glass windows, more beautiful than realistic. It was the posture struck by Duse on the stage and imitated by Sara herself in her early photographic portraits: haughtily aloof with averted eyes and a touch of indefinable sadness. Her tragic women are all caught at a moment of reflective stillness, looking quietly back and measuring the agony of their lives. Helen is seen turning from the funeral pyre of Troy to the prospect of being slain by the furious Greeks, gradually realizing that the very obsession with her beauty that destroyed Troy will cause her life to be preserved now. She is an indestructible principle. "Beatrice" speaks from her deathbed, an old woman remembering how she might have loved Dante if only he had spoken to her. It is yet another treatment of the chivalric code that Sara believed caused men to idealize women but blocked communication between them and ultimately deprived women of love. Marianna Alcoforando, the "Portuguese Nun," is also shown in old age, still glad to have been loved even if seduced and abandoned, for "lack of love is bitterest of all." "Sappho" disturbed one reviewer because Sara depicted her as a mother finding peace in total concentration on her child after having been tormented by all other forms of love. This unique Sappho-Madonna was probably Sara's answer to Sappho's accusers.

Many of the love lyrics are still overly chaste and girlish, valentines rather than serious poems. Yet almost any of them has the saving grace of its skilled discipline and clean simplicity, its strength achieved through understatement. These qualities have been more frequently remarked in her later work, but the direction was established early. For example,

"November" in *Helen of Troy* has an echo, perhaps, of the early *fin de siecle* Yeats in its first stanza:

> The world is tired, the year is old,
>     The little leaves are glad to die,
> The wind goes shivering with cold
>     Among the rushes dry.

When republishing it later, she made changes in two lines, aiming in revision as Yeats did at more austere language:

> The world is tired, the year is old,
>     The faded leaves are glad to die,
> The wind goes shivering with cold
>     Where the brown reeds are dry.[22]

The word *little* was a typically feminine adjective that appeared occasionally in her early poems, giving them an air of girlish preciosity. Her revised last line deliberately breaks and slows the rhythm to establish a more severe and restrained mood; both changes lessen the attribution of personality to leaves and wind.

The appearance of her book in October coincided with the publication of an article she had written for *The Magazine Maker* (October 1911), edited by Homer Croy, which she titled "The Unknown Poet and the Magazines." The extent of her reputation by 1911 is evident in her being invited to advise "unknown" poets from the viewpoint of a successful professional. She took to task the lofty poets who considered their work too good for the magazines but who went wild with joy when they actually sold a poem, for this meant logically that the poem could not be any good. The moral was to write to satisfy oneself rather than the market and to be patient about publication. Choose appropriate magazines, wait, and be persistent, she advised. And, above all, be a sincere and dedicated artist: "Poetry is a concise and beautiful way of telling the truth. . . . If a writer asks himself frankly and exactly what he feels about a certain object, provided that he has felt real emotion in regard to it, and provided that the subject is worth the emotion, his answer to the question, if it is simple, direct, and musical, will be a poem." The poet should read widely in the literature of all ages and times from Sappho to Swinburne, but then put out of mind what has been said before. "He should look steadily into his own soul to find the exact feeling with which it is stirred, and then into his brain to find the word to express accurately that feeling." From the fusion of personal emotion and traditional form would arise the poet's inimitable identity. The "subject" of a poem was the sensibility of the poet: "Every human being has something to say of himself which could not be said by another. Never in all the ages past nor in those to come will the same combination of emotions possess a human being as those which possess him. Let him express them quickly, for soon the night comes; and in expressing them he will find that after all, 'What is commonest, cheapest, nearest, easiest, is Me.' "

At the time she wrote this statement, poetry was searching for a discriminating audience among the general public, and there was not the spectacle of clashing movements and ideologies that erupted a few years later. She refused to participate in those controversies, feeling they had little to do with the value of a poem whatever its school or style, and thereafter she made few public statements of the theories she held about her own work. When the first little magazines appeared in 1912, *Poetry* and *The Poetry Journal*, she felt they were superfluous, for the general magazines were doing a sufficient job. Her professional career was well established before the period of revolt, and although later she too published extensively in the little magazines, she never relied on them to carry her reputation. In fact, she rather enjoyed making money from her work and the sense of independence as a woman it gave her. She was an entrepreneur in the arts, not a bohemian.

Homer Croy wrote Sara shortly that her article had "made a hit" with the readers; and in praising *Helen of Troy*, he singled out "Union Square" as "my favorite by far. . . . I'd give my magazine if I could do a thing like that." A Miss H., he said, "is reading it now and passing it around, telling how she has actually seen the author of it sitting on the bureau, on a pile of sofa cushions, a flickering jet on each side, eating candy with one hand and writing poetry with the other."[23]

Success meant that the public expected her to be "interesting." But she resisted every opportunity to display "temperament," even at the risk of seeming not to have any. Newspaper reporters annoyed her again, trying to find some way to capitalize on the occasion of her new book. A writer in the *St. Louis Republic* contrasted her poetic world of love and beauty with the grimy reality and "gum-chewing" mundane commercialism of St. Louis, struck by how often her poems referred to kissing: " 'It is not a subject that I should care to discuss,' says Miss Teasdale." The *Post-Dispatch* exclaimed, "That a girl could live in St. Louis and produce such verse has been a world wonder."

While sending out copies of her book and answering her rapidly increasing mail, she and Will Parrish sat down with Zoë Akins to help her get her first book of poems, *Interpretations*, in shape for publication. Zoë had had a well-known love affair a few years before with William Marion Reedy, who doubtless "feels a very fatherly love for the poems," Sara told John. Zoë's book was "vastly improved over the mss.," she confided in Marion, "and, sub rosa, I think S. T. T. and W. P. . . . are to be thanked for the change. We went over it line by line and poem by poem and got Zoë to take out half a dozen of the weakest poems, and scores of poor lines. You know she has a tendency . . . to 'swim in Greece' as Will calls it—you can guess what that means." Sara's remarks had no malice in them. "As it stands, the volume is a perfect beauty," she said generously. "Down in my soul I can only hope that mine compares with it."

Orrick Johns, now working for Reedy, wrote a careful review of *Helen of Troy* for *The Mirror*, and Reedy himself dashed off a note to her, saying, "It's beautiful—that's all. St. Louis ought to be proud of you." Sara was delighted; "It almost made me forgive him for weighing 260 pounds," she wrote John. Reedy thought she ought to do "a long poem, dramatic and lyric," and Orrick told her he especially liked her verse play. There were probably other pressures to launch into more rhetorical, large-scale verse now that she had established her genuine talent, her professionalism, and her capacity for growth. But she had already assessed her position differently.

As autumn of 1911 wore into winter, Sara sank into a deep exhaustion, spending up to twelve hours a day in bed in a futile attempt to regain strength by resting. The doctor was advising her to go south, but she was privately thinking of New York again now that the Poetry Society's winter season was in full swing and Jessie Rittenhouse had read some of her work from *Helen of Troy* at the meeting in early November. Miss Rittenhouse had also invited Sara to join her and a young woman from Michigan on a long tour of Europe the next summer, but Sara feared that "I should be sure to upset the plans by getting sick."

The publication of *Helen of Troy* carried her into the orbit of another poet, who, with his wife Jean, was to become a lifelong friend—the young Louis Untermeyer. When B. Russell Herts, editor of *International*, wrote her that he would request a review copy of *Helen of Troy* for Untermeyer, Sara seized the occasion to write the poet directly herself, praising his work and asking for his autograph. Untermeyer had just published his first book of poems—"a long-drawn-out sigh of self-dramatization called *First Love*,"[24] as he later described it—and was flattered by her attention, complimenting her work in return: "I have already spoken to the little circle in no uncertain terms about it." Writing to her again in December after the review appeared, he said if he had had more space, he "would have pointed out that what was particularly admirable about your poetry was that, even in your most intense love lyrics, the attitude was that of a woman—a most grateful change from the eternal (and usual awkward) impersonation of masculinity which the Elsabarkers of our and other times mishandle so consistently."[25] Sara was pleased at the recognition of "my consistently feminine attitude in the love lyrics. I have a theory that the only way women can hope to make their work compare with men's work, is not by trying to rival what men say, but by trying to supplement it."

Sara was not yet aware that men no less than women were trapped in the conflict that classified sexuality as either pornographic or pure, and she must have been puzzled by their confused and sentimentally moral response to "Union Square." In spite of his endorsement of the feminine attitude, Louis Untermeyer had not liked the poem as much as other critics had: "The last lines are climacterally [sic] true but literally false. . . . Of course you know what the girls in Union Square ask for is a very different thing from love. . . . And so is what they get—! I have seen too many of these poor, broken, and bedraggled butterflies to confuse the swift flame of any passion with the bitter ashes of their trade."[26] John Myers O'Hara admired the poem immensely: "It shows what you can do with material that has never been touched before." But he wondered whether it was the right thing to do: "Of course, it is for you to choose whether you should strike at these vital things in life—perhaps it is better, after all, to pursue the lovelier side of existence, and only give expression to what is unmarred in the realm of beauty."[27] Orrick Johns went the other way: "To me it is a miracle that a woman of Camille's life can have the wonderful soul that I know is hers. . . . I am almost sure nobody is bad. Aren't you?"[28]

Stirred by the favorable reception of her book and by letters from Jessie Rittenhouse reporting the success of her poems at the Poetry Society, Sara began pressing her parents and doctors for permission to go to New York again. Orrick Johns, who had been in a "steady grouch" all fall and unable to write because of the "shackles" of St. Louis, had finally broken free and gone to New York, staying at Sara's old boarding house on Irving Place, which meant that another friend was there to escort her around if need be. Sara found her energy returning, as it always did when escape was at hand, and zestfully wrote to Jessie Rittenhouse on New Year's Eve: "Praises be to all the kind gods! I am *really* going! The doctor says I can, and my parents say so. . . . I think of nothing else but going." At twenty-seven, she was still cast in the role of a dependent child who could not go anywhere without permission. She planned to arrive just in time for Miss Rittenhouse's annual party for the poets on January 21, 1912.

Sara's second visit to New York lasted until April. It marked the end of her life in St. Louis psychologically, if not actually. New York became the center of everything: all her new friends and professional associates, her career, her future.

Jessie Rittenhouse had persuaded her to stay at a rooming house for young women at 300 West 85th Street, run by a Mrs. Coates, but Sara could not bear the constant noise, and the location was inconvenient. At the end of the first week, she moved to the Martha Washington Hotel at 29 East 29th Street, a sedate hotel exclusively for women, where from her window on the eleventh floor she could view "my beloved Metropolitan Tower" and the "marvelous" skyline. This "nunnery," as she called it, became her regular quarters whenever she stayed in New York thereafter.

Miss Rittenhouse's party was followed by the society's dinner meeting.

"Wasn't last night wonderful? I think it was the most beautiful night of my life," Sara exclaimed in a note to her the next day. "I never loved people so much before. I've just been marking on the index of seats all the people that I know. Do you know that I owe all of this to you?" People were inviting her everywhere now. "I feel quite like a New Yorker, and I'm so happy if people like me a little." She was soon telling John O'Hara: "I am simply wild with the joy of life and with the most wonderful city that ever existed."

The wave of joy was accompanied, however, by its usual dark undertow. Although St. Louis had been left suddenly far behind, she carried with her the inescapable fears that welled up along with the energy of her happiness. "My head is as full of songs as the street-organ that is playing way down out of sight under my window," she wrote Jessie Rittenhouse. "I shiver to think *how* far down. . . . Isn't life glorious? I love it so much that the only dreadful thing in the whole world is to have to leave it so soon. The thought of death is like a terrible dream. Haven't you waked up after such torture and said 'It *must* be a dream. It is too terrible to be anything else'?" The dizzy height was an invitation to throw herself to her death, as it was for her princess on the tower. On Valentine's Day, feeling "in the very bottom of the pit of despair. . . as tho' I should like to crawl into a dark cave where I couldn't feel anything or see anything and where even thought couldn't come," she wrote a poem, "I Looked at Death, I Looked at Love":

> I heard Death calling, calling me,
> "Leap from your window to my breast."

Death promised rest to all lovers, crushed in his arms; but she chose to follow Love, "Love who stood sullen in the sun" with "no gift" to offer. On a lonely Valentine's Day, when men were sending other girls candy and flowers, the choice seemed to be between death and a life deprived of love.

The freedom of New York had loosened, as it had the year before, a great upsurge of feeling. Love might have seemed impossible to her in St. Louis, lying in her bed, imprisoned in the emotional atmosphere of her home. But here where all things seemed possible, it was hard to be fatalistic or to be satisfied with peeping at her hero from an upstairs window. She was almost twenty-eight and still waited for the grand involvement on which a woman, as she believed, staked her whole life. Her New York poems this year were poignant outcries for fulfillment, prayers begging for love. "Imeros," a sonnet written on February 12, two days before the Valentine's Day poem on death, explicitly states the yearning and the despair that held her teetering in a balance between hope and self-destruction:

> I am a wave that cannot reach the land,
> My strength is spent beneath a careless sky.

In the "lost mid-ocean," under the "cruel sea-gulls,"

> I am a woman who will live and die
> Without the one thing I have craved of God.

She is a singer "Who learns from longing all the songs she sings," who implores God, "Send me not back to death unsatisfied."

There were shy poems about first love, about catching glimpses of her lover in a crowd, or anticipating the hour when she will meet him— written, as she told Jessie Rittenhouse, "to nobody in particular." Even the titles—"Longing," "The Promised Land," "A Prayer"—underscore the constant theme. Give me "one minute with the man I love," she begged, "Then do whatever thing you will." Her poems were "tears distilled into a song"—

> . . .to my lover I must be
> Only a voice.[29]

One solution was never entertained: the nunlike "white election" of Emily Dickinson, the commitment to chastity, which transformed the deprivation of love into an act of spiritual self-denial. It was the solution of the pious and steely character of the nineteenth century, but not of hedonistic New York on the eve of World War I. For Sara, more vulnerable than the women of the previous century, the purpose of life was enjoyment, in the richest sense of the word:

> Poor saints—how could they ever know
> My heaven is on earth?

She had the courage to face the lack of love, if that had to be, but she was not inclined to bargain it for salvation, in spite of her Puritan ancestry. Exercises in self-denial were futile:

> I said, "I have shut my heart
>     As one shuts an open door,
> That Love may starve therein
>     And trouble me no more."
>
> But over the roofs there came
>     The wet new wind of May,
> And a tune blew up from the curb
>     Where the street-pianos play.
>
> My room was white with the sun
>     And Love cried out in me,

"I am strong, I will break your heart
Unless you set me free"'[30]

Although she scheduled regular hours for working on her poems, she by no means sat reclusively in her hotel room hoarding her emotions. Her life had become a continual social round—parties, luncheons, dinners, teas, lectures, opera, and theatre—sometimes forcing her to spend the morning in bed to recover her vitality, which she burned lavishly and seemed to exhaust quickly. In one week, she turned down twelve invitations, after a particularly heavy schedule.

Her new friends the Untermeyers were only peripheral to the Poetry Society, but she doubtless felt personally drawn to them more than to the older established poets or to the morbid John Myers O'Hara, who seemed more ridden with minor illnesses than Sara herself. She first met the Untermeyers in late January 1912. "Louis Untermeyer, the poet," she wrote to Jessie Rittenhouse, "wants me to spend the evening with him and Mrs. Untermeyer. I know him only thro' letters and so I must go to you for a 'reference'. I'm sure he must be all right tho', for he seems to be very nice. . . . Don't think that I'm foolish to ask you about these people—tho' it sounds so. You see, I promised mother that, unless a man was introduced to me by a friend, or unless I knew that he was a nice fellow, I'd not go out with him." Untermeyer had insisted on coming alone to pick her up rather than in the company of his wife, and Sara apparently thought a "reference" from the unimpeachable Jessie Rittenhouse would get around her mother's strict rule.

Jean Untermeyer later wrote that Sara was "of all the American women poets of my generation the one who came closest to me in the intimacies of friendship." She did not recall their first meeting; Sara's shyness and delicate coloring did not leave a vivid or accurate first impression, she felt. But "Almost imperceptibly, the little acts of kindness, the candor and good sense, the absence of pose, the gentleness rather than the gentility of a 'lady,' the gradual emergence of intellectual curiosity and good taste, built up a firmer and truer picture of the young woman." Before long Sara had opened up: "Once she felt confidence in her company she gave of herself freely, and seemingly without second thought."[31]

Louis Untermeyer had progressed from being a high school dropout and despair of his family, through an abortive career as a concert pianist, to his new role as a poet and reviewer. When Sara first met him, he had just joined the radical magazine *The Masses,* and supported himself by working at his family's jewelry business in Manhattan. "He has the most wonderful library I ever saw," she told John O'Hara. He was also a vigorous critic: "You've no idea how he scolds me for weak lines, and I almost always can fix them." One senses from the tone of her letters that

Sara found in the Untermeyers something of the youthful sophistication, the wit, and the freer atmosphere she looked for in New York, while they remained safely middle class.

One day in February 1912, she, the Untermeyers, and John Myers O'Hara, with Jessie Rittenhouse and her mother, made an expedition to Edwin Markham's home at West New Brighton on Staten Island, to pay a sort of impromptu tribute to the most famous living American poet "with a (figurative) laurel wreath and an (actual) frosted cake,"[32] as Untermeyer recalled. It was a long tiresome trip by elevated train, ferry, and trolley, and it ended in the rain. But the pilgrimage demonstrated that the younger poets still looked up to Markham, not so much, probably, for his poems as for his example of success and his liberal attitude, which gave them confidence in their commitment to poetry.

Sara's friendship with Jessie Rittenhouse deepened, too, during the spring, and she seemed no longer so awed by the busy, competent older woman who knew "everyone," and who had skillfully brought her out. And, as if the life in New York were not yet the culmination of delight, she found it possible to accept Jessie's invitation, after all, to spend the summer traveling in Europe. The young woman from Michigan was not able to go, and Sara's health was no longer a threat. She returned to St. Louis the first week in April, this time without a sinking heart, because she had only a month to prepare for the sailing.

Her status as a celebrity seemed to be well established in St. Louis by now, after the national success of *Helen of Troy* and her reception in New York. She and Zoë Akins, among others, were guests of honor at the Papyrus Club on April 14, where a poem by each had been set to music and was performed. The St. Louis *Censor* reported that no less a personage than Markham had "pronounced our own Sara Teasdale, the best young woman poet in America." The writer added, however, that "She is attractive but not particularly good looking. It is her modest manner and utter lack of conceit that are her chief charms and have won many admiring friends for her." It was an unpleasant reminder that she who longed for love and beauty—the standards by which women publicly were judged—was neither loved nor beautiful, and had to settle for talent, modesty, and friendship.

The summer of 1912 proved to be the most memorable season of her life. It was that rarest kind of travel—four leisurely months in which the weather was always perfect, even when it rained, and everything went right, and she and her companion were perfectly attuned to one another, as they idled through Italy and north through Switzerland and Germany. If one lived for the most intense experience of the beautiful, then this was surely it. In later years, she yearned to repeat the experience of that summer, "the most perfect days of my life," she told Jessie; but it proved impossible.

Their ship, of the Hamburg-American line, sailed from Hoboken on May 15, and Sara, remembering the miserable chill of her first trip abroad in 1905, brought along an electric heater. But the weather was remarkable, even for May. "Miss Teasdale and I," Jessie Rittenhouse wrote later in her memoir, "sat upon the deck without wraps and steeped ourselves in the beauty of the sea, while at intervals we talked of and wrote poetry."[33] Sara gathered all her forces and poured them into seventy-seven lines of blank verse, "From the Sea," which, having no typewriter, she had struck off by the ship's printer. It summed up her life of waiting, inexperience, and anticipation—a message from mid-ocean, addressed to an unnamed lover two thousand miles away, the fictitious ideal she summoned up to fill the vacant place in reality:

> All beauty calls you to me, and you seem,
> Past twice a thousand miles of shifting sea,
> To reach me.

The poem acts out the romantic dream of love as she anticipated it: the first meeting of the lovers, surrounded with speechless shyness; yet "in my heart there was a beating storm." This was the moment of discovery, when "to my life's high altar came its priest," when she bowed in ecstatic submission. It was the fulfillment of a destiny:

> ...long before I ever heard your name,
> Always the undertone's unchanging note
> In all my singing had prefigured you,
> Foretold you as a spark foretells a flame.

Nevertheless, she is still denied any fulfillment beyond the knowledge that at last she is really loved:

> Oh, my love
> To whom I cannot come with any gift
> Of body or of soul, I pass and go.

The awakening leaves an unsatisfiable restlessness like the "unborn evanescent stars" of phosphorescence in the ship's wake at night. The tragedy that lurks within anticipation is, as always, her fear that she may have too little to offer in response to the overwhelming demand and that inhibition will stifle the very thing she has desired:

> I strove
> To say too little lest I say too much,
> And from my eyes to drive love's happy shame.

Yet I was free as an untethered cloud
In the great space between the sky and sea,
And might have blown before the wind of joy
Like a bright banner woven by the sun.34

The Great Experience leaves behind only the gratitude for its having happened at all and the painful knowledge of the magnificence that might have been.

Sara and Jessie Rittenhouse soon discovered that the pain of unfulfilled love was something they had in common. "The poor dear was crying the other day over her love affair," Sara wrote to the Untermeyers, "and I suddenly felt ten years older than she instead of ten years younger. What a pity that she can't be happy—or at least happy in her unhappiness." Sara had come to find her "very dear and lovable. She has one of the most clear and beautiful souls that I ever saw."

Once through the Straits of Gibraltar, Sara turned to composing lyrics about the ports or cities they visited, some of which she later collected under the heading "Vignettes Overseas." Jessie Rittenhouse remembered the circumstances surrounding the composition of these poems, in Naples, Amalfi, or Florence; with "happy spontaneity she would toss off lyrics of the passing scene,"35 which seemed to fall from her lips in finished form. There is evidence that Sara did tend to compose not only lines but entire stanzas or poems in her mind before writing them down, and doubtless she often recited such lines to Jessie Rittenhouse. But Miss Rittenhouse wrote her account twenty years afterward and apparently refreshed her memory with the published versions of the poems, for Sara's notebooks clearly show that almost every one of the examples quoted had actually been painstakingly revised. In one case, "Florence," two lines of the second stanza are entirely new, the result of heavy revision in August 1913, and could not have been tossed off "with happy spontaneity" in July 1912. In fact, all of the poems quoted by Miss Rittenhouse had been published within a few years of the tour, while none of the many unpublished poems remaining in manuscript were cited by her.

Nevertheless, sentimentalized as it is in retrospect, Jessie Rittenhouse's account communicates the same sense of dreamlike perfection in the Italian portion of the trip that Sara's frequent letters and postcards also describe. Venice was a beautiful faded ruin, like woods in autumn; at Lake Como, there was "a Maxfield Parrish-picture look to everything." It was an endless feast of beauty, whose effect on the two romantic young spinsters was predictable: "I think that either of us would fall in love at a second's notice if an English-speaking man were within the radius of a mile," she wrote Louis.

Switzerland and Germany in August were pleasant enough, but they did not measure up to the Italian experience, as evidenced by the scant two or three lyrics they inspired. In Hamburg, at the end of August, Sara and Jessie had to transfer to a slow boat for the return trip, and after months of living in a kind of high-pitched romantic anticipation they might have suffered a letdown, except for one thing: quite unexpectedly, Sara did fall in love.

On board the ship was a young Englishman named Stafford Hatfield, with an array of talents in music, literature, and science, a charming conversationalist who spent the long, mild evenings talking with her under the stars. She described the experience in "Places," written in 1918:

> In the ship's deep churning the eerie phosphorescence
> Is like the souls of people who were drowned at sea,
> And I can hear a man's voice, speaking, hushed, insistent,
> At midnight, in mid-ocean, hour on hour to me.[36]

Unlike the gloomy John Myers O'Hara, Stafford Hatfield was outgoing, even mercurial, and by the time their ship docked in New York, he was almost irresistible. She stayed in New York instead of returning home, and as the days and then weeks passed, she was unable to make up her mind what to do about him. He planned to return shortly to the continent, but it isn't clear whether he urged her to go with him or simply pressured her to go to bed with him. In the midst of her emotional turmoil, she tried to see friends—the Untermeyers and John O'Hara again, and her old friend Marion Stanley, who had also come east. Even Will Parrish was in New York, on the eve of sailing for Europe with her sister Grace. Sara had again come down with a bad case of the grippe, always the penalty for a crisis. On September 24, 1912, when she had been reduced almost to a state of emotional helplessness, Will Parrish bundled her onto the train and sent her home to St. Louis. She wrote Jean Untermeyer about it from the train that night: "I am still rather dazed, for so much has happened today. . . . My friend Will Parrish . . . came this morning at eleven o'clock. She is a splendid friend and an old and very dear one, and I am certain that my good angel sent her down to me this morning. Heavens what a pitifully damp mess of nothing I was when she arrived! I was all the more ashamed of being such a baby because it has been years, literally, since I have made such a fool of myself, and I fancied in my conceit that I was quite beyond such things."

As she explained it later to Marion Stanley, "Mr Hatfield became more and more insistent and finally one morning Will Parrish came down and found me crying my eyes out. . . . Mr. H. will come to America again in the spring. He sailed home on the Olympic on Sept. 28."

Of the many poems that quickly followed about leave-taking, the brief-ness of love, or the absent lover, "Mr. Hatfield's progeny," she called them—one of them evoked again the image of "imeros," the wave in the sea, about to sweep her with its passion:

> But I feared the onward surge,
> Like a coward I turned aside.

When faced with the grand opportunity, she fled from it, as she had always been afraid she would do.

# CHAPTER FIVE

# "Now at Last I Can Live!"

**S**ara's failure of nerve with Stafford Hatfield shook her with the realization that at twenty-eight she could very well face a life of lonely spinsterhood if she did not do something about it soon. In two years, she would be thirty, that point of no return when unmarried virgins became unmarriageable "old maids." While her friends all moved about freely, living their own lives as they pleased, she was still a dependent, obedient child, whose parents had settled into old age and could die or become incapacitated at any time, leaving her unprepared to support herself, with no established life of her own. She had known only a few men very well; but John Myers O'Hara was out of the question, and Louis Untermeyer was married. Louis tended to take a ready interest in other women, and Sara, who found him attractive, had in fact, she told Marion, "just barely escaped an exciting time" with him before leaving New York. But an "affair" was morally unthinkable. Although she had written passionately about the "great loves" of women who were driven to defy law and custom, these were only the fantasies of a painfully conventional and inexperienced young woman, and she wanted a most conventional husband, not a lover, when it came down to actuality. The only possible candidate was Stafford Hatfield. To a young woman of Sara's background, Hatfield's storm of attentions could mean but one thing: that he was interested in marrying her. He may even have suggested it.

Back in St. Louis in the fall of 1912, instead of sinking into ennui and depression she filled her notebooks with new poems that reassuringly kept the relationship with Hatfield alive, shaping it into all the usual

95

patterns of unrequited love that was her constant theme: They had parted, but he would not forget her; he would come back; even if he forgot
her, their brief love would always sustain her; he might seem to forget
her, but remembrance would overwhelm him if he saw her again; she
would send him tormenting thoughts so he could not forget her. Of this
"progeny of Hatfield," the most telling is a piece of wish fulfillment, "The
Old Maid," which was accepted in December for publication by *The
Forum*:

> I saw her in a Broadway car,
>     The woman I might grow to be;
> I felt my lover look at her
>     And then turn suddenly to me.

The woman is "strangely like" the narrator herself in appearance, although

> Her body was a thing grown thin,
>     Hungry for love that never came;
> Her soul was frozen in the dark
>     Unwarmed forever by love's flame.

This would never happen to her, because her lover's

> eyes were magic to defy
> The woman I shall never be.[1]

She was counting too heavily on the seriousness of Hatfield's interest
in her. He had written Sara "several dear little letters" in the days before
sailing to Germany at the end of September and then she waited patiently
until mid-November before receiving even a postcard. "I suppose that he
is in the arms of the lyric lady, Helena Voight-something, I forget her last
name," she wrote sourly to Marion Stanley. Hatfield had told her about
this German friend, but Sara obviously believed herself to be his only
serious love interest and expected him to return to New York on business,
and to her, in the spring. After this first shade of disappointment and
alarm, her public enthusiasm for "the adorable Hatfield" became more
guarded.

Preoccupied so much with the paradox of misery that always accompanied love, she had been putting her thoughts in order for another long
monologue about Sappho, the archetypal feminine poet who had for all
time identified love and "song" with pain. "I'm wild to get at it," she
wrote the Untermeyers as soon as she had returned to St. Louis, "but I'm
going to let it simmer for several months." She was afraid of scattering
its impetus in short poems on similar themes. The experience with Hatfield may have prompted the idea; waiting through the autumn for some

confirmation of his promises must have reinforced her notion of love as an inevitable disappointment for a woman.

Hatfield's continued silence followed the ominous pattern she had twice before traced in her verse drama and her short story—the lover who persuades her to the brink of sexual involvement only to become suddenly indifferent, leaving her baffled, with injured pride and the urge toward suicide. Imagination seemed to be turning into reality, and to save her pride she assured her friends that Hatfield really meant little to her. "Don't think, Jean," she wrote to Mrs. Untermeyer, "that this affair has been a very deep thing—thank heaven, it hasn't." Hatfield was "as fresh-hearted as a child, and he knows—oh, almost everything. But alas, he has a child's selfishness and utter lack of the sense of responsibility. We had wonderful days on the steamer.... I was very unhappy to part with him—you know what a miserable state I was in that morning when you called up. But Percy Bysshe Shelleys aren't—well, they aren't a very good foundation to build one's house of happiness upon." Her disavowal revealed how seriously she had actually taken the affair; the alternatives were marriage or nothing.

The new monologue of Sappho was a meditation on the division between love in the ideal or general sense and love for particular persons, and it reflected her own troubled thoughts about herself. Sara completed the poem on Christmas Eve, 1912, and the next day sent a copy off to the Untermeyers, titling it "Sappho and the Leucadian Rock." She based her subject on one of the common Sapphic legends, the suicidal leap of the poetess from a white rocky promontory on an island in the Ionian Sea in order to rid herself of the madness of possession by love for a ferryman named Phaon. Her scholarly edition of Sappho's poems by Henry T. Wharton treated the lurid story as one of the more unlikely myths clustered around the name of Sappho, tracing it to various traditional sources. Sara sweepingly disregarded fact, legend, and scholarship, as she had done in her earlier feminine portraits, and created a figure who is clearly modeled on Sara herself.

"I wanted Sappho to be almost suave in her attitude and perfectly self-possessed," she wrote Jessie Rittenhouse. "I wanted to get away from the passionately hysterical Sappho that most people have done." Sara's genteel breeding would have found offensive the idea that a woman would go mad for love of a man; but there was also her deep-seated feminine pride, which would not stoop to such an act. Her Sappho does not dive from a cliff driven by passion in full view of a crowd, but slips out of her house in the stillness of moonlight while everyone sleeps, so as not to be stopped or questioned—in that respect, clinically true to a type of suicide. Her decision to take her life has been reached after careful and private reasoning. Contrary to the legends, it has nothing to do with an excess of "mad" love for any individual person; in fact, it is the opposite.

> How should they know that Sappho lived and died
> Faithful to love, not faithful to the lover,
> Never transfused and lost in what she loved.

Her intense idealizing of love has made the actual experience of being in love a disappointment:

> I asked for something greater than I found.

Driven by passion for ideal love and beauty, the poet suffers an unwilling torment in her real life, which ends only when she decides that through her art she has sufficiently repaid the gods for the gift of life and can seek rest in death:

> I have grown weary of the winds of heaven.
> I will not be a reed to hold the sound
> Of whatsoever breath the gods may blow,
> Turning my torment into music for them. . . .
>
> The gods have given life—I gave them song;
> The debt is paid and now I turn to go.[2]

"Sappho" had emerged climactically out of a long and sustained excitement—"When I wrote 'Sappho' I summed up all I had in me up to that time," she later wrote Louis Untermeyer. Sara's own poems had heretofore been written largely about the tensions of a desired but impossible love. Going one step further, "Sappho" was a confession of the fatigue, malaise, and distaste that she felt at actual love involvement with men, in contrast to the glorious promise that had held her in suspense. For the "mad" physical, sexual desire that had driven Sappho to her death in the legends, Sara substituted a repulsion. Sara's tragic heroines always came to their deaths alone, never together with their lovers, like Tristan and Isolde or Romeo and Juliet; that, too, would have been a kind of consummation beyond her limited experience to imagine.

She sent the poem enthusiastically to Jessie Rittenhouse for reading at the Poetry Society, but quickly regretted her impetuosity when she found herself rigorously revising it. "I have whacked at her endlessly, and I think she is a good bit better," she wrote on December 31. Jessie Rittenhouse did not particularly like the poem, and Sara hoped she would not present it before the society after all; "but as Touchstone says, it is 'a poor thing, but mine own.'" In her usual way, she accepted criticism meekly and with goodwill, but persisted in finishing the poem as she intended. *Scribner's* accepted it in January—"Heavens, I'm as mad with delight as if I'd never had a thing taken before!" she wrote Louis. It was published in December 1913.

Ever since returning home in late September, Sara fully expected to spend the spring again in New York, especially with the prospect of renewing her relationship with Stafford Hatfield. So in spite of sieges of the grippe, an ulcerated eye that curtailed her reading for a month, caged excitement, and love misery, she could endure St. Louis for the first winter in several years. The mails were full of letters from friends in New York keeping her abreast of the news and gossip. Zoë Akins, now established there, passed on the stories of "erotic goings-on" she gleaned every day from the poet Blanche Wagstaff. John Myers O'Hara's father had died at the end of November, and John entered a long period of morbid withdrawal from which Sara could not shake him. Harriet Monroe had founded *Poetry* in Chicago that fall, but its distinguished future lay unpredictably ahead, and no one suspected that 1912 would some day be designated the watershed year between modernism and the old order. At that point, the only objective was to gain a wider audience for poetry of any school. William Stanley Braithwaite had begun publishing *The Poetry Journal* in Boston about the same time, but Sara confessed to Marion Stanley about these magazines, "I take very little interest in either. I hate the fostering of an art so well able to care for itself as poetry, tho' I suppose they will do good in their way." Sara's own reputation continued to expand, and *Helen of Troy* went into a second edition in the fall of 1912, after only a year.

The big news was the much-awaited publication of *The Lyric Year* in November 1912, a first *"Annual Exhibition or salon,"* as the editor optimistically called it, of the 100 best poems of the year. The project had been got up by Ferdinand Earle, a wealthy poetaster, who offered a first prize of $500 and two second prizes of $250, with a panel of judges consisting of Braithwaite, Edward J. Wheeler, president of the Poetry Society of America, and Earle himself. As it turned out, the volume was thoroughly conventional, much of it already outmoded. Over 10,000 poems by two thousand poets were submitted. Sara's short lyric "I Shall Not Care" was among the 1 percent accepted for inclusion, although it did not win a prize.

The first prize, to Sara's ecstatic approval, went to her friend Orrick Johns, who needed the money, for "Second Avenue," an earnest but tedious piece of rhetorical uplift in rhymed stanzas about the immigrants crowding into New York's Lower East Side and their contribution to the destiny of the nation. The volume is most noteworthy for publishing "Renascence," the poem that brought sudden fame to Edna St. Vincent Millay at the age of nineteen. Many, including Orrick Johns, believed it should have won the prize. But in retrospect, even "Renascence" shares the cosmic posturing and pretentiousness that characterized so much of the volume. Critics were soon carping over the awards, and the disappointing project was never repeated.

Sara, who found the poems of *The Lyric Year* mostly without merit, made the discovery of a new poet, in early December 1912, that sent her reeling with excitement. "I am perfectly wild over John Hall Wheelock's 'The Human Fantasy,'" she wrote Jessie. "You *must* read it. The poems are good separately, but they gain vastly by their cumulative effect, and I am sure you would agree with me that nothing finer in the line of a love story in a sequence of poems has been done since George Meredith's 'Modern Love.' The book is the best thing done by an American in years. I am telling everybody about it, and am sure that you will find endless pleasure in its spontaneity, its vigor and its healthy passion. . . . I wrote a note to him last night—I do hope that he won't dislike me for it." As Wheelock recalled, her letter hailed him "as one of the world's greatest poets. She was coming up to New York, she said, and would like to look me up."[3]

Wheelock, son of a Long Island physician and for three years a doctoral student in Germany, was then working as a clerk in Scribner's Book Store, associated with the firm where he was later to become a distinguished editor. Sara's letter, coming as it did from a well-known poet and filled with enthusiasm, buoyed him up considerably. "She was like the answer to a poet's dream," he recalled, because of her generous and intelligent praise of what she liked. He quickly replied, "I confess it sent a thrill through me to see your name at the end. It is a name which already has a certain glamour—definitely represents a beautiful fact. Perhaps your words especially pleased me coming from one whom I associate with a very finished perfection."[4]

Sara's adoration of his work spread like a halo around him personally as well, and she immediately began to picture herself in love with him, as she had a tendency to do with every new interesting man. Within a week after receiving Wheelock's first letter, she wrote to her friend Orrick Johns, with whom she had been sharing her excitement:

> I've just got up, after having spent most of the night in a mixed worship of poetry and J. H. W., to find a letter from him. May the gods be praised! Tho' I could never forgive him if he stooped to love me even in the remotest sense (the chances of my ever having to do any forgiving are small!) Here is evidence of my madness:
>
>> I have not seen my lover's face,
>> And I have never heard his voice;
>> But I have seen his naked soul,
>> And I rejoice.
>>
>> It is enough for me by day
>> To walk the same bright earth with him,

Enough by night that over us
The same great roof of stars is dim.5

The second stanza, slightly revised, and a third in the same vein were
published the following July in *Smart Set* under the title "Enough." But
she dropped the first stanza, which was about her relationship with Wheelock at the time of the writing and would doubtless have been puzzling
to a reader.

On January 3, 1913, she sent Marion Stanley a copy of *The Beloved
Adventure*, "my beloved Wheelock's second book. . . . He and I are carrying on a rapid-fire correspondence and I am deep in love, having put Mr.
Hatfield out of my head and heart." She had not yet even met John Hall
Wheelock, of course, and one cannot take too seriously her claim that she
had disposed of her feelings for Hatfield, even though he had sent her
only one postcard and one letter in three months. Her delight in Wheelock's poetry was genuine, but inventing a love affair with him may well
have been a compensation for the disappointment in Hatfield. It was
essential to be "in love" at all times with someone.

Wheelock was a lyric poet of fastidious perfection, like Sara herself, and
his chief theme was also love, although his poems were affirmative, rather
than plaintive disappointments:

> Your body's motion is like music—
> Your stride, elastical and light,
> Moves to the rhythm of hushed music,
> The unheard music of delight.[6]

His presence in New York brightened the aura of anticipation as January
23 approached, the day when she could finally leave. This year she was
less concerned about the possibility of her own poor health preventing
her going than she was that of her parents. But everyone stayed well
enough, and by the last week in January she was installed in the Martha
Washington Hotel and was caught up again in her friendships. Only a day
or two after her arrival, in an action that was "very unlike her," as John
Hall Wheelock recalls, she "walked into the Scribner Book Store where
I was a clerk, and introduced herself, and had a copy of my book for me
to autograph." They were soon taking long evening walks together, and
she kept up her vivid enthusiasm for his work, prodding Louis Untermeyer and Orrick Johns into reviewing his new book. "He is decidedly *not*
disappointing," she confided to Orrick.[7] Within a month, she preferred
her evenings with him to anything else, and begged off attending a play
of Yeats with Jean Untermeyer: "Needless to tell you, who must have
guessed it some time ago, I'd rather be with him than see a procession
of Irish players stretching from Cork to Killarney. We had a wonderful
time last night—walked for two solid hours."

She invited the new luminary Edna St. Vincent Millay to tea, and the two went on a bus top ride, in a small burst of excitement that did not, however, develop into friendship. Her friendship with the Untermeyers had grown intimate in the year since they met, and she was now sharing with Jean the concerns of her personal emotional life, as she had with Marion Stanley. Jean and she had a tearful session one afternoon, apparently about Louis, and both ended feeling "noble" and much closer to each other. "Many months ago I conquered this—else I should hardly have come here this winter," Sara said. It probably had to do with the attraction she felt to Louis and with its consequences. "Only," she wrote the next day, "don't lets make a hash of our poor souls the next time we are together." It was to the Untermeyers she turned in early February 1913 when an emotional shock drove her for the first time to think seriously of taking her life.

What happened can only be pieced together from indirect evidence, which suggests that Stafford Hatfield wrote her a letter exploding the elaborate structure of dreams she had built around him. Since he no longer planned to return to America, he probably wrote to tell her so, although it must have gone beyond a broken promise to reveal an attitude she had not perceived in him before. In panic, she cast about for something secure to cling to, and found it in Louis Untermeyer's poem "Prayer," which had been recently published in the *Century*. It began:

> God, though this life is but a wraith,
> Although we know not what we use,
> Although we grope with little faith,
> Give me the heart to fight—and lose.[8]

She wrote Louis: "This is just to thank you for 'The Prayer'—I've been rereading it in the 'Century,' and I think it pulled me a foot or so up from the depths of woe. Heavens, but I've had a jolly day! Well, God did a good thing when he made *you*, anyway. I have been seriously weighing a good many things, but I think if I hadn't a father and were courageous (which I'm not in the least) I'd get out of this messy world. I'm not putting enough into it to pay for my keep—and I *won't* [underlined three times] grow old and sour like Harriet Monroe. Thank heaven you and Jean care for me." Whatever the shock of disappointment was, it came between January 27 and February 1, when the themes of her poems in her notebook changed abruptly to failure in love and the wish to die. In "Lonely," she depicted herself looking down from her high window through tears at a patch of sunlit courtyard where men played ball, shouting and laughing. She thinks of throwing herself to her death, "to lose myself forever," to forget her "crying heart," and rest. "A Cry" is a desperate appeal for love addressed to a distant person whom she loves "madly" and uncontrollably, although she struggles against those feelings, and against her will to die.

As she worked her way through this worst crisis, she wrote to Louis Untermeyer of the "thousand new things" she had been thinking as "the result of the various and sundry emotions that I've had during the past weeks. . . . Briefly here are one or two of them: 1. That it is perfectly useless to expect someone else to come into your soul and set it to rights for you—you must set your soul to rights yourself if it is ever going to be in order. 2. There is no use in thinking that you deserve all that you want simply because you want it very hard. Perhaps you'll be a lot better in the end by *not* having what you want. . . . you must take as joyously as possible every experience that comes to you, and not fret about the things that don't come. *There,* that is my belief, and I am happy to have someone to tell it to. Thank heaven I am alive. I guess my youth is over—it is time—it came perilously near taking me off with it when it left me."

A poem titled "Peace," dated February 1913, shows her making the kind of adjustment she prescribed in her letter to Louis Untermeyer. She "to whom no love was given," who loved without return, has nevertheless received "marvellous gifts" of beauty and insight from the "careless man" who gave them to her unconsciously. She releases him from her demand for love and will be saved by the love she feels whether it is returned or not. In effect, she forgave Hatfield for his unprincipled sexual advances and for not loving her, and she retreated to the high ground of her own idealism.

Stafford Hatfield remained a ghost to haunt many of her poems, although it is doubtful that he ever knew the emotional havoc he had unwittingly caused, and they continued exchanging letters from time to time. John Hall Wheelock, who had only just met her, was not aware of the seriousness of this crisis, but recalled that "there was a man somewhere in the picture whom she admired very much and who eventually proved to be not reciprocating her feelings about him. . . . Because of her unnecessary depreciation of herself as a woman of attraction, she took these things very hard." Wheelock believed it to be less a matter of rejection than simply the discovery that the man did not really care about her, that she had only imagined herself to be attractive to him. Momentarily, her latent self-destructive sense of personal worthlessness had risen frighteningly to the surface. As a child who heroized her father and disliked her mother, she placed an inordinately high value on being pleasing to a man, judging her own worth by its reflection in him, an attitude enhanced by the chivalric literature on which she had nourished herself. "I think if I hadn't a father. . . . I'd get out of this messy world," she had said.

Another way to cope with her problem was to minimize it by placing

it in the impersonal and sobering perspective of human suffering. A few
weeks later, she wrote "Testament," the only one of these unhappier
Hatfield poems she published:

> I said, "I will take my life
> And throw it away ..."
>
> But out of the night I heard,
>   Like the inland sound of the sea,
> The hushed and terrible sob
>   Of all humanity.
>
> Then I said, "Oh who am I
>   To scorn God to his face?
> I will bow my head and stay
>   And suffer with my race."[9]

She ordinarily had little concern for human suffering in the abstract, or
for its philosophical or theological implications. But in the spring of 1913
she was exposed to the surge of "social consciousness" among some
poets and friends, and it may have served to distract her from preoccupation with her own problem. Untermeyer's poem "Prayer," which helped
her maintain her balance, reflected his association with the newly reorga-
nized *The Masses,* for it not only echoed the spirit of "Invictus" but also
prayed that he might always remain as sympathetically aware of "the dirt/
And all that spawn and lie in it," "the bitter ballad of the slums," as he
was of idealized beauty and refinement. Orrick Johns' prize-winning
poem "Second Avenue" owed its success partly to a vogue for social
awareness, which meant championing the workers and practicing a sentimentalized gritty realism, while taunting the genteel middle class.

One of the more unlikely vignettes in the history of American radical-
ism is that of Sara Teasdale strolling the streets of New York on the
warmer March evenings of 1913 rapt in discussion with John Reed, a
month before his arrest and jail term for participating in the strike of
silk-mill workers at Paterson, New Jersey. Sara doubtless met him
through Untermeyer, as she may have other members of the *Masses*
group. Reed, the "playboy" radical of Dos Passos' portrait in *U.S.A.,* was
just on the eve of discovering his calling as a journalist-activist and still
had ambitions to be a poet. Like others, including Dos Passos, he began
with the moods and delicate colors of the estheticism of the nineties and
the Celtic twilight and then, on his political radicalization, found the
street life of the city a colorful and vital subject matter.

Sara liked Jack Reed immensely. Tall, pug-nosed, "a big-boned, broad-
shouldered, handsome, semi-theatrical figure" (in Untermeyer's
words),[10] Reed notoriously loved the company of women, and his candor

and high spirits must have lifted Sara out of her despondency. They exchanged volumes of poetry, she praised his work extravagantly, and he declared in return, "There is no better living writer of delicate lyrics! I loved your book. . . . Why on earth should people like you bother with injustice and dirty things? The merest drudging machine can tend to that. You go on and sing. I'll never depress and brow-beat you with 'social reform' again."[11]

"But you didn't 'brow-beat' me with 'social reform,'" she protested. "I didn't even think of it by so big a name as 's.r.' It seemed just very interesting talk."[12] They wrote to each other occasionally, and she tried to renew their brief friendship when in New York a year later, but Reed had in the meantime covered the Paterson strike and the revolution in Mexico as a radical journalist, befriending Pancho Villa, and had left New York on his way to becoming a legend.

Throughout the spring, she continued sifting the experience of love denied, trying to define more clearly the conviction that had been emerging since "Sappho" was conceived, that beauty was the transmutation of pain; as in "Alchemy," where like a yellow flower after spring rain,

> My heart will be a lovely cup,
> Altho' it holds but pain.

She would learn

> To change the lifeless wine of grief
> To living gold.[13]

Still, her work was haunted by the insufficiency of that formula, for it was in effect a substitution of art for an unfulfilled emotional life. "The Fountain," a poem that may at first glance seem merely pictorial, with its "deep blue night," "satyr carved in stone," and "milk-white peacocks," appears to make the transformation from pain to beauty so smoothly as to conceal any trace of her quandary in a dreamlike repose. But the fountain "sang alone" in the night to the "drowsy heart/ Of the satyr carved in stone," just as the poet had sung her love songs to unhearing ears of men. The water suggests life, vitality, perhaps feminine sexuality, while the satyr, overtly sexual, male, and uninhibited, is made of stone, its heart sleeping, unaroused by the fountain's appeal through music.

> The fountain sang and sang
> But the satyr never stirred—
> Only the great white moon
> In the empty heaven heard.[14]

The stillness is not peace, but frozen action, and the moon, which ought to preside over lovers, is a symbol of chaste loneliness.

And her impassioned poem "Central Park," a place she always associated with pairs of lovers walking or embracing on park benches, expresses

her enraptured worship of beauty in the veiled foggy night with its reflections of lights on water "like sunken swords," but asks

> Why am I unsatisfied ...
> O, beauty, are you not enough?
> Why am I crying after love?[15]

An untitled poem declares bleakly,

> Now I am one with all whose high hopes fail,
> The lonely and the broken and the blind.

Despite the rise and fall of her high hopes in Stafford Hatfield, Sara not
only went on living but also came out of the experience with a somewhat
more mature and realistic management of her own emotions. It was the
first and last time she would allow herself to stake her life on a romantic
expectation elaborated out of loneliness and need. In fact, even as she
explored her sense of failure, she had begun to develop a genuine fondness and admiration for John Hall Wheelock. He was tall, handsome,
talented, gentlemanly, excruciatingly shy and sensitive, enormously interesting to her, and unmarried. By the time she left New York around
April 6, 1913, she had reached the conclusion that she was in love again,
although this time she proceeded more cautiously.

April also found her submitting her lyrics to Harriet Monroe's *Poetry*,
in spite of her lack of faith in the magazine and her disapproval of Miss
Monroe for being a "sour" old maid, a feeling perhaps rising from her
own fear of that fate. ("I wonder if I shall be equally so at her age?" she
asked John O'Hara.) She had met Harriet Monroe in New York, probably
at a meeting of the Poetry Society. Miss Monroe had urged her to visit
Chicago, and Sara, happy that "you like me well enough to really want
to see me again," accepted the invitation, planning to stop off in early
June on the family's annual pilgrimage through Chicago to Charlevoix—
"if you can recommend me a hotel that will be so utterly proper that my
parents will be satisfied."[16] She also dutifully sent her dollar and a half
for a subscription to *Poetry*.

When Sara returned to St. Louis in mid-April, the train was nine hours
late because of flooding, and in the gloomy household of her aging and
ailing parents, "very forlorn in my little green study," as she wrote
O'Hara, she was desperately homesick for New York and concerned
about her own future. "Sometimes I am wild to be away and out of
vexations which I cannot bear for other people and must perforce bear
*with* them," she wrote to Louis and Jean. "If I felt it my duty to stay here,
it would be comparatively easy. But I am not at all sure that it *is* my duty.
There is scarcely anybody in St. Louis except my own family that I'd give
a straw for. Everybody has gone away to live or to travel indefinitely in
Europe. Sometimes I long to try to earn my own living. If I were a bit
stronger I'd go in for it. As it is,—well, this is a preface to saying that if

you should chance to hear of any sort of work that you think I might be able to do, tell me about it. I wish that I could talk this over with somebody. Of course, my family wouldn't understand it. But it does seem a pity to stay dawdling about and not doing anybody else or yourself either any good during the finest years of your life."

To add to the misery, a blistering heat wave made her anxious to go to Charlevoix to escape it, in spite of the loneliness she dreaded there. She was reading Strindberg, Havelock Ellis, and Dostoevsky, finding *Crime and Punishment,* she told John, "all horror and misery, and yet the most masterly thing of its kind that I ever read."

The trip to Charlevoix had been put off to mid-June, and Sara became engrossed in a project she had begun to think about in April, that seems anomalous for her, a "Ballad of the Carpenter's Son," a fourteen-stanza poem about the life of Jesus focusing on his leaving home for meditation in the desert, out of which he discovers his calling. It is vividly impressionistic, psychological in approach, and free of religiosity in feeling or tone. Perhaps her dwelling on thoughts of her father, whom she adored, and whose old-fashioned Baptist faith she respected, influenced her; she had occasionally turned to the Bible when distraught, probably less for anything it said than for its association with the sense of security. She worked hard on the poem for weeks, incorporating suggestions made by William Rose Benet, and in September wrote Marion Stanley that *The Century,* where Benet was an editor, had accepted it for their Christmas number.

The summer of 1913 proved to be more exciting than she had anticipated. Around June 14 or 15, she parted with her parents at Chicago for a brief visit with Harriet Monroe while they went ahead to Charlevoix. The visit extended to ten days, and drew her, to her astonishment, into the center of bohemian life, which she had not seen first-hand even in New York, although Jack Reed had talked and written about it amusingly.

"Of course Miss Monroe isn't like that lot," Sara wrote Louis and Jean. She had formed a different opinion of Harriet Monroe now: "She has been a dear to me—so much gentler and finer than I had thought her in New York. There is a tragedy—a woman so sensitive and loving that she is crying out for affection and yet so repressed and shy that everybody thinks her old-maidish and hard and bitter." Miss Monroe could fly into icy rages or catch fools in the steel trap of her mind, but with Sara she was unfailingly gentle. Sara's admiration for her grew steadily through the years, and she particularly welcomed, and applied, the outspoken and intelligent criticism Miss Monroe always gave her work when she asked it. They quickly became close friends; Harriet Monroe was one of the important influences in her life.

One of Miss Monroe's gifts was to bring people together. On June 17, she introduced Sara to Eunice Tietjens, then an amateurish young poet

who was to join the staff of *Poetry* in the fall, and with whom Sara had
exchanged a few letters during the past year because of their mutual
acquaintance with Zoë Akins; Mrs. Tietjens' composer-husband Paul was
from St. Louis. Sara and Eunice liked each other on the spot. Perhaps not
since Marion Stanley had Sara felt such an instantaneous rush of fondness
for another woman. Like Marion, Eunice Tietjens was comfortably open-
minded, reassuring, warm, and sensitive, and much less inhibited than
Sara. "Eunice was . . . tall and dark," Harriet Monroe wrote in her autobiography, "and her olive skin and midnight eyes were emphasized by a
heavy mass of brown hair. She was a clever talker in three or four languages, and she loved the new contacts . . . with writers."[17]

One of Mrs. Tietjens' first acts of friendship was to bring Sara to meet
some of her Chicago literary friends, particularly Floyd Dell, who was
then making his reputation as editor of the *Friday Literary Review,* a vigorously progressive critical journal. Sara had read and liked some of Dell's
articles and doubtless imagined that she would encounter the kind of
dignified literary culture she was familiar with in New York. To her
horror, she was plunged into a bohemian society where people lived and
slept with whomever they pleased, and drifted in and out of each other's
studios as if privacy no longer mattered.

"Heavens, Jean, what a world!" she exclaimed to Jean Untermeyer.
"You see SEX written over every inch of it. It is fairly screamed at you,
and yet the people I have met are exceedingly kind and fine in many ways.
Sometimes you can't help feeling a bit apologetic in regard to your lack
of experience. . . . Here if you speak of loving anybody it seems to mean
going as far as possible. It is my sense of taste as well as my conventional
bringing up that is jarred horribly by this. It seems to me to be an ugly
thing—just ugly. I would make the most terrible fiasco of being 'ad-
vanced' that ever was. It would set so unbecomingly on me. Well, there
is no danger of my ever trying it."

Floyd Dell and his wife Margery were early experimenters in open
marriage and were presently living apart. Margery, who was leaving town
for a while, offered Sara the use of her quarters—"called by courtesy a
'studio' "—a one-room old store on the South Side, on Stony Island
Avenue, with unlocked doors connecting to another store adjoining,
where two young men came in and out at all hours. "Now the joke of this
is the contrast of S. T.'s bringing up and the studio," she told Jean,
doubtless thinking of her Oriental rugs, private bath, and maid, to say
nothing of Baptist propriety. Of course, she declined the offer.

She was disappointed not to find Floyd Dell a man of character, after
having read his lively, crusading prose: "I have been so enthusiastic about
his articles that I could scarcely believe so weak looking a creature could
have written them. He is the essence of the decadent youth in appearance
—slight, nervous, terribly sensitive looking, with a tired manner and a

tired way of looking at you. He isn't half as enthusiastic as I had fancied him. He's burned out. The pity of it sort of breaks your heart."

It was almost a relief to flee to the loneliness of northern Michigan with its quiet woods and lake, where she found sadly that the place was unchanged, "with scraps of my girlhood lying about in the empty bureau-drawers,"[18] while she herself had changed much, after the "emotional vortex" of ten days in which, she wrote Jean, she "felt as tho' the whole world were slipping into a Swinburnian hell." The Chicago experience found its way into a "queer half mad ironic" poem, "very much out of the usual order of S. T.'s work," which she sent to Marion Stanley in July:

### THE STAR

A white star born in the evening glow
Looked to the round green world below,
And saw a pool in a wooded place
That held like a jewel her mirrored face.
The star was romantic and young and good,
And she thought she had never been understood.
She said to the pool: "Oh wondrous deep,
I love you, I give you my light to keep!
Oh more profound than the moving sea
That never has shown myself to me!
Oh fathomless as the sky is far,
Hold forever your tremulous star!

But out of the woods as night grew cool
A brown pig came to the little pool;
It grunted and splashed and waded in,
And the deepest place but reached its chin.
The water gurgled with tender glee
And the mud churned up in it turbidly.
The star grew pale and hid her face
In a bit of floating cloud like lace.[19]

The poem is an expression of mingled shock and self-satire. She is the white star, living aloft in isolation, seeking fulfillment in idealized relationships, perhaps like her friendship with Marion Stanley. Such relationships had held up a mirror of self-understanding. She even fancies this shallow pool to be "more profound than the moving sea," her symbol of love between men and women. But that supposedly pure virginal femininity, which had narcissistically reflected back her own light, receives the coarse, sensual pig "with tender glee," suddenly revealing her idealization of feminine nature to be mistaken. The star recoils in shock and embarrassment, but probably still peers curiously through the lace-like cover behind which she has hidden. The poem may record her emotional experience centering on Eunice Tietjens, whom she had approached with a rush of adolescent affection, only to be introduced by her to the bohemian way of life.

In retrospect, Chicago had been exhilarating as well as disturbing. She had fallen in love with the city, she said, and Harriet Monroe turned out to be "the finest addition to my friends that I've made for many a day. . . . She is not a lovable person on first acquaintance—but on the whole, she is one of the deepest, tenderest women I ever knew—and she is 'on to' herself as J. B. R. [Jessie Rittenhouse] and a lot of others could never be." Nevertheless, she told Jean, she could not agree with Harriet Monroe's "unfortunate adoration of Ezra," or about her taste in poetry: "She has a tendency to take things that are heavy and labored." Too much poor work was coming in to *Poetry*, Sara thought, because poets couldn't dispose of it elsewhere. The key to Harriet Monroe's heart, however, was not to challenge her, but to love her. "H. M. has the gentle art of making enemies down to such a fine point that Whistler would have sat at her feet. . . . She is an unpleasant person on the surface—full of sharp words. But she is waiting to be loved and you must love her ere she will seem worthy of your love, as the bard saith. And then, when you have boldly leapt into her soul, you find it beautiful and gentle and full of sympathy. She is old enough to be my mother and yet her heart is as young and wildly beating as a girl's—and that is the tragedy, and thence comes the bitterness."

Luckily for Sara, her new friend Eunice Tietjens had an opportunity to spend much of the summer at Charlevoix too, conducting a kindergarten for the many small grandchildren of Mrs. Daniel Burnham, widow of a prominent architect. Eunice and Sara spent long evenings walking or sitting in the little summer-house perched forty feet above the lake, talking about poetry and love and John Hall Wheelock into the darkness.

In mid-July 1913 Sara received a casual note from Vachel Lindsay introducing himself: "I look forward to a most profitable friendship with you by letter—if you are so inclined. Miss Monroe told me grand things about you."[20] Harriet Monroe was busy getting her poets to meet each other. In this case, she probably had match-making in the back of her mind. "Miss Monroe told me you were a very lovely young lady—and that it would be much worth my while to stay over in Chicago till the end of the week—when you arrived—just to meet you," he explained.[21] Failing that, he began writing letters, his interest piqued. Sara responded cheerfully, although she was doubtless unprepared for his persistence or for the flood of ten- and fifteen-page letters that were soon to follow, sometimes at the rate of one or more a day. Lindsay was entering his most productive period and the beginning of his fame. Harriet Monroe had published his "General William Booth Enters into Heaven" in the January 1913 issue of *Poetry*, a turning point for his career. He was eagerly defining his beliefs, and Sara was not only a sympathetic and responsive listener but also a professional poet with a national reputation. It was six months, however, before they met.

In the summer of 1913 in Charlevoix, it was not yet Vachel Lindsay but John Hall Wheelock on whom she fastened her thoughts. They had continued writing to each other, and by now Sara had decided she was genuinely and seriously in love. Her problem, however, was in determining how Wheelock felt about her. "I do not understand him," she wrote the Untermeyers. "He has been an enigma to me—and his letters are equally beyond my understanding." She watched carefully for any signs from the reserved and oversensitive young man that he might be in love with her; although there was nothing she could point to with certainty, there was at least a constant show of promise, an enigmatic interest in her that might—or might not—be love.

By September, she had decided to take matters into her own hands and go to New York and find out. It was a bold move for her; the rules of respectability that required her to find a husband also forbade her to take any overt initiative in obtaining one. She was "miserable" in St. Louis and wrote the Untermeyers, rather exaggeratedly, that worry over her parents' health had brought her to the "verge of a nervous breakdown." She told Marion Stanley that her parents were ill, "not very ill, but enough to have worried me a great deal," and she needed relief: "I am going to New York all on my own money. Of course they may make a big fuss—but I don't think they will."

Money was the key to independence; being self-supporting would have freed her from the constant, oppressive sense of duty and obligation to her parents. This doubtless lent a strong motivation to her ceaseless efforts to publish in the major magazines and be paid for it, for it was the only skill on which she could capitalize. She received an average of $10 or $12 for each poem from the national magazines. It was far from enough to live on, but it allowed her the luxury of occasionally doing things she pleased without begging permission.

She was back in New York at the Martha Washington Hotel by September 16, almost directly from Charlevoix, and only Eunice Tietjens seems to have shared her secret reason for returning so soon. She told John O'Hara and Vachel Lindsay that she had come for a week of shopping—a "week" that would stretch to five months. But to Eunice she poured a stream of cards and letters charting the fever of her love affair. "All goes fairly well," she declared on arrival. "The Most Wonderful was looking handsomer than ever last night, and we had an endless walk on the East Side—*but* no love whatever—and I rather dreary and fagged. . . . Of course he *is* a love—and yet I'm afraid that I can't keep at this high temperature if he's always at so tepid a one." She was excruciatingly careful to appear "so *reserved*" and "un-running-after-him in any way." But it was exasperating to be so eager and yet pretend not to be, while waiting for Wheelock, who was equally reserved, to make some sign.

After a month, Sara had little progress to report: "The mills of the gods are slow. In my case Eros has no wings."

She had written a great deal in the two years since publishing *Helen of Troy,* and was busy now putting together a new volume of poems with a title—*Rivers to the Sea*—taken from a poem by Wheelock. As he remembered the autumn of 1913, Sara "had come to have an exaggerated regard for my critical judgment, where poetry was concerned, and consulted me constantly on what to leave in and what to take out. I gave my opinions, for whatever they might be worth, and she acted on them often; not always, however. The question of a title for the volume troubled her greatly. Many were proposed and discarded, until one day I suggested 'Rivers to the Sea,' part of the second line of the last stanza of a poem of mine, without title, on page 116 of my third book, *Love and Liberation,* then recently published. Sara had taken a special fancy to this poem. Her approval was instant. With characteristic impetuosity she blazoned the new title across the first page of her manuscript, striking out all the other, tentative ones. About a week later, if memory serves me, Sara came to the Scribner Book Store and handed me a package that I was not to open till I went home. Impatient, I untied it almost the moment she was safely out of the store, and found in my hands the autograph manuscript, complete up to that date, of what was to appear in 1915, after certain additions and subtractions, as one of Sara Teasdale's most important books, *Rivers to the Sea.*" It was inscribed, "For John Hall Wheelock, October 1913."[22]

The impenetrable mystery of Wheelock's real feelings served only to intensify her interest in him and her determination to make him love her. But to him, her behavior was at times equally bewildering, hidden as its meaning was behind the proprieties she scrupulously observed. One night after they had returned to the Martha Washington Hotel from a walk in Central Park, and he said goodbye to her at the door, "she came up and took my hand and then she sort of muttered under her breath, but quite clearly, 'You love me and I love you,' and then turned away quickly and went upstairs. This was a signal to me to know where she stood, and that worried me quite a lot. I didn't know what to say, so in a cowardly way I never said anything. . . . I hadn't said that I loved her. Of course I loved her in the sense that you love any fine human being, but there was nothing romantic about it for me, absolutely not." Sara's fervid hopes, however, cast Wheelock in a different light: "He does love me, of that I am sure," she wrote Eunice Tietjens in November. "Heavens, what a man! I *know* that he isn't in love with anybody else—that's one comfort—and you know I'm a bit unlikely to pull the shielding wool over my eyes."

Wheelock was the occasion for many poems during that autumn, often written after their evening walks. For example, a stanza from "Swans," entered in her notebook on October 23, 1913, that sums up the unspoken questions lying between them, where the sleeping swans, like the satyr at the fountain, form an image of hushed anticipation:

> We watch the swans that sleep in a shadowy place,
>     And now and again one wakes and uplifts its head;
> How still you are—your gaze is on my face—
> We watch the swans and never a word is said.[23]

Her fine lyric, "The Kiss"—"Before you kissed me only winds of heaven/ Had kissed me, and the tenderness of rain"[24]—was written on September 24, with the marginal notation "Latest song included in book made in N.Y. Oct. 1913 for J. H. W." "At Night" depicts her lying in bed thinking of her lover—"Five streets divide us, and on them the moonlight lies"— wondering if he is awake, as she sends her thoughts to him like "a flock of wild birds."[25] Her poem "After Parting," written at Charlevoix during the summer, was, as Wheelock recalled, "written about us in such a way that I would never be able to forget":

> I set my shadow in his sight
>     And I have winged it with desire,
> That it may be a cloud by day
>     And in the night a shaft of fire.[26]

One of the most ambitious is an eighty-line poem, "A November Night," depicting a walk in Central Park on a foggy night, where she plays girlish games of imagination with him:

> You smile at me
> As though I were a little dreamy child.

All her chaotic thoughts and impressions take proper form and shape only when seen through his eyes. Then the fog closes in to isolate them from the world, and for one moment even he, walking ahead, nearly vanishes—"You, too, grown strange to me and far."[27] For an instant there is a glimpse of the possible estrangement that haunts any close relationship, or of the uncertainty that Wheelock might be lost to her after all. It was in such passages, as in "The Swans" and "The Fountain," that she was learning to project wordless suggestions not through metaphor but the simple presentation of a scene, anticipating an aspect of Imagism.

Wheelock took her to his family's country place in East Hampton on Long Island, a house built by his father within sound of the sea, with attractive walks around it. "Sara was deliriously happy there," Wheelock said. "Sometimes she'd spend a whole week. My mother liked her very much and they got along very well together." In late November, she wrote another long poem, "The Mother of a Poet," for Mrs. Wheelock. It depicts the child growing up under the loving protection of its mother, but in maturity striking out on alien adventures of the mind and imagination, "Winged on a flight she could not follow." The cosmic purpose of the poet is to voice for the inarticulate mass of mankind the joyous life force, which, over evolutionary time, creates conditions of beauty:

> So, in the man who sings,
> All of the voiceless horde
> From the cold dawn of things
> Have their reward.

The mother fears for her son and "would soothe and set him free" from his mission, but of course cannot.[28] The theme is reminiscent of Sara's depiction of Mary in "The Carpenter's Son" as a mother who cannot understand or accept her son's divine calling. The two poems were printed adjacent to each other in *Rivers to the Sea,* accentuating the parallel idea.

Wheelock's own early life had been troubled because his father had discouraged his hopes for a career as a poet—"you can't make a living writing verse"—and had sent him instead to Germany to earn a doctoral degree so he could become a teacher. "I just spent my time writing a lot more verse," Wheelock said, "and came back after three years without a Ph.D." He then found a job at Scribner's Book Store and went about writing in earnest.

Sara's friendship with Wheelock was idyllic, although as a love affair it did not seem to be going anywhere. In early December, she wrote Eunice Tietjens that "tho' I may never have what I want most, at least I have in him the finest man friend I have ever had. . . . For heaven's sake never mention J. H. W.'s name in connection with mine. It is already being whispered about that we are engaged, and the situation is very unpleasant for me because I wish so hard that it were true!"

In her usual fashion, she was able to be both love intoxicated and shrewdly objective in her appraisal of a man's character whom she loved. She had seen Stafford Hatfield's irresponsible impulsiveness even while she dreamed of a perfect marriage. She wrote about John Hall Wheelock to Harriet Monroe: "He *is* cold and abstracted and un-get-atable at first. . . . He is the shyest person I ever knew—so *very* shy that out of the mere torture of it he has invented this seeming calm abstraction. He has told me with utter humiliation of the real terror that it is to him to meet people. I remember once a little incident that will prove it. It shows too that his trouble amounts almost to a nervous disease. We were at a large formal dinner together and had to sit opposite each other. He talked in his company manners way with the woman next him, who happened to be a stranger to him. When we finally left the table and stood together, he said in a low voice absolutely grey and tortured: 'This has been terrible.' A little minute afterward I noticed a drop of blood on his hand. 'Where did that come from?' I said. And then I was ready to beat myself for my lack of care for his feelings, for I saw his pain at my question. The foolish creature had pressed his finger nail into his hand out of sheer nervous torture. And yet he had seemed *perfectly* at ease during the dinner—only very un-merry. You can have no real notion of a man like that unless you have known him intimately."

Yet, "of all the men I have known, he has the deepest and surest knowledge of me. I have never said anything to him in my life that he didn't understand and treat with a sort of gentle humor and tenderness. . . . [He] has given me many of the happiest hours of my life—a sort of absolute freedom that I have never known with any man before—I can't help being grateful to him."

As the Christmas of 1913 approached, and she had to economize more and more to stretch her dwindling funds, Sara could not bear to leave New York and Jack, although she felt she ought to. It was the first Christmas she had spent away from her parents in her twenty-nine years. Vachel Lindsay, writing from Springfield, Illinois, now consumed by curiosity to meet her, was urging her to come home to the Midwest where he felt she belonged. His new acquaintance with Harriet Monroe had intensified his conviction that a cultural revolution was in the making: "*not* the Socialist Revolution, either. But just such another set of infinite tiny momentary changes as we have seen in dancing and in Dress and in songs are going to take place in all the ways of life. . . . By the time women have voted at two Presidential Elections we will be doing things as different as the Tokugawa Shogunate from modern Japan." In this new blossoming of the popular culture, the artist belonged in his region, in his home town, to help it along.

When Sara had sent him an "ardent invitation" to visit New York in the fall of 1913 and meet her friends, he had replied: "And as for New York—get away from there. Go back home and write poems about St. Louis. If all the prodigal sons and daughters were gathered there—would return to their native heaths, America would be remade in a generation. Temperament set atremble in that exotic air has nothing to do with cornfed America."

Sara defended New York, the city that had liberated her from the morbid oppressiveness of her own Midwestern home; but Lindsay was only stimulated to develop his argument more vigorously. He saw them as representing two dominant directions in American literary culture that were at odds with each other, he, the native tradition of people like Lincoln and Twain, she, the imported hot-house culture of Europe. After reading her poem "Sappho," he was moved to "talk to you like a dutch uncle. I was just exactly in your frame of mind toward Beauty—I was as steeped in the Greek mood—in certain moments—five years ago—as you are today. . . . I feel vastly older than you in esthetics. The Greek standards are in you for all time—and I know it is possible—still keeping those standards in the core of your heart—to look the West straight in the face and admire it. I can remember when a corn-field seemed the most horrible slashing thing in the world to me—and a small town newspaper a masterpiece of bad grammar and stupidity. But now I look on both with the same joy with which one observes squirming bouncing ruddy children.... I know it is possible for you to move on in this way though the transition cannot come in a day.... I do really, most seriously covet a fellow warrior in this middle Western fight." And so he tried to enlist her.

"You have indeed a singing voice. That's it—precisely, and therefore you are a rare bird," he wrote her in November, and then followed with a proposal that must have roused the greatest amusement she had felt in months:

> I only wish I could take you harvesting. It would give you a rest from this nightingale business. The women ... never can be emancipated till they can be disguised in the flesh and bones of men and go out and have the dogs bark at them six months at a time, and sweat like troopers and eat like threshing machines and work like blazes. I wish you would give this passionate little breast of yours to the middle West—instead of always to particular persons—or your own moods.... We accept the proposition that you are an individual, you have abundantly proved it—now show us that you are a voter and a citizen. I think you ought to be cook in a farm house one whole season and then write it all in poems from the dishwashing to weeding the radishes....
>
> The middle West needs to be glorified and gilded. It needs to sing—it needs to be pounded to a pulp by us resolute poets. You quiver in the wind when you should be going out against the enemy with a baseball bat, as it were.... It is my conviction that you should write up your special social history.... You are Sara Teasdale—living by the Mississippi. Write a poem about that river that shall bring tears to the eyes of Huckleberry Finn himself. You are Sara Teasdale—living in the state of Missouri. I walked through that state and it is full of poems.... You are Sara Teasdale—graduate of the St. Louis High School. Write a poem about the Public School in the Middle West.... Burn yourself to ashes—scatter yourself over a field in the spring and come up the World's most wonderful corn-song in the autumn. What the Sam Hill are you doing in New York—anyway?

In the year since he had completed his great walk across most of the West from Illinois to California, working as a harvest hand, picking up odd jobs along the way and spreading his leaflet, "The Gospel of Beauty," Lindsay at the age of thirty-four had at last been "discovered." His name had begun to appear in the national magazines, and he could look back with a certain comfortable mellowness on several years of pain, frustration, and near paranoia over his failures. But Sara's warm invitation to join the Poetry Society and present his work in New York was to him the siren voice of the establishment, and as a self-styled radical he had no intention of yielding to it in order to enhance his growing reputation. "I want them to join my gang. I want Rome to come to Camelot.

Camelot does not want to go to Rome. . . . There never was a person, not even Mohammed with so much uncrushed arrogance in him—or faith that he had the true religion to reveal, as I have. And I know well enough New York even *Poetry* New York—is in no state of mind to receive it from me. . . . Meanwhile it is far more fun to play beggar and bide my time. I would rather beg than not have my way. You know nothing of the Love of God, child, if you think it is less than the love of Woman. It has come between me and every woman I ever knew."

It was fair warning. In a remarkable burst of self-exposure—"showing you my naked bones until I ought to be ashamed"—Lindsay told her of the mystical strain that was passed down in his family: "There has been in one branch of my people a peculiar tradition. My great grandfather used to have peculiar and very confidential interviews with my mother when she was only six years old—and of course—later—as the only one of his grandchildren who showed symptoms of 'carrying on the light.' He laid his hands on her head and blessed her and enjoined her—endowed her as it were with her office. She has been a passionate religious leader all her life. . . . She began on me when *I* was six years old—with this tale of the Light, and of grandfather Austen. Till I was seventeen I was under the complete domination of her most powerful mind. Then for years I had to fight for myself and my personality—it was a heart-breaking struggle. . . . If I can in the end, be to the people who listen to me with loyalty, what my mother is to *her* friends, who listen to her loyally—I will have achieved my life."

Lindsay's own vision of his mission as an artist-evangelist had shaken him out of sleep at two o'clock one morning on a boat coming back from Europe with his family in 1906: "The vision of Christ-Apollo. . . . woke me with terrible power—it shook me from head to foot—and I was in a daze for two or three days—and with the feeling of the completest triumph I have ever known. It was the turning point of my life." This had occurred after "years of struggle between the Hebrew and the Greek in my soul when I was almost torn to shreds with it."

Sara had once described her own inner conflict in nearly the same terms to John Myers O'Hara: Greek versus Puritan. Both she and Vachel Lindsay were offspring of an intensely puritanical, evangelical Protestantism, and they had initially responded guiltily to the hedonistic appeal of European art; Lindsay was awe-struck by the Venus de Milo in the Louvre much as Sara had been. He found his resolution by absorbing art into religion, Sara hers by sublimating religion in art.

Although Vachel Lindsay struggled hard to keep women at the bottom of his list of interests—"My first love is the Good God—the second the Devil—the third my Ink Bottle—the fourth mine own people—(Papa, Mama, and little sister) and fifth the road. Yes—Woman is number six, I can't help it"—he nevertheless found himself continually attracted to women and involved in spite of himself. For three years he had been in love, off and on, with a young Springfield woman, Octavia Roberts, who found him impossible, and his hopeless interest in her was beginning to wear itself out when Sara Teasdale was gently pushed toward him by Harriet Monroe. In September 1913, Octavia Roberts firmly broke off the relationship and burned his letters, announcing her plans to marry someone else in December, a disappointment that may have turned his curiosity more seriously toward Sara.

Lindsay took playful liberties in his letters, always careful, however, never to offend with his teasing and lecturing, always gentle and respectful. She was the well-known romantic, genteel lady poet: "My Dear Sara Ravena Trevenian Tremain Trevor Teasdale," one letter mockingly began. She was also "Excellent Rascal—Sara Teasdale." He became intensely interested to know what she looked like. "Miss Monroe writes me that you are a 'prize package,' " he said, but the solemn face of Martha Washington always stared back at him from the letterhead of her hotel stationery until he began to have the uncanny feeling that Sara looked like her. At Christmas she finally sent him a photograph, and he studied her face carefully, declaring that she was "elfin" and had "wise eyes" and a "great deal of curiosity and kindness in your mouth." She also promised to invite him to St. Louis to meet her as soon as she returned, a date that to his disappointment was constantly being postponed as she found reasons to stay in New York.

Sara was immune to his efforts to enlist her in his campaign, and too deeply preoccupied with Wheelock to pay attention to any romantic tinge to his interest in her, although she wrote appreciatively of his beliefs. He increasingly protested that the love of women was at odds with his religious calling, for he had been frustrated by Octavia Roberts and uncertain of how to feel toward Sara. "I am always getting all snarled up with complete pagans and then preaching myself hoarse at them and getting all tangled up in their hair and leaving in the end with my sermons fallen to the ground. The real serious kind of people are apt to be so lacking in dimples." Still, he begged her for a lock of her hair—woman's hair was one of the most femininely appealing things to him—and she sent it. And now he sat down every night when the house was quiet for his daily letter to her, which had become a kind of spiritual communion like meditation in a church.

As the day of meeting Sara approached, he became more preoccupied with defining the kind of relationship they should have. "I never settled down to what might be called a professional comradeship in the nightingale business," he wrote. She was not only the first woman poet he had ever known, unless one counted Harriet Monroe, but also the first poet of national reputation. She was neither a dimpled pagan, a religious comrade in arms, nor the feminine poetic voice the Midwest needed. The obvious answer was to remold her in a new image: "I would like *so* much to have a professional interest in your life—you are *bound* to *grow*—I would like to have something to do with the direction in which you grow. Your letters tell me of this friendship and that—but nothing of your dreams as a priestess and citizen. . . . The woman heart of America must needs sing itself. . . . You ought to make yourself the little mother of the whole United States and especially the Middle West."

But when Lindsay told her that her life lacked direction—"You zigzag from one romance to the next"—she took offense and delighted him by replying spiritedly that she was actually a snob, and considered St. Louis a very unromantic place. "You certainly are a willful miss. I begin to get *that* all right," he said. "And a very proud one—in your secret artistic pride. . . . I'll take you out and show you your city someday. Women—sensitive women are so sensitive to the finished side of civilization—they are after all such shut-ins. It is impossible for them to do any deep sea diving—as it were—and come up—and they remain on the shore forever." That summed up better than anything the gulf that lay between them, in spite of all they might share.

Sara put off her return to St. Louis until after the Poetry Society dinner on January 28, 1914, and a formal luncheon for Yeats on February 10. In five months she had become thoroughly immersed in the literary life of New York, the gossip, the parties, theatre, and evenings with friends, more actively than she had ever been or would be again. The shy girlishness had begun to wear off, her tortured inhibitions had relaxed into greater forthrightness and poise, and her critical judgment had sharpened. She had gained in professional self-assurance. But in spite of the hours spent each week with Jack Wheelock, she had not been able to get a declaration of love out of him. "My lover and I are still dragging along," she wrote Eunice Tietjens, "both of us terribly unhappy and both of us confiding it shyly to the other and every now and then having heart-breaking discussions as to how a man can support a wife and still keep true to his ideal of being a poet. Heaven knows how it will turn out. Both of us will be grey if this keeps up. The poor boy can't sleep and is evidently suffering about as much as I—which I suppose I should consider a good thing. Well, I am thankful to God for this much if I never have more. He is so much finer than any other man that I ever knew that I could kneel to him gladly. I wish I had more skill in managing."

She reached home on February 14 or 15, more disconsolate than ever at the dreariness of St. Louis. After New York, "where everybody is so full of life and enthusiasm it is deadly to come back to this place where poetry is an unknown art, as dead as the embalming of the ancient Egyptians," she wrote Jessie Rittenhouse. To Will Parrish in Germany, she cried, "Oh, lucky that you are, to be out of this STODGE hole of a city; I am wearying my soul out for Broadway and my boy."[29] Her gloom was darkened still more by her father's declining health. At seventy-five, and unwell, he insisted on going down to his business and returning exhausted, while Sara feared momentarily hearing of a heart attack or stroke.

Vachel Lindsay, on the other hand, had been building to a crest of emotional excitement. His letters had grown almost flirtatious, at times even silly, then suddenly remote and somber, by turns. He had written a poem about her "golden" hair which he constantly revised, sending her a new version every week. On the invitation of Sara's parents, he had arranged to arrive around 6 P M on Wednesday, February 18, stay the night in the house, and return to Springfield by train the next day.

It was a vastly more important meeting for him than it was for her. He regaled the family with performances of "The Congo" and "The Kal-lyope Yell" and he and Sara talked for hours in her little study, as he had anticipated. But she was not quite what he expected. The gentleness of her poems, the obliging softness of her letters, had not prepared him for her firm ambition, her artistic tough-mindedness, and her air of New York professionalism. It left him feeling further away from her rather than closer. His ambition for her as the "Little Mother of the United States" must suddenly have seemed hopelessly inappropriate. Over the next week, as he prepared to leave for Chicago for the banquet sponsored by *Poetry* in honor of Yeats on March 1, he analyzed his impressions in letter after letter to her, trying to get at her identity for his own satisfaction.

He was acutely conscious of her dependence on literary society, while his sprawling world had taken him "everywhere but in jail almost—and in a way hardened to it all." He was not prepared for her "remarkable eyes . . . the velvet of the Gods—the eyes of your genius. . . . watching watching me. . . . Your face is much longer and more sensitive than in your pictures. . . . I do not want to live in your alleged heart. Everyone does(!) But in your eyes. They are more exclusive. . . . You are certainly an intense egotist, and have a most sharp tang and savor to your egotism, and a great delicacy and charm to it as well."

His second letter was addressed to "My Dear Velvet-Eyes," and after that "Dearest Saraphim," a nickname his sister Joy had invented. "Velvet-eyed lady—I can see in you the same art-egotism and ambition that I know in myself. I can see you value your kingdom, I can see you wish to more strongly grip those that like your songs. . . . But I detect you, fellow conspirator. I apprehend one half of why you like New York. You get more fish lines into your hand, you rascal. You fight a merry little battle for your dreams' sake. More friends, more listeners!"

He tried to come to terms with the fact that she was a woman. "As a singer-of-love I have little to say to you. The kind of love you sing about—realized or desperately attempted between man and woman has never brought me anything but desperate sorrow—a house burned down as it were.... Yet—if you were not a woman—I know I would not be writing to you. I am stealing a man's consolation from your womanhood by writing to you." He was soon saying, "I don't want to be your sweetheart. I don't want to ever love anyone again, in the Romeo sense, for years. It's too deadly. But I want you for the dearest kind of faithful friend."

Since Sara felt no attraction to him as a potential lover, she had no such problem with her emotions as he did. "He is a fine fellow but full of mannerisms, which are rather lovable on the whole," she wrote Jessie Rittenhouse. "He is blonde, medium height, 34 years old, has keen grey-blue eyes, a nice voice, *great* capacity for sustained converse.... He read me a number of his poems and I give you my word that it was a thrilling experience. He shook the house, also my nerves.... His new poem 'The Congo' ... has a lot of substance and for want of a measuring rod for exactly that kind of poetry, it is hard to tell whether it is good or not.... He fondly hopes to reach 'the man in the street.' But the man in the street is looking for lyrics of the high order of 'I heard it first at mother's knee' and will have none of this new-fangled nonsense." To Louis Untermeyer, she wrote that Lindsay was "full of eccentricities—aggressively himself.... almost a monologist if he gets on a familiar and favorite train of thought. His voice is good, but too loud much of the time and *very* Middle-West.... Yet the fresh humanity of the man—his beautiful exuberance, fills you with delight.... You forgive the celluloid collar and the long craning neck that seems to grow unspeakably when he lifts his head in recitation.... He has, quite literally, clean hands and a pure heart."

Harriet Monroe had invited Vachel Lindsay to read "The Congo" at the Yeats dinner in Chicago, but Sara felt it would be a mistake: "I fear that it is in direct opposition to every law that Yeats laid down so splendidly in his speech [in New York]," she told Jessie. But it was Sara who was mistaken. Miss Monroe had taken care to place on Yeats's bedside table the issue of *Poetry* containing "General William Booth Enters into Heaven." Yeats not only read it but praised it highly in his speech the next day; and this was followed by Lindsay's rousing performance of "The Congo," the first time an influential audience had heard him. It thrust him suddenly, and with mixed feelings, into a limelight he had both sought and resisted. Harriet Monroe chalked up the banquet as one of her most exhilarating triumphs.

The burden of Yeats's remarks in Chicago was probably much the same as had impressed Sara in New York. He formulated a theory of lyric poetry like that which she herself had developed over the past six years, which was in the air of the new times: freedom from rhetoric, sentimentality, and moral uplift; austerity rather than preachiness; natural speech rather than artificial diction; "a style of speech as simple as the simplest prose, like the cry of the heart. . . . It is not the business of the poet to instruct his age. His business is merely to express himself, whatever that self may be." The poet should strive for simplicity, humility, "giving you his emotions before the world." He should seek "instantaneousness of effect."[30]

Sara did not attend the banquet, feeling she could not leave her parents again so soon after returning home, and so had spent "two grey lonely weeks," enlivened only by Lindsay's brief visit. Eunice Tietjens, in Chicago, was her nearest friend, and Sara soon began contriving a way for her to visit St. Louis, since she herself was unable to go to Chicago. The two had been thick in plans of all sorts throughout the year since their meeting, not only Sara's hopeless conquest of Wheelock's affections, but literary schemes as well. Eunice had taken up with Margaret Anderson's new *Little Review,* in addition to *Poetry,* and her work was appearing in almost every issue.

Sara's exposure to bohemianism in Chicago and New York had set her to thinking seriously about the revolutionary change in sexual mores and attitudes going on about her. If she recognized herself as excessively proper and Victorian for the time in which she lived, she also, once the shock began to wear off, wished to come to terms with the new mentality as open-mindedly as possible. To this end, she wrote an essay, unusual for her, on H. G. Wells for *The Little Review,* under the pseudonym "Frances Trevor." It appeared in the April 1914 issue, entitled "Two Views of H. G. Wells," a debate between a fictitious conservative named "Mary Martha" and a tougher-minded modern, Frances Trevor, thus reflecting the conflicting currents within herself. Mary Martha, whose father purportedly is a minister, has read Wells' *The Passionate Friends* and finds that her reactions are governed by her conscience, which she personifies as "a little old Victorian lady," sitting "in the background of my consciousness" knitting. "Meanwhile I go blithely about, espousing all sorts of causes and thinking out all sorts of theories—imagining, you know, that I'm perfectly free. Suddenly she wakes up—she lays aside her knitting with a determined air and says, 'Mary Martha, *what* are you thinking about! Stop that right now, I'm ashamed of you.' And she has authority, too, you know. I stop. Ridiculous, isn't it?—but it is so."

The little old Victorian lady disapproves strongly of Wells, who appears to advocate the abolishment of monogamous relationships on the grounds that they are "shams," artificial restraints on natural human tendencies. But human nature is not to be trusted; character must be built by strenuous attention to duty, self-denial, and devotion to hard work, which keeps irresponsible males out of trouble. "Nature is still unbearably ugly in lots of ways. When we can train it to be unselfish and disinterested then it will be time to tear down barriers."

Frances Trevor counters with the charge that the Victorian lady is a sentimentalist who wishes to lay a fine gloss of pretense over the realities of life. Wells "discloses to her scandalized eyes various unfortunate facts which she has done her best to conceal, as for instance the fact that there is such a thing as sex." To Wells, sex is "*the* disturbing element in life," making it impossible "that life should be the sweetly pretty parlor game our little Victorian lady would have it." Wells has taught us "to look at life squarely, without moral cant, and with a scientific disregard as to whether it pleased us personally or not. . . . No, the day of Victorianism is past. We are slashing away at the web, we are learning to *think.* It is a slow and painful process and we know not where the struggle will end. But at least we shall be nearer to the divine nakedness of truth."[31]

Although Sara gave the edge to Wells in this debate, the struggle was only defined, and was far from being won. She had been watching Zoë Akins in New York "fluttering around the candle of SIN as assiduously as possible," getting herself "talked about in a messy way." When Zoë returned to St. Louis for a visit in late spring, Sara found her offensively addicted to telling sexual anecdotes about her rich bohemian friends. "I heard so much about sex," she wrote Eunice, "that I should like to forget it forever and be as the angels in heaven who have none." To Sara's amazement, Zoë's set discussed homosexuality and "excesses" all the time as calmly as any ordinary happening.

Eunice recommended that she read August Forel's *The Sexual Question,* and Sara not only did so but urged Marion Stanley to read it, too, as a help in her marital difficulties. Marion had separated from her husband Bruce and had come to New York in mid-winter to start a new life only to be stunned and guilt-stricken by the sudden death of her mother in Tucson. Marion was floundering, and Sara seemed to have moved too far out of her life now to be of any help. But she believed Forel to be a sensible guide, "interesting and exhaustive. . . . It is not messy at all— indeed only a small part of the book is devoted to abnormal states."

*The Sexual Question,* first published in America in 1906, is a perfect compendium of conventional middle-class assumptions about sexuality, which avant-garde Americans spent the next three generations trying to demolish. "In normal women especially young girls, the sexual appetite is subordinate to love," Forel declared, thus separating love and sex in the very way that was the source of Sara's confusion. "In the young girl love is a mixture of exalted admiration for masculine courage and gran- deur, and an ardent desire for affection and maternity. She wishes to be outwardly dominated by a man, but to dominate him by her heart." She is sentimental, ecstatic in submission, "vanquished by his embraces," so that men have a dangerous advantage. Women need to be treated re- spectfully. "The first coitus is usually painful to woman, often repug- nant." Forel stressed the innocent idealism of women, the shocking "lewdness" of men. He deplored "old maids," who, unlike old bachelors, needed to compensate for lack of love by involving themselves in art, literature, or good works, to avoid becoming "dried-up beings or useless egoists." He also criticized American women for their increasing desire to remain young and attractive and avoid hard work or childbearing. "A woman's ideal ought not to consist in reading novels and lolling in rocking chairs, nor in working only in offices and shops."[32] Otherwise, the Aryan racial stock would decline and gradually be replaced by Negroes and Chinese.

Ironically, Forel reinforced for Sara the social conventions that H. G. Wells attacked. But he candidly covered the full range of sexuality, including the physiology of sex, pornography, and abortion. He was surprisingly tolerant of a wide range of sexual behavior between consenting adults, even homosexuality, calling only for discretion and the protection of children, and he considered adultery not a crime but merely a reason for divorce. Sara, in short, found him liberal, wholesome, and informative in her own badly neglected education.

"I think that the whole world of sex is a bit upheaved in the spring," Sara wrote Eunice. She had been receiving love letters from a brickyard laborer in New York named Charles Cummings, addressed to her through magazines in which she published. She wrote to Robert Sterling Yard, editor of *Century*, requesting that her home address not be given to him should he ask for it. The semi-illiterate letters touched her, for they were respectful and passionate, and "once in a while he says something almost beautiful. This, for instance: 'Last night I walked for a long time through the loving fields thinking about you.' . . . When he speaks of enduring 'cruel and colored dreams' (the phrase is his own, and I think it good, don't you?) I feel a sort of tenderness for the poor soul." He wrote of his sexual desire for her very plainly and with "a childlike simplicity, and yet, to use my favorite word, he is not 'messy.' " If it weren't for "the gulf between us," she was all for answering him.

Sara was desperate for someone to talk to, and also to help in reviewing her manuscript of *Rivers to the Sea*. "I am still entirely in love with J. H. W. and our parting was sad enough—but since he loves his poetry better than anything else, I suppose that he must keep his freedom," she wrote Eunice, but "I'm always hoping to win the battle in the end." So she sent Eunice $10 for train fare, from the sale of a poem to *Harper's*, and asked her to visit for a few days in St. Louis near the end of March 1914 to talk over the state of her life.

Eunice did far more than Sara had anticipated. On her last day in St. Louis, she had lunch with an acquaintance named Ernst Filsinger, a business man who was passionately fond of poetry and the arts. According to her account, Eunice discovered at the luncheon that he knew a great many of Sara's poems by heart and had "loved Sara for years through her poems, but that he had never met her. . . . He had joined a literary group to which she belonged with the hope of meeting her; but she seldom came, and he had always missed her. Would I now introduce him?"[33] Eunice was as dedicated as Harriet Monroe to finding Sara a husband, and she disagreed with Miss Monroe's backing of Vachel Lindsay. They both knew that Sara was wearing herself out for John Hall Wheelock and would gladly have seen her develop an interest in someone else. Perhaps with this in mind, she quickly arranged the introduction and Ernst Filsinger called on her Sunday evening, April 5.

"I spent last evening with Miss Teasdale," he reported to Eunice promptly. "What an extraordinarily interesting girl she is! It was for me an epoch—and I am greatly indebted to you for the privilege of her acquaintance. We discussed many things—but especially the modern poets. How vivid were her comments on men and women. I wish I had time to tell you in detail of our talks about the feminist movement—of her naive opinions as to feminine instinct versus art and artistic endeavor."[34]

"Your friend Filsinger turns out to be *most* charming and nice," Sara wrote her, "and best of all, he reminds me to a really thrilling extent of Jack. Jack is a little taller and a good deal younger and handsomer, but they have *exactly* the same coloring and their manners are much alike. Every now and then I can almost believe that he is Jack—just for a second. Jack has more fire and humor, but the same outward sedateness, and the philosophical temper of the men is much alike. . . . Wednesday night he took me to dinner at the Contemporary Club and Sunday he is coming to take me to the Ethical Culture lecture, so he has done quite a bit to break the monotony of St. Louis."

Filsinger's reference to Sara's opinions on women in the arts suggests that she was still anxious not to be considered unfeminine for being a professional writer. She had been asked recently by an old friend, Thekla Bernays—"the best that St. Louis has to offer in the way of a cultured woman," she told Louis Untermeyer—to write a poem for a suffrage edition of the St. Louis *Times,* and produced for the occasion another poem titled "The Old Maid," "a feminist document that had nothing to do with suffrage, but was 'in line,' generally speaking." After the woman's death, her friends open a locked bureau drawer and find a scrapbook filled with pictures of children, and inscribed on it, "The children that might have come to me." To Sara's hilarious amusement, the editors changed the line "They opened her drawers" to "They opened her dresser": "The phrase was too much for Middle-Western morality." And, to top it off, they mistakenly printed another woman's picture captioned with Sara's name. Sara's idea of "feminism" was to assert the essential femininity of women: that is, their maternal role. She admitted to being "only a lukewarm suffragist."

Vachel Lindsay had also been preparing for another visit, and when

Harriet Monroe sent him a check for $5 for a review he had written, he scrambled to the train for a trip to St. Louis on Wednesday, April 8. When he had visited Harriet Monroe in Chicago, she called Sara a "darling" and "was determined to make me silly about you," he said. Although he had only met Sara once before, Lindsay was obviously falling in love with her, against all his efforts at monastic self-discipline. He was always teetering on the brink between his religion and the sensuous appeal of women, he said, and urged Sara, "When I come to see you you must keep Baptist thoughts in your head—but ambrosia in your hair. . . . I have as much obsession for the gossamer cataract of a woman's hair as W. B. Yeats. . . . The day before I come you must put your hair up in papers or shampoo it or something, and make it look as much like . . . golden fleece and fuzzy-wuzzy and halo and aureole and—well—" He asked her to send him a hairpin, so he could imagine himself undoing her hair and letting it fall. He admitted to being jealous of Wheelock.

They went to the movies on this April visit. It was one of Lindsay's passions; he wrote fan letters and poems to movie actresses and in 1915 published *The Art of the Moving Picture,* one of the first studies of its kind. After the visit he was somewhat subdued. "Why do I always feel so bold in Springfield and so timid in St. Louis?" he asked. He hinted that on the next visit he would try to kiss her. "Yet the only place I would have a legitimate right to kiss you would be on the edge of a wheatfield—the thermometer at 108 degrees." Her civilized delicacy was at odds with his need for earthiness, to have "all America flow through my veins," the rough and the smooth alike. "I do *not* want to climb on your honey island."

But Sara did not yet take any of it very seriously. "His daily letters are a delight," she wrote Louis, "tho' I realize I am only a peg to hang correspondence on. There never is and never could be anything but friendship between us—but since he adores to pretend devotion, and since he does it with charm and humor, and since he doesn't expect any return, all is well." Neither Lindsay nor Filsinger, however, with all their charm, could save her from boredom and frustration and worry over her future. "St. Louis is a howling wilderness. I don't see how I'm going to stand it."

The poems she wrote returned to the mystery of pain. A long poem, "In Sorrow," written in mid-April, is astonishing in its grimness and austerity. She is lost for once, she says, "in a sea shoreless and black," the infinite sorrow of the world. A child is born and dies in an hour, but the idiot "with hanging hands cannot die." An old man begs pitifully with his eyes for comfort against approaching death; a young man dies suddenly, a life unlived. The millions cry for joy before they die, and the "undreamed of millions" of the dead—"What are we who have come from their sorrow and pain?" She goes into the spring orchards for solace, but only sees a cat with a red bird in its mouth creeping by a fence. No pleasure evolves from this pain, only additional pain—and this cannot be forgiven in the scheme of things.

> Where can I shed my blood
> That those who are thirsty may drink?
> Is my life a useless gift,
> Even my life?

In May she wrote a third and final monologue on Sappho. This time the poet speaks from beyond death:

> I was a sister of the stars, and yet
> Shaken with pain . . .
> And I was sick of all things—even song.
> In the dull autumn dawn I turned to death,
> Buried my living body in the sea . . .

Waking from sleep and finding a lover bent over her would be joy—

> But if you came
> Not from the sunny shallow pool of sleep,
> But from the sea of death, the strangling sea
> Of night and nothingness, and waked to find
> Love looking down upon you, glad and still,
> Strange and yet known forever, that is peace.[35]

Love comes to her perfectly in death, encircled by her lover's arms. Death proves to be the sought-for goal of passion, for it pays life back for the pain, sorrow, and guilt that life has inflicted. Sara had finally thought her way through to an equation that balanced her sense of obligation to life with her unwillingness to accept its pain. Death paid the debt while offering escape and rest.

In late April, her father's health took a turn for the worse—the doctor was concerned about a possible stroke—and, with her mother away on a ten-day trip, Sara took responsibility for his care. The worry for her father nearly drove her to distraction. In the midst of it, Vachel Lindsay sent her the manuscript of *The Congo and Other Poems* for criticism—"Go at it, cut and slash," he urged. Harriet Monroe, who had recently been in New York arranging for the publication of her own volume of poems, had sold Macmillian on publishing Lindsay's, too, and he was readying the manuscript for submission. Although Lindsay invited her to return the manuscript unread when he learned of her father's illness, she tackled it promptly and sent him her recommendations within a few days. She advised cutting about twenty poems in addition to ones he had eliminated. Later he credited her editorial advice for the rapidity with which Macmillan accepted the manuscript without asking for further changes.

Lindsay also reported making notes for "The Chinese Nightingale," a poem whose central image mesmerised him before he quite knew what to do with it. It was actually a kind of dream vision of Sara, whom he saw as the voice of refinement and literary culture, identified here with ancient Chinese aristocratic elegance. "You are really the lady in The Chinese Nightingale," he told her, "though much covered up with costume." It was her power, through the nightingale's singing, to transform the mundane world into a vision of beauty and the humble Chinese laundryman, through her love, into a king. The happiness of working on the poem "has made my whole life worth while," he told her.

Sara, however, had her mind continually on Jack Wheelock and had urged Harriet Monroe to meet him while in New York. Unluckily, the two didn't hit it off, she learned from both sides. "Jack is the hardest person to get at under the sun, anyway," she wrote Eunice. "And meeting him all unprepared in that way at Scribner's was trying for him. He'd have preferred several cocktails at first, I know."

Her campaign to win Jack Wheelock, such as it was, could not go on indefinitely. She had waited nearly a year for him, and it would soon be two years since her experience with Hatfield had jolted her abruptly into maturity. Her thirtieth birthday would arrive in three months, and her father's precarious health was a forecast of the inevitable future. By the end of April 1914, she had decided to return to New York in June when the family made its annual move to Charlevoix, her father's health permitting, and to try to bring her long exertion for Wheelock to a conclusion, one way or another. If that did not work out, she could consider Vachel Lindsay, who was obviously falling in love with her, and Ernst Filsinger, who seemed interested and even reminded her of Wheelock, but whose perfect politeness was impenetrable. She needed to know both of them better.

When her mother returned to St. Louis in early May, Sara was emotionally exhausted from taking care of her father and went off to "the greenest hills in the world" at Saxton's Farm, she wrote Harriet, "to forget it all." She invited Vachel to visit her there from Wednesday, May 6, until Friday; and then Ernst Filsinger immediately afterward, for the weekend. Ernst "is really a love," she told Eunice, "and much like Jack only not so shy—and without Jack's subtle sense of humor, which is simply adorable." The full moon poured luxuriantly on the countryside during their stay. Ernst read aloud to her from Francis Thompson's *Shelley*, she and Vachel talked poetry: "A heavenly week it was," she told Louis.

But after the idyllic walks in the woods, and the moonlight, she returned home to grim reality. Her father had fallen down and cut his head, and her mother had come down with a terrible cold. She could bear to face their deaths, she wrote Louis, "but to see them so weak and unlike themselves breaks my heart. And there seems to be no escape from it. It stretches ahead for years. I have gone to pieces over it to such an extent that I am utterly unlike myself."

May was therefore a month of intense thinking, and at Saxton's Farm Sara had begun to discuss her situation with Vachel and apparently talked frankly about her wish to marry Wheelock. The alarming decline of her father's health over the past year proved to her that she could not wait long. As she told Harriet Monroe, too, at thirty she could not postpone marriage much longer if she expected to have any children. The week at Saxton's Farm showed that Vachel and Ernst both cared about her, and offered the only possible alternatives to Wheelock in the brief time left in which to act. Stafford Hatfield had written her again, and there are hints that he tried to reestablish an intimacy, but Sara had closed that door once and for all. "Do you know Ethel Barrymore's remark?" she asked Harriet Monroe. " 'The men I love and the men who love me are never the same.' "

Ernst Filsinger actually worshiped Sara without reservation, but lacking the fluency with words that the poets had in abundance, he said nothing and tried to let his attentiveness speak for him. He probably did not seriously think at first that so divine a creature might actually marry him. But Sara considered the possibility as soon, probably, as he did. When in late May Vachel wrote her a "horrid cross letter," she sent it back to him and extracted a humble apology. "There is a certain streak of 'bully' in Vachel," she told Eunice. "I do wish that E. F. *did* love me—but I don't feel that he does, and you are too kind to be frank with me if you think he doesn't." Eunice, of course, insisted that he did.

Vachel, for his part, was becoming increasingly agitated at his steady uncontrolled drift toward the idea of marriage, to find himself tangled and lost in a woman's hair, when his instincts were all for renouncing love, fame, and money for the open road. He and Sara must also have talked at Saxton's Farm about where their own relationship was going, for immediately on returning to Springfield he began turning the problem over and over, trying to see how the irreconcilable pieces might fit. He had a mystical commitment to his home town, where like Blake he was possessed by a vision of what it might be:

> New-built, the Holy City
> Gleamed in the murmuring plain.[36]

But it was hard to see how a New York person like Sara could accept Springfield, Illinois, when she could not even bear St. Louis. Before the idyll at Saxton's Farm, he had considered himself only "a playmate that plays the same game—and understands the same world of words." Opposite as they were to each other, they could maintain a kind of hydrostatic balance through an inspired friendship. But choices were being forced:

"Whichever I am: (1) A man of the Road, (2) a man of Springfield or (3) Sara's man renouncing all other allegiances—I love you dearly—and I must henceforth keep thinking on your real place and mission in my destiny, and my real place and mission in your destiny."

He had a very clear idea of what he wanted her place in his destiny to be: his "conscience to whip me back to the road and the Earth—and not the power that makes me forget them." Always battling with himself and with the world, he needed a woman, he said, who would support him in his fight and help him to win, a "man-maker." "America and art are far apart—that is—when we follow the art currents we run counter to the American currents." His big objection was that she was "not a daughter of the soil," not an embodiment of the native spirit who could pressure him constantly to be true to himself, but a representative of that beautiful but rootless literary culture he feared. In spite of his months of trying to proselytize her, it was he and not she who was now yielding inch by inch. "You are the hardest person to refuse anything I ever dealt with that you set your thoughts upon," he appealed, "and I pray you to ask of me the deepest and most serious things I used to ask of myself."

No matter how he looked at it, a successful marriage would require "scads of money" and a career that would draw him into a vain quest for fame and compromising obligations. "I have a dread of being contaminated with money," he had confessed. After his sensational appearance in Chicago, the invitations to read publicly became more frequent, and he could see the path of a highly successful career opening up. But after each triumph he felt both a glow of satisfaction and a desperate fear that he was losing his personal integrity, and a need to cleanse himself by plunging into anonymity, hard physical labor, and an adventure on the road, to fight with himself and win. He loudly admitted his inability to resist the lure of women, success, and praise, but when they were actually at hand he cried out, "I want to break from the net before it chokes me." His passionate Tolstoyan, Buddhistic, Franciscan faith (as he called it), identified as it also was with the strong personality of his mother, was contradictory and destructive to the idea of marriage. But Sara's Baptist background was too sedate for her to recognize the fierceness of the evangelical fire that burned in him, and she may have taken it for poetical extravagance. He was aware of the danger, in any case, and wanted to proceed no faster than he could feel sure of himself: "We must not hurry the green fruit."

It should not be thought, however, that Sara would have suggested the possibility of marriage to him. It was not only unladylike, but far from an ideal solution for her. Lindsay had allowed himself to develop an emotionally complex relationship that was both literary and personal, on which he had come to depend for motivation in his work. Dominated all his life by the powerful presence of his mother, and still living at home, unemployed, like an ungrown boy, he had gradually turned Sara into a symbolic figure to inspire and nurture him as an artist, a kind of American muse-mother. He could not now bear to give her up, and in response to her expressed determination to marry he could only explore the possibility of being her husband in order to keep his peculiar love for her intact. Sara may have been gratified at this, but she hoped she would not deliberately mislead him.

Sara now planned to leave St. Louis on June 5 with her parents as they set out for Charlevoix, but intended to stop off at Chicago, as she had done the year before, and then go on to New York, joining her parents at Charlevoix later in the summer. She urged Vachel to join her in New York, but he balked at the suggestion if she were going "just to study your spiritual barometer in regard to Wheelock weather." He preferred that she stop off instead in Springfield and even threw himself into elaborate plans for such a visit. "I do not want to go to New York and divide you with other gentlemen. . . . Make up your mind who you belong to—and tell *him* and tell *me,* and go to one or the other. This world is a place of choices." He would not pull up stakes and abdicate Springfield for New York unless she loved him more than anyone else: "You will care for the rocks from which I was hewn, the pit from which I was digged."

Vachel visited St. Louis once more before Sara left. For months he had been working through Harriet Monroe to arrange a salon reading of his work, to be sponsored by a Mrs. Pettus, who would pay him a modest fee, enough for train fare and expenses. It was a scheme, of course, for a chance to see Sara again. The reading came off with great success on June 1 with both Sara and Ernst in the audience. Sara had heard him read only before a small group in her home, and was "thrilled by the added power that he seems to get from a room full," she told Harriet. He stayed overnight at her home again and left filled with the conviction that he must find a way to marry her.

On Vachel's insistence, she did debark at Springfield for a few hours on June 5, catching another train later in the day for Chicago. He had mowed the front lawn and busied himself making arrangements in the event she consented to stay longer. But she urged him again to come to New York and went on her way, agreeing to see him in Chicago a few days later.

After her departure, alone in his family home in Springfield, Vachel sat down to write her that he had decided to make the plunge: "I will come to New York. . . . I have come to the point where I am willing to make a considerable sacrifice of my plans to be with you a little while. It looks like a little to you but it is an enormous step for me. Please take it as seriously as possible." The immediate problem was how to raise $200 for the trip. Harriet Monroe would advance him $100 for "The Fireman's Ball," already accepted for publication in *Poetry,* and the rest could be raised by doing a series of readings in and around Chicago. But the long-range problem was how to develop a steady income on which he could eventually support her. His only possible hope was to exploit his new role as a performer, even though he dreaded a "falsely distended Chatauquaesque reputation as a speaker." He would spend the next weeks investigating the possibility—and then "If . . . I can come anywhere *near* the income that can keep you safe and happy and living your life as life has been for you—I shall certainly ask you for your heart forever. But I am afraid my dear—you are rather versatile—and after all your wanting me to take life and happiness in June seriously—you do not want any more progress—well—it will be very hard for me." Sara, however, would not allow him to set any conditions. They were both to be free.

Sara had just written to Harriet Monroe, "My heart is as stupidly constant as the north star. I can't get Wheelock out of my head." In Chicago, she laid the whole case before Harriet Monroe and Eunice Tietjens and asked their advice, as she sat between them on the floor of the *Poetry* office. "Harriet . . . thought that when one had a chance to marry a great poet like Vachel Lindsay one should accept it gratefully," Eunice Tietjens wrote in her memoir. But Sara was used to money, to a quiet, orderly life arranged as she liked it, and she lacked physical energy. Vachel was not only constantly penniless but also exhausting for Sara to be with for more than a short time. From a practical point of view, Ernst Filsinger was the answer. But he had not asked her to marry him. According to Eunice, Sara said she was "half in love with each of them."37

Sara spent ten days in Chicago, and Vachel was there for the last half of them. He "behaved like the fine gentleman that he is," she wrote Harriet Monroe afterward, "a noble person. I only hope that he will not someday be sorry that he ever knew me." He had proposed that they meet under the statue of Abraham Lincoln in Lincoln Park, so that his patron saint, "Father Abraham," might be witness to the possible betrayal of his principles, as he turned his back on Springfield for woman and career. It is doubtful that the meeting took place; Sara, the ironic realist, was not given to symbolic gestures. He even purchased an engagement ring, although it was too soon to present it to her, and valiantly began a series of readings and meetings with influential people to build his reputation and earn some money.

Sara arrived in New York on June 17, 1914 and saw Jack Wheelock the next evening. It was a dispiriting reunion. He was depressed and gloomy, and "I poured out my own perplexities," she wrote Harriet. "He undoubtedly loves me. I am *sure* of it—but he doesn't love me enough, and so I must try to forget him." He telephoned her the next day, still mysteriously distraught, telling her how much their walks together had meant to him, how he had been unable to sleep for months. "And *yet*, no word of loving me or anything of that sort. He said he couldn't confide his trouble to me." Sara irritatedly decided he would be "a really *terrible* husband.

He is so repressed and black about things." It made her yearn for Vachel. "I long to marry him—and yet I feel in my heart that both his love and mine will be terribly wried and perhaps twisted into hate almost by the material struggle. . . . He is a good deal of an idealist and would think me mercenary and extravagant when I needed things that he could not see the necessity for." After his free life, he could not really turn into a model husband and father overnight, and she lacked the strength to adapt to his way of life.

A day after the disturbing telephone call with Jack Wheelock, they had a leisurely dinner together and a long evening in Central Park, "where every bench held lovers locked in embrace." Sara had hoped all these months that her devotion to Wheelock would somehow be apparent without her having to say anything openly. It was up to him to speak first, and all she could honorably do was manipulate circumstances to encourage him to do so. By telling him now how besieged she was by two other lovers, how confused in her feelings and uncertain of her future, she hoped he would rise to the occasion and declare himself—"He could still have me if he wanted me—which he understood perfectly well, I am sure," she told Eunice. But to her intense chagrin he not only did not seize the opportunity but also told her she "would be happier married and that he advised me to marry."

Angered and hurt, she wrote Vachel the next day, summoning him to New York, "for I had definitely put Jack out of my mind forever as far as his being a lover goes. It was really startling to me to see with what ease I seemed to let all idea of marrying Jack slip out of my mind." Wheelock's "trouble," which he had all along been unable to talk about with her, was very simple: He was in love with another woman, "whom I had met and known well for many years because our families both summered in the same place." He could not afford to marry, and she could not wait; and so she married someone else, an Englishman. Wheelock had been unaware for months that Sara was in love with him, and then, suddenly surprised by the realization, found it too late to say anything without acute embarrassment. All spring, both of them had agonized in silence over a situation neither knew how to bring into the open. Wheelock finally did tell her his story, very probably that evening in Central Park, when telling the truth became inescapable. It was one detail that Sara never referred to in any of the many letters to her friends; she would not have wanted any of them to know that all this time he had preferred someone else to her.

But Vachel, on receiving her special delivery letter in Chicago, was more sobered than elated at the prospect of the trip to New York. Its symbolic meaning to his life and work was too vast to treat lightly, and he was deeply concerned about the financial commitment if he should marry her. Going to New York meant nothing less to him than a decision to marry, although she insisted not. "If you and I were just playing," he told her, "it would be grand." He had just sealed a letter to her asking for a year to get his life on a new footing, when her urgent plea arrived. Instead of impulsively coming directly to New York, he decided to go home "to *think* out our affair if I can" and to make a walk of Sangamon County—"Springfield is the only place for me just now." He feared being swept romantically into a decision they might both regret and insisted that before he came to New York she must agree to accept his ring and tell him how long she was willing to wait for him. "I love you child for your impetuous fire and eagerness," he said. But "be fair to friend Whee-lock and give him a square chance."

Besides, he had glimmerings of a scheme that might induce Sara to return to the Midwest. Harriet Monroe had hinted that if Eunice Tietjens went abroad next year, as she talked of doing, Sara might be invited to take her place in the *Poetry* office. He would be willing to compromise on a location only 150 miles from Springfield; Sara would have the cultural delights of a big city and the friendship of poets and artists, and she might even, in time, learn to share his "New Localism."

But on arriving home in Springfield on June 24, he found a letter from her that persuaded him to come to New York immediately, in spite of all his misgivings: "Your last letter . . . has stated your position so clearly and beautifully, your chain of logic is such I cannot but be bound with it. . . . I am coming to New York on the terms of your last letter—on probation, so to speak. . . . I have been struggling with myself ever since I reached home—and your letter has decided me. My heart fought my head every minute. Now my head is quite convinced." One can only surmise what she wrote him. Probably it was the honest truth: that Wheelock was out of the picture and that she needed to find out without delay, by their spending some time together, how she really felt about Vachel in order to choose between him and Ernst. In spite of the "cataracts of ink" that had flowed between them, they had actually met only half a dozen times, and then only for a day or two. "But I do not think you ought to let Filsinger put in his bid at the same time if you are considering me seriously," he admonished, "let him come *after* I leave New York or let him come to Charlevoix."

And so Vachel Lindsay arrived in New York the evening of June 30, like a knight in a fairytale competing for the hand of a princess. She made him wait until six o'clock the following day to see her, while she sat in her hotel room speculating about their relationship in a letter to Harriet Monroe: "I still feel that our marriage would be a disastrous thing, but I love him. . . . And yet, in a queer way, his love does not seem to me quite like the love that I want from the man who is going to own me. . . . He *never* (even in his most passionate moments) makes me forget myself. And I feel that it is the same way with him. He himself never *loses* him-self." They both loved with too many misgivings about the future to pretend they had drunk the magic potion of Tristram and Iseult. "I have quite definitely put Jack out of my mind," she added. "But I still feel that the best thing for both Vachel and me would be for me to marry Filsinger (if he asks me!) Vachel knows that I feel this way." The parks were crowded with lovers, "and they are all kissing very hard. . . . There is something pitiful about so many people all trying to get some sort of peace out of each other."

The following days with Vachel were exciting, "among the very happiest of my life." The day after his arrival, Edward J. Wheeler—president of the Poetry Society—gave a party for Vachel and Sara: "Jack and Louis and Vachel all in one room at the same minute was a bit thrilling," she confided to Eunice. "Oh, Eunice, isn't it wonderful to have a body when a man loves it so much? If only V. had some money! Or if I were strong enough to work! Or if the world weren't so exacting about marriage licenses!" But such independence and freedom were only to be dreamed about. She had long since bowed to custom and necessity and had determined that marriage was the only possible solution for her life.

Still, in spite of the boundless energy with which Vachel courted her and his insistence that she marry him, "I am not desperately in love," she confessed to Eunice. "I hear from Filsinger often—I suppose you do too. I do not know what will become of me. I wish that somebody would sweep me off my feet. But nobody seems to."

Eunice took these remarks as a cue to alarm Ernst that "if he was really interested in Sara it was time he acted,"[38] suggesting that she was not leaning very strongly toward accepting Vachel. Perhaps she felt Sara had hinted for her to do so. Ernst was so shaken he could scarcely write. "I must go out and think," he scrawled in a hurried note to her. "Never have I been so terribly moved—as no one has ever meant so much to me as Sara. Yet I'm sure she doesn't care a fig for me! Can't you give me some hope?"

Eunice relayed the word that "in her last letter she wished for someone to carry her off her feet. Keep on bombarding her," she advised, "I think there is still hope." Ernst telephoned Eunice long distance, almost inarticulate with worry over "the horror of what you wrote me," and throughout the next month clung to her for advice. The only reason he hadn't asked Sara to marry him was the fear that he might create an unwelcome interference during her visit in New York. He hoped for an invitation afterward to Charlevoix in August, where he would have his turn. "I'm sure she's forgotten my very existence," he moaned. . . . "Has she never suspected how I felt?" In desperation, he wrote the best letter he could, after tearing up a dozen drafts, asking Sara to marry him, followed it with flowers, and then proceeded to "bombard" her indeed.

"My St. Louis man, Ernst Filsinger, is sending me a flood of special delivery letters and telegrams imploring me to marry him," she wrote to

Harriet Monroe on July 14, a few days after Eunice had prodded him into action. "His letters are as mad as hatters, and he is sending me such quantities of flowers that the market for roses orchids and carnations must have gone up in consequence." And to Eunice she quipped, "At last my ships seem to be coming in *all* at once." Although Sara had suspected for weeks that she would probably marry him if he ever asked her, she replied with a letter so analytical and cool that he was discouraged: "At present I can not possibly say anything definite. I have known you for such a short time and in such a simply friendly way that I feel as tho' either of us may be quite hopelessly ignorant of the other's real self." She insisted on being completely frank, explaining that in the past month she had come to love Vachel Lindsay. "He loves me very deeply, and his surface faults are drowned in his innate chivalry and tenderness. He wants me to marry him as soon as he can be assured of a steady income." But "I do not love Vachel desperately. My feeling for him is a real affection, but I do not feel that he is absolutely necessary for me. . . . I value you very highly and if we knew each other better, perhaps I should love you. I do not know. . . . In so many ways you are at most a stranger to me, and I realize that I am equally a stranger to you."39 Ernst believed he had headed off any immediate catastrophe, but worried how he could develop her esteem for him into a "deeper sentiment."

Ernst's vigorous campaign was actually more effective than he knew, for Sara had been waiting for it. As soon as he declared himself and she realized how genuinely he did love her, she began to reach a decision regarding Vachel. They were "having wonderful times together," she told Eunice, "but I realize either that I am not as passionate as I have always believed myself, or else that with all of his fire and tenderness Vachel cannot stir me to the depths. . . . He still feels that he can support me after a year or so. But if I must wait a year or so for him, I cannot ask Ernst to do the same thing." She would "give Vachel until the end of the month to see if he can make me *desperately* in love. If he can, of course I suppose that I will marry him regardless of finances. If he can not, I will go up to Charlevoix and see if I love Ernst. . . . My room is filled with flowers. . . . How I should have adored four years ago some of this love that is going to waste now. . . . I have told Ernst everything very frankly. I do not know how he will feel about it. But it is all a part of me and he must take me as I am. I do not love him now, but probably I shall in a month! I am suddenly grown beyond my own forecasting."

It was more difficult explaining to Harriet Monroe, who was Vachel's advocate. She could not see her way to marrying him, Sara announced flatly. "I feel honestly that I am not strong enough physically to go thro' the years of poverty that would be ahead of us, and secondly I want him to be free to follow his art, which continual efforts at money-making would destroy." But Harriet responded promptly with a lecture, suggesting that Sara had been trifling with his affections by letting him come to New York. "When I asked Vachel to come to New York," Sara returned, "there was an absolute understanding on his side that I felt that we could never marry, but that I wanted to be with him." The "portable paradise" of their weeks in New York were splendid enough, whether they led to marriage or not, and the trip had established Vachel's career on a solid footing with the people who mattered there: "Neither of us needs any sympathy." Harriet had suggested that perhaps their families could help support them. "I could not live in the Lindsay family home. . . . It would kill me," she said. "As for my own family, I am too proud to accept help from them. They do not understand the artistic attitude anyway, and they would feel terribly abused to have to help support me and a man who (according to them) would not earn a living. And Vachel *will* not take a position drawing a regular salary—not that I want him to, but I have sounded him. . . . My darling lady, I don't see what we can do but let it go as a beautiful dream."

In the midst of furious attention from all sides, she took to her bed with a severe case of the grippe and tonsillitis, of the kind that used to incapacitate her in an emotional crisis. She was sorry to spoil Vachel's last week, "the darlingest most interesting soul alive," she told Eunice, "*but* I *can't* marry him, Harriet notwithstanding."

In the meantime, she had written a somewhat more encouraging letter to Ernst, who still imagined that he needed to proceed with utmost caution to avoid making any move that might upset her or threaten his slender hope. He agonized in sympathy over each headache she reported —"How she must suffer!" he exclaimed to Eunice—feared she might try too soon after her illness to travel to Charlevoix and finally was made deliriously happy when she gave him permission to come to New York for a few days in early August instead of waiting until Charlevoix.

Vachel left New York at the end of July knowing that Ernst would arrive in a few days. Sara did not know whether she could love Ernst, she told Eunice, "but I seem to have a versatile heart. It can turn with a good deal of ease from Wheelock to Lindsay and why not still further? I hate myself for this, quite frankly I hate myself. But I am glad that it is so even if I have to hate myself." Sara's judgment on her possible future with Vachel Lindsay was grim: "It would resolve itself into my family's supporting us most of the time, and that would make a nerve-wracking life of squabble and torture." Vachel did not want to marry her immediately any more than she did and at best hoped she would wait for him. But to wait "a year or two or three for him to earn something and *then* have to give it up, it will be all the harder for us," she told Harriet Monroe, "and for me it will mean that I shall never marry. And I must marry, for at the bottom I am a mother more intensely than I am a lover." This confession, surprising as it may seem, was completely sincere. She had repeatedly insisted during the summer that she wanted to have children. And one remembers her portrayal of Sappho as a mother, her "feminist" poem, her poems of John Hall Wheelock's mother, and of Mary, mother of Christ, and her discovery that she might not, after all, be a person capable of the grand passion celebrated in literature, to say nothing of her highly conventional idea of marriage.

Sara lay in bed reading the flood of love letters Vachel sped to her from Springfield on his return home. "Oh if I only had $4000 a year and health, how I'd gladly be Mrs. Lindsay!" she exclaimed to Eunice. "Heavens, how much has happened to me in the past year! Before that my life was almost all in my imagination. And yet I long for the calm of an unrequited affection! It is a real rest cure. Three letters to-day from Vachel, two from Ernst and a telegram. It is a somewhat wearying ordeal. . . . And it seems *impossible* for Vachel to get it thro' his head that I'm *not* going to marry him."

Sara had intended to join her parents in Charlevoix in time to celebrate her thirtieth birthday on August 8, but her illness forced the postponement of Ernst's visit until August 4, delaying all her plans. His visit was absolutely essential, however, whether she was exhausted or not, for he had to be introduced to her "most particular friends," she told Harriet. "If I marry him, I don't want to seem to be marrying a dark horse, as it were." There was a systematic plan to be carried out, which she had foreseen in early May at Saxton's Farm. She couldn't just "sit in a corner by myself and decide which of two men I will marry without allowing either of them to make love to me," she wrote Harriet, using the term in its old-fashioned sense of "to court." It had taxed her strength to the utmost, but it had to be done, partly for the sake of appearances, partly to keep herself straight with everyone. She had probably known all along that Ernst was the inevitable choice.

Unaware that there was a certain predetermined air about the progress of his courtship, Ernst Filsinger arrived in New York "in raptures of ecstatic joy," grateful for even the few hours she allotted him out the time she needed to rest. There was nothing of the high excitement of Vachel's visit. She was worn out. Her friends did indeed like Ernst, for it would have been hard not to. He was eminently presentable, a man of culture, warmth, and deep sincerity, passionately interested in what was going on in the arts, and in some respects more liberal in his tastes than Sara. She sought Jack Wheelock's advice on the marriage question, since she had not allowed, nor could very well allow, her disappointment in failing to marry him to disturb their friendship. Wheelock had lunch with Ernst at the City Club, liked him very much, and did not hesitate to urge her to marry him, although he doubted whether Sara really cared for Ernst very deeply. She had hesitated too much, asked too many friends for advice.

With these preliminaries out of the way, Sara set out for Charlevoix on August 9 for the final stage of what now seemed the inevitable unfolding of a foregone conclusion: the approval of her parents and the discovery that she truly loved Ernst Filsinger. Ernst could hardly believe his good fortune and feared every moment that some obstacle might arise to shatter his beautiful dream. Sara insisted on making the long train ride alone, with Ernst to follow the next day. "We've decided it best not to risk offending anyone by failure to observe the conventions," he told Eunice. "Ridiculous and tough on me, but I'm in hearty accord as I won't take any risk, *now.*" Sara's train was late arriving, and she was forced to spend half a day in Grand Rapids, where she wrote to Harriet Monroe that she wouldn't let Ernst travel with her "for the sake of the silly conventions. My conventionality crops up in strange places—usually, I fear, where it chimes in with my desires—for really I prefer to travel alone. It is quite tiring enough without having to talk all the time to somebody." She begged for Harriet's understanding about Ernst: "I can see that I am pretty likely to love him. . . . You must not blame me, oh you *must* not. . . . I am doing what seems right to me. I may be all wrong, but I can't help it."

On the day she left New York for Michigan, Vachel sat down to write her a letter aimed at forestalling a marriage that now seemed ominously near at hand: "It is your mind and your plans that put me out of your life at the next turn of the road—your heart is for me." He had been deeply concerned about her health in New York, for it was the first time he had seen her in collapse, and had realized that such spells were part of her nature. "Stay single for me," he argued, for it would allow her to pay attention to remaining well, and guarantee her the hours of solitude she needed. "You are in a sense my saint. . . . Isn't our life together worth keeping?" He begged her to pledge with him a platonic marriage of the spirit and of poetry. She had given him her bracelet one day in New York as a memento, as they sat in a Catholic church listening to the nuns singing: Now they could pledge themselves as monks and nuns do, "not a marriage in the world's sense—but . . . infinitely preferred to giving you up to a reckless experiment. . . . Poets are few—life is not planned for them—they must make such plans as they can with honor. And they have to pay the price of being different. You are trying to avoid the price."

There was too much truth in his accusation for it not to have caused her some pain. She had ventured out of her girlish world of dreams of love and beauty to confront the game of love in all seriousness and found herself promptly retreating to the safety of convention and respectability in which she had been so rigidly brought up. Society required a husband, not a lover. She was helpless to do otherwise. She had written in her notebook six months earlier,

> I am a woman, I am weak,
> And custom leads me as one blind.

Since there was no escape from the prison walls of propriety that through the fear and weakness implanted by her mother closed her in on all sides, she could only make her restricted place as habitable as possible, and find her freedom in her poetry:

> Only my songs go where they will,
> Free as the wind.

Mrs. Teasdale met Ernst at the station in Charlevoix on August 12 in the family surrey and brought him to Sara, whose mood was somewhat distant. He was still not sure she would marry him, and he went to the most extreme lengths to behave exactly as he thought she would want him to. In his mind, he was in a battle to win her away from Vachel Lindsay. He wrote a long letter that day to his parents, probably while Sara rested, telling them the news, for they had no idea their son was on the verge of marriage. Describing her as "my ideal for whom I have hoped since boyhood," he wrote that "Sara, I am sure, loves me too but is in no hurry to tell me so" and went on to characterize her as a "glorious, *womanly* woman—no 'female rights' sort of person. . . . Ever since I knew her she has put the duties of true womanhood (motherhood and wife-hood) above *any* art and would I believe rather be the fond mother of a child than the author of the most glorious poem in the language. . . . She is given to no extravagant tastes and extreme simplicity seems her prefer-ence in everything. . . . She is one of the if not *the* most well-ordered-methodical—sane and sensible women I ever knew."[40]

Ernst's father was a native of St. Louis and had built up his own business as a monument dealer. Unlike Sara's father, who was a Republi-can and a Baptist, he was a Democrat, a member of the Ethical Society rather than of a church, and shared the progressive ideas of the German intellectual community, with their vigorous belief in education and self-culture. He had wanted Ernst to study for law school, but family circum-stances did not allow it. A tornado in 1896 had severely damaged the family home and pinned his mother in the wreckage, hospitalizing her for weeks. The proud and self-sufficient family refused outside help, and sixteen-year-old Ernst dropped out of high school to get a job in a wholesale shoe company, studying at night, working his way up in the business. He learned Spanish at the Berlitz School, spent a season walk-ing the length of the Panama Canal while it was under construction, interviewed President Diaz of Mexico, and served as the consul for Costa Rica in St. Louis. When Sara met him, he was a partner in his own shoe-manufacturing company and was already known as a specialist in Latin American trade through his book *Trading with Latin America*, published in 1911. He was not by any means wealthy—his business life was still something of a struggle—but he had the capability of supporting Sara's needs, and he idolized her to the point of letting her have her own way in everything.

Sara, who already knew she was going to marry Ernst, apparently did not wish to prolong the fatigue of courtship, and only two days after his arrival, and after drives along the lake, walks on the shore, and evening conversations in her look-out above the water, told him she now loved him. "She told me this morning it had all gone more quickly than she had any idea," Ernst wrote to Eunice. "I think I have really swept her off her feet now, as she did me." On August 18, they announced their engagement and sent Eunice Tietjens a telegram: "Thanks to you we are the happiest people in the world." A week later Sara wrote her, "There isn't a shadow of a doubt that I am deeply in love and that Ernst is the man for me. . . . Everybody in New York who met Ernst is wild about him—so are my parents. It is all *too* good."

Sara was honorable, like her father. She had been careful never to misrepresent her position to anyone and to accept no obligation without paying. Having committed herself to Ernst, she would show him and the world a perfect picture of happiness and devotion. If it were true, as Vachel thought, that she was not willing to pay the price of an unconventional love, she was on the other hand quite ready to pay the price of a conventional one, and if she had any misgivings she hid them scrupulously from everyone. Having painfully learned that one did not always get what one wanted, she had made a reasonable settlement and was free of the burden of uncertainty. Happy poems were harder to write than unhappy ones, but she tried to celebrate her new condition:

> I am sandaled with wind and with flame,
>   I have heart-fire and singing to give,
> I can tread on the grass or the stars,
>   Now at last I can live![41]

# CHAPTER SIX

# "Caught in the Web of the Years"

In the autumn of 1914, Sara exhibited all the girlish romantic idealism about her approaching marriage that she had always known she would feel, that everyone might have expected of her. Letters had duly gone out to her many friends, exclaiming that she loved "deeply," that Ernst was perfect, that they were unbelievably happy. "She is deeply, devotedly attached to me," Ernst wrote to his sisters on announcing the engagement, "and her love for me is as great as mine for her." Sara, too, was amazed: "It has surpassed my highest hopes. The most sacred and the greatest desire of my life is to make him happy always." They wept to think of all the lonely years they had lived in the same city deprived of the happiness that might have been theirs, and Sara wrote a poem on the subject, "The Years." She sincerely intended to submerge her life in her husband's.

Years later, she confessed to a friend that after she promised herself to Ernst she stood alone in the garden at Charlevoix wondering dismally how she could have done such a thing. An equally serious concern was how it would affect her work. She had written virtually nothing for five months, as she laid poetry aside for the marriage question to be settled. Up to that point, she had developed the theory that "song" was the transmutation of pain, particularly, the pain of loneliness and unreturned love. If she were suddenly to become ideally happy, what would happen to her creativity, which would have no frustration to feed on? And if her much-awaited happiness did not actually occur, how could she dare write in contradiction to what everyone expected? "I am writing a brief happy lyric once in a while," she wrote Harriet Monroe; "I do hope that I won't turn into a sort of jelly-fish when I am married."

Vachel Lindsay was distraught when he received the news of her engagement, even though she had tried to prepare him. He mailed Sara's bracelet, a love token of the summer, to his sister Joy in Cleveland, burned all her letters in a ritual of misery, and threatened to go to China where his brother-in-law was a medical missionary and where his parents had been visiting since May. "And yet I can not bear to leave you," he wrote, as he worked the "black-beast" anger out of his system. "You shall be my Beatrice." He mounted her photograph and placed it "between my two pictures of Buddha which I have brought down stairs today with the Nuremburg Madonna," hoping to sublimate his love for her into the worship of a saint, knowing even as he did it that loneliness and the seductive appeal of women would soon attract him to someone else.

Sara received his letters silently as he battled with himself for several weeks, unable to reconcile himself to his loss until the pain had been exhausted and she had been forced to go through it with him. Then she wrote to him calmly and rationally, and he was at peace again. Even though he could not marry her, her influence on his life had been considerable. A year ago, he had announced his intention to recruit her away from New York literary society and educate her to become the voice of the Midwestern farmlands. She, in her delicacy and frailty, proved to be the more firm and immovable. "I feel so different—having been to New York," he told her on returning to Springfield. "I must thank you and thank you—for noble new friends, and for all that has happened to my external fortunes—for a changed and refreshed point of view—for a tremendous head of steam to go at my work." She had insisted he leave the isolation of his small town, introduced him to people who could help promote his career, and provided new friends with whom he could talk as one professional to another. "I know in my own heart I've given 'value received' to Vachel," she told Eunice Tietjens. When his parents returned from China in November, he sent her some embroidered Chinese silks as a wedding present and then launched on his first speaking tour arranged by a New York agent, although he did not want to see her again for a long time.

The wedding was set for Saturday, December 19, 1914. "Poetess to Wed Maker of Shoes," the Chicago *Tribune* announced inelegantly, a headline that probably saddened Harriet Monroe, who had wanted her Elizabeth Barrett to marry a Robert Browning. Sara came to know Ernst better as they saw each other frequently during the fall, and she seemed to grow more genuinely reconciled to the prospect of marrying him. She had always loved new clothes, and the preparation of the trousseau was a delight. "I show him everything," she wrote Eunice, "even the combinations [lingerie]. We are about 2/3 married already and the other 1/3 will come with much less embarrassment on the part of each of us because we have been sensible beforehand and done a lot of things that lead gently up to the climax. Ernst has a tremendous lot of self-control and yet there is a good deal of healthy animal in him, the darling."

Still, despite her deep respect for Ernst and her gratitude for his "nearly perfect" love, "to a woman of your temperament and mine," she wrote Eunice, "there is no absolute goal." On December 4, only two weeks before the wedding, she wrote the first poem since May that probed one of her deepest misgivings, "I Am Not Yours." It was an admission of her inability to lose herself in her lover, although she desperately wanted to be plunged "deep in love," obliterated, totally possessed. To her disappointment, she remained her same self:

> Yet I am I, who long to be
> Lost as a light is lost in light.[1]

It was a last-minute prayer that she might fall in love with the man she was about to marry, couched in the terms of conventional feminine submissiveness—although frankly admitting the stubborn survival of her own willful identity.

The December wedding was a small and quiet affair in the Teasdale home on Kingsbury Place, with only members of the immediate families present, to avoid unnecessary strain for her parents. She was elaborately gowned in "soft cream satin with a lot of tulle and real lace and orange blossoms and pearls," she told Harriet Monroe, "as bridy as possible." The couple left immediately for a honeymoon in Boston, where, at the Essex Hotel, she wrote the Untermeyers, they found "a cozy place far from everybody."

From Boston came a stream of letters to their families exclaiming over their incredible bliss. "Married life seems to agree mightily with us," said Ernst to his mother, "and particularly with my adorable Sara, who has gained several pounds— has a complexion like peaches and cream—two exquisite dimples—and is so altogether sweet that it is a perfect joy to be with her." Sara was no less overwhelmed: "We are so happy that the days go by like an ecstatic dream. Neither of us can realize that all of this happiness for which we have longed is really ours. It is too good to be true."

The weather was cold and wintry, and they hung Christmas wreaths in their hotel room windows. On Christmas Eve, they set up a miniature artificial tree with real candles on it and, after dinner in their room, turned out the lights "and sat in the beautiful darkness looking at our little tree with its fast-burning tiny candles." On Christmas Day, in the "fine, nipping cold," they traveled out to Concord, the place founded by Sara's Puritan ancestors, where freshly fallen snow covered the streets and houses. They hired a closed carriage and drove about to see the houses of Emerson, Thoreau, and Hawthorne, and the battlefield and bridge, ending the day with tea, toast, and marmalade before a fireplace at the Concord Inn. "Everything seems to have a holy enchantment," Sara wrote her sisters-in-law.

Yet, it is unreasonable to believe that two such idealizing people, particularly with Sara's deeply troubled background, could have made an adjustment to married life so smoothly and rapidly and in full accord with the conventions of romantic love. Some years later, when she had reestablished her friendship with John Hall Wheelock, she laughingly admitted to him that the first week of marriage had actually been a "fiasco."

On December 29, after having declined all other invitations for the week alone together, they went down to New York and a meeting of the Poetry Society, where three of her love poems to Ernst were read and they were the beaming guests of honor. Marriage had not eradicated Sara's deeply ingrained Puritanical fastidiousness, and on New Year's Day, 1915, in their hotel room, she wrote a poem strangely jarring to come out of a honeymoon: "New Year's Dawn—Broadway." After the raucous noise, the coarseness and ribaldry of New Year's Eve, which have driven silence—personified as feminine—back to the stars, the drunken revelers crawl home to bed,

> And the dawn awakes,
> Like a youth who steals from a brothel,
> Dizzy and sick.[2]

Probably she thought of it only as a piece of realism, for it was in vers libre, the new style that was being used by Masters and others for realistic subjects. But, like her poem on the star and the pig, it communicates her revulsion toward sensuality. She placed the two poems adjoining each other in her next book.

One would think that after having virtually transferred her life to New York, she would have had some regrets in returning to St. Louis to settle down, when less than a year ago she had called it a "howling wilderness." But now, because of Ernst, "For the first time in years St. Louis seems really a good sort of place," she told the Untermeyers. They took rooms at the Arthur Hotel, at Berlin Avenue and Skinner Road, for Sara was not particularly anxious to assume the unaccustomed role of housewife. It was just as well, for no sooner had they begun the routine of married life in January than Sara was plagued again with constant chronic illnesses, as she had been during her troubled late adolescence. It started first with a severe cold that drained her energy and continued with a bladder inflammation, with spasms so painful at times she could hardly walk.

The main thing, however, was to gather in hand the strands of her work and career. *Rivers to the Sea* still awaited a publisher, and she needed to resume her regular habits of composition. The landscape of poetry had changed radically in the past two years. Edgar Lee Masters' Spoon River poems had been running serially in Reedy's *Mirror*, and, along with the work of Sandburg, Lindsay, Robinson, and now Frost, there was suddenly an air of powerful realism, ironic or pessimistic in attitude, plain of speech, modern in spirit, and closer to American life. The era of genteel poetry, with its antiquated rhetoric derivative from British romantic poetry, its slavish regard for the past, escapist daydreaming, lyrical effusion, and moral cliché, was clearly at an end, and once-popular poets such as Madison Cawein slid into oblivion with astonishing rapidity. The latest phenomena were Imagism and free verse, both the center of swirling and confused, often pointless, controversy. Eunice Tietjens had entered the fight in November with an article in *The Little Review* on "The Spiritual Dangers of Writing Vers Libre." She argued, as did others, that formal poetry forced the mind to sift and refine its ideas and language, while free verse allowed a flaccid expansion to cover a "paucity of ideas." It was a form, or lack of it, which encouraged indulgence in "brutality," ego gratification, and the grotesque.

But Sara was always ready to learn, and Ernst was excited about the new trends, Masters' work in particular and then Frost's, after the publication in 1915 of Frost's *North of Boston*. During the spring, he and Sara wrote several free verse poems jointly, as well as others in conventional form. The one that shows his hand most strongly is "The Lighted Window," which they composed in February. Sara later told Amy Lowell that the poem was more Ernst's than hers. A man, "Hurried, harrassed" by life, passes a lighted toy store window in a rainy winter dusk and is attracted by the marbles, which in a spontaneous return of feeling he suddenly desires as covetously as he did when a child. But he hurries on his way, and there in the lighted window, "I left my boyhood." When the poem—not a very impressive one—appeared in *The Century* in June 1915, it startled many, who were surprised not only to hear Sara Teasdale speaking in masculine tones but to see the formal perfectionist flirting with free verse. It was not really a radical departure for her, for she had turned to a similarly loose form nearly a year earlier for "In Sorrow" and had been practicing irregularities in rhythm and line length, with more natural and varied speech patterns. "Free verse" was, anyway, an ill-defined term, which generally meant little more than irregular line lengths and the absence of rhymed stanzas. Sara's "free verse" actually had carefully controlled rhythms, with lines based on natural phrases. These techniques were as old as Milton. "New Year's Dawn—Broadway" is built almost entirely out of such units, which carry either two or three stresses that alternate and fall roughly into patterns.

About half a dozen poems written during January and February 1915 are initialed in her notebook "S. T. and E. B. F." Several of these dealt with the misery of the European war in ironic contrast to the approaching spring. She was instinctively a pacifist and shared Ernst's sympathy with the German-American community. One antiwar poem, for which she was solely responsible, "Spring in Naugatuck Valley," attacked the manufacture of munitions. It was published in *The Century* in April and was widely reprinted. She tried again to give shape to "In Sorrow," her despairing poem of the previous year, although in the rewriting it lost its ragged forcefulness while gaining smoothness. She could not successfully fit these large impersonal subjects into the small framework of her lyrics, and, besides, she disliked poems that suggested a message. Ernst's coauthorship was very soon abandoned, and she seemed more at ease when she turned again to the personal voice and the quiet fatalism that had characterized her previous work:

> Come, for life is a frail moth flying
>    Caught in the web of the years that pass,
> And soon we two, so warm and eager,
>    Will be as the gray stones in the grass.[3]

By the end of spring her work had recovered its necessary sadness as she began to face the consequences of her marriage, and she could ask, in "Midnight Rain," why, when the tree trembles with ecstasy to the rain,

> alone for me
> Is there no ecstasy?

The torment of her bladder pain had been constant since January, and she was annoyed with her doctor, who, instead of having her lie flat "to conserve strength"—her own favored method of treatment—had her come down "to his office for irrigations when I was not able to go—and he did it so awkwardly that I suffered *agony,*" she told her sister-in-law Irma. In spite of it, however, she managed to get the manuscript of *Rivers to the Sea* off to Macmillan, following the example of Harriet Monroe and Vachel Lindsay; and on May 2 she and Ernst had met Edgar Lee Masters, who, Sara told Jessie, was "not particularly fascinating. . . .He looks just like Thackeray." Ernst had also written a letter complimenting Frost on *North of Boston*, and Frost replied that "I know your wife's poetry and admire it," while angling for a possible invitation to read his own work in St. Louis.[4]

Sara was finally forced to bed for a week of total rest, but by early June was "hobbling around," preparing to leave their "lovable rooms" in the hotel and move into her parents' home for the summer while they went, as usual, to Charlevoix. Macmillan had returned her manuscript, saying they would like to see it again. Sara believed that war conditions had made the publishing business chancy. Vachel's book had not created the sensation it should have, she thought, for people's minds were on the European conflict. She resubmitted her manuscript with further revisions to Macmillan on June 19, begging Jessie Rittenhouse to write the editor, Edward Marsh, and urge him to publish it. To her surprise, they did accept it, on July 1, offering 10 percent royalties. Sara thought it "a really strong book . . . for it has four full years of work very carefully weeded . . . a far more vital book than 'Helen of Troy.'"

Throughout these six months, Sara was undergoing a profound self-searching as a result of her marriage. The brief unsatisfactory honeymoon had been followed immediately by six months of continuous pain that would have precluded sexual relations. Ernst was patient, protective, and sympathetic. From the beginning, she had insisted that they sleep in separate bedrooms, for she had never in her life slept in the same room with another person and did not feel she could rest if she had to do so. Her romantic belief in the forgetting of self through the ecstasy of love had failed miserably; she had felt nothing of such love. She had even tried briefly to share a creative companionship through the writing of poems, but that experiment, too, had been quickly abandoned. When her sister-in-law, Irma Filsinger, was having an unhappy love affair that summer, Sara wrote her:

> And above everything remember your own fineness and be proud of it. . . . It is the women without pride who go to pieces—the women who give themselves *too much*. I do not mean by this that they necessarily give more or otherwise than convention allows. I mean that they give too much of their *souls* away. No highly developed, thoroughly self-conscious modern woman can really give her soul and be proud of it. I used to always think that I wanted to lose myself in the man I loved. I see now that I can never do that, and that I was foolish to wish that I could. The man who wants a woman's brain, soul and body wants really only a slave. And the woman who wants to give *all* of herself, spirit and intellect and flesh, really doesn't want a lover but a master—and that isn't beautiful except in books, and not *really* beautiful then. I am saying all this for myself, just to put on paper some random thoughts that have come to me as a sort of shock since my marriage.

Sara's shock was much more complex and disturbing than might be supposed from this straightforward statement. For months she had been living an unreal life, ever since she had committed herself to a conventional marriage that did not arise from her true feelings. She had bowed to necessity, as she saw it, and settled for security and respectability. She had been robbed of her youth, and there were no choices left. Sara was supremely logical in all the arrangements that led up to the marriage itself; but the conventions governed not only how she should marry but also how she should feel—overwhelmed by perfect love, devoted to her husband, and blissfully happy. Sara was adept at the genteel social graces, which required a certain amount of sophisticated artificiality, but she was profoundly self-honest and could never endure the counterfeiting of emotion. Yet for months she had been pretending to feel what she was supposed to feel, saying what she was supposed to say, endeavoring to fulfill the conventional image of a dutiful wife. Having made the choice, it was what she owed, a debt to be paid. But it violated her true emotions, out of which came her poetry and her sense of being a singular identity. The sacrifice was greater than she thought, for the freedom to love was the focus of her creative energy, and when suppressed it burst forth destructively like a nightmare, as she had written in "Dreams" only a month after becoming engaged:

> I gave my life to another lover,
>   I gave my love, and all, and all—
> But over a dream the past will hover,
>   Out of a dream the past will call.
>
> I tear myself from sleep with a shiver
>   But on my breast a kiss is hot,
> And by my bed the ghostly giver
>   Is waiting tho' I see him not.[5]

Although she had once deplored the new feminism of writers like Ibsen and Shaw and had sided with the world of her mother against them, she now took their position in a gesture of self-preservation.

John Hall Wheelock said that in the early days of their marriage Sara and Ernst "lost their way." An intimate relationship proved to be more complex and precarious than either of them was prepared for, and adjustment did not occur spontaneously. Sara had deep respect for Ernst and gratitude for his unfailing patience and understanding, but it must have been more than she could bear to submit to sexual love without being genuinely in love, a repugnance compounded by the fear and guilt instilled in her by her mother, who had doubtless felt the same way. Sara had reverted to the same childlike state of helpless illness she experienced when she had first begun to suffer the emotional conflicts of oncoming maturity half a dozen years earlier. Sara's emotions were an endless battle between rebellion and submission. It was her own life that she described as "a frail moth . . . caught in the web."

By midsummer 1915, in spite of illness and the problem of coming to terms with marriage, she had sold a dozen new poems to major magazines and had signed a contract for the publication of her book in the fall, a burst of activity that not only made up for lost time but proved that marriage had not diminished her creativity. Some of her poems went back to the memorable times of the previous summer, and it is hard to tell which of her three loves—Vachel, Ernst, or Jack— is the occasion for each, although Ernst may not figure in any of them because she spent so

little time with him in New York. "Summer Night, Riverside" is undoubtedly about Vachel, with its kisses under a floweting tree whose falling
petals tangle in her hair. "The India Wharf" suggests one of the long
exploratory walks with Jack Wheelock, for she

> felt alive, defiant of all death and sorrow,
> Sure and elated.

> That was the gift you gave me.

And its wistful ending hints at a relationship that might have been:

> I always felt we could have taken ship
> And crossed the bright green seas
> To dreaming cities set on sacred streams.[6]

In August, she marked the end of those loves with "Afterwards": "I do
not love you now,/ Nor do you love me," for love has passed like a
splendid summer storm, leaving small things to remember, like raindrops
clinging to cobwebs, "while the distance/ And days drift between us."

Sara and Ernst spent the last ten days of July with her parents in a cold,
grey Charlevoix where she corrected the proofs of her book. Then she
returned, after Ernst, to St. Louis and her doomed efforts to keep house,
which, with her still constant crippling bladder pain, threatened to overcome her, even though she had a cook and a maid. Besides, she had
important work to do to see that her book was properly launched. Never
before or afterward did she mount such an energetic campaign to promote her work. One might suppose that her marriage to a businessman
had something to do with this, except that Sara had as much business
acumen of her own. She had always circulated her work diligently, undaunted by rejections, working constantly for improvement, and keeping
records and accounts, a model poet-entrepreneur. She would not con-
tribute poems to magazines that did not pay, feeling that poets should
place a value on their work.

*Rivers to the Sea* was scheduled for release on October 6, 1915 and Sara
began a campaign in September to guarantee that it would be widely
noticed. Macmillan planned an initial run of 1,640 copies, nearly twice as
many as she expected, and had advertisements ready for release in newspapers across the country, featuring her new work along with Masefield's.
Sara had supplied lists of names, including Poetry Society members and
"several hundred of our friends," for a special mailing, and St. Louis's
largest bookstore, Stix, Baer and Fuller, were mailing a similar announce-
ment to 2,500 people. Sara also diligently sent hand written letters to
college and university libraries around the country, gracefully urging
them to support the too-neglected art of poetry by seeing that her new
book was available for wide circulation. Reedy would give it a big splash

in the *Mirror,* of course, and Braithwaite would feature it in his regular page in the Boston *Transcript.* She begged Jessie Rittenhouse to do the review for the *New York Times,* in spite of the burden of her fall lecture series, and even sent her a check to supplement the meagre fee the *Times* would pay.

Sara's exhilaration was somewhat dampened by her finally being sent to the hospital by her doctors, for the bladder pain had become insupportable. She was lying in her bed in St. John's Hospital when the first copy of *Rivers to the Sea* was brought to her on Wednesday, October 6. "I am bubbling over with joy," she wrote Jessie. "The binding, print and paper are all that could be desired." Two years earlier, the manuscript had been presented as a love gift to John Hall Wheelock. Now the dedication was changed—"To Ernst"—and the lines from Wheelock's poem no longer served as an epigraph to identify the source of the title.

Wheelock himself came upon the book in the shipping room of Scribner's Book Store, where he had gone to give instructions to a clerk, and saw there "a volume that looked up at me like a living creature," with the "not unfamiliar title, 'Rivers to the Sea.' " His eight-page letter to Sara was filled with generous praise: "Most of the poems are so well known to me they are part of myself." What gave her work stature, he felt, was its direct presentation of emotion without comment or analysis or intellectualizing, through concrete images of life and utter simplicity of statement. Lesser poets would get between the reader and the poem with their attitudes. To him, the book was a single poem, not only because of the unity of its sensibility but also because of its careful arrangement, which led the reader through cycles of experience, and because it presented "a world, complete even to its smallest details—the swans, the park, the subway. . . .a miniature world grouped and ordered to point the symbol of your own experience, culled from the less personal order of the outer world."7

The reviews were more laudatory than she hoped for. Even Harriet Monroe's was "a very sweet one for so acid a critic," she told Jessie. Reviewers found the feminine point of view in her work to be one of its chief points of interest—a revelation of women's emotion. Macmillan capitalized on this in their blurbs, saying the book "reveals the soul of a woman." But most praised her restraint, her formal perfection, her confined energy, her sincerity and freedom from sentimentality. Louis Untermeyer had written a kind and enthusiastic personal letter—"The book is splendid"—and promised to review it in the *Chicago Evening Post.* But when he sent her a draft of his article a few weeks later, it was loaded with negative criticism: too narrow a range, too patterned, even tending to descend into bathos and cliché. "I have not treated you as a novice to be politely and deprecatingly patronized," he said. "And so here's the ointment and the flies."8 Sara was hurt. "You count the flies in the ointment so carefully that the number of them seems enormously large," she re-torted. Untermeyer was riding a new bandwagon; for Frost and Masters were now the rage, and since his reviews were always self-conscious displays of his current position he may have decided to use the occasion to remove himself from too close an association with his own idealistic, lyrical past.

Sara and Ernst finally moved from her parents' home at the end of October, when she had managed to get on her feet again, although they took rooms at the Usona Hotel at King's Highway and Waterman Avenue, Sara being unable to keep house—a fact that in itself did not make her unhappy. She had mountains of letters to answer and copies of her book to send to poets in both England America. Rudolf Rieder, a young profes-sor of German at the University of Wisconsin, where Ernst's sister Irma was working on her master's degree, had translated seventy or more of Sara's poems, and with Macmillan's permission was hoping to bring out an edition in Munich at the end of the war. Stafford Hatfield, who had kept up a sporadic correspondence with Sara, had vanished into a Ger-man prison camp earlier in the year but now reported himself safe and well cared for.

And Sara, who had gone through half a dozen doctors desperately seeking help, spent a few days again in the hospital in mid-November, in another futile effort at relief from pain. The year-long misery had gradu-ally become the chief subject of her poems, and she collected a group of seven of them under the heading "In a Hospital" in a later book. They are not particularly memorable and are oddly childlike in attitude, al-though one, "The Broken Field," ends with a strong figure of speech that touches the depth of her sadness:

> Great Sower when you tread
>   My field again,
> Scatter the furrows there
>   With better grain.9

The fall of 1915 also saw the beginning of Sara's acquaintance with Amy Lowell and a correspondence that lasted until Miss Lowell's death ten years later. Amy Lowell's *Sword Blades and Poppy Seeds* had been pub-lished in 1914, when her work had just begun to show the influence of her enthusiasm for the Imagistes. Since then she had published her anthology, *Some Imagist Poets,* and, after a recent explosive parting of the ways with Ezra Pound, was about to begin her role as the "demon sales-woman" of the new poetry, in Eliot's words. Sara had read *Sword Blades and Poppy Seeds* the previous spring but only wrote Miss Lowell from her hospital bed in October. It was an ingenuous letter, full of measured praise, and no doubt timed to draw Miss Lowell's attention to *Rivers to the Sea* without actually appearing to do so. Sara was adept at such maneuvers to gain friendly attention, although her praise and her interest were never insincere.

After somewhat nervously exploring the new trends in her lectures, anxious to shed her conservative label and jealous of Harriet Monroe, Jessie Rittenhouse had invited Miss Lowell to speak at the Poetry Society meeting on November 30. Miss Lowell's talk shook the meeting into life, and when Jessie Rittenhouse recognized that here was a rising star worth catching she paid her the supreme compliment of inviting her to the private party she always threw for her friends just before the annual dinner meeting of the society in January. Miss Lowell, in the meantime, read *Rivers to the Sea,* and marveled, as she always did, "with a feeling of painful envy," at how Sara accomplished "that beautiful lyric touch." She did succeed in breaking Sara of a habit others had found annoying too: "Why will you spell 'through' 'thru'?"[10] Oscar Firkins' review in *Nation* also complained that "she sears her pages with the spelling 'thru.' " Sara immediately dropped it, along with 'tho.' "

Sara's book, in addition to its own merits, rode the crest of the popular vogue for poetry, stimulated by the controversy over Imagism and free verse. Her work seemed to bridge the comfortably traditional and the new, with its skillful lyricism and modern urban subjects. Lecturers like Amy Lowell, Jessie Rittenhouse, and Harriet Monroe were in demand for club meetings and banquets, and Sara was frequently invited too, although she declined because of her ill health. She had gone to every noted specialist in St. Louis and found no diagnosis but "chronic inflammation," and in December they could suggest only that she spend several months in bed. But she was too engrossed in her work. Pulled down, crippled, and almost paralyzed at times by the seemingly causeless pain and weakness, she also faced boundless opportunities, and her mind was constantly active with new poems and ideas. In January 1916, she and Ernst hit on a solution to the problem of meeting her public: He would accept the invitations for public readings, since she was unable to. And so beginning in January, and continuing through the spring, Ernst, who had a good voice, read her work before clubs and civic groups in St. Louis, sometimes to audiences of several hundred, and apparently with success.

Ernst was a "dear," Sara told everyone, attentive, caring, anxious to promote her work. "It was a matter of great pride with him," John Hall Wheelock later recalled, "that he should be married to this very remarkable creature." Yet he must have wondered what kind of marriage he had come to, after those conversations along the shore of Lake Michigan in 1914 when she seemed to want nothing more passionately than to be a wife and mother. Now her poetry and her career were everything, and her incurable, though indefinable, illness kept her from being a wife in any sense but the close companionship that had developed between them.

One reason Sara did not want to be hospitalized was that she aimed to attend the Poetry Society annual dinner meeting in New York on January 25, 1916 as she had done faithfully for the past four years. Now that she had arrived at the top, the temptation must have been irresistible to enjoy it to the full. So they went, and Ernst sat with her proudly at the head table, where Jessie had also placed the Frosts, the Untermeyers, the Markhams, E. A. Robinson, Mary Austin, and John Hall Wheelock. Afterward, he went on to Boston on business for a few days, while Sara, installed in the Martha Washington Hotel as of old, was brought up to date on all the latest news by her friends.

Being in New York also meant revisiting the emotionally charged scene of that most important year in her life, when she had thrown herself into the vain and exhausting effort to marry John Hall Wheelock. She was accustomed to getting what she wanted, as Vachel Lindsay had pointed out to her, but this most imperative of all desires had been frustrated. She stayed on alone in New York for a week, very much aware of the emotions she had to come to terms with, and wanted to stay longer. But her friends were fearful that her presence at the time of Vachel Lindsay's arrival in February to begin his spring tour would be too disturbing to him, for "Vachel fostered the idea in everybody's mind that we were engaged because he wanted everybody to feel so and because he really felt in his own heart that we *were,* in spite of my never having given him a promise." Although she herself had no qualms about meeting him, the attitude of her friends made it impossible for her to stay on. If they believed "that I broke the engagement and wantonly hurt him in order to marry you," she wrote Ernst, "you can see that there is nothing for me to do but to go," rather than explain.[11]

From New York, the place "where all the happiest hours of my life (until I met you) had been passed," she wrote to Ernst to remind him, and perhaps herself, how much she loved him. "I wonder sometimes whether you can ever take the time in that busy harrassed life of yours to feel the beauty of all this. As I write, I am half-blinded by tears. . . . I cannot be happy away from you. I want you to know this in all its fullness. You have given me so much—and I want to give you an equal gift." The key to her love for Ernst was this sense of responsibility and indebtedness, which was aroused by revisiting the scene of her love for Wheelock.

On returning to St. Louis, she wrote a poem "The Ghost," about a love that still haunted her. Her other love, the one "who had loved me madly" (that is, Vachel), was no threat, for "The past was buried too deep to fear." But the other, the one that was "never spoken/ Goes like a ghost through the winding years" and "it was then that the terror took me/ Of words unuttered that breathed and stirred." The notebooks are filled increasingly with poems on her love for Ernst, which have little to say beyond her gratitude for its enduring stability and for the meaning it has brought to her life. In mood they are quiet and appreciative, lacking in intensity. "Lyrics of love fulfilled are hard to write," she told him. "They so easily seem sentimental."

Ernst had been diligently at work finishing another book, *Exporting to Latin America,* which Appleton was planning to bring out in April. It was done partly for extra income, since his business was in trouble and he had begun to fear for the future. Sara had her own modest earnings to cover the expenses arising from her work and perhaps an occasional extravagance she felt guilty about Ernst's paying for. *Rivers to the Sea* had sold out in three months and a new printing was issued in February 1916, which meant that, with royalties of $.15 a copy, Sara had earned more in three months than the $200 that Harriet Monroe said was a poet's average annual income from his work.

Sara was patient enough about living in St. Louis, although her heart had been set on New York ever since she first visited it in 1911. The "Chicago Renaissance" had little attraction for her, in spite of her personal friendship with Harriet Monroe and Eunice Tietjens, neither of whom she had seen for over a year. In the competition between Chicago and New York, she always sided with the latter. Harriet Monroe came down to St. Louis on February 11 to lecture at the Art League; Sara thought it an incredible performance under the circumstances: "You may gather something of Harriet's tact," she told Jessie, "when I tell you that she did not so much as mention either Zoë's name or mine during the lecture," although she was Sara's house guest and speaking in her home city, where Sara was believed to be one of the most important living American poets. "Her subject was 'The New Poetry' and it was all CHICAGO and nothing else. I think that Sandburg, Ezra Pound, Aldington et al got on people's nerves a little." Harriet boasted privately that her Chicago banquets had "a far finer crowd" than New York's. Sara urged Jessie to set up an annual prize larger than the $250 offered by *Poetry,* which Vachel Lindsay had won in 1915 for "The Chinese Nightingale": "It is the only way to get ourselves into the Chicagoans' field of vision."

A more charming visitor was John Masefield, whose reputation in America was then very high and who was on a celebrity tour like Yeats's of 1914. He was Sara and Ernst's guest in St. Louis, where to Sara's amazement he insisted on their calling each other by first names. He offered to approach English publishers about bringing out a selection of her work and left them with an aura of warmth and kindness.

Macmillan began to press Sara for a new book of poems after the remarkable success of *Rivers to the Sea.* It was much too soon, of course; she could not hope for another volume for several years, for although she might write five or six poems in a month, no more than half would be publishable, at least in her judgment, in the magazines. And even these would be further culled for collection in a book. So as she lay abed in

March 1916, stricken first with the grippe and then two weeks of "stomach trouble," she conceived of a plan that might interest Macmillan: an anthology of love lyrics by women poets of the previous fifty or sixty years. It would be a very choice selection, limited to seventy short poems, beautifully printed one to a page, with an attractive binding.

Sara immediately, and in characteristic fashion, threw herself headlong into the project, enlisting her sister Mamie and Ernst, who carried home armfuls of library books for her to sort through. Needing someone in New York to find material unavailable in St. Louis and to advise her on copyright problems, she appealed to Thomas Jones, one of the conservative sonnet-writing poets of her generation, who was among her circle of New York friends. Jones generously tracked down answers to her questions and copied poems she had not been able to locate, and in a few weeks she had begun to assemble her collection.

It was a curious act of retracing her steps and defining her own taste and the attitudes that she believed to be distinctively feminine; it was, in short, almost as much an expression of herself as one of her own books, for she limited the verse to love lyrics beginning with the women whom she had liked since girlhood. In the process, she rediscovered her old enthusiasms. "I ADORE Mary Robinson," she exclaimed to Jones, "and have for ten years. I daresay I owe more to her than to anybody else except Christina. . . . I had not reread her for years. . . . but I found that I still knew many by heart. She is of the *absolutely* perfect few—every line exquisite, simple, and full of the thrill that only comes when real poets sing."[12] A. Mary F. Robinson was a Victorian Englishwoman who lived much of her life on the continent and published a number of critical studies of French literature under her married name, Madame Duclaux. Like Sara, she said, "I have never been able to write about what was not known to me and near."[13] Sara emulated Mary Robinson's songlike simple stanzas, her ironic juxtaposition of personal mood and impersonal surroundings, and especially her variations on the constant themes of unsatisfied love and death. Sara's early work is full of echoes of Mary Robinson's *An Italian Garden,* a little book her mother had given her for Christmas in 1906, as a typical stanza will illustrate:

> Out of the window the trees in the Square
>   Are covered with crimson May—
> You, that were all of my love and my care,
>   Have broken my heart to-day.

If it had not been for the challenge of changing times and styles, which led Sara to write much stronger work, she might have remained a writer of such dainty verses.

Sara had hired a secretary to come in for three hours a week and now put her to work preparing the manuscript, although complaining to Jones that she "nearly drives me crazy—she has no initiative whatever." She wanted the project kept a secret, in case she couldn't find a publisher, but finally asked a few other friends for advice—Harriet, Jessie, Jack, and Louis—and, after bringing the number of poems up to a hundred and accepting Wheelock's suggestion of a title—*The Answering Voice*—she sent the manuscript off to Macmillan around June 1. She had little faith in their ability to design an attractive book; "I nearly drove them crazy over my fussiness to get 'Rivers to the Sea' as decent as it is," she wrote Jones. And she had qualms about copyrights, many of which were held by Houghton Mifflin, who might charge more than the volume could bear.

The year 1916 was also the tercentenary of the death of Shakespeare, and it unleashed as much bad poetry as the centenary of Browning's birth had done in 1912. Sara was asked by William Stanley Braithwaite to do a commemorative poem for his page in the Boston *Transcript,* and the Drama League of America wanted an "ode" from her to read at their special celebration at the statue of Shakespeare in Tower Grove Park in St. Louis. She managed to turn out a short, trite poem on Mary Arden, Shakespeare's mother, for Braithwaite, but froze with horror over the ode, procrastinating until it was almost too late. Only four days before the celebration she dashed off the worst poem she had ever written, and it was read with theatrical flourishes by the actor William Faversham on April 28, as a tree was ceremonially planted and girls danced, draped in gauze. It was, of course, a success, although one that Sara tried as rapidly as possible to forget.

Over the past year, Sara had gradually retreated to the same state of "emotional prostration" that had brought her to Cromwell, Connecticut, for a "rest cure" in 1909. She could see no other help than to go there again. "Oh let me be alone, far from eyes and faces," a poem titled "Weariness" began, "Let me be alone, awhile, even from you." As soon as the manuscript of *The Answering Voice* had been put in the mail to Macmillan, she boarded the train for Cromwell on June 6, leaving Ernst to see the book through the press with the help of Williamina Parrish, who had returned to St. Louis from Europe with the outbreak of war. Macmillan did not accept the book, but Houghton Mifflin subsequently did, on July 17.

Weaving rugs and raffia baskets and taking evening walks to her favorite spots in the woods, she seemed to cheer up markedly and used the time alone to take measure of herself and her life—the reason, apparently, why she had come there. Although the regimen at Cromwell Hall was supposed to forbid any exertion whatever, she worked at her poetry and wrote almost daily letters to Ernst. She had been thinking her way through the controversies surrounding imagism and vers libre with a view to defending traditional lyric poetry and would have liked to write a critical essay, although she believed she "should not do critical nor combative writing," feeling herself "a creator and not a critic—at least if I ever turn critic," she told Ernst, "it will be as a critic of life and society and not as a critic of literature." The gist of her argument was that poetry traditionally needed "melody" as a means of making itself easy to remember and of communicating emotions that could not be communicated through metaphor or intellectual statement. Like Frost, she saw the new forms as subtractive, exploiting limited existing aspects of poetry, not introducing anything actually new. But she did write up her ideas in spite of her hesitancy, taking pains to avoid too argumentative a tone, and she allowed Braithwaite to publish them in the Boston *Evening Transcript* on August 5 in a large feature article called, misleadingly, "America's New Shelley—A Woman."

Sara attributed the decline of melody "in the most fashionable kinds of poetry today" to a reaction against its over exploitation by Swinburne and the poets of a generation earlier. The new forms were simply the development of tendencies always present in poetry, and the new poets were to be thanked, for they "have emphasized the necessity for precision, compression, and visualization, and they have infinitely enlarged the subject matter of poetry." In her letter to Ernst sketching her views, she had gone further to say that they "are compressing and hardening their work until their poems are like pellets of condensed food—they may contain a great deal, but they aren't palatable." In her published remarks, Sara criticized the Imagists for dwelling "with a sort of self-conscious satisfaction on very frail and isolated beauties in nature or emotion, and this tendency is as artificial in its way as the toying with complex and fragile French verse-forms that occupied so much time twenty-five years ago." Instead of such "highly specialized trifles of emotions," the poet "must give himself freely to us in his work, and he must be honest in the most literal sense. . . . After all it makes little difference whether the poet accomplishes his object by the use of regular metre and rhyme or not." She had invited Amy Lowell over from Boston in July to help her in "hashing over a lot of questions about art in general and poetry in particular," but Miss Lowell was off for her own respite at her country place and had to decline.

Sara also thought of inviting Wallace Stevens down from Hartford for tea, having just read a verse play by him and liking "the occasional verbal magic and the fine music once in a while," although she told Ernst it was hard to make head or tail of him.

Sara had arranged the contents of *The Answering Voice* in a sequence that reflected the progression of the love experience from lonely yearning for a lover, through adoration, to loss and remembrance. It began with Christina Rossetti's "Somewhere or Other"—"Somewhere or other there must surely be/ The face not seen, the voice not heard"—and ended with Emily Brontë's "Remembrance," "When the days of the golden dream had perish'd." This cycle summed up the painful view of love common to the poets of the feminine tradition from the mid-nine-teenth century onward. Sara's arrangement is a perceptive definition of it, for she saw how each individual poem fit into the pattern. There is no place in it for love as something realized or sustaining. Even when love fastens on a particular person, he is so idealized and hidden behind a blinding halo that the woman, unequal to her lover, always seems alone with her worshipful emotion. It was the essence of love that it should be unrealizable even while it was so desperately desired. The intense craving for love seems curiously negated by a refusual to believe in the possibility of it.

If Sara herself is representative—psychologically and in her back-ground—of the feminine poets who created this body of love poetry, then it would seem that the self-contradictory, self-defeating attitude toward love resulted in large part from the extreme suppression of emotional freedom of middle-class women in their relations with men. They were suspended, as it were, between an anxiety to love and a fear of loving that could not be resolved, and they therefore found themselves ill and in rebellion against their own lives. Love was the predestined pursuit of the impossible. Sara was aware that her poems sprang from the pain of knowing that what she desired most in life was unattainable, and one can guess that her chronic illness was the form that her own rebellion took. Beset with contradiction, she could write to Ernst from Cromwell Hall, where she had gone to escape from marriage for a while, "I long to be near you and to feel the pressure of your arms so much that sometimes I have a strange but very real ache all over my body that seems to be crying to you," and could mean it in all sincerity. She lay there in bed with insomnia, and wrote

> My heart cried like a beaten child
>   Ceaselessly all night long;
> I had to take my own cries
>   And thread them into a song.

This poem, called "Song Making," is a reiteration of the equation between pain and poetry that she had worked out in "Sappho." It ends:

> Life, you have put me in your debt
>   And I must serve you long—
> But oh, the debt is terrible
>   That must be paid in song.[14]

The first draft of "Song Making" was lighter and self-mocking:

> My heart cries like a beaten child,
>   And I must listen, stark and terse,
> Dry eyed and critical, to see
>   What I can turn into a verse.

> This was a sob at the hour of three,
>   And this when the first cock crew—
> I wove them into a dainty song,
>   But no one thought them true!

Caught in the suspense of that formula, however, there was no way to go either forward or backward, and her poems began to reflect the air of resignation, which became more pronounced as time passed, that she called wisdom. For her, the bitter lesson of life was to accept the fact that nearly everything one ardently desires must be given up, and that one is essentially alone. In "Lessons," she expresses the idea that she cannot lean on persons weaker than herself or accept protection and comfort from those who are stronger. Another "wisdom" poem begins with her well-known lines,

> When I have ceased to break my wings
> Against the faultiness of things . . .

and concludes:

> Life will have given me the Truth,
> And taken in exchange—my youth.[15]

With even one's own identity lost in death, life would seem pointless but for one thing: beauty. Although there is no clear line of demarcation, it seems generally true that the focus of her poems before her marriage is the anticipation of love, or its disappointments, while after her marriage it shifts to the "ecstasy" and solace of beauty as the ultimate value of experience. The poignancy of such ecstasy lay, of course, in its stark contrast to the loss of all else, for that was the price exacted. Her creating songs out of pain and loneliness paralleled the exchange of one's hopes and desires for those ecstatic moments when life assumed positive value. Life was a gift, whether asked for or not, and one had an obligation to repay it with some sense of value received. Beauty for her is that value: "But oh, the debt is terrible."

One of her most popular poems, "Barter," written in September 1916 after her return from Cromwell, states the transaction concisely:

> Spend all you have for loveliness,
>   Buy it and never count the cost;
> For one white singing hour of peace
>   Count many a year of strife well lost,
> And for a breath of ecstasy
>   Give all you have been, or could be.[16]

She originally titled it "Buying Loveliness," and among some altered lines was "Life will not give, but she will sell." Another poem, "August

Moonrise," written either at Cromwell or shortly after her return, describes her experience on an evening walk in the woods there, where, filled with impressions of beauty in the landscape, she comes to a "shining pool" that suggests the "cup" out of which she has drunk beauty all her life. She feels a deep assurance that "no bitterness can bend/And no sorrow wholly bow" her because of this love, even the threat of death:

> Let this single hour atone
> For the theft of all of me.[17]

In her letters to Ernst from Cromwell, Sara scolded him for spending too many evenings at the office and worrying too much about his business affairs. But the Filsinger-Boette Shoe Company was failing, and Ernst was desperately trying to rearrange his affairs. Sara returned from Cromwell to Charlevoix, after a side trip to Nahant, Massachusetts, in August, while Ernst stayed with his own family, not taking new quarters as he waited to see whether he would remain in St. Louis. He had decided to close out the debt-ridden business and look for a position somewhere else. Sara hoped he would settle in New York. But in October, to her frantic distress, he was on the verge of accepting a position with the U.S. Department of Foreign and Domestic Commerce in Buenos Aires. She tried discreetly to persuade his family to intercede. She would be isolated in a strange city where she did not even know the language, while he traveled a great deal. Her parents were too old for her to live so far away, and her anthology would be held up or even abandoned because of the great distances for mail to travel by boat. It was "only a small matter, I know," she told her sister-in-law, Irma, "and yet it can't help meaning something to me." Harriet Monroe advised her, "Be *sure* not to hold Ernst back from S.A. or anywhere else he ought to go. Besides you would like it";[18] and Sara tried "not to stand in the way of Ernst's ambition, whatever it may be." But Ernst went to New York in November to investigate the possibilities there, and disaster was averted when he found a position with Lawrence and Co., textile dealers. He and Sara both went "wild with delight," she reported to Harriet. Only two days after his telephone call to her on November 24, Sara was on the train to New York, leaving St. Louis for good, at last, abruptly leaving the scattered pieces of her life to be gathered together later.

During the autumn, she had carried forward the complex planning for *The Answering Voice,* with its many permissions to obtain and possible changes to make, fearing with good reason that a move to Argentina might render it impossible to finish. And she had also found a solution to the problem of publishing a new book soon on the heels of the last one. This would be to bring out a collection of the best of her previous work combined with as many new poems as she could muster to warrant a new volume. Macmillan accepted it on December 14 for publication in the spring, without even seeing the new poems, still anxious to capitalize on the popularity of *Rivers to the Sea*, which had gone into a third printing in July. The new volume, *Love Songs*, would include a half dozen of the somber poems that resulted from her summer of self-questioning, grouped under the heading "Interlude: Songs out of Sorrow." This "interlude" was the first foreshadowing of the mood that would gradually spread to dominate her work.

Sara disliked the burden and the clutter of the business side of being a successful author, which seemed to consume too much of her well-measured supply of energy. She circulated her poems sometimes to three or four magazines before acceptance, and at this time she was publishing dozens of poems a year. She had to respond to requests for permission to reprint or set her poems to music as well as countless inquiries to join literary societies, serve as a judge in contests, read her work publicly, and the like. Invitations of this kind she almost always declined. In the fall of 1916, she tried the services of a literary agent, Mrs. Julia R. Tutweiler of New York, who sold several poems for her. But, given the deduction of fees and the bother of constant communication with her agent, she soon went back to handling her own business affairs, at which she was expert and needed no advice.

In October, she had supported a project with which few today would associate her name—Mencken's petition against the censors on behalf of Dreiser's *The Genius*, which the Western Society for the Prevention of Vice had succeeded in banning from bookstores and the U.S. mails. The publisher had withdrawn the book to avoid litigation. Dreiser had refused to compromise, and Mencken circulated a petition among well-known and respected authors endorsing Dreiser's stand. Sara and Ernst both enthusiastically signed the petition that was filed, uselessly as it turned out, with the Postmaster General. Ernst, an admirer of Shaw, had progressive sympathies, and Sara believed strongly in the right of artistic self-expression, no matter how unpalatable it might be to others, as she had defended the new movements in poetry while disagreeing with them.

Their open-mindedness was put to the test in New York, which they found feverish with increasing sentiment for the United States to enter the war against Germany. Sara watched the approaching involvement as a kind of insanity, curious at the reflex behavior of people who had previously seemed rational. She and Ernst hoped the United States would stay out.

Because of the abrupt move to New York, they took rooms for several months at the Hotel Bonta, 94th and Broadway, planning to find an apartment later. Sara quickly came down with her "old enemy the grippe," as she nearly always did after some unusual excitement, while Ernst, burdened with worry over the problems surrounding the dissolution of his company, was attending lectures on the textile industry two or three evenings a week at the YWCA to help him in his new job. They were showered with invitations from friends, but kept to themselves. *The Answering Voice* went to press in mid-January, less than a year after Sara had conceived the idea.

When Ernst's business had started to collapse in the summer of 1916, Sara viewed his intense concern and long hours of work as an alarming symptom. And now, in New York, his anxiety to succeed and his continued nervousness over the possible bankruptcy of his shoe company caused her to lecture him about relaxing and caring for his health. All the hidden strain in their marriage, which seemed reasonably happy to their friends, was brought to focus in this issue. Ernst was energetic and active, while Sara was always "frail" and ill, perhaps a poor judge of "excessive" activity. She was the child of settled, well-to-do parents, for whom everything had always been provided. He saw himself as rising from a humble background through ambition and hard work and did not at all think of himself as obsessively "driven" by ambition. In fact, those who knew him did not see him in that light either. But he did have an almost excruciating sense of responsibility, an anxiety to live up to what he felt was expected of him, that had dominated him since boyhood. It was shown in the quality of his worshipful love for Sara, whom he would not dream of contradicting or depriving of anything she wanted, and in his work, where he welcomed the burden of worry over a thousand outcomes. Her retreat from marriage, her need to be alone, required adjustments on his part, too, and his most conspicuous reaction seemed to be to throw himself ever more intensely into his work. He had no feeling whatever of competition with her because of her fame; it was a thing totally apart. And Sara, with her ironic self-humor, was equally incapable of being the prima donna with a slavish consort, as Edna St. Vincent Millay later became. Ernst's absorption in his work expressed everything that could not be spoken about the tensions in their marriage. It not only roused Sara's concern; it frightened her. Marriage had not cured her acute sense of inadequacy, with its accompanying fear of being abandoned. Ernst's obsessive overworking, as she thought it, was like a deliberate neglect of her.

When Ernst left in late January 1917 on a short business trip, Sara wrote him: "Dearest boy, I know that you have been and always will be the dearest husband in the world, and I am very sorry that I have not been more cheerful the last few days. But I *shall* be from now on, and you may rely on my not worrying." It was a promise she found impossible to keep.

Her constant desire to repay Ernst with something equal to his devotion led in January 1917 to a poem, "Because," that shows a further working out of the problem of independence in marriage, which had given her many troubled hours:

> Oh, because you never tried
> To bow my will or break my pride,
> And nothing of the cave-man made
> You want to keep me half afraid. . . .
> Take me, for I love you more
> Than I ever loved before. . . .
> Take my dreams and take my mind
> That were masterless as wind;
> And "Master!" I shall say to you
> Since you never asked me to.[19]

And yet two months later she wrote "Doubt," in which her soul is sometimes

> less your own
> Than a wild, gay adventurer . . .
> Oh, I am sure of my body's faith,
> But what if my soul broke faith with you?[20]

In "The Game," she sees life as a game that she has played with "head held high," according to the rules, so that no one could laugh at her when it is finished, a game "for love and a little fame." She has won the game and has what she wanted, but is now "alone and very tired," and her heart cries silently "As blood wells up in an open wound." Her notebook shows her experimenting during these months to obtain a more vivid and vigorous sense of physical objects, to get a modern "bite" into her work by dealing with negative emotions with crispness and clarity, the hard truths that modern life demanded. She was engaged in a gradual transformation of her work reflecting both the new developments in poetry as well as her own maturing outlook. Because of the lag between composition and the publication of her books, her public image and her popular reputation rested on the earlier work that she had outgrown, the "dainty" verses she mocked in "Song Making."

As spring approached, the war hysteria mounted. The national anthem was played at every conceivable occasion, and there were food riots and police guarding the water depots. Isadora Duncan, at a performance Sara attended with Ernst in March, and described to her sister-in-law Irma, dropped off her gown at the end revealing herself draped in the flag "amid storms of applause and the strains of the Star-Spangled Banner." Sara observed the drift with detachment and dread.

Ernst's crisis over the shoe company continued worsening for months, and he feared it might affect his position with the Lawrence Company. Sara, in spite of her determination to face life more stoically, was continuously "weak and good-for-nothing" and had spent a few days in January 1917 at Cromwell again, consulting Dr. Lord, "who knows my whole make-up so well." He attributed her condition to "anxiety," she told Irma, and encouraged her to believe that she would feel better "when the effects of this perturbed fall and winter wear off." She hoped she could regain health as good as she had had before marriage. Contributing to her depression was the news of the death of her brother, John Warren Teasdale, Jr., at the age of only-forty-seven, after years of suffering the consequences of a stroke, probably stirring her fear for her own health. Her poem "The Silent Battle," published in *The Mirror* at Easter, commemorates his death.

Still, she made an effort to fight against her own illness, her incurable "open wound." She attended social functions when she felt able and saw her old friends regularly. Around the eighth of February, she at last met Vachel again for the first time in two and a half years. Even in the summer of 1916, he had declined an invitation to visit her and Ernst, saying he was still not ready, his pride was still too sensitive. His occasional letters had been ceremonially distant. Arriving in New York for a recital on February 5, 1917, he felt ready to see her again, and she threw a party for him with some of their old friends—Witter Bynner, Jessie Rittenhouse, Joyce and Aline Kilmer, and a few others. It was "a sort of homecoming," he said, and he became friends with Sara again, and with Ernst, whom he liked.

Corrine Roosevelt Robinson invited her to tea, where she met Teddy. Around February 1, she and Ernst finally met Amy Lowell, who gave them an audience and dinner in her room at the St. Regis Hotel, which "was *wonderful* and must have cost a fortune." Sara told Ernst's sister Irma that she was "*fearfully* fat (has no shape at all) and affects a masculine manner, even smoking two large black cigars in our presence." These were the observations one was expected to make about Amy Lowell. Sara followed her work with interest and admiration mingled with impatience at her mannerisms. She visited Miss Lowell again for an hour on April 29 at Sevenels, the Lowell family home in Brookline, a "fairy-tale palace," while staying at the Concord Inn in nearby Concord. They had moved from the Hotel Bonta in April because of the poor food and noise, to the Beresford at 1 West 81st Street, and Sara, who intensely disliked moving, had treated herself to another rest cure, using the money she had received from *Good Housekeeping* for a twenty-eight-line poem, "The Gardener's Prayer," commissioned and written to order for the August number. She was sensitive about spending money on these trips away from Ernst during his financial crisis and so tried to pay for them from her own earnings. Within the past year, she had made three such trips to be alone, and they were rapidly becoming habitual. For whatever reason, her bladder inflammation had finally disappeared in the spring of 1917, after two years of nearly constant pain.

After the declaration of war against Germany on April 6, the city had become increasingly "rabid," Sara thought. "It makes me heart-sick to see how autocratic our country is becoming," she wrote Ernst's sisters, "and how avidly people are going into war—not as though from necessity, but with a certain fanaticism and ferocity which makes me feel that the world has almost gone into lunacy." They had invited a pro-German friend to dinner but had to take him to a small, quiet restaurant where "his vociferous espousal of the German cause might not get us in trouble." In spite of her good intentions, she had grown fretful again about Ernst's working and worrying too much, and she complained to his family, the first of many such appeals she would make for them to persuade him to relax and rest. There was also the threat of a draft of men between the ages of thirty-one to forty within a year, which could sweep in Ernst and many of her other friends.

In June they moved again, for their apartment on the third floor was too near the noise and dirt of the street in warm weather, and took rooms in Pelham Manor at the northern outskirts of New York City, with a Mrs. Arthur, widow of a popular playwright, who to Sara's incredulity had just sold the motion picture rights to one of his plays, called "Blue Jeans," for $10,000 cash. They had arranged for an unfurnished apartment in a better location in the Beresford for September 1 and planned to ship furniture from St. Louis. The summer passed pleasantly, with a weekend in the mountains and a Fourth of July picnic up the Hudson with friends, although Ernst now had to spend nearly an hour commuting each way. He had begun to speak on foreign trade at business conferences, and in June had delivered two addresses in Springfield and another in Boston. But to Sara's dismay he had gone down to Washington in July to consult with the Department of Commerce about doing a commercial traveler's guide to Latin America. "I dread *terribly* his taking it upon himself," she wrote his sister, "but you know how strong a will he has." It meant more long evenings of work on top of long days in his office. But bankruptcy of the shoe company now seemed almost inevitable, and Ernst's pride was deeply wounded by the failure of his business. He grasped at any opportunity to build a reputation. Any extra earnings were welcome too, since they always seemed to live to the limit of their income. "I am constantly marvelling at the ease with which people get through the world—people who don't seem to struggle and who aren't either energetic or conscientious," Sara wrote Irma Filsinger. "I preach to Ernst to take their example unto himself."

She herself was piling success upon success, even though her outlook had gradually grown more pessimistic. In June 1917, she was given the Poetry Society of America annual award of $150 for the best poems read before the society during the previous year. These were "Songs out of Sorrow," the group that had signaled a turning point in her work. Her two new books were both scheduled for publication in September.

Although Ernst would not take a vacation, she managed to persuade him to spend a few hours on Sundays away from his work, and he took off the afternoon of her birthday on August 8 to be with her. "We surely have a capacity for enjoying each other that few people ever experience, I believe," she wrote Ernst's parents, "and we are happy mortals to have such a deep love to share." Her notebook of this period is filled with appreciative poems about their love and the assurance it gives her. But these are encroached on by blacker moods and by a more desperate affirmation of beauty as her only salvation:

> The rest may die—but is there not
>   Some shining strange escape for me
> Who sought in Beauty the bright wine
>   Of immortality?[21]

In "Debtor," she wrote, "I am a debtor to life,/Not life to me."

The move into their apartment at the Beresford on September 1 was a triumph in logistics, Sara thought, for she had arranged all details in advance so well that they could sleep there the first night with almost everything in place, except for the bathroom tissue, which had accidentally blown out the open window. Sara's sister Mamie, who had returned to St. Louis while her husband Joe Wheless served in the army, had managed the shipment of the furniture for her. But Sara was so done in by the effort that she had to go to Cromwell again for a week, where she tried to recover from her constant "indigestion" with massages, salt rubs, bed rest, and a diet of nothing but a glass of hot milk every two hours. But this time her weakness, pain, and extreme depression suggest a problem more serious than nervous exhaustion.

"I feel so grateful for your never-ceasing tenderness," she wrote Ernst, "that I feel, my darling, that no woman has ever lived who loved her husband more deeply or with more reason than I love my darling." She pleaded with him again to control his constant annoyances and worries over his business affairs and spend some time outdoors, playing tennis or golf. "Things never get ship-shape in this life, never," she advised him. She herself had gone off to Cromwell leaving two buttons of his shirt unsewed, and, since her sewing woman hadn't come, she sent him two safety pins "at the risk of making you laugh."

The somber fall of 1917 saw a greater outpouring of her published work than she would ever see again. *The Answering Voice, Love Songs,* and a fourth reprinting of *Rivers to the Sea* all came out in September, and *Love Songs,* which proved to be her most popular single volume, went into a second printing only two months later. Readings from *Love Songs* before large audiences were scheduled at the New York Public Library and the National Arts Club. Ernst no longer read her work publicly, "because," she wrote his parents, "as a businessman, it is probably best that [he] should not be thought to be giving his time to such things."

Although women had been publishing poetry in unprecedented numbers for decades, Sara was the first to gain a reputation as voicing a woman's point of view and emotions and the first to compile an anthology setting forth a coherent picture of women's attitudes toward love. Reviewers noted that in the last century it had been considered immodest for women to write about love. In her preface, Sara said that, before the recent period, "for reasons well known to the student of feminism, sincere love poems by women were very rare in England and America."[22] But Sara's collection presented the conventional point of view, and this puzzled reviewers who looked for distinctions between the love poetry of men and women. Braithwaite decided that men were more free to express themselves and women were more subject to convention, although that, he thought, was their charm. Conrad Aiken, reviewing *The Answering Voice* in the Chicago *News* on October 10, was not satisfied:

> We must remember, of course, that women develop their minds on a man-made literature. . . . They are taught a man's language. But even so, is it not possible, will it not be possible, for some women to unfold at last to us what a woman really thinks? . . . One searches in vain [in this volume] . . .for an awareness of what is, to them, specifically the masculine attraction. One searches in vain, also, for any close analysis of the evolution of a love affair. . . . Does a woman regard love as a simple entity, rather than (as Freud tells us) a complex, many parts of which are at least dubiously attractive, and all parts of which are penetrable by analysis? Are there no qualifications to a woman's love—are no aspects of it repellent, or transitory, or in any sense variable? . . . The female remains sphinxlike as before. She tells us merely—what we tell her.

It was the peculiarity of Sara's own work that she should expose her feelings with excruciating honesty, and yet no one seemed to see its meaning, as if she were dramatizing conventional attitudes with which she only sympathized for artistic purposes, as though conventions could not contain the most intense emotion. One of the penalties she paid for this, she told Amy Lowell, was "a growing shyness, and a positive horror of hearing any well-meaning soul try to read my poetry in public. My lyrics were never meant for reading aloud—or, if they are read so, for being listened to by more than two or three people. . . . Of course not all of my stuff is bang out of my own life (thank the kind gods!)—but it is tinged so deeply and directly with my own feelings that the idea of its being read or recited to a roomful of people (especially if I have to be present) gives me a longing to die at once." Ernst was fond of reading her new work to visiting friends, a practice in which she indulged him, although she was often acutely embarrassed, especially when his voice broke at times with emotion and he found it hard to continue.

As the winter came on, Sara modified her pacifism to the extent of believing that Germany ought to be prevented from winning the war. She wanted to have a party for Max Eastman but had too much trouble making up a guest list of friends who would not come to blows with him over his pacifist views. "The feeling here is growing more and more acrid all the time," she wrote Irma Filsinger. "America" and the "Star-Spangled Banner" were sung at virtually all concerts and theatrical performances, and women knitted everywhere constantly, even during dinner at the hotel dining room. "How much of this is bona fide patriotism, I don't know. It all makes me heart-sick, for it represents such terrible loads of sorrow to be borne later when our men are maimed and killed by the thousands. It is staggering when one thinks of the four thousand years of so-called civilization on this planet—that it culminates now in the most brutal and tremendous bloodshed that the world has ever seen."

Eunice Tietjens had gone to France as a war correspondent for the Chicago *Daily News,* and even Blanche Wagstaff, a New York poet of several years' acquaintance, hoped to go to "dear France in her dire need. Then, too, with all one's dear ones and relatives going to the front, what is one to do?"[23] By January 1918, New York City was running out of coal, and many apartment houses and businesses were without heat in sub-zero weather. Sara had four electric heaters going in her apartment, and Ernst several times came home at noon because his office was too cold for work. The drain of young men from the work force was beginning to be felt, and, to Sara's astonishment, women were delivering telegrams and operating elevators. She had never been a newspaper reader but now avidly read the war news every day, and by April 1918 could say to her sisters-in-law, "Don't you both long to be in France? If I were strong and unmarried I'd be there doing something more vital just now than poetry." Still, she could not endure to think about the misery and the killing or the suffering of women over the loss of sons and husbands. She wrote a number of poems about the war through the winter, as if trying to find some secure value to hold to against the spectacle of mindless obliteration—even one worshipful poem about Woodrow Wilson, whom she and Ernst admired. These are weaker than her usual work, and she left uncollected those she published in the magazines. One, titled "Sons," printed in *Everybody's* for January 1918, describes a mother pointing out her son marching with his regiment that moved "like a great machine," as she grasps someone's arm, faint with dread. The ending lines,

> And still they passed with kits and guns,
> Mothers' sons,

were featured shortly in a full-page newspaper advertisement for War Savings Stamps. "The war has made me hideously unhappy these last months," she wrote Harriet Monroe in February, "and now that it seems to be about to end without really attaining anything, I feel pretty much as though God were making an awful mess of his experiment on this planet." The war intensified her deep depression which had sources of its own. Her bladder ailment had returned in the fall, and her physical weakness finally sent her off on another rest cure. Ernst now suggested these trips himself, which relieved her conscience, although she tried to pay for them from her own earnings. On January 9, she was at the Pudding Stone Inn in Boonton, New Jersey, for a week, where she worked at a play, a project she probably thought would bring in additional income, but which was soon abandoned. "This is the first time for some months that I have not felt utterly exhausted all the time," she wrote Ernst, complaining about the requests for readings of her work and the volume of her mail. "All of these details simply keep me sick and miserable so that I am no good to you or to myself or to the world—it is so much more important that I get work done, which I can't do when I'm giving my energy to other things." Washing her hair one day, she was "melancholy to see so much grey."

On moving to New York from St. Louis, she had resumed seeing John Hall Wheelock, after an absence of a year and a half. Her relationship with Vachel had been conducted in public view, as it were, and afterward was much exaggerated by gossipers. Sara admired and respected him with a warmth to the end, but her three delightful weeks with him in New York cannot accurately be called a "love affair," even though he wished it to be. It was the paradox, or perversity, of her emotions to want the man who did not respond to her, while remaining unstirred by the two who competed for her so strenuously. Her baffled feelings for Wheelock remained to pique her, although now there was no possibility of their ever being more than good friends. They saw each other often, as before, sharing their work and their ideas and she kept up her friendship with his mother. He was an intimate guest in her and Ernst's home. In her quiet, tenacious way, she clung to the best in their relationship and expected no more. It provided that perfect suspense of the unattainable that to her was the essence of love, rendered more bittersweet now because it had no future, only a past to remember.

Gradually Wheelock became the subject of some of her poems again, some of which have probably been attributed to her love for Ernst. Many of those with sea imagery refer to Wheelock and are associated with visiting his family home in Long Island. In "Spray," written in October 1917, "I knew you thought of me all night,/I knew, though you were far away," and she felt his love "blow over me" like the sea spray.

> Then be content to come to me
> Only as spray the beating sea
> Drives inland through the night.[24]

It was only a wishful attempt to bridge the distance. Many of her poems since girlhood had followed a similar pattern: the cry of loneliness in the night, and the lover being pulled invisibly by the force of her love to answer. She had written "To One Away" in May 1911:

> I heard a cry in the night,
>     A thousand miles it came,
> Sharp as a flash of light,
>     My name, my name![25]

To this telepathic projection of love, she replies, "I know, I know." She titled her anthology *The Answering Voice*. In "The Storm," another poem about Wheelock, written two years later, she is awakened in the night "By a wind that made me glad and afraid," roaring in the trees like the sound of the sea, while

> I thought it was you who had come to find me,
>     You were the wind.[26]

But if she drew a certain poignant satisfaction from these rehearsals of an impossible love, her mood was more often much bleaker. "I am alone, in spite of love,/In spite of all I take and give," she wrote in January 1918. "Sometimes I am not glad to live."

> I am alone, as though I stood
>     On the highest peak of the tired grey world. . . .
>
> And only my own spirit's pride
> To keep me from the peace of those
> Who are not lonely, having died.[27]

She had begun to look back, as if hoping to embalm her happier memories and thus save something from the slow, inexorable annihilation of her inner self. In "The Nights Remember," another poem about her love for Wheelock, she thinks the memories of "The kingly hours that once you made so great" should be allowed to rest like buried kings in their tombs, "Let them not wake again, better to lie there":

> Many a ghostly king has wakened from death-sleep
> And found his crown stolen and his throne decayed.[28]

"Remember me as I was then," she wrote in "Change," still another poem from the early months of 1918, in

> that one year of youth we had,
> The only youth we ever knew—
> Turn from me now, or you will see
> What other years have done to me.[29]

Her tension and depression had been growing alarmingly throughout the fall and winter. The yearning for a return to her idealized love for Wheelock, the sense of a life exhausted and pointless that she expressed in her poems, were danger signals. By mid-March, her physical and emotional condition was so near the point of breaking that she went back again to the Pudding Stone Inn at Boonton, New Jersey. She was unable even to answer letters. "I have so little strength," she wrote Ernst, "that it seemed to me the wisest thing to use it to write poetry rather than letters, so that for about four months now I have not attempted to answer any but requests for permission, etc." Here she wrote "The Wind in the Hemlock," a passionate forty-line poem again reaffirming beauty as the only escape from death, looking up at the immortal stars and moon with "envious dark rage," "heart-broken in my hate." "What has man done that only he/Is slave to death. . . ?"30 She takes shelter within the hemlock tree, closing her eyes to the stars and identifying herself with natural life, which seems serene and beautiful and uncaring about death, living only for the moment.

Sara's illness and emotional exhaustion beginning in September 1917 had, in all probability, a specific and serious cause. She had confided in John Hall Wheelock at some point in the early years of her marriage that she was pregnant—but she could not decide whether she really wanted to have the child. Although at one time she claimed a genuine desire for motherhood, her life was not the same now. Marriage had brought insoluble problems and a deepened sense of inadequacy, not fulfillment, and a child would consume the limited energy she needed for her work. It seemed to be a choice between having a child or a career, and she was not only riding the crest of popularity but also developing rapidly in technique and style. Wheelock refused to advise her, feeling that the decision was too serious to be any but her own. After it was over, she told him she had had an abortion.

"It took quite a toll of her," Wheelock said, both physically and in emotional conflict. It seems likely to have occurred in August 1917, when she wrote in her notebook a ruthlessly self-flaying poem "Duty": "Fool," she addresses herself, do not flail at the empty air, "The wrong is done, the seed is sown,/The evil stands." Her duty now is only to create "Out of the web of wrong," from the "ill-woven deeds," her "thread of song." With her rigidly conventional upbringing and her view of life as a set of moral transactions, she would have felt there was a heavy price to pay for this. She would almost certainly, however, have convinced herself that the abortion was necessary on the grounds of health and would have found a legitimate physician who agreed with her. And no doubt it was a threat, for having a child would have destroyed the fragile structure of her life. Still, she would not have been able to escape a sense of guilt toward Ernst or a feeling of failure as a woman, given the assumptions of her life.

By May 1918, she was feeling somewhat improved and went down to Boonton again on May 9 for the spring weather, where Jessie Rittenhouse visited her on the weekend and told her the inside story of an unprecedented honor Sara was about to receive. This was a $500 poetry prize for the best book of poems published in America in 1917, offered jointly by Columbia University and the Poetry Society of America. The Pulitzer prizes had just been established that year, to be awarded through the Columbia University journalism department, although there was no provision for poetry. Edward J. Wheeler, president of the Poetry Society, lobbied for the inclusion of poetry, and managed to secure a $500 gift from a donor for a special prize to supplement the Pulitzer awards. Sara's prize was the first of such temporary awards until the regular series was established in 1922.

Jessie Rittenhouse was one of the three judges selected by the Poetry Society of America, along with Bliss Perry and William Marion Reedy. Although Reedy had helped launch Sara's career in St. Louis, he voted instead for Witter Bynner, his objection to *Love Songs* being that fewer than half of the poems were actually new. Jessie reported his remark that he would "have more credit in St. Louis than he deserves."

The award was the climax of the steady rise of Sara's reputation since the publication of *Rivers to the Sea* in October 1915. Seven years before, she had glimpsed the meaning of success when she sat shyly against the wall and listened to the New York literati debate, and she had aimed for it unswervingly ever since, as a skilled professional who wanted her work to be judged on its quality. The excitement lifted her out of her depression, and, with the spring wildflowers, she was "intoxicated . . . as near heaven as I have been since I was in Italy." She begged Ernst to come down for the weekend, although she knew he couldn't.

Ernst was in for another serious scolding about overworking. Sara had even persuaded his sister Irma to write him, for she had "talked until I am tired out." Against her advice, he had agreed to do the commercial traveler's guide to Latin America for the U.S. Department of Commerce and was taking six language lessons a week, preparing for trips abroad that Lawrence had discussed with him. When she "told him a lot of plain truths about his appearance . . . all he said was '*Please*, darling, let up on this. You are spoiling the few minutes that we have together.'" When he was unmoved by her terrible predictions of a "complete physical and nervous breakdown," she decided that "*two* people could be stubborn," and threatened to go away and not return until he had dropped either the three French or the three Russian lessons. He yielded and gave up the Russian lessons.

Their income ran about $500 a year short of expenses, and they had borrowed from Ernst's family to get through the financial crisis surrounding the dissolution of the shoe company, which had finally been settled without public disgrace. "I have been thinking seriously of trying to get a steady job as critic," she wrote Ernst, "so that I could add $25 to $50 a month to what I already make. You would then not have so much to worry you—and as we both prefer to *make* money rather than be saving of it, I think this is a good plan. . . . I can't let you ruin your health and spirits by continued hack-work like the books you have done in the last three years. . . . Your words that you intend to try to get another job like the guide, as soon as it is finished, have made me nearly frantic. After my prize award, my services as critic should be worth more than they are now." She also thought of turning to short story writing, which paid well in comparison with poetry. But neither of these proposals, like play writing, came to anything.

Sara's close friends could see that Ernst's way of filling up all his waking hours with work, days and evenings and weekends, was related to the many frustrations of his marriage. He was a highly emotional and excitable person who exercised great self-control, who would never contradict or criticize Sara or allow her to think he was disappointed in her in any way. He was immensely proud of her achievements and had memorized much of her poetry. Although never expressing anger at her, he was given to occasional violent outbursts over small things, like the frayed cuffs on shirts returned from the laundry. Sara seemed oddly imperceptive about the intensity with which he drove himself, although her uneasiness and constant complaining about it suggest that his behavior touched some sense of guilt within herself.

Her own life was as relentlessly orderly as it had always been, with breakfasts brought up from the hotel kitchen and dinners, too, when she felt ill. Otherwise, they took all their meals in the dining room. She had a maid, a black girl, once a week; and she avoided excitement, fleeing to some country retreat whenever the demands on her time or energy seemed too great. Her gentleness, her very helplessness, had, as Vachel Lindsay had perceptively observed, a quality of ironlike strength that managed to shape the affairs of life to her liking. She enjoyed her prominence as a popular poet, and, as John Hall Wheelock remarked, she had a keen "political" sense of how to be successful, withholding poems that might confuse her public image or disturb her followers. Yet she insisted that she wrote from a deep sense of obligation, as if it were unwomanly to write poetry and enjoy success simply because she wanted to.

She returned from Boonton refreshed and elated over the prize and the publicity in newspapers across the country. She received the check for $500 on June 7, and issued a written statement that was printed in newspapers as an "interview." She declared herself on the matter of controversy among schools of poetry, saying that "poetic form is not of any real importance at all. The only vital thing about a poem is its content.

If a poem is of any value it must spring directly from the experience of the writer—not necessarily from an external experience, but at least from a spiritual one. If a poem is sincere and springs from deep emotion, no matter what the form, it will be of value to us." She recommended that children be taught to write and enjoy poetry early in life, but not by being forced to memorize Longfellow, as she had been, which had nearly stifled her love of poetry. "Children, who are all really barbarians, should be given the sort of poetry that semi-barbarous people make and enjoy—ballads full of primitive and even brutal feeling. If this were done, there would be joy and not disgust whenever a poem appears on the page of a school reader." She added a reason that was peculiarly her own: "It is the best antidote for the morbid repression that many of us have inherited from generations of Puritan ancestors."

Harriet Monroe congratulated Sara editorially in *Poetry*, but only after taking well-measured slaps at the Poetry Society of America and the credentials of the three judges, on the grounds that the prize winner should have been selected by a jury of her peers, reputable poets in their own right. The Poetry Society had been in the habit of awarding its previous annual prizes in a "singularly provincial and haphazard way," she said.[31] Miss Monroe would have preferred to see the prize go to Ezra Pound or H. D., but H. D. was no longer an American citizen, and Pound's *Lustra* did not qualify, since it had been first published in England in 1916. Sara seemed to win by default.

Jessie Rittenhouse, nettled by Harriet Monroe's remark that her own "recent small volume of verse could hardly be accepted as evidence that she is one of the more distinguished poets on [the Poetry Society's] rolls," fumed to Braithwaite that Harriet was trying to steal all the credit again: After "we had practically created the field and the public attitude had changed, came Harriet Monroe with a blare of trumpets proclaiming from the housetops that *Poetry* created the renaissance. . . . Miss Monroe has no use for my judgment of poetry and I am free to confess I have no use for hers."[32] It was one of Sara's miracles of diplomacy that she managed all her life to remain a good friend of both these women. Amy Lowell congratulated Jessie Rittenhouse on the judges' decision: Sara has "a power over lyrics which is not equaled by any one in this contry. She is a despair to me. I read her things again and again and wonder how she does them. They are the utmost economy of means and yet the result is adequate."

The excitement, however, brought Sara down with prolonged indigestion and facial neuralgia, and on July 19, 1918 she went to Nahant, Massachusetts for a month, her fifth such trip in the past year. "For all her triumphs she has been in miserable health, poor girl," Ernst wrote Irma. Sara could not walk for more than fifteen or twenty minutes at a time and had written almost nothing for weeks. Ernst had been approached by the Department of Commerce about going on an assignment to Brazil, and Sara thought she would go with him, although she did not relish the bother of packing and storing their things. Still, she wrote Eunice Tietjens, who was in France, "New York isn't so much to me now as it was. Ernst is the dearest man that ever a woman loved, and if I can be with him, all is well." She was trying "to pull myself together after much worry. . . . You would not know America. It is a different country from the one you left ten months ago—soldiers everywhere and food very restricted. . . . I wonder if things will ever return—that is during our lifetimes—to the old careless plenty that we grew up in? When I think of the days when we first knew each other, how utterly like a nightmare it would have seemed then to be told that every man between 18 and 45 would be at the absolute command of the government in five years time. Five years only since then, and the world is so different I often wonder if I am sane and wide awake."

When the draft age had been raised to forty-five, Sara did not wait to see whether Ernst would be drafted—he was thirty-eight—but persuaded several of her doctors to testify that ill health made it impossible for her to earn a living and that he was needed to support and care for her. As a result, he was classified 4-B.

The assignment to Brazil did not materialize, to Sara's satisfaction, but by the time the armistice came on November 11 he was considering a business trip to Cuba. Sara stayed indoors during the tumultuous celebration in the streets, but Ernst reported that "the most thrilling feature was the indiscriminate kissing of soldiers and sailors by young women," she told her sisters-in-law. "He said that it was most wildly done and very common all along the streets. Isn't that a strange return to the old Bacchic orgies?"

She was ill for a month with influenza, spent another few days at Cromwell, and continued to write little. Her mood was retrospective—"I Have Loved Hours at Sea," and "Places"—"Places I love come back to me like music"—the poem that concludes with a description of her shipboard romance with Hatfield. He had been on her mind since August, when an English composer named Treharne visited her and Ernst in New York with news that Hatfield was actually thriving in the German prison camp at Ruhleben, organizing an Arts and Science Union among the prisoners. But a more interesting poem is "Only in Sleep," about her dreams of children she had played with when a child, revised before publication to soften its negative tone. The second stanza begins "Only in sleep Time is forgotten," but in manuscript reads "Only in sleep Time cannot hurt us." In her dream, "we played last night as long ago/With stealthy secrets whispered low," the second line being changed to the more innocuous "And the doll-house stood at the head of the stair"—

Sara Teasdale, age 7.
She was not fond
of dolls.
Photo courtesy of
Margaret C. Conklin.

Sara Teasdale, about 5, with fist
clenched in rebellious mood.
Photo courtesy of
Margaret C. Conklin.

Sara Teasdale,
about 1913.
Photo courtesy of
Margaret C. Conklin.

Sara Teasdale, about the time of her marriage, 1914.
Photo courtesy of Margaret C. Conklin.

John Hall Wheelock,
about 1918.
Photo courtesy of Mrs.
John Hall Wheelock.

Vachel Lindsay, 1913.
Photo courtesy of
Eleanor Ruggles.

Sara Teasdale,
about 1920.
Photo courtesy of
Nikolas Muray.

Ernst Filsinger,
about 1920.
Photo courtesy of
Mrs. Irma Wetteroth.

Sara Teasdale, 1927.
Photo courtesy of
E.O. Hoppé, London.

Ernst Filsinger and
Captain Bentley in
South Africa, before
Johannesburg-to-
Berlin flight, 1929.

Ernst Filsinger,
South Africa, 1929,
after receiving news
of the divorce.
Photo courtesy of
Mrs. Irma Wetteroth.

Margaret Conklin, 1932.
Photo courtesy of
Margaret C. Conklin.

John Hall Wheelock,
about 1930.
Photo courtesy of
Charles Scribner's Sons.

Sara Teasdale, 1932.
Photo courtesy of
E.O. Hoppé, London.

proper little girls played with dolls rather than exchanging "stealthy secrets." The poem as published ends with the lines

> Do they, too, dream of me, I wonder,
> And for them am I, too, a child?[33]

In her notebook she had originally written:

> I, an eager shadowy child
> Care had not darkened, nor pain defiled.

The revision was an effort to shut out her morbid thoughts, but they were like the ominous figure in "The Strong House," written in November 1918 and published in the *Pictorial Review* but never collected. "Our love is like a strong house," it begins,

> The doors are fast, the lamps are lit,
>   We sit together talking low—
> Who is it in the ghostly dusk
>   Goes to and fro?
>
> Surely ours is a strong house,
>   I will not trouble anymore—
> Who comes stealing at midnight
>   To try the locked door?

Sara had a secret obsessive fear of a threat to her marriage, doubtless intensified by the abortion, and once was so troubled by an incident that she asked Jack Wheelock's advice. She had gone into Ernst's bedroom to wake him one morning, and half asleep, he muttered—or she thought he did—"She'll never die, she'll never die." It happened more than once, she said. Sara jumped to the conclusion that Ernst had another woman and that she was in the way and he wanted to get rid of her. Wheelock burst out laughing at the absurdity of it and assured her that no husband was ever more genuinely devoted than Ernst. But the incident always haunted her. It never occured to her that these words could also have expressed his deep anxiety over her health and his determination that she live, if indeed they had any reference to her at all.

They sailed for Havana around December 8, 1918. Sara paid her own expenses out of her prize money in order to be with him, for although she often left him to be alone with her work she felt a panic when it was he who left her, unless it were for only a day or two. The trip proved to be not very successful, for a general strike broke out creating countless inconveniences. They attended the opera on December 17, she wrote Irma, and "saw the flower of Cuban society. It was really a wonderfully brilliant and beautiful sight." But she had carried her fears with her, and a poem she wrote in Havana on December 20—"In a Cuban Garden"—

expresses, like "The Strong House," her clinging to love for security against some lurking deadly threat:

> Hibiscus flowers are cups of fire,
>     (Love me, my lover, life will not stay)
> The bright poinsettia shakes in the wind,
>     A scarlet leaf is blowing away.
>
> A lizard lifts his head and listens—
>     Kiss me before the noon goes by,
> Here in the shade of the ceiba hide me
>     From the great black vulture circling the sky.[34]

This poem marks an important psychological change in her treatment of death, which had heretofore been depicted as rest or sleep, relief from conflict. Here it becomes a menacing presence, like the muffled figure who tries the lock on her house of love where she had hidden for safety. When she wrote of yearning for rest, of being kept among the living by the force of her pride, she was in command of her feelings about death. "In a Cuban Garden" reveals a terror at losing that control, of being stalked by death, and appeals for help. The poem is artistically perfect in its way, an example of the mastery that Amy Lowell admired so greatly, in its utmost economy of means—without obvious metaphor, simply the presentation of vividly contrasting images of love and death whose impact makes superfluous any other kind of statement.

On December 23, on the return voyage, she wrote "At Sea," describing herself on the deck of the ship alone in a wild storm at night, with earth and sea hostile: "I must fight always and die fighting/With fear an unhealing wound in my breast."[35]

With dismay, she learned in January 1919 that Ernst was to be sent shortly to Europe to open up new trade connections for the Lawrence Company following the peace and the rebuilding of the European countries' economies. She dreaded the prospect of the months alone, and wrote to Eunice Tietjens asking if she could be "warm and confortably well-fed" if she stationed herself in Paris while Ernst rushed about Europe on his mission. "I have been in miserable health for ages and so life is not such a thrilling adventure as I wish it were," she said wryly. The European cities were suffering shortages of food and fuel, and she thought it would be foolish to go abroad where she would likely be uncomfortable and almost as lonely as in New York. She decided to stay. "I almost break down when we talk of his going," she told her friend Marguerite Wilkinson. "Yet I want him to go."[36]

The preparations for the long trip were immense, and the time was short. The night before Ernst sailed, a secretary typed late to finish the manuscript of his book, while he gathered together his hundred letters of introduction, textile samples, price lists, and sales materials, and Sara packed his steamer trunk. She had taken charge of organizing him in her usual methodical and thorough fashion. His Scandinavian-American Line ship sailed for Copenhagen on Wednesday, February 8, 1919.

Depressed at his absence and annoyed at the heavy volume of mail to answer, which now included Ernst's, she decided in less than a week to go down to Boonton, New Jersey, again. She was prompted to leave sooner than she intended by a note from Harriet Monroe announcing that she was coming to New York and would stay with Sara in the apartment. Horrified at this intrusion into her privacy, Sara wired her that she had the flu and was just leaving for the country to take care of herself, as she had promised Ernst she would do.

Ernst, meanwhile, was having a delightful time, which he desperately wished Sara could share with him. He was outgoing, made friends easily, and loved to have fun with groups of people, exactly opposite in temperament from Sara. As his ship moved through the Gulf Stream, the nights grew warm and there was dancing on the deck, with entertainment by Norwegian folk singers and Danish and Swedish folk dancers. The champagne flowed freely, and there were jolly times in the smoker. The trip was Ernst's great opportunity; neither he nor Sara felt he could refuse it because of her health. She had come to live virtually the life of an invalid. In the past year, she had attended only two meetings of the Poetry Society and had sent Ernst to functions where she had to be represented—even to the opera or theatre with friends like Jean Untermeyer, so he could enjoy an occasional evening of amusement without having to depend on her.

Sara stayed at the Pudding Stone Inn for a month, avoiding mail and the ringing telephone. Harriet Monroe came down to visit her there, with her usual mixture of sentimental warmth and acerbity. Sara found Miss Monroe's possessiveness toward her poets annoying as well as her obsession with taking credit for everything new in poetry. But Sara admired her incisive mind and her staunch integrity, and she had come to share something of Harriet Monroe's disdain for the Poetry Society of America, "often a hopeless place if one is expecting any spiritual awakening." But "it is always entertaining from the human standpoint—and you meet your friends in a pleasantly informal way. . . . I'm sure if you could sit way in the back of the room with Ernst and me you would find it delightful. That is the only place where you can laugh and not be found out." The air of jingoistic patriotism at so many of the meetings during the war must have been offensive to her and Ernst. Even Amy Lowell had paranoid moments about German spies. In any case, her friendships with Jessie Rittenhouse and others were personal, not dependent on the society.

The conversations with Harriet Monroe at the Pudding Stone Inn, followed by a reading of her editorial on Max Eastman in the March 1919

*Poetry,* criticizing his "lingering conservatism," stimulated Sara to write a vigorous letter to the editor in response. Having put it in the mail, however, she was seized with misgivings and wired Harriet Monroe the next day, withdrawing permission to print it. "It is not that I have gone back on anything I have said in the letter—far from it. But it was borne in upon me . . . that I had no business engaging in controversies." Sara bridled whenever anyone judged poetry according to the fashionableness of its form.

> Of the five poets (Carl Sandburg, H. D., Aldington, Amy Lowell and Ezra Pound) whose work H. M. mentions as examples of "severely modelled classic shape," all but one (Sandburg), are associated in our minds with translations that they have made of poems from other languages, or poems of theirs based on the spirit of those in another language. With unbounded admiration for poems in Greek, Provençal or Japanese, composed according to the most exacting rules, why is it that their own poems in English are for the most part in free verse? I imagine, for the very good reason that they feel they can render what H. M. called "the old pagan clarity" better in this way. The charm of the strangeness of a foreign tongue, has its counterpart for them in the strangeness and the freshness of poetry that has set aside old measures and old rules. No one could be more grateful than I, for the beauty that they have given us in the new forms.

It seemed contradictory, then, to "speak regretfully of Mr. Eastman's championship of exact metrics" when this was the very essence of the highly traditional poetry in other languages admired by the free verse poets. "There seems to be a feeling that if more of us could free our poetry of lines having approximately the same number of syllables, and stanzas each having the same number of lines, we should be happier and better poets. But is it not evident to the editor that fairly regular rhythm, modified by variations within itself, and regular recurrence of rhymes are joy and freedom, not bondage, to those poets who choose them of their own free will and who use them with ease? They enhance the fun of the game as the conventions enhance the fun of life." The vogue for free verse really depended on the public's love of novelty rather than on any intrinsic superiority of form, she concluded.

Nevertheless, Sara had come to agree that *Poetry* had been "the greatest single factor in the re-birth of poetry in this country. In almost every case it has printed the best work of a given author—never his second best." Sara had not only survived the upheaval that accompanied the advent of literary modernism, but had learned many valuable lessons: self-irony, freedom from formula, rigorous craftsmanship, a concern for theory, and a firmer sense of her own mode. The poet she admired most was Yeats. "I've been reading Yeats furiously again," she told Harriet Monroe. "He is the greatest poet living without the shadow of a doubt."

At the end of April, back at Boonton, New Jersey, again with a severe case of depression and a sore throat, Sara accepted appointment as a judge for the Columbia-Poetry Society prize for the best work of 1918. The other two judges were professors Richard Burton and William Lyon Phelps, who were "in absolute accord at first that no new free verse poetry should be recognized at all," as Sara confided to Harriet Monroe. "If professors ever are in the vanguard, it will be at a very distant date." The prize money had not been secured until the last week of April, and the judges were required to reach a decision by May 24, so there was no time for announcements to appear in most of the journals. As a result, few nominations were made, and Sara was concerned that this might give the conservative judges an excuse for ignoring books they did not care to read. She had been reading virtually every book of poetry published in 1918 and felt that Sandburg's *Cornhuskers* was "head and shoulders above everything else." She was free to vote for it even though it hadn't been nominated, but she took the precaution of having Harriet Monroe nominate it and send a copy to the judges. Her second choice was Masters, and her third was either Conrad Aiken or Lola Ridge. None of her potential nominees were associated with the Poetry Society; all were identified in the public mind with "modernism," and Lola Ridge's *The Ghetto and Other Poems* was furthermore politically leftist. Sara considered Aiken's work to be "preoccupied with over-sophisticated states of mind," she told Harriet, and Ridge's to be artistically uneven, although both appeared superior to most of the other entries.

To her dismay, both of the other judges wanted to award the prize to Margaret Widdemer and would not listen to any of her recommendations, a judgment "typically professorial," she declared. Not easily discouraged from pressing her point, Sara "fought, bled, and nearly died . . . and finally made the judges agree to split the prize" between Sandburg and Widdemer, since neither side could agree with the other on a single candidate. She feared she had made enemies in the Poetry Society by her action. But she believed that the prize ought to go to poetry artistically more challenging than the innocuous lyricism the Poetry Society fostered.

Ernst's leaving her for such a long trip was more disturbing than the mere loneliness she felt. In spite of her frequent admonishments to herself that no one could put her soul in order but herself alone, she had come to depend on Ernst's presence to keep her morbid moods at bay. And the more she relied on her marriage for a sense of safety from her own destructive thoughts, the more fearful she became that Ernst might be unfaithful. His worry-ridden, work-filled evenings and weekends, his business trips, were like a reproach for her lack of strangth, a deliberate defiance. Just at the time when her emotions had taken a worse turn, he set off on a six-months absence, and she was alone with her problems, hovering between the emotional dependence she could not escape, with its sense of neglect, and the stoical self-sufficiency she believed to be her salvation.

After having fended off her threatening emotional problems for months, she spent the lonely spring of 1919 trying once more to define and come to terms with them through her poetry. The poems she wrote were unflinching studies of her losses, and at times even the poetry seemed a worthless and little-understood residue of a life that had been spent in a slow, silent bleeding to death. Her sleepless nights and restless days, her nerves like "the ceaseless cry/Of wind in a tight-drawn wire," years and years of them, had left her

> nothing
> But a handful of songs like these
> That people think were happily written
> In an hour of ease.

When she looks into her heart as into a mirror "that once reflected what will not return," she sees that all the other faces are gone, only the image of her own eyes remains, and "the unsatisfied/ Dark fires with which they burn." The great moments that she had treasured like jewels have turned into "These songs, as useless as ashes."

In "Dust," she also likens one such memory to a jewel and goes to it trembling, "for I thought to see its dark deep fire—/ But only a pinch of dust blew up in my face." This particular memory is probably of Stafford Hatfield, for she continues

> I almost gave my life long ago for a thing
> That has gone to dust now, stinging my eyes.[37]

She was allowing herself to resurrect in Ernst's absence the desire for love, which had never been fulfilled in her marriage; "imeros" still irritated the wound that would not be healed. She had been unable to feel any passionate love for Ernst, even though she had tried, and was trapped now, with no hope of ever being free to love anyone else. But the problem lay much deeper within herself, even beyond this frustration. In marriage she had only perpetuated the lethal struggle between passion and inhibition that had crippled her since girlhood. One can surmise that she had instinctively grasped at a conventional and loveless marriage rather than face a relationship that would have incited unmanageable guilt and fear, no matter how much she desired that relationship. The terms of the conflict were within herself, and external circumstances only had a fatal way of conforming. The safe, "strong house" of her marriage was also a prison, where she slowly wasted away; but the other kind of love that lurked outside was both tempting and terrifying. Like the storm wind, it made her "glad and afraid." The figure that waited to seize her was not only love—it was death. The identification of passionate love with death had been implicit in her poems almost from the beginning, not only in the ecstatic desire for loss of self "as a light is lost in light," but more overtly in "Sappho," where suicide in the sea expressed Sappho's escape from the compulsion of love, and yet its perfect fulfillment. In April 1919, she explored her ambivalent emotions more openly than she had dared to do before. In "Night after Night," a shadowy figure paces back and forth beneath her window. "Is it a lover wanting me?" she asks. She abruptly draws shut the curtain "with caught breath—/I make no sign, I am free of blame."

> Oh is it Love or is it Death,
> Are they the same?

"Spring is a hard time to live through," she wrote Harriet Monroe, because spring embodied the promise of love. "Why am I waking/ To the old longing in the old way?" she asked herself. She walked on the avenue, and "Many and many a man passed,/ But not one was mine." Home was the place for her—"There I can lock the door/ And keep spring away." It was inevitable that in a mood like this she should dwell on John Hall Wheelock again. He was still an enigma: "I cannot tell if you love me/ Or do not love me at all," she wrote;

> I know many things,
>   But the years come and go,
> I shall die not knowing
>   The thing I long to know.[38]

"I understood the rest too well/ . . . But you I never understood."[39] She endured an enforced silence, "Like a rock that knows the cry of the waters/ And cannot answer at all."[40] But the mood of fatalistic resignation began to permeate even this last source of consolation. No love had ever been spoken between them or even communicated silently by looks and gestures. She had "only a hush of the heart. . . . Only memories waking/ That sleep so light a sleep."[41] In the spring of 1919, she wrote a lyric about her love for Wheelock that has often been considered one of her finest: "Let It Be Forgotten." With its repetition of the word *forgotten* six times in eight short lines, its ambiguous but evocative imagery—"Forgotten as a fire that once was singing gold/ . . . as a hushed footfall/ In a long forgotten snow"[42] —it was "one of the best songs I've ever done," she told Harriet Monroe, "and comes nearer in music and a sort of silence at the end, to what I mean by a lyric, than anything else of mine that I can think of." Sara collected eight of these poems on Wheelock, in which she tried to write an end to her long infatuation, all but one of them written in 1918 and 1919, and published them as an untitled group—section V—in her next book *Flame and Shadow*, in 1920. One of these poems, "Nightfall," had been composed in New York on July 3, 1914, when she finally decided that he would never marry her: "We will never walk again/ As we used to walk at night."43

But although Sara ritualistically laid this hopeless love to rest over and over again, it would not remain buried. On June 18, she visited Jack Wheelock's mother at the family home in East Hampton, Long Island, and within a few weeks had produced another set of poems centering either on Wheelock or on the beaches and landscape around the Wheelock home. These also were published as a group in *Flame and Shadow*, appearing as Section IX, "By the Sea." Bowing to her hopelessness, she now envisaged the possibility of a love-meeting of their spirits after death:

> If life was small, if it has made me scornful,
>   Forgive me; I shall straighten like a flame
> In the great calm of death, and if you want me
>   Stand on the sea-ward dunes and call my name.44

"We shall be happy," she says, "for the dead are free."45

A retrospective stillness settled on her work in 1919, suggesting the end of her hopes for an escape. "What is it all for?" she asked Harriet Monroe in May. "If I could only grow up—but for all my thirty-four years I'm as tragic inside as I was at twenty-two. . . . Oh Harriet, what a mess life is, especially when you are as damned good-for-nothing physically as I have been these past years, so love me—I need it." Her bleak assessment of the future was summed up in "The Long Hill," where she saw her life passing its crest without her knowing it: "But it's no use now to think of turning back,/ The rest of the way will be only going down."46

Sara took pains to present her emotions honestly and to define herself as precisely as possible. She could have written, she said of "the world" and what people said of it, but chose instead to tell of herself, for it was the only thing she knew—

> I have made a chart of a small sea
> But the chart I made is true.

Still, no one, even among her friends, seemed able to read the chart so carefully drawn, in part because she kept hidden in her notebooks the poems that were too revealing, in part because she never abandoned, but only modernized, the Victorian practice of discreetly veiling love in allegory and ambiguity. Occasionally her friends might observe lapses in her good-humored, rational, and orderly public self, but she kept increasingly alone with her hidden problems. She was reading Krafft-Ebing's *Psychopathia Sexualis* in 1919 and displayed a morbid interest in sexual pathology in conversation with her friends. She even wrote erotic limericks, which her close friends considered some of the cleverest they had ever heard, although she took pains to guarantee that none were ever preserved. When Louis Untermeyer complained that her poems did not show her intellect, Sara wrote the poem "What Do I Care?" in response. She considered her intellect equal to that of any of the men she had known well, but accepted Untermeyer's verdict that "my songs do not show me at all"—"It is my heart that makes my songs, not I." This poem is a curious exercise in distancing herself from the emotions that caused her so much torment, while asserting that her "mind is proud and strong enough to be silent." "I am an answer," she says, her songs "are only a call."47

During Ernst's absence, she had explored the guilty emotions that she had not been able to channel into marriage but that had no place else to go. The only alternative was to kill her feelings by an act of will, since she could neither live with them nor assert them through rebellion. Her gradual retreat within herself to a position of immobile, ironic resignation was the pattern she had followed all her life when emotional conflict became unendurable. It was the nearest equivalent to the "rest" she so often wrote of craving in death.

Ernst's adventurous trip through Europe only six months after the armistice frightened Sara, who pictured him facing incalculable danger because of the hard terms of the peace imposed by the Allies. After the Scandinavian countries he had gone on to Poland, Austria, and Germany, where he was the first American businessman to enter following the war. But the Germans seemed cordial, peaceful, well dressed, and well nourished, and had begun a surprisingly rapid recovery. Ernst was convinced that German militarism would never rise again. In early May he cabled Sara to join him in Italy, but after an initial enthusiasm, she decided the trip would be too much for her. Ernst was at Versailles the day the peace was signed, standing in the crowd to watch the great men enter and leave. He had intended to remain in Europe through July, but Lawrence called him home early for consultation. Exhilarated with success—"my sales ran into the millions," he told his parents—he sailed for New York in mid-July on the S.S. *Rotterdam*, which also carried home members of the U.S. peace mission. Sara was at the pier to meet him on July 22, and his wild hugs and kisses knocked the hat-pins out of her hair.

She had changed during Ernst's long absence. Her withdrawal into herself, into a mood of isolated, self-sufficient fatalism, had become pronounced. It was her way of coping with the emotional disorder that Ernst's presence had formerly helped to keep under control. In June, she had written "To E. in Switzerland," where she liked to think of him among the high mountains, which wore "bright immemorial capes of snow. . . . Far above noise and struggle of things." Here his hurried spirit might find a "cold white hour of calm," as if he looked into a polished crystal at "Life, its vast trifles and yourself and me." But the restless Ernst was not easily to be placed under the same glass bell with herself. When she received the news that he was returning earlier than expected, her joy was qualified. "How will hungry Time put by the hours till then?" she asked, and then

> But why does it anger my heart to long so
> For one man out of the world of men?
>
> Oh I would live in myself only
>     And build my life lightly and still as a dream—
> Are not my thoughts clearer than your thoughts
>     And colored like stones in a running stream?

As the moon rises and "The stars are ready, the night is here," the love night of his return,

> Oh why must I lose myself to love you
>     My dear?[48]

And the next day she wrote "The Sanctuary":

> If I could keep my innermost Me
> Fearless, aloof and free
> Of the least breath of love or hate. . .
> If I could keep a sanctuary there
> Free even of prayer. . .
> I could look even at God with grave forgiving eyes.[49]

Sara's instinctive rebellion against marriage had reasserted itself during the six-month separation, and Ernst's return was to some extent an intrusion into her quiet, self-contained life. Shortly after his arrival, she was ill in bed again with flu and bladder pain, after nearly a year and a half of freedom from it. She had decided, she told Harriet Monroe, that women were mistaken to think that men were "rocks" to cling to—"men are never rocks. *I've* never found one. Women are less likely to turn out un-rock-like than men. Women are solider than men—less likely to get all worked up and light-headed. A man is almost always light-headed and somehow you don't mind it after you've learned you have to put up with it. By that I don't mean emotional instability any more than any other kind. Ernst, for instance, is emotionally, so far as likelihood of falling in love with any other woman goes, very stable, but in a general way, more excitable than I—and that's going some."

Their period of readjustment was short-lived. In early August 1919 Ernst learned that he was to be sent on a four-month business tour of South America, to leave on September 6 for Peru. He was to go on south to Valparaiso and Santiago, then over the Andes to Buenos Aires, and up the coast to Rio de Janiero. He begged Sara to accompany him, and at first she agreed. But in the end her fear of over exertion and hardship won out. The hotels were said to be bad and traveling conditions primitive. Again, she dreaded that her weakness, her inability to keep up with Ernst's pace, would create tension between them. And besides, her expenses would run to $2,500, far more than she felt they could afford.

Sara dreaded the continued separation. "Never did I realize before how completely and tremendously I love him," she wrote Jessie. She could not bear to stay in New York alone through the autumn, after the ordeal of nerves she had endured in the spring, which only frequent rest cures in the country could mitigate. She decided to spend the months of Ernst's absence in California, where she would be far away from the ringing telephone and well-meaning friends and could immerse herself in the total peace of isolation and a mild climate that might forestall her annual bout of colds and sore throats. "I fear from my going to California that people may think me a worse invalid than I am," she told Jessie, urging her to come out for a visit.

In haste, they subleased their apartment, furnished, until March 1, and Sara arranged to stay at the El Encanto Hotel in Santa Barbara. Ernst's departure on September 6 left her depressed and annoyed, with countless details to settle. Unable to leave by the fifteenth, she was forced to stay in a guest room for a week, where her irritability mounted. By September 23, she was at last on her way to St. Louis for a brief stopover before traveling on to the West coast. The ten-day visit with her parents was painful, because of their feeble old age and the squabbles over "family finances and politics" between her brother and her father. But, once arrived in Santa Barbara in early October, she recovered her spirits rapidly, as she always did when visiting an attractive new place, before the problems she had left behind could catch up with her.

Santa Barbara reminded her of the Bay of Naples and her heavenly summer in Italy with Jessie Rittenhouse. "This is an adorable place," she wrote Harriet Monroe—"mountains and sea, and air so transparent that you feel as though you could touch the stars with your hand." It seemed drenched in the motionless quiet she loved, an antidote to the tumult of life that always threatened her equilibrium and that seemed personified in her restless, ambitious husband. She organized her life in her usual methodical way, with hours of work on her poems and correspondence, an afternoon nap, and a program of studying French—three lessons a week—and astronomy. She had begun to plan her next book, for which Macmillan had offered a contract at 15 percent royalties, 5 percent more than for her previous book, even though it might be a year and a half away. Her pace had slowed.

The hotel gave Sara a special rate because she was a celebrity, and the local poetesses were soon approaching her for criticism of their work, "all bad," which she gave patiently and courteously. She soon began to rank Santa Barbara above any place in the United States—"Indeed I *am* wild over this place," she wrote Ernst, although its inaction would pall on him, she feared—and she had even taken walks of three or four miles up to a ridgetop for the magnificent wind-swept views of mountain ranges and ocean. The El Encanto Hotel stood on a hilltop about 500 feet above sea level; from her room on the ground floor she had an unobstructed view down the slopes to the sea, and could watch the sunsets, the moonlight, the "madly bright" stars, and the fog rising in. Marguerite Wilkinson had given Sara letters of introduction to friends there, which she had not used, and Harriet Monroe offered letters too. But Sara declined, saying "It's lots of fun to be alone, and with sea and mountains somehow I've not needed people much."

Just as she was leaving New York, she had received from Amy Lowell a copy of her new book *Pictures of the Floating World* and acknowledged it from St. Louis, where she had time only to leaf through it. But on the afternoon of November 20, she reread it in earnest, and the effect was electric. She lay down for her habitual nap but was too excited to sleep:

> There is no way that I can tell you of the *impact* that this book made on rereading it here in this golden air with the quiet and the distance all around me. As I finished it the mountains were royal purple with sunset. And it seemed to me that I realized for the first time what you are. I have liked you and been interested in you for so long—but this was quite different. Suddenly I knew you—the violence and the delicacy—I found you something that I can love in my own way. When we have met, New York or Boston, or my ill-health or your own hurry, or other people, or something else—has always been like a sort of half-lifted veil through which we talked. And it is easier to talk through veils, after all. I take great pains to keep veils between myself and most people, and I suppose you do too. It is too terribly exhausting to talk without veils, to be ones own self and as purely ones self as one may be. I suppose that most people count on their fingers the ones to whom they have been willing to be their whole selves. Usually a very small piece of oneself is quite enough to give even close friends. And it is much simpler so, all around. Well, I wish you were out here now, that's all. But then you aren't—and maybe if you were I'd find myself putting up the veil on one side and tacking it neatly, while you, on your side were hammering at a nail to keep it secure at the other end. And we'd talk of editors and publishers and the latest English poet to come over—just as we usually do. And my mind, which is a neat little machine, would keep itself pleasantly concealed, while you were cutting yours down so as to fit the apparent size of mine—and there we'd be. Well, there's no use—only there are so few women in the world who interest me at all—I'm sorry that one of them who interests me mightily at this minute, is so far away.

It was Sara's test of poetry that it should bring one in touch with a living presence, and Amy Lowell's book did that for her. "Every word in these poems is new washed, clean, burning with brightness," she said. A few of the poems seemed "defiled by your own splendid technique by exhibiting it too openly. . . . The book as a whole is so full of you, so vital, that it is not the technique one wants to think of but the human being behind it." Afterward, she feared that her own burst of self-exposure was a "bit too impetuous" and would prove embarassing, but was relieved when Amy responded with kindly warmth. "I've never quite outgrown my childhood," Sara apologized, and "and it is all too evident in moments of enthusiasm." But as Sara agonized over the horror of self-exhibition, Amy Lowell observed ironically, "I think it is very curious how we people do manage to get ourselves down on paper and publish it and let the world read it and not turn a hair. It seems to go with the gift somehow, for even you, although you balk at hearing [your poems] read in public, print them for all the world to see. Surely we poets are a queer lot, and no wonder our psychology puzzles the layman."

Sara's study of the stars in the autumn of 1919 was a search for a principle of permanence in a universe where everything of value, including one's own life, would eventually be lost. In July, she had written "Since There Is No Escape":

> . . .since at the end
> My body will be utterly destroyed. . . .
> Since there is no escape even for me
> Who love life with a love too sharp to bear. . .
> Let me go down as waves sweep to the shore
> In pride; and let me sing with my last breath.[50]

Her poems of late summer and early fall dwelt on the happy free days with Wheelock that could never return, on her love for her father, on her loneliness. "It comforts me a little," she wrote, that the stars

> will not change at all
> Though change takes everything.

The stars in their obedient and orderly paths were a reminder of the law that decreed a system of things in which love of life and beauty were given only to be ironically and cruelly canceled by death. One's spirit was torn between rebellion and submission to the inevitable. In "November Stars," she recited a catalog of the names of stars she had learned:

> The noiseless marching of the stars
> Sweeps above me all night long. . .
> Without haste, without rest.[51]

She published the poem in 1930 as "Rhyme of November Stars" in her book for children, *Stars To-Night,* but omitted the concluding lines that expressed her profound frustration and questioning:

> Splendor of many stars and the unknown
> Invisible lights with which all space is strown,

With what unwearied patience you submit
To the One Will that must be infinite—
Your steadfast immortality
Half angers and half comforts me,
Serenely ordered, on and on
You will shine—I shall be gone.

She would be happy, she wrote in "Compensation" on November 13, to produce one poem

As hushed and brief as a falling star
On a winter night.[52]

The flight of the falling star, although brief, was free. But she was ambivalent toward the vast network of fixed stars, whose submissive serenity was bought at the cost of all she lived for.

Stars appear in Christian tradition as sparks of divine intelligence, or as the illumination of consciousness, identified with individual souls. Jung sees such imagery as having a "uniting character" for the troubled individual.[53] For Sara, the stars were the soul's counterpart, but mocked human mortality rather than giving promise.

Throughout most of the autumn of 1919, Sara felt "more perky than for a long time," she wrote Amy Lowell, "and if it weren't that I miss Ernst, I'd be completely happy—or *almost,* at any rate, as happy as a human being has a right to be." Life at Santa Barbara was a distillation of all appealing things—the dry golden warmth, the gardens incredibly banked with flowers, the Mediterranean blue of the sea, the delicious food, and above all the magnificent silent spaces. She did not force herself to work. "Maybe a poem comes to me at night, maybe not," she wrote Jessie. Yet by the time the winter rains began at the end of November, her depression had returned, she reported to Ernst, along with a bad cold "that manifested itself in one of my colossal fever blisters, general malaise, and weakness." She had not expected to become ill in the mild climate and was also disappointed that two months' rest and idling had done nothing to bring back the strength she had lost at the time of the abortion. She missed Ernst keenly, writing a poem on November 29 about the "sound of useless rain in the desolate courtyard" at night:

If you were here, if you were only here—
My blood calls out to you all night in vain.

The approaching Christmas would be the first they had not spent together since their marriage five years before. "Aren't we growing to be an old couple?" she wrote him. To memorialize their wedding anniversary on December 19, she wrote "It Will Not Change," originally titling it "Love" (which explains the reference to "it"):

It will not change now
    After so many years;
Life has not broken it
    With parting or tears;
Death will not alter it,
    It will live on
In all my songs for you
    When I am gone.54

In this nostalgic mood, ill and lonely in the Christmas season and restless for Ernst's return early the next year, she received a cable from him, sometime before December 21, that upset her violently: Lawrence had asked him to sail directly from South America to meet him in London on February 1, 1920 for a special mission in Europe without returning home first. Ernst would continue to be gone at least until late spring; to mitigate the disappointment, he urged Sara to join him abroad.

Sara's cold had turned to bronchitis, and she lay in bed with a bad cough trying unenthusiastically to seem more cheerful for Ernst than she felt, "though I should be more sincerely myself if I were to curse heaven and my abominable health." She felt petulant and annoyed about everything, even to her stoicism in having got along without a trained nurse throughout their five years of marriage, "a record which may have been foolish on my part if longevity is a thing to be desired," on the assumption that each cold lessened her long-range resistance a little more. "I do hope you will not have to keep this traveling up indefinitely," she begged Ernst. "Yet, after all, a life of action is the happy life. A life like mine which consists almost wholly of meditation is damned gloomy. If only I had better health I would have no cause for complaint. I could go with you and that would be jolly all around. . . . I truly envy you your travels. How I long for bodily health to take them!"

She went outdoors on Christmas Day for the first time in a week, to sit in the warm sunshine, feeling how strange it was that they should be worlds away from each other, and then wrote Ernst at length about some changes in her will she had been considering. She would rather they leave money for prizes to young poets than for relatives who didn't need it. "To be frank, my own life does not seem to me so tough an affair as to make death necessarily quite remote. For this reason, I am the more anxious to enjoy as much as I can, and therefore I hope to go abroad in the late spring, even if I am not up to doing much but taking things quietly when I get there, and even though my going should cost more than it might at first seem worth. I do wish that Jessie were going over! She is an almost ideal traveling companion, and as I shall have to be alone so much after I reach Europe or England—especially if I am no stronger than I have been during the last years." There was a certain pathos, even defiance, in Sara's proposal to join Ernst in Europe and be with him as much as his busy schedule and her weakness would allow, so she could crowd some enjoyment into her own life. His suddenly extended absence had again roused her fear of being neglected and betrayed. "I am sorry for anybody, no matter what mistakes he or she has made," she said apropos of a recent affair of Edgar Lee Masters, "who has loved anyone deeply and been deceived.... Life for me would cease to be life under such conditions. Oh my darling, I love you, I love you! Kiss me, over and over!"

Sara had begun work on her new book in early December, whose title was taken from some lines of Hugo she had read, "Reçois la flamme ou l'ombre/ De tous mes jours," and she had counted on Ernst's returning to help her put it together. The critical task of selecting and grouping the poems was next in importance to composing them, and she needed him. Macmillan wanted the manuscript by June 1920. Other practical problems crowded in on her. The apartment in New York would have to be subleased again until October 1, arrangements had to be made for her to go abroad, and their tangled problems with New York State income tax needed to be straightened out, all from the distance of 3,000 miles. She could not blame Ernst for following the path of ambition, as she saw it, but he was leaving her to her own resources too long, and she was drifting into the hopelessness she perennially fought against.

She was homesick, she wrote in "I Am Borne Onward," for the "triumphant certainties" of the religious faith of her ancestors, for she had to weigh everything in fragile scales of her own making; they each had a guardian angel to lean on—"I am alone." Santa Barbara no longer gave her any solace. Instead of stars and sunlight, she wrote about the fog, the "cold white ghost of the sea," which rose to inundate the land, "the whole world gone blind," blotting out even herself:

> I put my head on my hands before me,
>     There is nothing left to be done or said,
> There is nothing to hope for, I am tired,
>     And heavy as the dead.[55]

In "White Fog," written in March, she again described the engulfed world, where

> The one unchanging thing is I,
>     Myself remains to comfort me.[56]

California was overrated, she wrote the Untermeyers. She had suffered several colds by mid-February in spite of its famous climate: "So much for the golden coast." She was disgusted with the idle rich who dominated Santa Barbara, who "fritter their lives away on polo, golf, 'motoring' (as they call it) and such stuff with a sort of 'well-bred ennui' no matter what is going on."

Sara finally received Ernst's letters explaining why he had been sent so urgently to Europe. The Lawrence Company had combined with several other firms—bankers, cotton brokers, and engineers—to form a commission to investigate the purchasing of shares in textile mills in central Europe. They were to meet in London, then visit Germany, Austria, Czechoslovakia, and Poland, where he and Lawrence would negotiate with prominent international business and political figures. As Ernst wrote his parents, "I wonder if you can appreciate what it means to me to have this great chance?"

Sara contemplated the gradually diverging paths of their lives as they both achieved success in their careers. Despite their being apart, "let us be glad that you are doing such wonderfully interesting work and that you are having a chance to prove to the world the great ability that is in you! What a tragedy it would be if you, of all people, had had to spend your life as a hinterlander, drudging in a small way at small things! When a soul has power, the greatest blessing that life can give us is an opportunity to use that power. . . . The fact that we can't be together is the bitter drop in a cup overflowing with rich wine."

Sara was less despondent as spring approached and Ernst wrote that he would be returning on May 1. She canceled her plans to meet him abroad, glad to avoid the trip, having heard from friends that conditions in Europe were still unsettled and uncomfortable. She was buoyed, too, by a flood of enthusiastic reports on his European adventure. His letters arrived more regularly than they had from South America. She had been reading the *Vie d'une Ame* of Thérèse Martin, soon to be canonized as Saint Thérèse, the "Little Flower," and drew her own conclusions: "Not much *life* in such an existence, but somehow the account of her cramped little soul throws light on the working of the human mind. And from that standpoint it is valuable. The more one comes to think about life, the more one realizes that it is necessary to get a certain amount of 'kick' out of it. But whether the 'kick' is obtained from sorrow or joy, love, war, religion or art makes very little difference in the end."

Santa Barbara was enlivened in late spring by the impending visit of Yeats, who was scheduled to speak at the Women's Club on April 7. Harriet Monroe's sister, Mrs. Calhoun, was in Santa Barbara and attended the lecture with Sara, passing a note to Yeats beforehand for her, asking him and his wife to tea afterward. Harriet had written Sara that the great poet had been "crusty" in Chicago; but he was charming, full of humor, and without condescension before the Santa Barbara women, reminiscing about the Abbey Theatre. "Although we had been told that there would be no reception for Yeats afterward," she wrote Ernst, "we waylaid him in a side room and he was very cordial. I was so embarrassed and excited that I could hardly speak. There is no other artist in the world for whom I feel the same veneration and enthusiasm. He spoke of knowing my name and liking my work, but he is a rather vague person so that I suppose his knowledge of S. T. is very limited."

The women were disappointed not to meet the wife of their hero, for whom they had a devouring curiosity, but she had not attended the lecture. The Yeatses were guests of a rich Chicagoan who whisked the poet away in a waiting automobile as Sara and Mrs. Calhoun were stepping into their own car. Suspecting that Mrs. Yeats was in the other automobile, they sped past it and indeed got a glimpse of a "ruddy and well-developed, rather pretty" woman in her mid-thirties. They shortly found themselves "by chance" at a tea room in the old De la Guerra mansion, "much frequented by the elite," where the Yeatses had been taken for tea, and installed themselves at a nearby table with a full view of Yeats and his wife. "She looks aboundingly healthy and muscular," Sara reported, "somewhat masculine. . . . I agree with the verdict that I have heard from Harriet. . .that *Mrs.* Yeats is the 'the boss.' . . . Knowing Mr. Yeats' poetry as well as I do, I think that I absolutely understand the attraction between them. His feminine streak is offset by her masculine one and the balance is good, but I should think there would probably be more thoroughgoing admiration and affection than romantic love on either side." Sara herself had avoided socializing with the local people, maintaining a strict privacy throughout the year. "I could be a lioness with a regal air and be fearfully sought after, if I cared to and had the strength," she wrote Ernst. "But you know how little such a course appeals to me: Indiscriminate admiration is easy to have—and not worth the having." She had been invited to receive an honorary Doctor of Letters degree from Baylor University in June 1920, along with Amy Lowell, Vachel Lindsay, and Edwin Markham, although she privately called it "flapdoodle" and declined. The others accepted.

Then, in the happy flush of the Yeats visit, she received a letter from Ernst telling of a further delay in his return. It gave her "a nightmare of the most hideous kind. . . . I woke up in a dreadful state of anguish. I had dreamed that as soon as you came home, you told me that you had to go away again. I was both heartbroken and rebellious and I kept saying: 'I can't live this way, I won't live this way.' "

She had given up hope of his helping her with her book, since he now would not be back until June, and she worked through it alone as she prepared to leave Santa Barbara and return to New York to find them a place to live. As her train pulled out of Santa Barbara on April 26, she felt "a mingled feeling of sadness and elation that always comes to me when I leave a place where I have been for some time. The strange way that your soul carries your body around—or is it that your body carries your soul around?—always comes to me at such times with a sharp shock. I say to myself: 'I'll die and never see it again.' It isn't that I care especially to go back or that I leave anything I love; it is simply the queer feeling of the unrelenting destiny that pushes onward and never turns back."

She stopped for a day at the Grand Canyon, where she had to rest for an afternoon because the spectacle overwhelmed her, and then she was on her way to St. Louis. For three days on the train, she arranged and rearranged her poems in her loose-leaf notebook, planning a sequence that "will serve to show that the many short poems are in reality one life poem, or parts of it. . . .'Flame and Shadow' *is* a good book, if a somewhat sad one," she told Ernst. "If you stay away any longer, any poems will have to be written with tears instead of a pencil."

Finally back in New York in mid-May, after another melancholy visit with her parents, she took rooms at the Schuyler Hotel on West 45th Street, and busied herself with getting *Flame and Shadow* into press and ironically observing the antics of her friends. Ernst, to her dismay postponed his homecoming yet again, to July, and disturbed her by proposing that he take a position as Lawrence's liaison officer in Europe, to be stationed in Cologne. Sara discouraged him with her faint-hearted response, although the proposal might well have fallen through anyway.

As the season wore into summer, she sank into deeper despondency and stopped writing poetry entirely. It was a barren spell that would last until nearly November, the longest she had ever gone without writing. The Untermeyers annoyed her with their marital instability, she wrote Ernst. Jean flirted outrageously with other men to even the score with Louis, in order, she said, to make him love her the more—although Sara couldn't imagine "desiring a love which I had to purchase in such a manner." When they threw a party for Siegfried Sassoon, a poet "somewhat over-impressed with his own worth," Jean professed to be in love with him "somewhat the *way* she was with 'Bennie' Huebsch—that is, she sits on the arm of his chair and attempts to caress him, etc. At one time she sat on the floor at his feet. He seems quite indifferent—in fact I think he has very little use for women." Even a drive with Jean in the country exhausted her because "She is in a very unhealthy state of mind and poured so many of her neurotic and erotic worries into my ears."

Her glumness had something to do with her fastidious disgust with the "messy" sexual life of New York, from which she had been absent for nearly eight months. Even Amy Lowell had disappointed her by writing a poem about a lonely woman watching men pass on the street, "knowing their terrible lusts and how naked they are under their clothes. . . . Unfortunately a mere catalog of sexual acts and feelings does not evoke anything lasting in the way of emotion." In July she read Joyce's *Portrait of the Artist as a Young Man,* finding it "vivid," "coarse," "as raw as I ever read." It was an impressive record of adolescence, she told Ernst, though "It is always. . . an open question just how near art should come to reality."

In July Ernst wrote that he was to sail at last on August 14. "I think I could never live through another year of longing like the last," Sara replied. Ernst himself was full of high spirits. His commission had acquired an interest in a big spinning mill in Czechoslovakia and had arranged to act as sales agents for others. He frequently served as a translator—on one occasion for the chancellor of Austria. The lawyer for the group was John Foster Dulles, who had recently served on the reparations commission of the peace conference. Ernst believed the peace had been botched, that the United States ought to be involved in the rebuilding of Europe, and that it was nonsense to consider Bolshevism a threat. In April he had motored through southwestern Germany near the French border, visiting the small town of Maikammer, where the Filsinger family had originated. Ernst despised the arrogant French soldiers stationed in the town, feeling that French militarism was a more serious threat than the German. And just before sailing home from England, always alert to new technological developments, he booked one of the early commercial flights from Paris to London, in a two-motored plane seating eleven passengers. The three-and-a-half hour flight at an altitude of 2,500 feet was so noisy the passengers stuffed cotton in their ears and passed notes back and forth, unable to carry on a conversation. Ernst overcame his fear of heights on this flight, he said, and would have become an aviator if he were younger. Sara, on the other hand, was horror-stricken at this supposedly reckless escapade when she learned of it.

On board the luxurious R.M.S. *Aquitania* of the Cunard Line, which reminded him of the St. Regis Hotel or of Claridge's, Ernst wrote his parents that "my greatest joy in the voyage is the fact that every moment brings me nearer Sara. I don't think that anything could ever persuade me to remain away again for such a long period." In the past year and a half, Sara and he had lived together for only six weeks. She seemed to dread his approaching arrival on August 21 almost as much as she welcomed it. The last poems she wrote in the summer before silence set in were wistfully reminiscent of Wheelock rather than of Ernst, celebrating the free spirit that could not realize itself rather than the love that was a trap. In the paralysis of emotion, she had to counterfeit a joyous excitement, although her nights were often filled with insomniac brooding, see-sawing between self-blame and her utter incapacity to do other than she had done. When her poetic voice returned some months later, she wrote "Sleepless Night":

> They love me, and I have not made them happy,
> (Rush of the wind and river-whistles moaning)

They love me and I can not give them peace,
  (The city shifts in sleep with a low groaning.)

They love me and I watch their faces aging
  And growing pinched as the slow winter dawn;
I give them nothing but a few sad poems,
  And life is short and we shall soon be gone.57

# CHAPTER SEVEN

# "A Dream Lost Among Dreams"

**S**ara claimed to be ecstatically happy after Ernst's return on August 21, 1920, nervous though she was about the "volcanoes" of emotion with which he threatened to engulf her. She had secured their apartment again at the Beresford in early summer and had even repainted the woodwork herself in a surge of domesticity. Nevertheless, her deeper apprehensiveness won out, and by mid-September she was suffering from a bad cold and was ready for another rest cure in the country. Ernst took her to Buck Hill Falls, Pennsylvania, returning the next day to New York. But her room at the hotel was too chilly, and she stayed only a few days. Depressed by the long drought in her productivity and still unable to feel well, she finally settled on the remedy reserved for extreme circumstances: another stay at Cromwell Hall. She left Ernst again around October 25 and this time did not return until nearly the end of November. It was "a terrible struggle" to be away from him for so long, she told Jessie Rittenhouse, but she grew markedly more cheerful and gradually began to write again.

Her poems turned repeatedly to the one subject of central interest: the need to preserve herself through some kind of resignation and withdrawal from the struggle. "If I should make no poems any more," she wrote in "Leisure" at the end of November, "There would be rest at least." She would retreat into the enjoyment of the few things that gave her pleasure,

> Sharing with no one but myself the frosty
> And half ironic musings of my mind.[1]

The mood was a recovery of the attitude into which she had settled before the jarring disturbance of Ernst's return, and with it her poems began to come again with some regularity.

But if the self-isolation was peaceful, it had an underlying ominousness, because it also meant surrender to the sense of a fatal entrapment, a relinquishing of her will. "There is no way out of the web of things," she wrote in February 1921; it is a snare, she says, that will break her wings if she continues her rebellious struggle. She can only be quiet and "brood on beauty" for a while:

> Caught in the trap of space that has no end,
> See how the stars, august in their submission
> Take their Great Captor for their changeless friend.

None of her relationships escaped the "half-ironic" detachment with which she viewed life. "It is one to me that they come or go," she wrote in "The Solitary":

> Let them think I love them more than I do,
> Let them think I care, though I go alone;
> If it lifts their pride, what is it to me
> Who am self-complete as a flower or a stone.[2]

In "The Crystal Gazer," she portrayed herself fusing all her "scattered selves" into a crystal ball, into which she gazed at

> the little shifting pictures of people rushing
> In restless self-importance to and fro.[3]

When she and Jean Untermeyer visited the Cloisters on a pale, sunny March afternoon in 1921, they decided that each should write a poem about the sixteenth-century figure of a nun lying in death. Sara's "Effigy of a Nun" is a somber self-portrait, of one

> Content to look at life with the high, insolent
> Air of an audience watching a play.

She is a woman of "infinite gentleness, infinite irony," of loneliness and "warring thoughts," who, in the "subtle pride of her mind," has hoarded her complex inner life against the world.

> She must have told herself that love was great,
> But that the lacking it might be as great a thing
> If she held fast to it, challenging fate.[4]

The figure was like someone frozen in the trance of her dream of life, interchangeable with death. "She was an inscrutable, arrogant person and she has interested me," Sara told John Gould Fletcher.[5]

If Sara's life had come to seem dreamlike to her, trapped as she was in a silent, private inner conflict, in circumstances she did not have the strength to change, she managed to lead a convincing double existence.

Even the few close friends who sensed the tensions in her marriage believed that she and Ernst were reasonably happy and comfortable together. John Hall Wheelock, who spent many evenings with them, thought of Sara as a singularly sane and practical manager of her life. Habits that might have seemed odd in others—her frequent need to be alone in the country, her perpetual undefined illness, her preference for prewar long dresses and high shoes, her refusal to socialize, the insomniac nights when she worked on her poetry, and the late mornings in bed—all seemed natural and unnoteworthy in one whose visible manner was of gentleness, poise, quick wit, shrewd insight, and extreme orderliness.

There were only occasional glimpses of the irrational obsessions that underlay her marriage. Sara's jealous fear that Ernst would fall in love with someone else, and leave her, erupted at intervals. According to Wheelock, she held Ernst strictly to account whenever they were apart, which was often; he was expected to avoid other women, except a few close friends of Sara's, and not to be seen having lunch or dinner with them or escorting them out for an evening unless Sara herself had arranged or approved it. When traveling on business, he telephoned her regularly. Once, during such an absence, Wheelock told, Sara came across a letter written to Ernst by a woman unknown to her, in a manner that seemed overly familiar. Although the letter suggested nothing compromising in Ernst's behavior, it disturbed her. When he telephoned, she confronted him with it quietly, making no direct accusations, but pressing him relentlessly until he was in tears, sobbing, trying to explain what appeared to need no explanation. And then, apparently feeling she had gone too far, she apologized and soothed him again in her gentle way. As Sara grew more reclusive and more selective, she became also more mercilessly exacting in the proper behavior she expected not only of herself but also of her husband and her friends.

Sara's career no longer needed the intense promoting she formerly gave it. When *Flame and Shadow* appeared in October 1920, Sara saw to it that her friends Jessie Rittenhouse and Marguerite Wilkinson wrote well-placed reviews, even suggesting what they might say. Untermeyer, John Gould Fletcher, Braithwaite, and Lindsay had all seen the plate proof and agreed, she told Jessie, that "It is my best book and shows a stronger grasp of life as well as more flexible technique than the earlier books. . . . It is certainly more mature and it seems to me a more rounded testament than the others. If you feel something like this on re-reading the book, it would be fine if you found it in your heart to say so in the review." But beyond this, she captained no effort to publicize it, as she had done for *Rivers to the Sea,* and seemed to feel less the extravagant excitement of former years than a measured satisfaction in her achievement. She had become one of the most popular poets in America. The income from her work—royalties from her books, sales to magazines, permissions to set poems to music—ran to $2,500 a year, even during the postwar recession, allowing her the luxury of country retreats, travel, and expensive dresses.

Her intense privacy and reticence created an air of enigmatic reserve around her, as she withdrew from public appearances and her poetry assumed its tinge of unexplained sadness, confessing an emotion without revealing its cause. On her return from Santa Barbara, where in the months alone she had come to accept her isolation and self-completeness, she seemed more aloof and critical of the poets she knew, more inclined to give time only to those whose friendship mattered to her. "The 'major poets' of the U.S., with the exception of Vachel and one or two others, aren't the most lovable and the noblest lot of men one could imagine, are they?" she wrote Ernst in the fall of 1920 from Cromwell. "Witness what we saw of Frost's ill-temper under criticism that evening at our house, and also other things about him, such as his fulsome and evidently so false praise of Louis' poems—the most *terribly* overdone thing I ever saw, and Louis seemed to swallow it. Masters with his marital infidelities and his quarrelsome conceit, Robinson with his attempt to 'pass the buck' in the matter of his judgeship—Why go on? 'Human, all too human!'"

Sara often asked Ernst to meet people on her behalf or to handle her business affairs when she thought a man, particularly a husband, might be more effective. In England in the spring of 1920, he looked up Stafford Hatfield for her—the shipboard romance of 1912 had never been forgotten—and the two men found each other congenial. She also asked him while there to meet John Gould Fletcher, some of whose work she liked and who might be helpful to her reputation abroad. Fletcher left London shortly afterward for New York and, touched by the praise Ernst had relayed, called on Sara on June 21. She primed herself for the visit by reading through his work in the library and having the bookstore send over a copy of his latest volume to lay out prominently on a table. He was charmed by these attentions, and she liked him, she told Ernst, even if he seemed "somewhat egotistical" and "his fingernails were not clean." Fletcher arranged for her to meet a representative of the English publisher John Lane, who had taken the lead in printing the work of new poets, but nothing came of it. In comparison with *Flame and Shadow*, then only in page proof, she believed her earlier work unworthy to be published abroad.

Fletcher perceived Sara as "Markedly fragile in appearance and shrinking from contact with humanity," reminding him of H. D., though she lacked H. D.'s "cultivated archaism. . . which sometimes had seemed to me, in H. D.'s presence, almost an affectation. Sara Teasdale had refined her lyricism to a simplicity of statement that was very moving and very human, and that seemed to me. . . far removed from the elaborate and sophisticated self-exploitation that was now being practiced by such a figure as Edna St. Vincent Millay. I admired her art, equally compounded of the quietism of Christina Rossetti and the emotional intensity of Emily Dickinson, though she herself declared that she did not value it, finding, she said, her lyricism one-sided, and her own personality somewhat tiresome."[6] This self-deprecation was characteristic of her, especially in the deeply despondent mood of June 1920.

Later that summer, a week before Ernst's return, she entertained Vachel Lindsay and his mother at dinner just before their departure on August 14 for England, where he was to perform his work. According to Lindsay, when *General William Booth Enters into Heaven and Other Poems* was published in England in 1919 to a favorable response, the Macmillan Company pressured him to follow up with a recitation tour. At first he refused "to go through the weird land of England and be hanged as I was in Bryn Mawr or Boston (the two most English spots in America)." He was also exhausted from the constant cross-country tours of America, the endless repeating of himself, desperate to write poetry that satisfied him again and to finish his cherished project, the visionary *Golden Book of Springfield*. "What is the use of howling across the country," he asked Sara, "when all is over you do not remember any of it, and care less?" As Sara agreed privately to Ernst, "Good poetry can't be written in a hullabaloo. Look at Vachel, who has done scarcely anything really his best since he has been racing all over the country constantly." But the insistence of friends and publishers overcame Vachel's reluctance to expose himself to the condescending British, and he agreed to a series of readings in England in September 1920.

Sara had not met Vachel's formidable mother before, but described her benignly to Harriet Monroe as "a nice old soul—somewhat of a schoolteacher but very up and coming for a seventy-two year old—and full of humor." The mother and son made a striking impression in England, where Vachel was a resounding success at Oxford and Cambridge, culminating his trip with a sensational appearance at Westminster Hall in London. The expatriate writers, whom he despised, resented his reception as America's foremost poet. Fletcher, who like Pound had turned his back on America a dozen years earlier, had returned to England in September in time to witness Lindsay's triumph. What impressed him most was Lindsay's "extraordinary juvenility of mind." His was "a talent turned back on itself, arrested, inhibited from finding ultimate expression. He had escaped, not by facing his own obstacles and overcoming them, but by becoming a mixture of backwoods evangelist and playboy. . . .The secret of his arrested development lay less, however, in himself than in the gaunt figure with withered face, white hair, and spectacles who stood at his side and accompanied him everywhere around

London—his mother. . . .The type was familiar: the pioneer schoolteach-er, who satisfies her secret and shamefaced craving for beauty vicariously through another's destiny while forbidding beauty to express itself out-wardly in the body as well as the inward imagination." Lindsay was "his mother's victim," unable to "attain to final greatness as a poet because of this handicap." T. S. Eliot told Fletcher, "I am appalled at Lindsay," and Pound decided that Lindsay was only a "librettist" who needed his voice and personality to project his work.7

Vachel had taken his fight into the very citadel of the enemy, the dominant British tradition that seemed to him to sap the creative life of native American writers who were subservient to it. But he was obsessed with the fear that "my English trip was a mess," that he had been only a curiosity to the British, like a traveling Wild West show, a failure after all. In November 1920, *The Golden Book of Springfield* appeared, and for weeks went amost unnoticed. This confused utopian vision summed up all he had dedicated his life to, the apotheosis of his home town. Feeling "dull and baffled and demoralized" by what he believed to be another crushing defeat, he appealed to Sara for advice, criticism, and help. She responded generously by sending him copies of the few reviews she had seen and trying to support his self-esteem. He was in debt, forced to go on the recitation circuit again, "the slave of my past," unable to throw himself into the kind of battle that made him feel alive. "If I cannot use my body and blood to write with, as it were on the walls of a town," he told her, "I do not want to be a citizen and do not even seem to be living. . . .The only thing that awakens me is the leap in the dark." Despite his charismatic control of audiences and the undeniable pleasure he took in his public successes, his public and private selves were always at war with each other. The clamoring audience was a monster; he craved only the close companionship of a few friends, he said, and the sense of unfettered personal freedom. It was an irresolvable strife that slowly dragged him through the years to his ruin, and Sara always remained the tender, understanding friend to whom he could unfailingly turn for sup-port. As she sardonically observed the combative egos and political maneuvering among the poets, Vachel, although something of a Quixote, was an honorable and devoted knight.

*Flame and Shadow* proved to be as popular as her earlier work, going into a second printing in December 1920, after only two months, with a total of four printings in its first year. Although not obviously so to the reader, the volume was more personal. She grouped the ninety-two po-ems, which had been written between 1914 and 1920, in twelve sections, with a progression of moods from affirmation of beauty through pessi-mistic meditation on death to a qualified reaffirmation. Some of the sections were titled—"Memories," "In a Hospital," "The Dark Cup,"

"By the Sea," and "Songs for Myself"—and others were silently centered on Ernst (Section III) and Jack Wheelock (Section V). The last poem in each section seems to have been placed for emphasis, often summing up the theme of the group. "The Mystery," which concludes the poems about Ernst, describes the gulf that lies between them in spite of their long intimacy:

> Can I ever know you
> Or you know me?[8]

And the section on Wheelock ends with "Let It Be Forgotten."

Only the first two sections are predominantly positive in tone—beauty, and the memory of beauty—but even these are tinged with the painful sense of death and loss, the shadow behind the flame. The title suggests that she strove for a balance between her affirmation of values and her fatalism. Her careful placement of "The Wind in the Hemlock" at the end of the volume, with its rage against death and its compensating belief that if she can maintain an inner peacefulness, like the tree, she can subsist on beauty and be comforted, suggests a key to the overall design of the book as well as to her beliefs. The volume was dedicated "To E.," with the epigraph from Hugo: "Reçois la flamme ou l'ombre/ De tous mes jours."

Sara's Puritan background had left her with all the inhibitions but none of the faith of her forebears. "I read to-day Socrates defence before the court at Athens when he was condemned to death," she wrote to Ernst from Cromwell in October 1920 "—a noble speech. Christianity hasn't much to boast of when you put it along side the teachings of some of the old fellows I've been reading. So far as I can see, the new thing Christ had to offer was love (no mean gift) and pity—and his teachings got twisted into a sort of glorification of suffering. I'm sure he never intended that." The war had convinced her that suffering could not be a part of any divine plan. And to the individual it meant at best a tragic test of one's pride and fortitude. The grandeur of nature on a large scale, and the long-range evolutionary process, seemed to argue for some sort of purposeful order. After visiting the Grand Canyon, she had written Harriet Monroe, "It makes me feel that immortality must *be,* after all, since the ages have worked for such harmonious splendor there."

In spite of the success of *Flame and Shadow,* the winter of 1920–1921 was worrisome, for Ernst had returned from a year's absence to find the affairs of his office in a shambles and business down because of the recession. To Sara's dismay, he was working long and fretful hours again and taking two Italian lessons a week. Her own emotional problems had sent her off for the month at Cromwell, and she was fearful over her eighty-two-year-old father's precarious health. There was one happy week in February 1921, when Ernst joined her in Lenox, Massachusetts, in the Berkshires and they seemed to be free of all the oppressive problems that weighed on their lives. They were the only two guests at the hotel, and the landscape was buried in glittering snow. "Our days were the most care-free and the happiest we have had since our marriage, I think," she wrote her sister-in-law Irma, "and Ernst was just like a boy. I never saw him so full of spirits before. It was a never ending delight to be together, and we walked and read aloud and enjoyed it more than I can say." One of the books Sara read was James' *Wings of the Dove*, about which, she told Fletcher, she was "vastly enthusiastic." Her dream of quieting Ernst's restlessly driven life and keeping him entirely to herself for a while seemed for a moment to be realized. She even persuaded him to drop his language lessons. "But he is so incurably ambitious," she wrote Irma, "that I never know what new thing will crop up for him to wear himself out on." She commemorated this vacation in the poem "Winter Sun (Lenox)," which ended with the somewhat doubtful lines

> "Let come what may," your eyes were saying,
> "At least we two have had today."9

Sara's father's health worsened in the spring, to the point where she expected to be called to St. Louis at any moment. The possibility of his sudden death had been a source of morbid worry for her over the past several years. Her attachment to her father was intense. In the winter of 1918–1919, she had written a poem titled "The First Thing I Remember" about her father, "my first lover," singing a lullaby to her as she was cuddled against his shoulder. She had watched his decline into frail and trembling old age with agonized solicitude and dread. It may be that her own morbid fear of death in these years was related to her deep concern for her father, who had been her main source of strength since childhood and the model of honor and fortitude for her own character.

But this crisis passed, as the others had. In late April, she went off to the Pudding Stone Inn at Boonton, New Jersey, again, her favorite place to watch spring come in. She no longer tried to rationalize these periodic weeks in the country; they had become part of the regular pattern of her life. She usually took along the flower guide that Ernst had given her in 1918 and on her walks in the woods identified wild flowers and entered notations in her book.

In the summer of 1921, her parents prepared to escape the heat of St. Louis by going to Charlevoix as they had done for so many years, although they seemed almost too feeble for the effort. Sara and Ernst planned to visit them there at the end of July. Sara was fretting about money again. They seemed scarcely able to keep up the expense of their apartment at the Beresford, and, since "we can't bear to move from this place," she turned to her only reliable source of additional income—the compiling of another anthology. Her feminine point of view again determined her focus. Her first anthology had been of love poems by women; this one would be a collection of poems for children. By mid-July she had signed a contract with Macmillan to do a volume called *Rainbow Gold* and had begun to solicit her friends for suggestions of their four or five favorite poems. The volume would include no poems written especially for children but would consist of standard English classics and a few contemporary poems, with the intent of appealing to children between the ages of ten and fourteen and helping to shape their taste for good poetry. "I shall try to avoid poems teaching a moral lesson," she told Amy Lowell. "I shall use 'La Belle Dame Sans Merci,' " she added, "in spite of Miss Lawlor's telling me that she feels such an inclusion will damn the book in the eyes of some virtuous parents."

In July, Jessie Rittenhouse sent Sara a copy of the recently published *The Story of a Poet: The Life of Madison Cawein,* by Otto A. Rothert. Cawein, a prominent poet of the twilight generation, and the one who had proposed Sara's name for membership in the Poetry Society, had died suddenly in 1914 at the age of forty-nine, and the volume, published in Louisville, was a collection of reminiscences, newspaper extracts, and appreciations. The effect on Sara was to jolt her underlying morbidity again. "I read it for several hours yesterday," she wrote Jessie, "and it made me so blue—the desperately sad end of the man—that I could scarcely get a wink of sleep." On December 4, 1914, Cawein had gone into the bathroom to shave and was heard to fall. He was found "fully dressed, . . .lying in the dry bath tub. Blood trickled from a wound in the left side of his head."[10] He was believed to have suffered a stroke and fallen into the tub, where the blow to his head caused a blood clot that led to his death four days later. He had never regained consciousness. Sara believed that a tendency to strokes ran in her own family. Her brother John Warren, Jr., had died of a stroke at about the same age as Cawein, and her father was expected to suffer an attack at any time. Shortly before her own death twelve years later at the age of forty-eight, she became obsessed with the idea that her blood vessels were beginning to break (although they were not), and she too was found dead in her bath tub.

Reading of Cawein's death touched deep and lasting sources of anxiety. She did not try to put it out of her mind but went back to a poem she had written in May, called "So Be It," another fatalistic lyric on death as symbolized by autumn, and retitled it "Epitaph (In Memory of M. C.)." When she submitted the poem to Harriet Monroe in 1924 for publication in *Poetry,* she asked, "Would you prefer to call the verses that I call 'Epitaph,' 'Epitaph for a Poet,' or 'Epitaph for M. C.'? They are that."

The brief, delightful week with Ernst in January had, as Sara feared, not led to any change in his way of life. "If only he did not have so many business worries!" she wrote to her sister-in-law Wanda Filsinger. "I am always anxious about him for he keeps so keyed-up and madly energetic every minute." He had lectured in April and May at Harvard's Graduate School of Business Administration, and in the previous autumn the federal government had published his *Commercial Travelers' Guide to Latin America*. International problems, however, had made Ernst's business "terribly trying," and Sara worried about her own income because of the depression in the book business. She hoped to make "real money," she told her sister-in-law, from her anthology, *Rainbow Gold*. In spite of having won the $200 Brookes More Prize for the best work published in *Contemporary Verse* for 1920—for some of the poems appearing in *Flame and Shadow* as "The Dark Cup"—she felt little enthusiasm for her own work. "I am writing very little," she wrote Wanda Filsinger, "and I begin to wonder if I shall ever publish another book. At the rate I am writing I shall not have enough material until ten years from now!" She sent Ernst off for a Fourth of July camping trip at Lake George with their friend Jim Wilkinson, in her tireless effort to make him take care of his health. He had gained nearly thirty pounds since their marriage, and now, at 180 pounds, needed some exercise, she believed. But fearful that he might catch cold sleeping in the open air, she made him take six blankets.

They traveled the long journey to Michigan in late July to visit Sara's parents, whom they found disturbingly feeble. They tried to enliven the trip by going by a Great Lakes steamer, but found the boat "not absolutely first class" and crowded, and so did not enjoy it, except for seeing Niagara Falls.

Then in early August 1921, Sara's father died at Charlevoix. Although she had long expected it, his death affected her profoundly. The first poem she wrote afterward, in late September, was "Never Again":

> Never again the music blown as brightly
>   Off of my heart as foam blown off a wave;
> Never again the melody that lightly
>   Caressed my grief and healed the wounds it gave.
>
> Never again—I hear my dark thoughts clashing
>   Sullen and blind as waves that beat a wall—
> Age that is coming, summer that is going,
>   All I have lost or never found at all.[11]

With this, she wrote an end to her long-held belief that the writing of her poems could exorcise her personal anguish, a belief that here seems to be identified with the comfort she had always received from her father. With his passing, her work lost some of its point. The thought of her father had also once stood between her and the urge to take her own life, and that barrier against death was gone, leaving her vulnerable to a keener sense that her own life would end.

She displayed her grief to none of her friends, writing few letters and fewer poems and busying herself with *Rainbow Gold,* which she now saw as a tribute to her father's memory. She spent a week in September 1921 in the country, probably at Cromwell, in total isolation and silence, to recover her stability. Her father's death had also left a tangle of problems in his affairs. Her brother George had encumbered the dried fruit business heavily, and a large mortgage on another property at Ninth and Pine Streets further reduced the estate. Each child's share would be only one-eighth, which would yield far less than they had once assumed it would. She and Ernst had sometimes talked of living in Europe for a few years, and he was, as always, full of restless plans to travel abroad. "I almost get sick when my Ernst talks of hoping to go to the Far East sometime," she confided in his sister Irma. The future, as always, seemed vaguely threatening.

Sara felt unwell through the fall and winter and seems to have made little effort to see anyone. Since returning from Santa Barbara she had become, she told Eunice Tietjens, "a recluse of recluses and never go anyplace." The poems she wrote were reflections of the emotional turmoil that lay beneath the unusually calm surface she displayed. In December, she wrote "Ashes to Ashes," a grim picture of her inner self as a burning house: "Keep it shut on the shuddering cries and the roar,/ There is nothing new about this fire in your heart." It would soon be over, and those who passed by would see only the light ashes lifted by the wind, "Too white to stain the clear cold blue of the sky."

The poems written over these months reveal the progression of her emotions from the despair at losing her father to a sense of her own weakening identity. In "Shadows," drawing perhaps on Plato's imagery of physical reality as a world of shadows, she saw only a sense of loss of the definition of her life rather than an inner light:

> We saw our shadows walking before us,
>   Etched on the hard sand, flat and grey,
> The last thin edge of the waves crept near us,
>   The autumn sunshine tried to be gay.
>
> Chained to the shadows our bodies made there,
>   Slowly we walked in the dwindling light;
> Our shadows faded, like wraiths we wandered
>   With the dark sea booming into the night.[12]

"It is Not I" is a further portrayal of a receding identity:

> It is not I they love
>   Although they think they love me,
> It is that picture of themselves they see
>   As though a mirror hung above me.

I can reflect them with a grace
   That lets them talk and makes them shine,
And if they tell their troubles to me
   I do not bother them with mine.

It is not I they love, there is no I
   Except for you who have me for your own,
And for the rest my heart may hide or seem
   A thing as light as snow, as still as stone.[13]

The genteel requirement that as a lady she be always "good" and pleasing to others, left her in the end with a sense that she had betrayed her own personality. She seemed constantly consumed with regret—"shall I die regretting/ All that was never said and never done?"—and wondering how all the things desired in life but never realized would be resolved in the end.

Her ironic edge had sharpened, as she counted her losses, although she seldom let it show in her poetry. It was only hinted at in "It Is Not I," but was displayed openly in "A Man Who Understood Women," another poem written in November 1921 and published but never collected:

He meets her twice or thrice a year,
   Sometimes less and sometimes more,
Each time they meet the stage is set
   Exactly as the time before.

He is most glossy and most gay,
   Witty, omniscient and bland,
She is inscrutable and mild,
   She lets him play his hand.

And if his pyrotechnics pale
   A little on her moonlit sky
He scarcely knows that it is so,
   And only vaguely wonders why.

And if he finds her eyes too wide,
   A shade too deep, a shade too cool,
She lets him wonder which she is,
   A saint, a sinner, or a fool.[14]

She also had a gift for epigrammatic succinctness, which she displayed most often in her "wisdom" poems. In February 1922, she summed up in a few lines the essential irony of life that she had probed for many months, in "Wisdom," one of several poems she gave that title. It described a "spring that never came," by implication a springtime of awakened feelings, promised but never realized.

> But we have lived enough to know
> What we have never had, remains;
> It is the things we have that go.[15]

She had lost ten pounds during the winter and felt "run down." In mid-March she went to the Colonial Inn in Concord, Massachusetts—"a change always does me good"—and stayed for about a month. "The thought of spring coming without my father to enjoy it and to watch for each loveliness, sends a sorrow to my heart," she wrote Irma Filsinger Wetteroth. "I think of him so very, very often and dream of him far too often for my own good—but I don't seem able to break off." She had written a few pathetic lines about him in her notebook:

> He loved all lovely things,
> And till the very last
> Named each soft open flower,
> Each bright-eyed bird that passed.

In the Concord public library, she studiously researched the records of the town's early history and her ancestor Simon Willard, copying several pages about his life, which she sent to her mother. She tried her hand at a longer, but unsuccessful, poem about the Revolutionary War battleground and spent a day as a guest of Wellesley College, carefully timing it for the spring vacation so as to avoid fatigue. "I am writing very little poetry," she complained to Irma, "and I fear it will be a long time before I have another book of it."

Sara, who metaphorically identified the seasons with a cycle of hope, fulfillment, and death, actually experienced a corresponding cycle of moods through the year. She dreaded cold weather, feeling it was the cause of her frequent respiratory illnesses, and usually felt restored both physically and psychologically by the coming of warm summer weather. In late May, she tried to find a comfortable hotel first at Marlboro and then at Cornwall on the Hudson above New York, but gave up and returned on May 27 to the apartment, where she persuaded Ernst to take Memorial Day with her at a guest house in Easthampton. They returned there over the Fourth of July, spending a total of two weeks near the Wheelock family home in Long Island. It was "the best and longest vacation we have had together," she wrote Irma, and she stayed on alone for ten more days. Visiting the place had never failed to produce several good poems. This year they included "Land's End," depicting a desolate stretch of beach at the far reaches of the world, where she and the usual unnamed companion "leave our lost footprints" for the passionate sea to erase.[16] According to John Hall Wheelock, it was written for him, as was the urgent love poem "When I Am Not with You," written that August; and so was "The Beloved," written in April at Concord. "August Midnight," published in *Scribner's* in December 1923 as "Absence," but not collected, returned to the Sapphic theme of torment in love, which had been absent from her work for over two years:

> I cannot sleep, the night is hot and empty,
>   My thoughts leave nothing lovely in my heart,
> You love me and I love you, life is passing,
>   We are apart.
>
> The August midnight vibrates with the voices
>   Of insects and their passions frail and shrill—
> Oh from what whips, oh from what secret scourgings
>   All of Earth's children bow before her will!

One might suppose that the occasion of the poem was Ernst's absence at that time on a trip to Washington, except that the emotion seems inappropriate. It is as though she combined the circumstance of Ernst's absence with her feeling for Wheelock. In October 1922, she wrote "I Shall Await You," on a theme she had employed before in poems about Wheelock. She will wait for him after death, "if you care to have me"—

> I can await you, or I can avoid you—
>   We shall not meet unless you want to meet.

Although some of the love poems written during the year doubtless have reference to Ernst, particularly those expressing appreciation for love's durability, it is evident that another resurgence of her hopeless affection for Jack Wheelock inspired many of them.

Sara and her sister Mamie Wheless felt obligated to go to St. Louis in September to help settle their father's estate. Their brother had filed a claim in probate court for $35,000 to set aside a codicil to their father's will that had deducted $20,000 from his share because of a large debt he owed the company. George Teasdale claimed the right to an equal share with his sisters. Sara found the trouble distasteful and was heartbroken at her mother's condition. "She is so broken and changed," she wrote to Amy Lowell afterward, "both physically and mentally, that I could hardly bear it. The doctors thought she would not live a week (she is seventy-eight) but she grew better, and I came back to New York, but only after getting so ill that our old family doctor insisted that I ought to go to a hospital in St. Louis. . . . My mother's death is a matter of only a few months at most, they think. You know what it means to have the thought of her poor frail tottering self, that until a few years ago was fire and energy, always on my mind night and day."

Sara's state of mind was evident in a poem, "Hide and Seek," written in early October after her return. Recalling the nerve-wracking "terrible game" of childhood, she realizes now that it is the pattern of all life, a "game in the dark,/ A groping in shadows," with the same wild exultance and dread of lurking figures, leaving unsaid what one wants to say, certain only of "the long sleep/ When the game is over and we are put to bed."

*Rainbow Gold* was published during the distraught days of September 1922, and was dedicated "to the beautiful memory of my father John Warren Teasdale." Publication had been delayed for two months while Dugald Walker completed the charming illustrations—"really inexcusable," Sara complained to Irma, "for he had the complete ms. the early part of January. But he is temperamental!!" The book was an immediate success and for a time outsold all her other work. Its seventy-nine poems ranged from anonymous English ballads to Frost, Yeats, Dickinson, Lindsay, and Graves, arranged roughly according to the seasons, from spring to Christmas, with an emphasis on delight in nature. She was guided, she said in her preface, by what she and her friends had enjoyed as children, particularly poems "with highly accented rhythms. . . .They enjoyed certain sad poems as much as merry ones, but meditative, moralistic and gloomy poems were never read but once, if they were read at all. And I am glad to say that poems full of sentimentality fared no better."[17] The collection is still a classic of its kind, although changing taste and the difficulty young people now find in reading complex poetic language and earlier forms of English have rendered it less accessible than it was when published. She prepared a written "interview," as had become her custom, for the publisher to distribute to the newspapers.

The grim mood of the fall and winter drained her strength. When her name was put on the ballot for election to the executive board of the Poetry Society of America in November, Sara begged off. "I could not serve on account of ill-health, if elected, for I never go out at night, and rarely in the day time," she wrote Mrs. Markham.[18] She had high hopes of capturing Ernst for a short Thanksgiving holiday out of town, for she was at odds with him again over the intensity with which he drove himself, but the Lawrence Company were changing office arrangements that weekend and he was required to oversee the move. Sara went off alone the day after Thanksgiving to the Mayflower Inn in Washington, Connecticut, in the Berkshires, for a week. "If I want to get any work done (composing poetry) it seems about necessary to get away from the apartment, where the 'phone and the ever-increasing business mail make my small amount of strength vanish all too soon," she wrote Irma. It was an exciting season in New York, but Sara never felt "strong enough" to go out, sending Ernst alone or with friends, "for he finds relaxation in company whereas I find fatigue in it." The winter was oppressive, an anxious watch for news of her mother, whose mind now wandered fitfully.

She had forgotten that Sara had visited her in the fall. She required a constant companion and seemed to fail so rapidly at intervals that they did not think she could live much longer. But to everyone's surprise, she survived each crisis, refusing to leave the large house that Mamie and Sara felt was too expensive to keep up for only one person. Her expenses had, in fact, begun to eat into her capital.

Sara's long flirtation with death had gradually progressed from dread to fearful fascination and now finally to submission. In December, she wrote "The Old Enemy":

> Rebellion against death, the old rebellion
> Is over; I have nothing left to fight...
>
> Therefore I make no songs—I have grown certain
> Save when he comes too late, death is a friend.[19]

Her poetic output had, indeed, declined to an average of only one poem a month, and she seemed unconcerned. Her poems repeatedly expressed the attitude that all was over, and she was only waiting for the end. "Arcturus in Autumn," written in October 1922, was her favorite poem, she said in later years. The star that came in spring, signaling the rebirth of the year, left her in October as the trees were stripped of their leaves in the dark,

> Oh then I knew at last that my own autumn
> was upon me...[20]

In "An End," she recognized that it was not merely an inexorable movement of nature that brought her nearer death, but an act of her own choosing:

> And I have said good-bye to what I love;
> With my own will I vanquished my own heart.
>
> With my own will I turned the summer from me.[21]

Her life had withdrawn to an inner place out of the cold and snow, alone with her memories: "I shall have winter now and lessening days."[22] And in "Winter Night Song," if her lover comes singing to the window, reminding her of the green season, she will not rush to open it, but will turn her back and drowse by the fire as time ticks away and the falling snow closes her in. The agitation and rebellion, followed by withdrawal, was the fixed emotional pattern of her life. She expressed it neatly in "Prescription Against Anger," written in September 1922. "Let be, let be, let battles be," she advised. Instead of fighting, find an isolated stretch of beach and lie there all day and into the night, count the stars until "the peace of the eternities" comes to you, "And then go home to bed."

But life went on. She was keenly interested in what the poets were doing, although she viewed the scene as rife with politics and jealous maneuverings. She had written to John Gould Fletcher, "I long to go to a country where I am a stranger to the politics of the literary cliques. I know too much of the inside of things here." The publication of Eliot's *The Waste Land* in 1922 exacerbated the ideological squabbles among the poets. Sara agreed with Untermeyer's assessment in his review, "Disillusion and Dogma," in *The Freeman* in January 1923. Although Untermeyer was later to come round when Eliot's prestige was established, he attacked *The Waste Land* violently at first as a "pompous parade of erudition," displaying a "twitching disillusion, a persistent though muffled hyperaesthesia," and a "mingling of willful obscurity and weak vaudeville," lacking "an integrated design." Eliot, an "analyst of dessicated sensations," failed to meet the human need for an ideal, only meeting despair with despair.

Although Sara seldom went out, she kept abreast of the literary gossip by lengthy telephone conversations. She was fascinated by the rise and fall of careers and the antagonisms among poets and critics, viewing it all as an ironically amused spectator. One of her closest friends and informants on literary politics during the 1920s was Marguerite Wilkinson, a poet, anthologist, and reviewer for the *New York Times,* whose husband Jim was a high school principal at New Rochelle, New York. They saw each other only once in three or four months, but they telephoned each other almost daily for years. Sara called their conversations the "Teasdaily Wilkinsonian." She reported one such session to Jessie Rittenhouse, on the rapid rise of Elinor Wylie: "I'd have lots of gossip to retail if you were in ear shot, but none of it is important, and it concerns chiefly Elinor Wylie, who continues to climb the slopes of Parnassus before a dazzled multitude. Her work becomes more cryptic, crabbed and queer every week—there is so much of it printed you can keep track of her poetic temperature almost daily. . . . She has started a sort of poet's club, and means, I think to be the king-pin in the whole game, controlling, as she seems to do, a good many of the avenues to fame. So be it! She is undoubtedly an attractive and clever person—but a great spirit? I wonder."

Although Sara had shrunk from the dissension and skirmishing over poetry, it had nevertheless caused her to think about her own work, and she did not always reject an invitation to discuss it. She responded in March 1923 to a request from a Professor Lewis for comments on her poetry. She preserved her answers to his questions, although the questions themselves are lacking. In a paragraph titled "The Pattern of a Poem," she wrote:

The planning of the pattern of a poem is largely subconscious with me. Naturally the idea needs more or less space according to whether it is simply a statement of an emotion, or whether added to the statement, a deduction is made. The patterns of most of my lyrics are a matter of balance and speed rather than a matter of design which can be perceived by the eye. The pattern of "The Unchanging" in "Flame and Shadow" is necessarily very simple for the poem is only 8 lines long. It consists of the balancing of a picture of the sea shore against the mood of the maker of the poem. The poem rises swiftly for the first three lines and subsides on the slower fourth line. It rises again for two lines and subsides finally on the slow last two lines. The short and very slow last line is an emotional echo of the 4th line.

"The better the lyric is the less I consciously plan it," she added. She had moved away from the regular metrics of her early work, she said. "The best modern poets can not be pinned down to regular and exact metres for very long." And on the matter of intention, she said, "Often I am seeking not so much communication with my reader as a better understanding of myself."

When Marguerite Wilkinson had asked her for a statement on the writing of poetry for her *New Voices* in 1919, Sara had provided one of her rare comments for publication. She wrote from the observation of herself:

My theory is that poems are written because of a state of emotional irritation. It may be present for some time before the poet is conscious of what is tormenting him. The emotional irritation springs, probably, from subconscious combinations of partly forgotten thoughts and feelings. Coming together, like electrical currents in a thunder storm, they produce a poem. A poem springs from emotions produced by an actual experience, or, almost as forcefully, from those produced by an imaginary experience. In either case, the poem is written to free the poet from an emotional burden. Any poem not so written is only a piece of craftsmanship.

She went on to describe the process in detail:

Out of the fog of emotional restlessness from which a poem springs, the basic idea emerges sometimes slowly, sometimes in a flash. This idea is known at once to be the light toward which the poet is groping. He now walks round and round it, so to speak, looking at it from all sides, trying to see which aspect of it is most vivid. When he has hit upon what he believes is his peculiar angle of vision, the poem is fairly begun.

Sara defended traditional poetic forms on the grounds that they had become so familiar over the centuries that the reader was carried instantly into the poem without being bewildered or put off by the challenge of language and form. But this also placed a heavy burden on the traditional poet to avoid both triteness and tricks. "The poet must put far from him the amazing word, the learned allusion, the facile inversion, the clever twist of thought, for all of these things will blur his poem and distract his reader. He must not overcrowd his lines with figures of speech, because, in piling these one upon another, he defeats his own purpose. The mind of the reader cannot hold many impressions at one time. The poet should try to give his poem the quiet swiftness of flame, so that the reader will feel and not think while he is reading. But the thinking will come afterward." She deplored poetry with a message: "If a poet has a great gift, he may be able to speak for a whole race, creed, or class simply by speaking for himself. But for a poet consciously to appoint himself the mouthpiece of a certain class or creed *en masse,* is dangerous business."[23]

Sara's concept of the pure lyric might apply, with qualifications, to much of the work of Yeats, Housman, Frost, and lesser poets of the post-Swinburne generation to which she belonged. It was essential to the theory of the lyric that the poet develop his own distinctively personal voice, and Sara only occasionally echoed her influential contemporaries. "Water Lilies," which Frost told Untermeyer he liked, faintly suggests Frost, as does "Mountain Water." And "Those Who Love" has more than a suggestion of her idol Yeats, particularly in its second stanza:

> And a woman I used to know
> Who loved one man from her youth,
> Against the strength of the fates
> Fighting in somber pride,
> Never spoke of this thing,
> But hearing his name by chance,
> A light would pass over her face.[24]

When Harriet Monroe left for a trip in spring of 1923, Eunice Tietjens took over the editorship of *Poetry* and conceived the idea of publishing a collection of the juvenilia of the older poets. Sara did not care for the idea, feeling that the work of the "older poets (I suppose we must knuckle down to being that now, alas!)" would look doubly poor next to that of the younger poets because of changes in style. "I confess I'm willing for my juvenilia to be burned up and be damned to it." She would allow one of the sonnets to Duse to be trotted out again, but preferred to forget the rest of her "poor draggled baby clothes."

Eunice also inquired about "poems written in dreams or in other subconscious states such as delirium": "I never wrote one," Sara replied. "I've dreamed lines many a time, and some of them aren't bad, but the context had always faded into nothingness when I woke up. I had a full remembrance that there *was* a poem (or what seemed to be one) all composed, but by the time I was fully awake it had gone. Nothing is left usually but a phrase or a line. One such line is in a sonnet in 'Helen of

Troy and Other Poems': 'Great Spring came surging upward from the south.' Of course the subconscious plays a predominant part in the making of lyrics, as no one knows better than you. But with me the conscious mind is on the job at the same time as a sort of governess to the child. For instance, that song of mine that begins 'Let it be forgotten as a flower is forgotten' was written almost entirely without intervention by my brains. It simply was in my mind. But I was broad awake all the time and could not be said to be in a subconscious state."

Ernst was to go abroad for an extended business trip through Europe in the summer of 1923, and this time Sara was determined to accompany him to England, where she would stay for the summer while he traveled on the continent. But in mid-May her mother was reported critically ill, and Mamie went "rushing pell mell on the noon train and I am holding myself in readiness to go at any time," she wrote Amy Lowell. "I fear my English trip has gone glimmering." She planned, in any case, to visit her mother before sailing, although in the end, she told Jessie, "The strain of not knowing when I should have to hear the worst from St. Louis put me down sick and I had to give up my trip to see my mother by doctor's orders." Mrs. Teasdale rallied again, however, and Sara decided to go abroad after all, although "terribly tired and frazzled."

Sara and Ernst sailed on the French Line ship, the *France*, on Wednesday, June 13. Landing probably at Plymouth, they went first to Land's End in Cornwall, then back through Devon, staying at an inn in Exeter, where her room looked out on the cathedral. And on June 26 they headed north to the village of Church Stretton in Shropshire, on a pilgrimage to Housman country. Ernst left her there, going on for business in Chester and Manchester, planning to rejoin her a week later in Oxford and then proceed to London. But after three days huddled among the Shropshire hills, most of them cold, damp, and cloudy, Sara decided to cut short her stay and flee south before she came down with one of her dreaded colds. She begged off the planned meeting in Oxford—"I am not in a state to meet anybody—I look too pinched and miserable. . . . I will not feel any enjoyment in life until I am warm again." She would go on to London alone. "The pleasure of being with you is not great enough to counterbalance the danger of illness, and the misunderstandings that my utter inability to keep up with you, cause between us."

She settled down at the American Women's Club in London in July while Ernst went on to Paris and was soon cheerfully buying dresses at Liberty's and being fitted for a blue evening gown, attending an awful poetry reading, and introducing herself to literary people. She had tea with the de la Mares on July 22, a Sunday afternoon, at their modest home in the suburbs. "Had a beautiful time," she reported. "He is the simplest and sweetest person you could ever find and so is Mrs. de la

Mare." She shared honors with Violet Hunt (Mrs. Ford Madox Huefer), who had known Christina Rossetti and everyone from the Pre-Raphaelites on down, and went home tired "more from excitement than exertion."

She was soon into English literary gossip, delighted and interested as always in the interplay of personalities. Jean and Louis Untermeyer arrived in London on their way to the continent, where they would stay for a year and a half. They said "that the spirit of rivalry, even of bitter jealousy is far more rife here than in America," she told Ernst. "I wonder?!?" Sara was "much interested in Sylvia Beach, etc., but I doubt the wisdom of putting money into James Joyce's book," *Ulysses.*

Sara seemed more cheerful than she had been in years, probing the English scene that had long interested her from a distance. Through the link of her ancestors, who lay buried in English churches, she felt half as if she belonged there. But the unspoken complexity of manners, the occasional chilliness and condescension, reminded her at times that she was an alien, and she still, as at home, lay awake listening to the night sounds of the city or watching over the sleeping rooftops, feeling pointless among millions of strangers.

She was anxious to find an English publisher for *Flame and Shadow* and assiduously sought advice. She acted guardedly, trying to sense her way through the obstacle course of English manners that silently regulated what simply was "not done." "I try to step warily, not knowing where I am," she told Ernst. She wished to approach the English Macmillans, who were only loosely related to her American publishing firm, but she could not appear to push. She had lunch with Mrs. Macmillan and was invited to dinner, where she appeared to advantage, she thought, in her gown from Liberty's. It was the most formal occasion she had ever attended, a nine-course dinner, all very "stiff." When she left, the butler called a taxi for her, and agonizing over whether to tip him, she decided not to, the sins of omission being less serious in England than those of commission. But he made a "wry face" as he closed the taxi door for her, an expression that haunted her for days, especially after she found that she should have tipped him two shillings. "How *is* one to know all of these things? Lord!"

Sara also had occasion to exercise an exquisite diplomacy when she had tea with the poet Charlotte Mew, whose work she respected, "though I am sorry," she wrote Ernst, "that she seemed to be under the impression that I am doing a great deal of lion hunting." Sara's chief judgment of the English was that they abhorred anyone to be "forward." In spite of her careful approach, Miss Mew "apparently . . . lumps all Americans together as a bustling vulgar lot. . . . She thinks it un-understandable how people can publish personal love-poems. This was probably a direct slap and I took it as pleasantly and sincerely as I could. I said that it *was* a very hard thing to do and I felt that it was often done only because the writer felt that only in that way could he get complete freedom from the feelings expressed in the poetry. By externalizing them they ceased to be an annoyance to him, at least in some measure. . . . It rather bothers me to be considered a vulgarian, but they all secretly consider us as such—that is, her type do."

Sara's attitude toward Ernst on this trip had been punctuated by querulousness, perhaps in response to the pressure she felt he exerted and to his leaving her alone. She was irritated at business matters, some of which she had to refer to him. "I wish that I had asked you a few questions relative to these matters before you left," she complained—"but business questions seem to annoy you and I suppose it is better for me to work out my own problems." Still, she signed her letters with adoring kisses, and she addressed him as "My dearest Boy" and "My big Bunnie."

In the end, after her sensitive negotiations, Macmillan turned down her book. She could then decline Mrs. Macmillan's invitation to tea, for "We are quits as to social obligations. Besides, the formality of that house is a little greater than I am exactly at home in—and I'm glad not to have to meet that butler again!"

She next approached Jonathan Cape to publish *Flame and Shadow,* but he declined, feeling that "it will not have a sale in this country which will justify my incurring the expenses of production and publication."[25] He offered to publish it at Sara's own expense, although he would not be willing to use Macmillan's sheets, which Sara agreed were not attractively printed. Since Cape wanted fifty pounds, which she thought excessive, she continued her search for a publisher through August. But at the end of the summer, having been turned down also by Sidgwick and Jackson, Oxford University Press, and Cecil Palmer, she thought she might go back to Cape after all, hoping that Ernst would return in time to speak for her as a business man and better the terms.

In spite of her inability to walk at any length, Sara spent long delightful afternoons in museums, having "the time of my life and no mistake about it." In London, she had not been able to get Veronal, the sleeping tablet she had been taking regularly in New York to relieve the stress over her mother's illness, but she missed it less than she expected.

The Fletchers called on Sara, although she was embarrassed by his "rag man" appearance in the lounge of her hotel and decided to "put a little more ice into my manner." She had thought of meeting Aiken, who was also in England, but Fletcher and the Untermeyers advised her that she would not like him, "and I fear it would be a big tactical blunder to let him think I want to put myself out to see him. He is a sour, conceited man." Aiken had never liked her work and was later to exhibit his distaste openly.

The real highlight of her summer was a meeting again with Stafford

Hatfield after eleven years. She had not been able to locate him until August 8, her thirty-ninth birthday. "I had a real thrill in hearing Hatfield's nice voice over the 'phone," she told Ernst. It was the voice that she remembered in her poem "Places"

> speaking, hushed, insistent,
> At midnight, in mid-ocean, hour on hour to me.[26]

He took her to dinner at an Italian Restaurant on Soho Square, along with a friend, Mrs. Leigh Henry, who knew "the D. H. Lawrences and lots of other interesting people." Hatfield occupied an old house in Soho that Thackeray and other greats had once lived in, and with his wife, a singer, on concert tour on the continent, he was seeing a great deal of Mrs. Henry. "He actually looks younger than he did eleven years ago. . . . Strange as it may seem, I was disappointed. I wanted him to have become a more solid and grown-up person. Instead, he is still, as Mrs. Henry put it when we were alone together, 'incorrigibly innocent.' He will not take responsibilities. He is a dilettante at life in spite of his fineness and his wonderful mind." He and his wife weren't getting on, and he left his children with relatives and others to be cared for, a "part of his unwillingness to be anything but happy and carefree. But it doesn't please me. There is a certain sadness in his face."

Sara was terribly upset to find herself alone with Hatfield for a while at his home before her birthday dinner, for Mrs. Henry had not arrived on time. She promised Ernst it would not happen again. "I say this because, while you know how utterly un-Bohemian I am, and how sophisticated and ready to manage my own conduct, you might better know that this brief unconventional visit will not be repeated." She could not afford even the appearance of a contradiction to the strict code of propriety she applied to Ernst.

In the weeks afterward, she spent pleasant afternoons with Hatfield, walking for the view on Hampstead Heath, rowing on the Thames, visiting the Rodin sculptures at South Kensington Museum and the British Museum. Poor Hatfield was always out of work and in financial trouble, allowing others to help him, a trait Sara found "anything but admirable. But I am not in the business of reforming my friends." Perhaps her judgment of him was harsher in her letters to Ernst than she really felt, for she was clearly anxious for Ernst not to think that there was any renewal of her interest in her one-time lover. She enjoyed the time with him immensely, however much she disapproved his half-bohemian way of life in middle age. At idle times, he composed musical settings for some of her poems. And one evening, after dinner at his house, Leigh Henry entertained them with piano improvisations and comic impressions of poets—Aldington, H. D., the Sitwells. Henry, himself a poet, read from his forthcoming book—"not very gripping, nor human. . . . How much all such people are alike!" She decided finally that the friendly Henrys were hoping she would offer to take his poems to the United States in order to find a publisher.

Ernst, meanwhile, by late August was heading for Russia, on an itinerary that took him from Berlin to Stockholm, Helsingfors, Petrograd, and Moscow. Sara read each letter from Russia "hungrily," thrilled at his vivid impressions of what they thought of as a new country. "You will realize, though," she advised him, "that business men in America or here will be loathe to believe in anything but chaos there. They don't want to believe in anything else." One remembers her fondness for John Reed. But the Russian trip meant a postponement of their return until late September and countless difficulties in changing their reservations and obtaining staterooms. They not only kept separate bedrooms at home but also stayed in separate hotel rooms and staterooms aboard ship when traveling. And as autumn wore on, Sara began to fret about the chilly, wet weather, in her anxiety to return before catching the inevitable September cold, a matter of no small consequence to her.

Nevertheless, the summer in London had been a magnificent success. "I believe that I might be willing, or even glad, to live here for a year or so sometime," she wrote Ernst. She had not been so active in years, not only in rich visits to museums, theatres, and Regent Street shops but also in the stimulating meetings with poets, writers, and publishers, her inside view of literary politics and English character, and, above all, Stafford Hatfield to escort her on dozens of outings, even as far as Brighton.

Ernst's long-awaited return was sadly marred by her catching a cold after all. She took to her bed with sprays and gargles and canceled a trip to Oxford to visit Robert Graves, who was something of a hero for having arranged Vachel's triumphant appearance there in 1920. "My summer too would have been a perfect one (as earthly things go)," she told Ernst reproachfully, "except for this cold. If I had realized I'd be taken ill, I'd have gone home alone on Sept. 8, and so have escaped." She sailed home on the *France* on September 29, ahead of Ernst, arriving on Saturday, October 6, 1923.

Sara's return to New York was a hideously dismal letdown after the glorious summer. She was "weak and miserable" with the aftermath of her cold, the apartment was dirty after being closed for four months and was scheduled for partial redecorating, so it would be torn up for weeks; and there was a mountain of mail to face. Unable to leave the city because of the press of responsibilities, she tried to practice her customary quietist resignation. In late October, she wrote one of the nearly perfect lyrics typical of her later work, "The Tune." The "certain tune that my life plays" rises in an arc with mounting swiftness until it pauses at the top, "High over time, high even over doubt," then "faltering blindly down the air, goes out."[27] It combines the abstractness of music with a physical sense of movement and balance, like the path of a skyrocket, although nowhere is such a comparison actually suggested. She becomes a detached observer of the pattern of her own life, watching without emotion its predictable end.

In "I Could Snatch a Day," she asserts her capability of turning an autumn day into spring—always her symbol of the recovery of love and vitality—and even of breaking "the heavy wheel of the world," but instead

> We sit brooding while the ashes fall,
> Cowering over an old fire that dwindles,
> Waiting for nothing at all.[28]

At this time in her life, she was capable of a despair that brought her closer to T. S. Eliot than she would have admitted.

Although her poems came slowly, they were of consistently high quality. In November, she wrote one of her best-known poems, "There Will Be Stars," with its image of the return of two stars at midnight each autumnal equinox through eternity, while their house, their street, their lives, are long lost. In her first draft of the poem, the imagery was less personal, depicting the disappearance of all humanity, the reduction of the city to an empty field, with the permanent stars looking down. This conventional and openly stated theme was replaced by the more elusive metaphor of the pair of stars, which suggests a parallel with the lost lives of the two, as if the permanence of the stars mocked the briefness of human love, even while symbolically returning each year as a reminder of it. The stars teased one's mind with the reality of an incomprehensible design. She had written Eunice Tietjens from Santa Barbara, "I do nothing but dream and watch, and once in a long time make a song as light and useless as a sparrow's feather. . . . What did God do it all for anyway? What, what? I am learning a little something about the stars—it is all so big, seemingly so uselessly big. *What* is it for?" She told Harriet Monroe in 1926, "If I ever started a religion it would be star-worship."

In late January 1924, feeling "like a sort of fringe around nothing," she told Amy Lowell, she went for a few days to Crissey Place in Norfolk, Connecticut, in the zero cold and light snow. She also wished to have a good excuse to avoid the annual dinner meeting of the Poetry Society of America, where she was to be the guest of honor, and John Erskine, whom she disliked, was to read from her work, since they knew she would not. She had planned, too, to attend a concert of Fritz Kreisler with Ernst, "but I was so near the end of my rope that it was best to come here," she wrote him. She was reading Joyce's *Ulysses* and found it "a real contribution to psychology, but the sort of thing I hope will not become the fashion. It is the duty of art to select and coordinate as well as record."

Eleonora Duse was in America on her final tour—she was to die in

Pittsburgh in April 1924 before completing it—and Amy Lowell, uncontrollably seized with heroine worship, had been corresponding with her and writing a set of poems in the vein of Sara's early adoration. She sent the poems to Sara in January for criticism, while she was in Connecticut, but Sara, tired and no longer interested in Duse, responded only perfunctorily. "They moved me more than I can tell you," she declared. . . . "You have praised the lady as she deserves." She did not care to be reminded of her own early work or her schoolgirlish infatuations. "I wrote Amy to-day," she told Ernst, "and praised her poems. I do get a bit tired of being always a praiser. The poems, two of them, are very good though a bit over-done, perhaps just a bit gushing."

Amy Lowell's exertions to meet Duse and to arrange for translations of the poems into French, since Duse knew no English, came to nothing. In April, Sara wrote Ernst, who was traveling, "Amy Lowell is in town after her sad trip to Pittsburgh on account of Duse's death. . . . She is terribly grieved. Duse's body is lying in state in a Catholic church on Lexington Ave., and I shall try to go to pay my respects. Amy has arranged to have a huge wreath sent from the Poetry Society. The funeral will be on Thursday [May 1], admission by ticket only. The body will be taken to Genoa on a ship sailing Thursday or Friday. So ends one of the greatest geniuses of our time."

On February 20, 1924, Sara's mother died, after two years of sad decline and the anxious waiting of everyone around her. Sara wrote Harriet Monroe from St. Louis, where she had gone for the funeral and the settling of family affairs, "The house here is now my sister's and mine and is being dismantled and the furnishings divided between the heirs. It is a sad, hard job. The mingled pathos and the sardonic side of it would need a great artist to get them down. . . . It is better to keep as few belongings as you can." To Amy Lowell, she wrote after returning to New York, "I have been completely floored by the experience—I had thought that I had realized it all before it happened. But I hadn't. I went to St. Louis before I was well enough but had to hurry back to New York and am a good-for-nothing creature. Poetry seems so vague and far away! But I suppose I'll get back into it again." Her poetry notebook remained blank from February 1 until September 4, the longest period of emptiness in her writing in all the years of her career.

Sara and Ernst had planned to go abroad together again in the summer of 1924, but the settling of her mother's estate dragged through the wretched spring into the summer, forcing them to abandon the idea. The large house at 38 Kingsbury Place was slow to sell, and they had to drop their price before finally disposing of it. Ernst "needed a vacation badly— has had a rotten time at the office the past six months," she told Harriet, "and since nothing in the world ever thrilled me more than Yellowstone,

I engineered his going." Ernst traveled to Yellowstone for two weeks alone at the end of June, while Sara, who felt obligated to attend to business affairs, and in any case did not feel like making the long trip, stayed home, correcting proofs for the much rearranged and shortened version of *Flame and Shadow* she had paid Jonathan Cape to bring out in London in the fall. She had accepted an invitation from Jack Wheelock's mother to spend a few days at Easthampton as soon as Ernst returned and could go with her. But Ernst could not join her after all, and Sara went alone to saturate herself in peace and silence. Jack and his sister Emily had sailed for England on July 9, the Untermeyers were still abroad, and New York was hot and humid. She was longing for another grand escape, like the trip to Italy with Jessie in 1912 or even the recent summer in England.

Since neither Ernst nor any of her friends were free to travel with her, Sara arranged to go abroad after all, with her cousin Alice Teasdale, a woman fourteen years older than Sara, then living in Arizona, with whom she felt comfortable. Their itinerary was very sketchy. They planned to sail from New York for France on the S.S. *Zeeland* on Thursday, August 28, 1924, and, after Paris, to work their way south to Italy, returning in eight or ten weeks. Sara asked Harriet Monroe, "I wonder whether Ezra Pound and I could hit it off? I might drop him a line casually, if you think so." The unlikely meeting, however, never took place.

Sara and Ernst "said good-bye with more feeling than I like to exhibit," she told Marguerite Wilkinson. "If I didn't expect to see him in about six to eight weeks, I should feel desperately blue." But she thoroughly enjoyed the "lazy and dreamy" voyage on the modest second-class steamer, taking a French lesson daily and watching the stars at night; and a day out of Plymouth, their first port, she wrote her first poem since February, a faltering attempt to express her communion over the distance with Ernst. She and Alice decided not to leave the ship at Cherbourg, where only a slow nine-hour train to Paris was available, but to stay on till the last port, Antwerp, and do Belgium. To Sara's chagrin, the weather turned cooler and cloudy as they reached Europe; "I always curl up and wither as soon as it gets cold," she wrote Harriet. She had taken her electric heater on board, just in case, although it was not usable on the continent.

The trip seemed doomed from the moment they disembarked. After two sleepless nights in their windowless rooms in an Antwerp hotel, they skipped Brussels and took the train to Paris, but not without adventure. A French woman in their compartment had been put on board by her lover, who was trying to get rid of her, and she spoke unguardedly in French, believing Sara could not understand her. "I learned some phrases I can use when I am with my Bunnie," she told Ernst. At the French border, customs officers caught the woman hiding cigarettes, and

she claimed that Sara had planted them on her, a contretemps that resulted in a search of all their luggage.

They had been advised that Paris was uncrowded and hotel reservations were unnecessary. But the city was jammed with American tourists,
and all the hotels they sought were either booked up or beneath their
consideration. They finally stumbled on a small, adequate hotel by accident, while following a lead given them, and Sara cowered in her icy room
trying to extract comfort from the hot water pipes that crossed her ceiling. The outdoor cafés were too cold to sit in, and in the chill damp fog
they visited museums and historical sites. Sara fought off the symptoms
of a cold and ate all her meals for the rest of the trip bundled in coats
and sweaters. "When things are going well how I wish you were here,"
she wrote Ernst. "At other times I am glad you are not."

Sara believed in turning adversity to account, at least in her poetry, and
the cold grey days in Paris provided the imaginative stimulus for a set of
poems published in *Dark of the Moon* in 1926 under the heading "Pictures
of Autumn." The first of these, "Autumn (Parc Monceau)," was written
in Paris on September 25, and the others shortly after her return to New
York. After the dull months of burdensome worry and a life focused on
practical problems and personal ills, she produced another of the lyrics
that summed up her comprehension of life in perfectly realized imagery.
In "Autumn (Parc Monceau)" the colonnade curves along mirroring
water that is slowly covered with falling yellow leaves:

> And the marble Venus there—
> Is she pointing to her breasts or trying to hide them?
> There is no god to care.

The reflection of the colonnade among the leaves on the water is
"unavailing/ As a dream lost among dreams."[29] Too faintly to suggest
any kind of sensationalism, she touched on the psychological ambiguity
of her own Puritanism, and her belief that in the cosmic view one was
alone and it did not really matter. And the colonnade itself, like its own
reflection, is also only a "dream lost among dreams."

In "September Day (Pont de Neuilly)," the Seine receives the falling
leaves and carries them to the sea, flowing out of the milky mist and into
it again, as if from one dream into another. In the short moment of
consciousness that is the present, she is aware only of the inevitable
process of decay and loss. The autumnal mood produced her best work
in these years. "Fountainebleau," less personal than the other two poems, deserves to rank among the memorable poems in English on the *ubi
sunt* theme, with its echoes of vanished "heel taps" in cold empty corridors of the palace, the movement out into the geometric garden and then
into the corridors of the forest, which open into the mystery of time itself:

> The aisles lead into autumn, a damp wind grieves,
> Ghostly kings are hunting, the boar breaks cover,
>   But the sounds of horse and horn are hushed in falling leaves,
>   Four centuries of autumns, four centuries of leaves.[30]

"Fontainebleau is one of the most romantic as well as one of the saddest of places," she wrote her sister-in-law Wanda. "On a grey autumn day it is full of ghosts." All these poems employ the skillfully modulated sounds and rhythms of her maturest work to enhance the implications of imagery and theme.

Sara's annual September cold struck her in spite of all efforts to fend it off, although it probably was less severe than it often had been. In early October, she could no longer abide the cold of Paris and hurried south to the Riviera, where at least the midday hours were comfortably warm. Cannes was one of the most beautiful places she had seen, and she would have liked to sail to Sicily from Marseilles; but it was the off season, and few boats were scheduled. There had been nothing but mishaps and ill timing throughout the trip. She complained to Ernst that poor Alice, although "adorably sweet" and enjoying herself, was never able to understand French money, that she foolishly trusted everyone, forgot to pick up mail, and was unable to take responsibility for arrangements, which all then fell on Sara. They decided finally to take a ship at Marseilles that would call at Naples and Palermo before arriving in New York around November 1. She had come abroad for a rest, but was returning home exhausted. The return voyage was "one long nightmare."

After completing the few poems arising from the trip to Paris, Sara subsided into silence again, writing nothing between December 28, 1924, and May 4, 1925. Her last poem in December, "The Hawk," was another curious attempt to define the inner battle whose only possible outcome was death. Like "In a Cuban Garden," its central image was a deadly black bird of prey circling perpetually overhead, while down below, driven to and fro by "two quarrelling shepherds/ The Flesh and the Mind," people scurry and huddle as the hawk swoops down to kill. When she resumed writing in May, the theme remained the same. "Conflict" is much more explicit. Within herself, Spartan and Sybarite are gripped in combat, "evenly matched," struggling night and day, "my slow blood dripping wet." And no matter which one wins, in the end she will be "the defeated one."

Winters were hard to get through, and this one was rendered somewhat more complicated, emotionally, by a disturbing flood of letters from Vachel in early January 1925. Following the sudden death of his mother early in 1922, he had teetered on the edge of a breakdown, even violence, and in his now more frequent letters to Sara and Ernst he seemed at times lost in his tangle of idealistic dreams and hopelessness. In the summer of 1924, he had finally gone to the Mayo Clinic for his spells of mental haziness and had found that he was an epileptic, although he kept the diagnosis a secret from almost everyone, including Sara.

She had recently sent him a copy of the English edition of *Flame and Shadow,* and the effect was, in his own words, to open the floodgates. Living in the Davenport Hotel in Spokane, Washington, and desperate for a solution to his life, he suddenly saw her again as his focus and inspiration, the same as in the summer of 1914 when he wanted so urgently to marry her. She was still his artistic antithesis, but for that very reason necessary to his existence as a writer. "I cannot write or think or breathe in the exotic world which is your essence and to which your book pays tribute. Yet I pay them the same tribute from this distance, and I know you and yours are my final audience. Way way in my soul I know I am writing to please your sense of beauty and nothing else on earth. . . . I know till the day I die I should write and draw only for you. Your hand should always be on my wrist, or at least your letter in my pocket." She was "the deepest memory of my life. When I write to please you I write better clearer, more beautiful things than all else I have done. . . .and the Chinese Princess is my Sara. . . . I do not want to do anything wild or wicked, I want you and Ernst to help me to be very noble in this matter. . . . For my heart is coming home to you Sara—there is no other way out. . . . Really I must give you my heart—dear dreamer, I have held back too long. . . . Only my desperate need has shown me how deeply you were written on my heart."

This first seventeen-page letter was interspersed with rambling and repetitious references to problems with his publisher, his desire to marry and have twelve sons, and his conviction that his strength was at last returning. And then he sent a letter each day for four more days, one of them twenty-one pages long, scribbled in the late night by firelight in the deserted lobby of the hotel.

Alarmed, Sara replied soberly, urging him to read Yeats' *Wild Swans at Coole,* her own favorite volume of poems, which she would send him. To Harriet Monroe, she wrote, "Vachel has sent an avalanche of disturbing letters recently. I don't know what should be done about him. I had talked over all possible things with Dr. Wakefield [Vachel's brother-in-law and best friend] and it seemed decided that Vachel was to go to Egypt this winter. He could have made his expenses by writing newspaper or magazine articles. . . . But, as you know, he is in Spokane and underneath his thin layer of seeming to like it, is fearfully depressed and rudderless. He needs something to combat or preach to . . . a new background, a completely new set of ideas. . . . Of course if V. could find exactly the right woman to go with him, so much the better. I sometimes think that V's bringing up and mine might both better have laid less stress on the

Galahad idea. V. would be bound to be disillusioned by marriage (unless a miracle of a woman came along) and as far as a big family of children, nothing could be finer if there were money to support them. . . . What is to be done?"

There was a parallel in Sara's loss of her father and Vachel's loss of his mother. They each had a parent of the opposite sex to whom they were inordinately attached, and death left them bereft and vulnerable in their forties. Sara sensed correctly that he now needed a woman to restore the lost sense of stability. Sara had little to offer him but a kind of restrained and kindly warmth in which she took pains to include Ernst equally, with her usual insistence that the propriety of her married state be acknowledged. Vachel's letter of February 17 was a poem:

Dear Sara:—

> I
> Will not forget
> That golden queen
> For whom I wrote
> The best song
> Of my days.
> Her hand
> Was on my hand,
> And on my heart,
> And we were no more
> Than one breath apart,—
> The day we wrote
> The best song
> Of my days.

Then the volume of correspondence diminished, and Vachel's wild instability seemed to steady itself. "When I began to pour out the ink in your direction the first of the year," he wrote her in March, "you were surely a godsend. Tonight I am more the master of myself and your kind hand greatly helped."

Then there was silence until late May, when Vachel suddenly announced that he had married Elizabeth Conner on May 19. She was twenty-three and was then teaching in the Spokane high school. They had only met on April 10. As it turned out, if Vachel were to be married at all, he had unquestionably discovered the "miracle of a woman" Sara prescribed. Sara, always uncomfortable at being set up as Vachel's feminine inspiration, welcomed the marriage warmly and sent Elizabeth Lindsay the gift of a white silk Chinese shawl.

Earlier in 1925, Sara had gone to the "blue and white wilderness" of Lake Mohopac, New York, for two weeks in late January and early February for another of her periodic rest cures, and even did some tobogganing. She had notified Vachel, somewhat coolly, that she would neither receive nor send any letters while there, apparently with the intention of stanching the flood of his letters to her. But this was only a subterfuge, for she carried on her usual correspondence, and while there read two reviews of her work, opposite in point of view, that by coincidence appeared simultaneously—a brief essay by Harriet Monroe in the February 1925 issue of *Poetry*, and a lengthier treatment in an article on love poetry, "It Is in Truth a Pretty Toy," by Conrad Aiken in the February *Dial*. Aiken, whom Sara and her friends regarded as a touchy, waspish man, compared modern love poetry with that of the seventeenth century, using Sara's work as "the best version of the present 'tradition.' " This, he declared, "is, in the upshot, her undoing. For one cannot examine her work very long or very carefully without discovering that she is emphatically that sort of poet who, equipped with a very striking technical skill, yet lacks what we loosely term 'personality' and perforce relies wholly on a convention." He went on to find her work vacant, sentimental, lacking precision, her poems often padded, and too charmingly familiar, lacking psychological complexity. Although Sara might have accepted some of these criticisms if applied to her apprentice poems, she was angered at their unfairness as a critique of her recent mature work. And as a woman she knew more than Aiken did about the subtle tyrannies of convention and the condescension of male critics toward poetry by women, particularly their failure to recognize feminine personality as anything other than conventional.

Harriet Monroe's review found exactly the opposite: "This power of personality in her may prove the strongest factor in the persistence of her fame—indeed, fame, in the ultimate analysis, is always based on personality." Miss Monroe did not make Aiken's mistake of lumping all of her work together, but distinguished the stages of her growth from a "typical well-bred American girl" who "dreamed and rhymed over Duse's photographs" to "a fully developed fine spirit" expressing itself in work "austere and mature. . . with an economy of phrase and a simple lyric intensity."

Sara practiced her prescription for anger by quickly withdrawing from any concern over the matter. "Conrad Aiken reduces me to ashes in the Feb. Dial," she wrote Jessie Rittenhouse, "but I seem not to mind it particularly. He does the thing from his own ultra sophisticated standpoint as well as somewhat unfairly—not taking into account (apparently) what *are* and what are *not* love lyrics. For instance—oh well, I'll not bother you with it. My annoyance has cooled anyway."

In her present mood, Sara had withdrawn into inactivity, not even writing. Ernst had grown dissatisfied with his position at the Lawrence Company, but could not seem to find an alternative or to lessen the pace that kept Sara continually upset. "I am always preaching out-door exer-

cise," she told his sister Wanda, "but to very little purpose." The Untermeyers had returned from abroad, but Sara seldom saw them. "We have
seen few poets," she told Jessie, "and never go to the Poetry Society. It
is so changed from the old days."

Ernst was off in May 1925 on a business trip to Cuba and there was
hectic preparation for his departure to Europe on a trip that would take
him away for the summer, where he would address the International
Chamber of Commerce in Brussels on cooperation in credit. He had been
"so nervous and over-wrought from fatigue his state alarmed me," Sara
wrote Wanda Filsinger. "Sometimes I wonder just where this frantic
ambition of his will bring him. We rarely have a quiet evening together
and when we do he is so tired that I insist on going to bed early." The
affairs at his office were a tangle, and he seldom came home before 7:30
at night. "This whole winter and spring he has been under a frightful
strain. . . . Everything that I can do to calm and rest him, is done, but he
drives himself like a galley slave, accepting this and that and the other
invitation to do things that he thinks will bring him into greater prominence. I remonstrate in vain. Preaching quiet and exercise and relaxation
is like talking to the wind." They were never able to travel abroad together harmoniously because of this constant interference of business,
and "besides I did not want to be a hindrance—I simply *can* not travel
at his rate of speed."

Yet, Sara was proud of Ernst's successes, and when the *New York Times*
carried a story on the Brussels conference with prominent mention of
him, she wrote him excitedly, urging him not to stint but to see everyone
and go everywhere he needed to, she would cable more money. She
herself was off to Woodstock to sort through her poems and begin arranging them for another book, to be published in 1926. "I wish I were
in the mood to write," she said, "but perhaps I shall be soon." She was
reading Milton, Balzac, and Tolstoy, and a book on Kant. Ernst went to
Italy and then to Egypt, where he was forced to wait several weeks for his
textile samples to arrive, and his return was postponed until September.

During the summer, Sara served as a judge of the Witter Bynner Un-
dergraduate Poetry Contest, sponsored by the Poetry Society of America.
Although she usually begged off such responsibilities, she could not
refuse an old friend. Bynner, now in New Mexico, and a friend there of
D. H. Lawrence, was a link with her first days in New York. Sara recommended that first prize go to Countee Cullen, then a student at New York
University, as "by far the most interesting."[31] Cullen had won second
place the two previous years and was to publish his first book, *Color,* in
the fall of 1925.

Sara did write a few poems that summer after all. In Ernst's long
absence, she reviewed her life again and the curious, hopeless stagnation
into which she had drifted, and recorded it in a long poem, "I Lived in

My Life as a Dream," published in the *London Mercury* in September 1926, but never in the United States:

> I lived in my life as a dream,
> The unrest, the haste unending,
> Were as the unrest of a dream,
> The search was a search in a dream.
> But I said, "When I go home
> To the house we have known together,
> I shall tear myself out of this web
> Of spidery silver.
> The man's voice that waked me
> (If ever I was awakened),
> I can call to mind in that house...
> But when I had opened that door,
> When I stood again in that room
> It was empty,
> I could not recall
> The way his voice lived and its low
> Beating and violent beauty.
> I only knew it was lovely—I could not remember its ways.
>
> The chairs, the curtains, the cushions
> That had lived in that river of sound
> So many and many a night,
> They were saturated with sound
> Of the voice that I tried to hear,
> Left me still in the stillness.
> Then I cried to my mind
> "Call it back! Is memory nothing at all
> But a place to lose one's treasures?"
> Yet only the dusty voices
> Of many another came calling
> In a thin confusion and clamour—
> The voice that I loved was not there;
> I remembered all it had seemed like,
> I could not capture itself.
> I said, "It is peaceful as mountains
> Vague and great in the moonlight;
> It is clear as the word
> Of a cow-bell far off through soft rain
> In a place of moist fragrance and foliage;
> It is heavy as the eternal
> Unanswered questions of man;
> Insistent as the sudden
> Call of a plucked violin-string"—
> Ugh—these are words, I shall be
> Beseeching my brain no more.

> Let that sound be lost in my heart—
> Let me live out my life as a dream.

Whatever the lacks or tensions in their marriage, Sara had always instinctively expected from Ernst a sense of peace and security, as she had from her father. This is perhaps why his restless activity disturbed her so and why she could not abide his fretfulness and discontent. As she had closed all disconcerting elements out of her life, one by one, and withdrawn into the perfect peace and calm of self-containment, hoping to still the conflicts within herself, she began to find in the summer of 1925 that Ernst was being shut out also by that same relentless process, relegated like the rest to memory.

Such times of self-realization were usually followed by the nausea of nihilistic despair. In September, she wrote the sonnet "So this was all," which again foresaw an ending in pointlessness:

> So this was all there was to the great play
>   She had come so far to act in, this was all—
>   Except the short last act and the slow fall
> Of the final curtain, that might catch half-way,
> As final curtains do, and leave the grey
>   Lorn end of things too long exposed. The hall
>   Clapped faintly, and she took her curtain call,
> Knowing how little she had left to say.
> And in the pause before the last act started,
>   Slowly upinning the roses she had worn,
>   She reconsidered lines that had been said
> And found them hardly worthy the high-hearted
> Ardor that she had brought, nor the bright, torn
>   Roses that shattered round her, dripping red.[32]

But once having expressed the worst of her own thoughts, she found it easier to write, and the slim productivity resumed.

Ernst's return from Egypt in September did not restore a sense of closeness between them. His worry and ceaseless activity seemed to depress and annoy her more than ever; it had grown to be a fixed grievance with her. She kept to her own slow pace, no longer pressing herself to hurry her next book in to print.

The fall and winter of 1925 were more than usually depressing. "The cold grey days have started in early this year—I hate winter so!" she wrote to Irma on December 1. In early November, she had a tooth extracted, followed by complications, severe pain, a swollen face, with visits several times a week to the surgeon for a month and a half. And Ernst: "I am at my wit's end about him—he keeps himself so rushed every minute," she complained, "and works so much at night." His nervousness drove her frantic, and after a siege of the grippe she and Ernst both agreed that she needed more than the customary January escape to a New England inn for a week or two. She arranged to spend a month in Winter Park, Florida, where Jessie Rittenhouse and her husband of a few years, Clinton Scollard, whom Sara did not know well, now wintered. She would stay at the Alabama Inn, a resort hotel, and work "on getting my lyrics of the last five years together for the book I have promised so long to Macs." Her departure had to be delayed until January 24, 1926, while she recovered from a second bout of flu, ending this time in bronchitis, for which she stayed in bed under the care of a nurse.

Once in Winter Park, where it rained incessantly, Sara went straight to work on her book, now titled *Dark of the Moon,* with Jessie's help, and by February 15 the arrangement and typing had been completed, although it was "tedious and every poem has a reason for being where it is." Jessie "fell foul of some of the age-coming-on poems, not as poetry," she wrote Ernst, "but because she is constitutionally opposed to admitting unpleasant truths of certain kinds." Jessie busied herself preparing lectures for forthcoming meetings of the Poetry Society of Florida, wanting to give her audience "something sensational. This attitude toward poetry is a bit less austere than I like, but one must take people as one finds them and Jessie is so dear about my new poems that I'd forgive her even blacker sins." Her husband, a retired poet of the generation before Sara's, seemed to be a nice old gentleman who waited on Jessie, played golf, and read. "Too bad he is such a poor poet," she thought. Life in Winter Park was tedious, on the whole, with only Jessie Rittenhouse to interest her. "The people here are all so dear and sociable that they bore me to death." While palm trees and Spanish moss dripped in the rain, "the old ladies (there are no young ones) are talking about their warm houses in Peoria or Milwaukee." Quite a lot of them were "fabulously rich, which does, I will confess, increase the interest. It is something I should like to be!" When Jessie gave a talk at the local arts club, Sara pretended indigestion so as to escape going; she could not bear amateurish occasions. "She does the job grandly," she wrote Marguerite Wilkinson, "with touches of inimitable tact in asking this diamonded lady or that shabby college professor (there is a college here, too) what she or he thinks on this cloudy point." She was ready to leave a week before her intended departure, partly to escape the dear ladies who swarmed to meet her at the hotel in spite of the lies she told them when she wanted to be alone; "this town would never do as a place for me," she told Ernst. Florida was rapidly being covered with dreary developments, nothing but "a place where you can escape the cold and eat oranges."

She had urged Ernst tenderly to write her of all his problems and distresses; but when he sent her a very methodical, if somewhat wooden, account of his busy schedule of luncheons, addresses, meetings of the Export Managers Club, art shows and concerts, with the intention of demonstrating how well he was doing, she scolded him: "I really fear a nervous breakdown if you do not let up the pressure. You were so over-strung all fall and winter that you need rest instead of more strain." Although they both protested often how much they loved and missed each other, their loving relationship had come to show many small signs of strain: the soft sarcasms, the reminders of past annoyances that would not fade away, the readiness to be hurt over trifles. Ernst had grown defensive, with a reputation for explosions of temper, and Sara was quick to correct and counter. It seemed difficult for anything to go exactly right. When Ernst, with excruciating conscientiousness, sent her a night letter rather than a telegram, fearing it would disturb her by arriving too late in the evening, it made things worse by being delivered in the morning before she was up. And so she reminded him with a kind of chilly patience that she did not like to be disturbed before 9:30 AM. Life with Sara was a daily "challenge," he said later.

Always solicitous, Ernst urged Sara to remain in the warm South until spring in order to avoid a recurrence of the flu. "I really can't see myself exiled from home," she rejoined, "on the mere chance that I might take cold if I went to New York." But she did accept his suggestion to stop for a while at Charleston on the way. And so, after her complaints of a cold late train from Florida, he was delighted when she reported that she was "getting a tremendous kick" out of the old city. She was "almost in tears" at the romantic atmosphere of the eighteenth-century residences she visited, the camellias, the voices of mockingbirds, the museum exhib-its of Parisian wedding dresses and veils. "This place seems to me to be a very real work of art—made by people who loved it and made it for themselves—not to please the world at large," she reported to Ernst. "Whereas Florida is a factory-made product. . .to make money. I think the thing in life that appeals to me most is an unconscious but unshakable individuality—something that is impassioned in itself." The ladies of Charleston were "the best bred I have ever met. They beat the English all hollow. . . . though I imagine anyone would get awfully tired of the insistence on 'family' here, if one had to live in the midst of it." Still, she would rather live in Charleston than anywhere in the United States, except New York, she concluded.

Ernst begged her to meet him in Washington as her nine-day visit neared its end, but she declined. She would "peg out," she said, "and you'd be sorry and all and all." He always crowded her, she said, with "what is called 'making the most of every minute.' For me that doesn't work, as my darling knows." The continual physical exhaustion she had experienced ever since girlhood, except during the brief courtship years from 1912 to 1914, had grown even worse in recent years. "One short tour a day is all I can do with any comfort or get any real kick out of emotionally or spiritually." She was already surfeited from sightseeing in Charleston and "have the slight sore throat that always accompanies being tired with me." And so she returned to New York alone, it being better that way.

The only poem she had written during the Southern trip was "This Hand," on the theme of aging that Jessie Rittenhouse felt she dwelt on too much. Sara had always been proud of her small hands, which were not only shapely, she felt, but were the creative hands of a writer. "Must I watch this hand grow old?" she wrote. Like the oak leaves and the rose, one's body was helpless to resist the drift toward death:

> We hoard our prime, we dread its going
> And watch it while it goes.

Although Sara was too squeamish for the work of Joyce and Eliot, preferring Henry James, she discovered in the mid-1920s the writer whose temperament was irresistible: Proust. Her mastery of the language was now sophisticated enough for her to read the volumes of *À la Recherche du Temps Perdu* in French as they were issued. Ernst had ordered the latest ones for her, and she took them with her to Easthampton in April 1926 for her annual retreat to watch the coming in of spring and to visit Mrs. Wheelock. Proust's latest work was "the most concentrated and distinguished of the long novel," she told Ernst. "No man ever lived who understood the human spirit better, or who more patiently strove to set down what he had learned. It is a misfortune that certain strands of his theme make his work pathologic at times, but there are long stretches of pure poetry." And she wrote Witter Bynner, "Are you too a lover of Proust, and do you follow his fascinating miserable mind through thirteen volumes as I do? All my blood, and all of it is Puritan, more or less, rises against me, but it was a Puritan who said 'We love the things we love for what they are.' "33 Proust's curiosity for the labyrinths of human perversity, his exquisitely refined sensibility, his nocturnal insomniac imagination, his invalidism as the condition of his art, his acute sense of death and time, all were mirrored in herself. She must have recognized her own thoughts when she came finally on his words on death in *The Past Recaptured:* "This idea of death took up its permanent abode within me. . . . The thought of it adhered to the deepest stratum of my brain so completely that I could not turn my attention to anything without first relating it to the idea of death and, even if I was not occupied with anything but was in a state of complete repose, the idea of death was with me as continuously as the idea of myself."34

But the subtler and more pervasive impression of the vast work on Sara was its attempt to recover and measure the meaning of one's accumulated years and memories: "It did not seem," Proust wrote, "as if I should have the strength to carry much longer attached to me that past which already extended so far down and which I was bearing so painfully within me!" Man's past was something "which he must drag about with him from place to place, an ever increasing burden which overcomes him in the end. . . . And it is because they thus contain all the hours of days gone by that human bodies can do such injury to those who love them, because they contain so many past memories, joys and desires."35 Sara's attempt to recover the lost voice of her husband in "I Lived in My Life as a Dream" was a Proustian exercise, as was her brooding on memories of her father. She had come to a point where her life seemed to stand still with nothing before it except its ending. The burden of her own past was the history of an insoluble problem from which there was no conceivable escape, and her fatigue of spirit was like that of Proust when he attained the full realization of his own past existence.

April on Long Island was a series of "glistening" days, with a "frantic cold wind." The exhilarating spring weather, the comfort she derived from being near Mrs. Wheelock, stimulated several poems, as always. "On a March Day"—because the weather was more like March than April—was an oath that "I loved my life,/ All things that hurt me and all things that healed,"

> And that I ceased to fear, as once I feared,
> The last complete reunion with the earth.36

"Autumn on the Beaches," in which she also shifted her experience to another time of year, celebrates the exuberant, "stainless," cold blue sea, which "Never in all the million years" was "happier than today." The sea had recovered its "virgin" youthfulness:

> Only the forest and the hills
> Know that the year is old.37

To Sara, spring held out the promise of breaking the pattern of one's life and starting afresh, free of the burden of the past. Although she had gradually settled into a feeling that life was a trap without escape, some of her poems also hinted that she would go back to her youth and begin again, if she could.

The sea is always associated in her work with sexual freedom and fulfillment. It is the scene of many poems celebrating her feeling for John Hall Wheelock and was also connected in her mind with the magical, love-infatuated voyage with Stafford Hatfield. But in her ironic maturity she suspected that the beckoning freedom symbolized by the sea might be only an illusion. A few days after she had written "Autumn on the Beaches," she wrote "The Fountain":

> Fountain, fountain, what do you say
> Singing at night alone?

It seems to be a deliberate echo of "The Fountain" written in 1913:

> Oh in the deep blue night
> The fountain sang alone...

The musical voice of the fountain is her own poetic voice, singing of love. In 1913, the fountain sang to an unheeding "great white moon" and a "satyr carved in stone." In 1926, the fountain no longer yearns for a response:

> "It is enough to rise and fall
> Here in my basin of stone."

When asked,

> But are you content as you seem to be
> So near the freedom and rush of the sea?

the fountain answers that she has heard the laboring of the sea under the moon, and the sea too is captive:

> "Nothing escapes, nothing is free."[38]

For those few days in the bright sun and wind, she believed that the love of life could be asserted triumphantly, and death accepted calmly as a consequence.

Sara and Ernst were spending more time apart than ever. It was obvious by now that it was only a matter of time until he would leave the Lawrence Company. Sara was irritated by his saying he would have made a change sooner, except for her—apparently because it would entail pressures too upsetting to her. The conflict over his work was irresolvable, for Ernst could no more help dispersing his intense energy in a thousand directions than Sara could help shrinking from it into her shadowy stillness. Under his polished manner, and the somewhat stiff, although handsome, appearance, Ernst was impulsive and filled with easily excited feelings. Sara believed he needed firm management and had often called on his sisters and friends to intercede when she could not influence him. Ernst seems to have borne her criticism with a kind of annoyed patience and simply tried to avoid disturbing her as much as possible. As he once wrote Harriet Monroe during one of Sara's travels, "These are busy and lonely days for me. The strain of modern business is terrific. But, of course, I am not telling Sara."[39]

Sara was morbidly depressed during the spring of 1926, too, by the Untermeyers' separation and the approaching breakup of their marriage. For almost a year Louis had been involved in an affair with Virginia Moore, "a young woman," Sara said, "whose verse he feels is much better than it is." Sara had seen Louis only infrequently, but had kept closely in touch with Jean, with whom she felt deeply sympathetic. "Judge what a sorrow it is to me who have felt for so many years so close to them both," she wrote Vachel. "It is like a bad dream. . . . If you and Elizabeth lived in New York for always, you would come to realize how it frazzles you out and breaks your heart. The emotional and nervous strain is hellish. It is bad enough to visit here as you do—but just subject yourself to the hot blast from this roaring furnace for ten or twelve years and see what becomes of you. There is no escape except keeping away from people as much as you can even at the risk of seeming cold and downright unpleasant." Sara referred not only to marital infidelity, which was high on her list of sins, but also to sexual promiscuity generally. That spring she had written another short satirical poem, "To a Loose Woman," taking someone to task not for her lifestyle but for her lies and self-seeking character:

> You merely ride the crest of fashion;
> Ambition is your special ware
> And you dare to call it passion.

To Sara, "passion" was holy.

To offset the Untermeyers' marital tragedy, however, was the birth of Vachel and Elizabeth Lindsay's daughter Susan on May 28, 1926. "I can imagine some of the dark thoughts that must come into your bright golden head," she wrote Elizabeth, "when the pitfalls and the bleakness of this world seem almost too bad to bring a baby into." And in a Proustian vein, she marveled at the beginning of a baby's conscious existence: "Imagine having your eyes and your ears function for the first time! How unthinkable to be drawing in cool breath! I wonder how much of the whole affair is registered on the tiny brain?"[40]

Writing very little poetry of her own, Sara had been negotiating the transfer of her anthology of women's poems, *The Answering Voice*, from Houghton-Mifflin to Macmillan, who were to reissue it in November following publication of *Dark of the Moon*. She had little hope that it would sell very well because, she told Ernst, "I am not made to be an anthologist."

With Ernst tied up in business, as always, she went off alone for a Fourth of July holiday in Ogunquit, Maine, where she joined Harriet Curtis and her husband Paul, a friend of her early days at Cromwell with whom she had kept sporadically in touch. But she preferred her walks along the rocky shore to their rides in an open car, where the chilly wind tore at her sweater and winter coat and induced the predictable sore throat. When the Curtises returned to Boston, Sara extended her trip to Intervale, New Hampshire, in the White Mountains through the rest of July, where she worked over the proofs of *Dark of the Moon* and complained vehemently about the commercialization of the landscape and the horde of tourists. "Huge signs in execrable taste 'Food for the Famished' or 'Here's where you rest' add to my chagrin," she wrote Ernst. "God did well but man has done ill." She took spiritual refuge in viewing the soaring profiles of the mountains at sunset, writing "The Mountains (Intervale)," which in its first version depicted God ultimately smashing his handiwork, a doom doubtless brought on by man's desecration. Her puritanism had unexpected ways of surfacing.

When Sara was traveling or resting at some country inn, Ernst always handled her business affairs, screening her mail, replying to letters that needed answering, and forwarding only such items as she might want to see. Sometimes he misjudged and earned an explosion of annoyance for bothering her with a book or letter she would rather ignore. Fan letters almost always went unanswered, and requests for public appearances received a polite printed card of refusal. But in July 1926 a letter arrived from a young woman student at the University of Rochester asking for a photograph of Sara for a former high school teacher who had fostered her love of poetry, a letter written so winningly and sensitively that Ernst sent it on to Sara in spite of her prohibition. The letter touched Sara too, and she not only replied but even encouraged the correspondence to continue. The girl was Margaret Conklin, who was about to transfer that fall to the Connecticut College for Women in New London. The sudden acquaintance surprised both of them with its sense of an immediate understanding. Later that summer, Margaret sent Sara a box of wildflowers, packed with the roots and dirt just as they grew. It was the first of countless offerings that sprang from a deeply earnest desire to please.

Sara's interest in Margaret Conklin was almost the only pleasant aspect of a summer filled with frustrations and disappointment. She wrestled week after week with Macmillan over the printing of *Dark of the Moon* — "by far the worst job of printing on any of my books," she told Ernst— and finally had to let it go to press, delayed by a month, hoping that misprints and badly placed poems would be corrected as she asked. To mitigate this vexation, however, Jonathan Cape was bringing out an attractive edition in London at his own expense, *Flame and Shadow* having been successfully received.

Her summer away from Ernst stretched into August as she left New Hampshire for a week with Mrs. Wheelock on Long Island. There she learned with chagrin that a book written and published by her brother-in-law, Joseph Wheless, had been picked up and reissued by Alfred Knopf. "I do not like the book and regret that it was ever written," she wrote Ernst's parents. Sara was deeply fond of her sister, but had long since ceased to conceal her active dislike of Mamie's husband. Joe Wheless was a one-time Southern fundamentalist who had rebelled against his religious background by writing *Is It God's Will? An Exposition of the Fables and*

*Mythology of the Bible and the Impostures of Theology,* a nitpicking, legalistic foray against the virgin birth, the star of Bethlehem, and other matters he had been taught to believe literally. Sara cared nothing for the religious question, but considered his performance an embarrassment that became personal when she learned that he was advertising himself as Sara Teasdale's brother-in-law.

The stormy marital problems of the Untermeyers seemed momentarily to abate when Louis agreed to leave Virginia Moore and sail to England with Jean in mid-August in the hope that they might patch up their marriage. Jean was hysterical—on the verge of suicide, Sara believed—and Louis went reluctantly in order to ward off impending disaster. Sara's sympathies were usually with Jean, although Lesley Frost gave her Louis's version as reported by her father, and Sara, who had been in love with Louis once, in her fashion, admitted he had a case too. Sara was in a constant state of nerves and depression over their conflict, keenly sensitive to the suffering of their son Dick, a student at Yale, whose emotional life had already been warped, she felt, by the instability of his parents.

Sara returned to New York tired, losing weight, and dreading to face Ernst's continuing agony over his job at the Lawrence Company. He felt trapped, believing that if he took time to look for another position Lawrence would fire him. "The idea of 'being without a job' is apparently terrifying to him," she wrote Wanda Filsinger. "The failure in St. Louis all those years ago is still a source of chagrin to him and I think the unhappiness incident to it has kept him from going as far as he could have done if that great shock to his pride had not come to him." His moodiness and irritability doubtless gave her further reason to withdraw into the self-absorption that had gradually become her way of life.

After the rapid friendship that had developed through the mail, Sara and Margaret Conklin finally met in the fall of 1926 when Margaret had begun classes at Connecticut College. She came over to New York at Sara's invitation, staying at the inevitable Martha Washington Hotel, and visited Sara one evening in October at her apartment. Their meeting brought Sara a shock of recognition, for when the young woman entered the door, she realized the source of her attraction: Margaret was the reembodiment of herself, of the lost youth that she had longed to recover so she could find her way out of the maze of her adult years.

> I thought I should see her
> Never again,
> I thought she had gone
> From women and men,

she wrote in "The Self," a poem dedicated to Margaret,

I hoped, and then
I had given up hoping. . .

But the day she met Margaret,

I knew
The self I was
Came home with you.

Margaret, of course, was unaware of the role in which Sara cast her and was unaware, too, of the similarities in their emotional backgrounds that intuitively helped lead to their instant rapport. Margaret, like Sara, had been troubled by a deep-seated antagonism toward her mother, although she loved and admired her father, a doctor. Shy, keenly sensitive, intelligent, and strong willed, she suffered from a sense of personal worthlessness, the result of years of living in fear of her mother's abusive critisicm. As a high school student, she had read Sara's poetry while walking along the streets, and now could scarcely believe that this famous poet had actually befriended her, taken an interest in her, valued her as a person.

To Sara, Margaret was a child. Sara suddenly saw the opportunity that had seemed impossible—to grasp again her youthful hopefulness, the sense that life was still open, the freshness of response to beauty. She could do it vicariously through Margaret, whose alert sensitivity and interest in life delighted her. They became friends almost instantly, drawn together by subtle and complex needs that Proust himself would scarcely have had the delicacy to portray. Within a few months, Sara was writing Jessie Rittenhouse that she had "come to feel almost like a mother to her." Later she told Margaret, and other friends as well, that Margaret was the daughter she and Ernst had never had. Sara's childbearing years had passed, burdened by the memory of the abortion and the failure to fulfill an aspect of her womanhood about which she had once felt deeply. After she thought she had irrevocably closed that door on her emotional life, Margaret opened it again. Margaret thrived in the warmth of Sara's maternal affection, able at last to pour out her loyalty and her desire to please, grateful for the unaccustomed approval and support she received in return. It was a remarkable friendship, and it profoundly affected both their lives, coming just at the moment of need by that mysterious route of predestined "lovely chance" that Sara felt governed her life.

After Margaret had visited Sara twice in New York, she invited her to New London, promising not to tell her friends who her visitor was, so that Sara could avoid the fatigue of facing the predictable crowd of curious fans. Dark of the Moon had been published on October 12, 1926, and reviewers were again calling it her best book. The first printing of 5,000 copies had sold out immediately, and a second was already under way when Sara went off to New London on Friday, October 29. Margaret drove in from the college on Saturday and then took Sara on a tour of the campus, and the next day on a drive to Old Lyme, where Sara decided to move to a country inn more isolated and quiet than the hotel in New London. Settling down in a comfortable room with a fireplace and visited often by Margaret, free of telephone and business, she became positively cheerful and stayed on until November 17.

Sara had always been careful in arranging the poems in her books to offset the "dark" poems with those of an affirmative spirit. This reflected her ambivalent desire to please, on the one hand, but to express the truth of her emotions, on the other. She shrank from the self-exposure implicit in her somber work, still perhaps laboring under the lingering Victorian belief in which she had been reared, that in art one ought to stress the positive spirit. It was more a concession to her audience, however, than any real belief of her own, an adjustment to the image she felt her public demanded. Before sending a copy of her new book to Ernst's parents, she wrote them apologetically, "I often regret that my happy moods, which are almost habitual with me, so seldom get into my poetry, whereas the sad ones often bring forth poems. Often these poems are not in any sense a picture of my actual feelings though they are of course a reflection of a mood." And she wrote Eunice Tietjens, "I wish that I could get the happy amused part of me into my books. But you know my heart." And to Jessie Rittenhouse she stated the essential truth: *Dark of the Moon* was "the core of my life." The title indicated that she was exploring areas unlighted by the moon of traditional romantic love.

The emotional lift she received from her friendship with Margaret Conklin carried her through the fall with some measure of relief from the gnawing problems within herself. On Margaret's second visit to New York in October, Sara had given her an exquisite travel clock from Tiffany's, engraved with her initials, and a presentation poem that Margaret read over and over on the train back to New London. On one level of their friendship, they discussed books and authors, Sara's habits of composition, and Margaret's life and plans for her future; on another, Sara tacitly pretended that Margaret was a child.

Before the end of October, the Untermeyers had returned from England by separate ships, their marriage finally in ruins. Louis sped off to Mexico with Virginia Moore for a quick divorce and remarriage, although Sara predicted it would not last a year. She agonized over Jean's suicidal depression and proposed that Jean and her son Richard join her and Margaret for a summer in England. She was unavoidably pulled into the emotional vortex of the Untermeyers' marital breakup, and the symptoms of her own problems were increasingly obvious. She had been losing weight again, was stricken with malaise and a series of colds, and was wretched as always over Ernst's frustration in his work. In January 1927, she had to get away from it all again by retreating to one of her favorite winter places, the Grey House in Lenox, Massachusetts.

Ernst, always hovering solicitously over her reputation and successes, and anxious to show how well *Dark of the Moon* was doing—now on the bestseller lists—annoyed her by forwarding too many letters and reviews. "*Please* don't keep a great pile of boring clippings and hideous advertisements and other trash for me to go over," she chided. "The important thing is that I should not become so bored by the tread-mill of 'keeping a reputation' that I shall want to chuck the whole thing forever." She smoothed herself with rides to Pittsfield in the zero cold, dawdling at reading and writing in her warm room, and eating large meals to gain weight. Here she wrote one of the posthumously published lyrics, "All That Was Mortal," with its depiction of life as a brief alighting of a bird on the fresh snow of a field, leaving its footprints — a moment of consciousness in the immensity of death, a "flight begun and ended in the air."[41]

Then one day while she was reading in the Pittsfield library someone showed her a newspaper with the story that Richard Untermeyer had been found dead in his room at Yale on January 25, at the age of nineteen. He had hanged himself.

Sara rushed back to the inn to call Ernst, who had been trying to reach her. His voice was shaken. He had spent the evening before the suicide with Jean and dreaded what the death of her son would do to her. Sara thought the tragedy would end Louis's affair with Virginia Moore but doubted whether it would bring Louis and Jean back together. Later Jean told Sara that her son had left a confused, pathetic note accusing her of not having given him a large enough allowance. Sara placed the blame for Dick's death squarely on Louis. Later that year the Untermeyers tried to assuage their grief and guilt by privately publishing a collection of their son's poems. They claimed in a preface that there was absolutely no known reason for his act—it might have been a De Quincy case of trying to see how far he could go, and going too far. But they and their friends knew better.

Sara was "frightfully blue" over the tragedy for months, she told Jessie. When she finally talked with Jean on the telephone, "It was like talking with some bodiless spirit—the voice seemed utterly devoid of all but sorrow and so forlorn that I could scarcely find a word." But Sara had her own stoical persistent way of working through adversity and was busy revising her anthology *The Answering Voice*, which Macmillan had reissued in the fall. They now wanted an enlarged edition, adding another fifty poems to represent the immense amount of poetry by women which had burgeoned in the decade since her collection first appeared. She was not in tune with some of the new work by women, which could no longer be called love lyrics, but tried to find acceptable poems in order to be inclusive. Edith Sitwell's "sawdust and vinegar style," for example, was difficult to digest, and the only appropriate poem she could find was "By the Lake"—"pretty poor, between you and me," she confided to Jessie.

After the collapse of the plan to travel abroad with Jean and Dick Untermeyer, Sara decided to go with Margaret alone. Her annual April rest cure was spent at the Lighthouse Inn in New London, where Margaret, who could not really afford it, had readied her room with a basket of fruit, some candy, and a dozen roses. Sara's thoughts were, as always, deeper than they seemed. She methodically introduced Margaret to the important people in her life—Ernst, Jack Wheelock and his mother, Aline Kilmer, Vachel Lindsay when he visited New York, Morgan Guaranty Trust officers—for them to assess her, as though this investment in a new relationship required the appraisal and approval of her advisors. Margaret "passed," as it were; everyone liked her. But, close as she and Margaret were to become, she never shared her intimate problems as she had done with the few friends of her own age. Margaret was required to remain within the magic circle of youth, not to be stained by the suffering of the accumulated years.

And so preparations went excitedly ahead for a summer in England, the climax of the fairytale adventure that Sara wished to create for Margaret. It was a strange, perhaps risky, course she had allowed herself to follow: the effort to awaken from the frightening dream of her life by vicarious rebirth, and to have the child she had once sacrificed, without, however, the responsibility or the pain.

They sailed from New York on June 19, 1927, on the S.S. *Arabic,* on what promised to be, at last, a repeat of the youthful idyllic summer with Jessie Rittenhouse so many years before.

# CHAPTER EIGHT

# "Let There Be Night"

Ⓣhe summer of 1927 came close to being the perfect idyll Sara had hoped for. Margaret was "so happy that her eyes are almost dancing out of her head," she wrote Ernst, crossing the Atlantic in the June sunlight, watching schools of porpoises playing. It was a summer absorbed in the enjoyment of Margaret's spontaneous delight as Sara arranged the unfolding of one surprise and pleasure after another. Their relationship would never be closer than it was during these ten weeks.

They sailed from New York on Sunday, June 19, on the S.S. *Arabic*, landing at Plymouth on June 26, a day earlier than scheduled, which allowed them to stop over at Exeter. Sara and Ernst had stayed there in 1923 in the same hotel, the Royal Clarence, whose windows looked out on the cathedral. "Margaret is in the seventh heaven of delight," she wrote Ernst, "and is a sweet and helpful companion." Sara suffered as usual from the chill, but this time came fully prepared: "I am in two union suits and my heavy sweater and have the gas fire . . . going as hard as it can." Sara's enjoyment while traveling was never without a constant underlying strain of annoyances that kept her on the verge of invalidism. Margaret discreetly left her alone in the mornings, sightseeing on her own, while Sara rose late and kept to her room until lunch at one o'clock, preparing for the single chosen activity of the day, which would exhaust her. Sara suffered from indigestion and flatulence, which drove her to take an enema every day of the trip, and she soon developed "a huge fever blister" on her lip. These physical ailments, along with the insomnia, were symptoms of her chronic depression and nervous exhaustion, which had grown continually worse in spite of this effort to fight them off.

They settled in for twelve days at the Lee Abbey Hotel near Lynton on the north coast of Devon, "decidedly my kind," with motor trips, walks even in the rain, and ecstatic enthusiasm that eclipsed all other trips except those to "Villa Serbelloni and possibly the Riviera." The hotel was a renovated monastery perched above the sea, surrounded by meadows and wildflowers, and a wooded hill where Sara and Margaret walked in the evenings to watch the sunset and catch a glimpse of the rugged Welsh coastline far across the water. It was Sara's kind of hotel not only for its peaceful air of history and old time, its lovely garden walkways and espaliered fruit trees, its vaulted ceilings and fireplaces and generous afternoon tea, but also for its solid comfort: central heating as well as a fire on the hearth in her room, a private bath, and first-rate food, including fresh vegetables from the hotel's garden. Sara's letters to Ernst were effusions of tender affection, unusual for her in these years, filled with the wish that they could share these experiences, and with "all the love you can possibly want." To Margaret, it was "all so new and so unspeakably wonderful."[1]

They moved on to London, "always, always *my* city," on July 9, where all of Sara's plans continued to operate with a fine precision of which she was proud. Margaret was like a ten-year-old, she thought, appreciative and happy and subtly responsive to Sara's moods and wishes. Sara had given her in the spring a copy of *Muirhead's Guide to London,* inscribed with a poem in the flyleaf: "Margaret, may London be/ As dear to you as it is to me." She encouraged Margaret to ramble by herself while she rested. With her passion for anything from Liberty's, she had her usual fittings for new dresses, bought Margaret a thirty-dollar shawl there, and even ordered an expensive evening dress for her, which Margaret sensibly canceled as something she could not use. On her good days, they made trips out to Stoke Poges, Eton, and Windsor Castle, and then in mid-July Margaret went off to visit two aunts in Staffordshire and Wales while Sara took to her bed. "The doctor . . . was so definite and decided in his advice not to overdo," she wrote Ernst, "that I am trying to keep from getting exhausted. I find when I am overtired or excited that the blood pressure shows itself in unpleasant ways and the indigestion gets worse." Sara could always find a doctor to advise her according to her own preconceptions, and she dwelt more than ever on the fear of a stroke.

Sara avoided English literary society on this trip, for her chief purpose was to bring to Margaret a reenactment of her own youthful delight in beauty. But this time she did not reel off poems spontaneously, as she had done in Italy with Jessie Rittenhouse. She had grown too autumnal, too burdened with "the sad wisdom of age," to feel that kind of excitement again.[2] She nevertheless kept up a lively interest in the literary game, and just before leaving New York had written a vigorous letter to the *Saturday Review of Literature* protesting a review of the unrevised 1926 reissue of *The Answering Voice,* which the reviewer had found out of date; apparently he was unaware that it was a reprint and not a new anthology. It was important to set the record straight, with her revision of the book to appear soon. Ernst, always more adventurous in his taste than Sara, was reading Hemingway. "I was amused by your account of the people in 'The Sun Also Rises,'" she wrote him. "I'm afraid I couldn't stand them even in a book."

In her effort to recover her youthful attitude, Sara's interests ran nostalgically to the traditional English poets, and so she had scheduled the third segment of their trip for the Lake Country, a treat for Margaret, fresh from her English Literature classes. On July 27, they were off for Grasmere, leaving the "city of cities" ("Paris isn't in it") for the quiet countryside again, where Sara thought she would be more relaxed. She had had her portrait taken at Hoppé's, where, although they hadn't heard of her, she showed a Macmillan brochure and got a half-off professional discount.

Margaret proved to be the perfect traveling companion once again, when she scouted out a pleasant hotel at Grasmere, the Swan, mentioned once by Wordsworth, with not only a fireplace and a view but a "PRIVATE BATH!!!!" This, after arriving first at a hotel Sara could not endure. And then the days unfolded almost as perfectly as they had in north Devon, with drives around the lakes, a walk to Dove Cottage, and a row on Grasmere. Margaret was "very dear," massaging her head when she was incapacitated by one of her worst headaches and attending scrupulously to her needs.

But the trip failed to maintain its perfection to the end. From the Lake Country, they went north to Edinburgh, where they spent only a day, unable to find a hotel room, and were forced to stay the night in a wretched boarding house in Melrose. Margaret was relegated to a tiny room under the roof, up many flights of steps, where she huddled in a chair all night to avoid an infestation of bedbugs, although she said nothing about it to Sara. Sara, through her usual imperious insistence, managed to secure a room with light and an outlook. Throughout the trip, Margaret had dreaded that the strain and enforced intimacy of travel might cause Sara to regret having brought her, and so she watched carefully for the subtle signs of displeasure. In her queenly way, Sara seldom broached her dissatisfaction with people openly, but would simply freeze. Amusingly, however, she sensed Margaret's feelings and was trying just as hard on her part not to offend Margaret. "This has been a beautiful summer for me," she wrote Marguerite Wilkinson, "though in some ways less of a complete relaxation than I had hoped. Margaret is a darling and has understood the limitations of my strength in so far as physical exertion goes, but she is a most intense person and a hyper-sensitive one. I have had to keep my wits about me every second so as not to wound her by any slips of the tongue. Even my facial expression has had to be guarded. But she is very unselfish and full of the wildest joy in beauty I have almost ever seen."

From Scotland, they returned to Grasmere for a few days before sailing from Liverpool on August 20. But Sara could not enjoy even Grasmere now, since she had become increasingly preoccupied and distracted by news from Ernst that the Beresford had been taken over by new owners, who gave notice of a stiff increase in rent. Angered, Sara first demanded that the increase be offset by improvements she had long wanted; but then she decided they ought to move, since "most of the nicer people were leaving," and the owners, she felt, had not kept their word. She advised Ernst to take an apartment at the San Remo, on Central Park West at 74th Street facing the park, but he insisted on making no decision until her return.

The voyage home was miserable: "storms, terrific damp heat in the gulf stream and an inside cabin, so I was a bit the worse for wear," she wrote Marguerite Wilkinson. She arrived to face the dreaded move—to the San Remo, after all—and got herself into such a state that Ernst and Margaret sent her off to the Boxwood Inn in Old Lyme, Connecticut, in September while they assumed control. Sara felt somewhat sheepish, but hoped, she told Marguerite, that "all will go smoothly for the child and for Ernst—he is not much at taking responsibility." Margaret faithfully fulfilled Sara's demand for perfection by numbering each bookcase, lettering each shelf, and placing an identifying slip of paper in each book so that Sara could return to her new apartment and find her books in precisely the same careful order she had left them.

It was not only the move but also the return to Ernst's restless and depressed state of mind and his constant overwork that distressed her. Her own nerves were stretched taut. In spite of the brief weeks in England when she had succeeded in sharing Margaret's youth, her outlook had soured, and she had grown more fastidiously critical and withdrawn. "New York is so full of interesting people," she wrote Harriet Monroe, "but I make friends very slowly and if people annoy me in any way I greatly prefer to be without them." Her few close friends were therefore more necessary to her than ever, and it was a sickening shock in January 1928 when Marguerite Wilkinson died suddenly. Marguerite had been driven by religious anxiety, interpreting each crisis of her life as a divine test of her strength of character. She had suffered a nervous collapse in the summer of 1927, and, to recover, she had set herself one arduous challenge after another to prove herself unafraid. She had been taking flying lessons almost daily throughout the fall and had begun swimming regularly in the ocean in winter against the remonstrations of all her friends; "But knowing her mania for 'casting out all fear,' " Sara wrote Jessie Rittenhouse, "and her feeling that it was God's will that she do these things, I tried not to rouse her opposition too strongly." During one of these swims off Coney Island in January, Marguerite drowned. "My heart was saddened as it has never been before by the death of a friend," Sara said. Apart from Ernst, Marguerite Wilkinson was at this time almost the only person with whom she had regular close contact, Margaret Conklin being in New London for her last year of college.

The aftermath of Marguerite's death preoccupied Sara for weeks, as editorial tributes had to be arranged and Marguerite's poems collected and published. Sara assisted, but declined to take any responsibility, or to write a foreword to the proposed book. As always, she took careful measure of her strength and refused any involvement that would distract her from her own commitments. Her chief preoccupation now was completing the revision of *The Answering Voice,* which Macmillan planned to publish in the fall, with a new introduction and fifty additional poems written by women between 1917 and 1927. Margaret helped by scouring the library for material, although Sara found she had already read most of the work of British and American women poets at the time it was published. Sara's introduction expressed her view of the changes that had occurred in the revolutionary 1920s:

> The decade since 1917 has produced more good poetry by women than any other in the history of our language.... The work of to-day differs so radically in feeling from the work of twenty-five years ago as to furnish the clue to the reason for the unusual amount of verse written. Women have been forced to write because they found nothing to hand that expressed their thoughts.

> Though the passion called love has not changed appreciably during recorded time, our ideas about it have changed constantly, sometimes with great rapidity. The immediate cause of the new attitude may be traced to the growing economic independence of women consequent on education, and to the universal tendency to rationalize all emotion....
> There is a wider range of feeling as well as a less conventional treatment in contemporary poetry....To-day there is stated over and over, perhaps at times overstated, the woman's fearlessness, her love of change, her almost cruelly analytical attitude. The strident or flippant notes that occasionally mar the poems, arise from overstating new ideas, a habit that seems unavoidable until through long possession they become unselfconscious. This is a period of transition. The perfect balance between the heart and the mind, the body and the spirit, is still to be attained.[3]

Although Sara drew attention to the outpouring of work by other poets, her own writing had virtually ceased. "Remembering Porpoises off

Cuba," written in early January 1928, reflects her fatigue of spirit, "on a winter night when this planet seems sick of her journey," trying to remember a sight vivid with life and action that could cause her to "praise my Creator/ Till the night shuts down forever over me." And "Age," written in March, acknowledged the silence:

> I who sang in my youth
> Now hold my peace.4

The long frustration and distress over Ernst's work promised to reach its end when he was offered a position as foreign sales executive for the Royal Baking Powder Company in February 1928. He was elated, although Sara seems not to have believed it would make much difference. And indeed it did not, for in a few months his life seemed more hectic than ever, the hours of work longer and the pressure worse. Once when Sara had come to New London, Margaret met her at the hotel dining room and saw her, unguarded, across the room crying. Sara did not explain, although Margaret sensed it had to do with her marriage. Sara could no longer smother her almost constant wretchedness, or the growing feeling that the strain in her marriage could not be borne indefinitely. According to Ernst's sister Irma Wetteroth, Sara had broached the idea of divorce with him sometime in 1928, but he became frantic and refused to discuss it.

Ernst's new job called for another long trip overseas in the summer of 1928, and Sara at first thought of accompanying him as she had done in 1923, perhaps spending the summer in England again or, preferably, in Italy with Jessie Rittenhouse, in another restless attempt at recovering lost pleasures. But Jessie was not free, and an accident in a taxi spoiled all of Sara's alternative plans.

On March 25, a Sunday afternoon, Sara and Ernst had been out walking. Fatigued, she took a taxi home ahead of him, and in crossing Central Park West at Seventy-Second Street where the surface had been torn up for subway construction, the car struck a rut and threw her against the ceiling. Acutely sensitive to any kind of physical shock, she reacted violently, suffering pains in her back, neck, and head. When the pain did not abate, she went a few weeks later for a rest in Washington, Connecticut, but returned quickly to New York when she began to feel worse. X-rays showed no fractures, and the doctors could find no particular cause for her misery, which continued to increase as she became more agitated and distressed. Masseuses, osteopaths, and neurologists could not help, and in April she took to her bed under the care of a trained nurse. Ernst believed her problem to be only a "shock to her nervous system," he told his sister Wanda, recognizing that fear probably had exaggerated the effects of the accident. Sara's fears were indeed exacerbated by the incident, for "I know what blows on the head mean," she wrote Wanda, "and I have had great anxiety to add to the constant discomfort. It seems that rheumatism often develops from an injury of this sort, and it seems to have attacked me practically all over." As her life dwindled to anxiety and pain, along with the old frustration at the intensity of Ernst's pace, she decided to go to Cromwell once more, the place that had promised relief from her more serious crises almost since girlhood. She entered the sanitarium on June 6, leaving Ernst to complete his own arrangements for the business trip abroad. He visited her on June 24, five days before sailing aboard the *Ile de France* with Royal's vice-president in charge of advertising.

Sara's feeling of grievance against Ernst had increased to new proportions. "The accident came when I could least afford to have an extra strain," she complained to Wanda, "for I have been nearly frantic about Ernst for the past year. He has worked much harder than ever before (though that seems impossible, it is so) and has been under such a strain that his sweet temper and dear ways have almost completely disappeared. Indeed, I have often, after an outburst of violent temper on his part, wondered how long his nerves could hold out. All my coaxing and warning and pleading went for nothing."

Her long stay at Cromwell—from June 6 to August 13, 1928—did not provide relief, so she returned to New York and was admitted immediately to Presbyterian Hospital. Four days there, with more X-rays and examinations, proved to be fruitless. Restless and miserable in her apartment, she cast about for some new retreat where she might begin to feel well again, and so went up the Hudson to Lake Mohonk Mountain House in the Catskills, only to return to New York again in a few days because it was not quiet enough.

Margaret Conklin had graduated from Connecticut College in June and had gone to work as assistant to the director of the publicity department at Macmillan, having been promised a job by the well-known editor Harold Latham, to whom Sara had introduced her earlier. An energetic and conscientious worker, Margaret was soon greeting authors on arrival in New York, helping to stage cocktail parties, writing dust-jacket blurbs, and reading manuscripts for Latham. This swelled Sara's motherly pride, though she took comfort in little else.

Sara was undoubtedly struggling with one of the worst emotional crises of her life, almost sinking under the weight. Her writing had come to a stop, except for occasional poems about her unhappy relationship with Ernst. She probably also poured out her misery in her letters to him, growing more accusatory, for she had come to hold him in great part responsible for her emotional state. The record of her dissatisfaction with

Ernst has been almost obliterated, however, for she destroyed the poems, and only four of the thirty letters she wrote to him on this trip have been preserved.

In early September, word reached her from St. Louis that Ernst's father had died suddenly. Ernst was in Milan, unable to return, and Sara tried to offer sympathy to him and his family, although she scarcely seemed to have the strength. "They understood that I was not well enough to go to St. L. [for the funeral]," she told Ernst. Henry Filsinger had been a stonecutter, a man of simple dignity, high principle, and kindliness, whom Sara had always warmly admired. Ernst wrote his mother, "I like to think of father as a block of granite—one of the materials with which he worked so long."

The sympathy Sara felt for Ernst at the death of his father must have complicated even further the mixture of feelings she bore toward him. During the fall and winter of 1928, she was almost certainly thinking her way through the problem of divorce, a step that to her fastidious conscience could not be taken without careful planning and an excruciating appraisal of its moral losses and gains. She could not bear the thought of conflict, which she had tried to eliminate from her life in every form. Margaret once upset her by bringing her disturbed feelings from some office irritation to Sara one evening and found herself promptly banished for days until she could recover her equilibrium. Sara could not face a divorce action unless she planned it privately and with a free hand, avoiding opposition and struggle; she knew how desperately Ernst would oppose her. It seems probable that she even sought legal advice at this time, since her actions, in retrospect, followed a consistent pattern, as if planned. At the same time, she was bound by her own sense of honor to do nothing deceitful. It was not easy to reconcile these contradictory pulls. There was the additional dread of gossip and notoriety, for she was a public figure and had carefully cultivated a reputation for model respectability, even encouraging her marriage to be regarded in its early years as a kind of Elizabeth Barrett-Robert Browning ideal. For the popular poetess of love to be divorced was too much in the cynical new mode of the twenties that she despised.

With relentless irony, life had destroyed her girlish ideals one by one, and instead had brought her a failed marriage, an abortion, ill health, and a loss of the ecstasy that she believed to be one of the chief justifications for living. The future could only be worse: a decline into physical helplessness, for in her mind she was certain she would have a stroke unless she could find peace. And so she had begun a slow retreat, a search to recover the whole person she had once been. Her friendship with Margaret had miraculously taken her back to the premarital days when life was expansive in its breathless adoration of beauty and when friendships were less trying than marriage. It was almost a blind push for survival. Because her marriage to Ernst was the mistake that had begun her slow decline, divorce was the inevitable next step in retracing her way. If Ernst could not be reasoned with, she doubtless felt that she had given him fair warning and would proceed as she must.

In the fall of 1928, desperate for peace, she sent Margaret up to Amherst to look over the Lord Jeffrey Inn to determine whether it would be her kind of place. Amherst had associations for her because it held the home of Emily Dickinson and the college her grandfather Willard had attended. Margaret's report was favorable, so Sara tried it for a few days, only to return with unbearable restlessness. In mid-September, she went back to Cromwell, where she stayed for another six weeks, until early November.

Even at Cromwell Hall nothing seemed to go right. An unsigned, scathing review of her revised anthology, *The Answering Voice,* which had been published in August, appeared in the *Saturday Review of Literature* in October. Sara instantly recognized the hand of Louis Untermeyer and quietly consulted Jessie Rittenhouse and Harold Latham before confronting Louis. She had no doubt of his authorship: "I have not read his criticism for over fifteen years for nothing," she wrote Ernst. "In his desire to have the field as an anthologist all to himself, he wants to damn everybody else's anthology. . . . I do not want him to continue this sort of unfair treatment in other places—he is probably writing for several papers as usual. . . . I have little to gain from Louis anymore. I do not care for him as a friend for I have lost whatever respect I had for him. . . . He is a bully, and I might as well call his bluff."

She wrote Louis a cold but courteous letter, bearing down heavily on his loose language—that her anthology was "slipshod," "dated," "makeshift," a "compromise"—and defending her work point by point. Louis replied sheepishly, "in the weakest humblest fashion you ever saw," she wrote Harriet Monroe, who liked Untermeyer even less than Sara did, "full of flattery and saying the criticism was meant to be 'complimentary'(!!) but was written under 'stressful circumstances and in great haste' and did not express what he meant! How I hate insincerity." Their friendship survived, however, chiefly because of Jean Untermeyer, who returned from Austria that fall and remarried Louis, the affair with Virginia Moore having ended as Sara predicted it would. Sara began seeing them again occasionally, and Louis, having been disciplined, treated her more respectfully.

On October 24, Sara, still at Cromwell Hall, had a tooth extracted in nearby Hartford and suffered yet another trauma. The "fool dentist" broke off a portion of jawbone while pulling the tooth, and in addition to the excruciating pain, she felt her appearance would never be the same again. She returned to New York in December, the "worse for wear," to hear that the San Remo was to be demolished and would have to be vacated by April 1, 1929. "After all the illness and depression that I have had to fight," she wrote Ernst, "it seems rather too bad that I have to face moving again. I almost wish that I had no belongings but what could be put into a steamer trunk." She was "tired and blue," still annoyed by rheumatism, and fretful. "I sometimes wish I could store all the furniture, bedding, etc., and have nothing to look after but myself until I get stronger."

These "wishes" were hints of the plan that was gradually shaping in her mind for a separation, with the usual justification of her state of health. Ernst's business abroad had, predictably, stretched months longer than he had planned. He would not return until January, after a six-months' absence, only to leave for another long trip in March. It was the story of 1919 all over again. Sara's letters were a litany of suffering. "I am making as brave a fight as I can," she told him. "I think you have never realized what a fight it is." On the eve of his return, she was considering storing the furniture and going to California again, perhaps via the Panama Canal. She had wanted to go to Egypt, but her doctors thought it unwise.

Soon after Ernst returned in January 1929, Sara, in her paradoxical fashion, left for another "rest" at the Mayflower Inn in Washington, Connecticut, after having complained bitterly of his absence. She departed New York with the violent headache that bothered her every month, but she was soon soothed, taking pleasant walks and reading Proust in the quiet of her room. "I am enjoying the magnificent essay on the memory and its part in all creative art which opens the last volume of Proust's great novel," she wrote Ernst. "He makes a splendid plea for letting the subconscious mind do the work. . . . He was a great writer if ever one lived in our day. What a pity he was a sick man, and not only sick in body but at times, like Hodgson's old unhappy bull, sick in mind and body both." The first sixty pages of his last volume "are perhaps as fine an interpretation of the sources of creative work as exists in the world. I am mad with delight over them.—I suppose because I agree with him." In March 1928, she had written a letter to Edmund Wilson praising his reviews of Proust in *The New Republic,* for he was the only critic, she felt, who fully appreciated Proust's achievement and importance.

In the clear, cold weather, she made "real progress"; the "havoc" wrought by the hapless dentist in Hartford was clearing up, Ernst came down to see her, and she had become markedly cheerful, even writing a poem, "January Evening," about her surprise to find the planet Venus bright enough to cast a shadow. "Life has lovely surprises," she advised Ernst, "if one is patient and watchful." Her letters to him were tender and full of assurances of her affection. "I have found my eyes full of tears," she wrote, "when I remember your saying that being a vice-president and director of R. B. P. Co. was not so wonderful as all the dreams you had. That is so like you, to try to turn your sadness into a sweet little joke so as not to *seem* sad." Ernst had paraphrased one of her early poems, "The Kiss," which ended "His kiss was not so wonderful/ As all the dreams I had."5

But this two-week escape proved to be only an illusory calm before an intensification in the storm of her emotions. She returned to New York in the midst of Ernst's hectic preparations for his next departure on March 15 and the chaos of another move from their apartment. To her utter chagrin, he was swamped by a thousand activities she felt he could better avoid, including talks in Cleveland and Baltimore, when he scarcely had time to pack, to say nothing of overseeing the move. His forthcoming trip would be his most ambitious yet: England, Belgium, Holland, France, and Germany, where he had established a subsidiary company the previous fall; to England again, and then to Cape Town in May, where a new factory was to be built, followed by a trip up the east coast of Africa with several stops, and finally through the Suez Canal to Europe in late August, where he would spend another two months before returning to New York around November 1. The "million details" of planning as well as going over the work of the previous trip in so short a time had meant that "I have been leading a dog's life," he wrote his mother.

Sara again felt bitterly that he had abandoned all responsibility to her for the sake of his career, and she nearly collapsed at the prospect of the move, which this time had deeply disturbing implications. She had not searched for another apartment during the past months, having decided to store their furniture and take a small place for herself alone during Ernst's absence, fulfilling her long-held desire to live unencumbered by marriage or possessions. Her plans suggest that she had already decided to file for divorce while Ernst was gone, but it is likely that she was still indecisive, laying the groundwork for divorce but leaving the matter open as long as possible until something happened to tilt her into it with sufficient justification. Divorce was much like the idea of death—carefully studied and examined from every angle, inspiring fear yet attraction, as something forbidden but promising relief.

With the help of Margaret and her maid, and deeply resentful of Ernst's frantic schedule, Sara organized the move, sold part of the furniture and Ernst's books, and was in the midst of packing when "at Ernst's and my doctors' commands" she fled to the Mayflower Inn again in a state of nervous and physical exhaustion. Just previous to this, she and Ernst had attended a performance of Will Rogers in *Three Cheers* on March 2, her first evening out in nearly a year, belying to some extent her claim of total neglect, although she may have engineered it in a last-ditch effort to force him to relax.

Sara planned to stay several weeks in Connecticut, until after Ernst's departure, returning to a sunny penthouse perched atop the seventeen-story Cardinal Hotel at West End Avenue and 71st Street. But her mood in the days before Ernst left was grim. She wrote him urging that he cut back on some of his activities and avoid strain and fatigue, "but I have come to realize that I have very little influence with you, so I suppose you will continue whatever the spirit moves you." She remarked cryptically, "I have torn and burned the page in my poem-book that you asked me to burn." Margaret Conklin took over the responsibility for completing the move. Two days before he sailed, Sara wrote Ernst, apparently for the record, cataloging all his major business trips that had caused them to be separated for such long periods: to South America in 1919; Europe in 1919–1920; again in 1923, 1925, and 1928; and now for eight more months in 1929. "Well, you have seen this spinning planet as few see it, and with an avidity that few could equal. May this be one of your happiest trips." Unless her health "should take a turn for the worse"—a phrase now becoming habitual—she would go to England in the summer, sailing June 8 on the *Arabic*. "I long to go to Italy, but am not strong enough to battle with the Latin temperament just now." She signed her letter with a "good-bye kiss and a hug for good luck and a good voyage. With much love, your Sara."

Ernst's sister, Irma Wetteroth, on receiving a letter from Sara about the breakup of their apartment and Sara's moving to her own place, knew instantly and intuitively that a divorce was in the offing and tore up the letter in frustration and anger. Sara brooded on her sense of wrong over the next weeks, returning to the Mayflower Inn for yet another rest, even though she now had a place of her own and was, as she told Jessie Rittenhouse, "free as a bird." She found a particular grievance in the fact that Ernst did not come to visit her in Connecticut before sailing. She had relieved him of the burden of moving, she wrote Irma; he "did not have a single detail to attend to, nor did he lose a minute from the office. It hurt me that he did not make time to come to this inn to tell me goodbye, as he promised he would do. He is to be gone about a year. He has come to consider business more important than life. As this place is only about two and a half hours from his office, the sacrifice would not have been great." Pointedly, she wrote him scarcely at all on this trip, contrary to their custom of many years when they wrote each other almost daily when separated. It was intended to be a deliberate and meaningful silence.

When Ernst sailed from Southampton to Cape Town around May 10, 1929, Sara was ready to act. She had probably been waiting until he was too far away to return quickly and interfere with her plans. She had not discussed the idea of divorce with any of her friends, and only Margaret Conklin and Jack Wheelock, both sworn to secrecy, were to know about it beforehand. Wheelock was amazed to find that Sara believed she could go to Reno and divorce Ernst without his knowledge, so he advised her to be prepared for Ernst to be represented in the action. With an air of conspiracy, she arranged for Margaret to receive mail from her at a post office box and to answer friends' questions about her. Since she had let everyone think she would sail for England on June 8 and since few acquaintances saw her very often, she could safely spend the summer in Reno, fulfilling the residency requirement, and be granted a divorce before Ernst's return in the fall. It was evident that she had thought her way through the plan long before announcing it, though once she embarked on it her sense of grievance against Ernst turned to agonized pity and guilt at what she was doing.

In late May, she left secretly by train for Reno, accompanied by Louise Wardell, a trained nurse and close friend of Margaret Conklin, and on arrival engaged an attorney, W. M. Gardner, who advised her the most expeditious and amicable way to proceed. Since she did not wish to sue for alimony, would pay her own legal costs, and had no children, she needed only to convince Ernst not to contest the action. He could "answer" the complaint, denying the grounds for divorce without legally contesting, thus saving face and leaving it up to Sara, the plaintiff, to convince the court that reasonable grounds existed. Sara found the matter of grounds to be particularly distasteful, since it meant leveling charges that could only be humiliating to both of them, and she sought assurances that the grounds would not have to be made public.

On June 1, she wrote a letter to Ernst announcing the end of their marriage, enclosing a copy of a letter from her attorney with information on how he should handle his part:

Dear Ernst:
After so long a silence, you will not be surprised to learn that I have arrived at the decision announced in this letter. And because of my talks with you over a period of years, you will realize that complete freedom for each of us is the happiest, in fact is the only solution of our lives. I want you to know that though you have seen me in tears so seldom (I think only twice during all the years) I have wept many times when you did not see me. And during these last few months, while I have been coming to the decision which is now absolutely irrevocable, I have wept often.

I do not forget our early happy years together, nor all of the beautiful hours that I owe to you. I am very grateful for them and I want always to keep the remembrance unhurt. The only way we can keep it so is the way I am taking. It is the way that, but for the fact that you are a man, and must try to oppose, you would very likely choose.

Both of us are too high spirited to tolerate a patched-up relationship. I can not even consider it for a moment. There must be a clean break. I shall make it here and as quickly as possible. I have had excellent legal advice in New York, and I have excellent advice here also.

I am doing everything in my power to avoid publicity of any kind for either of us.

I am living with a Quaker couple who have only two other guests. As you know, my tendency to solitude makes such a life tolerable.

You will realize that I shall not ask for or accept any allowance (alimony). I can manage on my own money and what I can earn. Will you please instruct your company not to send me any more checks.

Your life is full to overflowing with your work. I am proud of what you have accomplished and hope that we can always be proud of each other.

I ask you now, more earnestly than I can express, to follow the suggestions in the letter from my lawyer enclosed herewith. If you do this, you will lighten the strain for me and hasten and facilitate matters here.

My decision is irrevocable. It is no sudden idea, as you know. Absolutely nothing can change the stand I have taken. I beg you to spare me emotional letters or cables. Let us take life as it is, and act like the disciplined and mature people we are.

I will, of course, pay the attorney's fees and costs of my side of the case.

I beg you to make this ordeal, which is for me truly a terrible one, as easy as you can. This is the last kindness you can do for me.

My lawyer's cable address is AYRGAR, RENO. Please cable your reply. Let us try to live so as to be worthy of the finest of our days.

Sincerely,
Sara

Ernst, in South Africa, was horror-stricken to receive the letter and cabled that she must stop immediately, that he would return at once and they would talk it out. But Sara replied, wildly upset, that his interference would destroy her, she could not endure any more, that he must let her go ahead. Feeling that he had no choice, Ernst acquiesced, and selected a Reno attorney to represent him from the list she had sent.

The grounds of the divorce were predictable. During their marriage, and particularly in the past two years, the action stated, "defendant over concentrated upon his work to such extent that he neglected plaintiff and his home. . . . [He] remained away from home at nights until late hours, frequently returned to his home after plaintiff had retired and left in the morning before plaintiff arose." She could not stay up late or rise early without jeopardizing her health; she had needed his attention and help, "and the lack of same caused her great suffering." He was engrossed in business and outside affairs, and responded to her entreaties with resentment. This led, it was claimed, to their formal separation on March 15, 1929.[6] Sara doubtless viewed the charges as a gross caricature of her complex and sensitive feelings. She sat in her rented room in silent anguish, while all around her other women were happily celebrating their divorces.

In Johannesburg, where his trip had become a "horrible nightmare," Ernst was undergoing his own silent suffering. He finally wrote to his sister Irma in July, breaking the news to the family:

That I am heart-broken goes without saying. If I did not love her, it would be much easier, but we could not have lived together for almost fifteen years without a step of this sort making life crash about one.

As to reasons, what does it really matter? You know Sara is very high-spirited, and one must try to understand her point of view. Bitter as it is for me, I shall try to do so. . . .

I suppose the manner in which I have been working the past few years, with its effect on myself, has had a good deal to do with it. Then, too, my long and frequent absences. Perhaps, too, a certain lack of interest, or Sara's inability to participate in things that especially appeal to me, and perhaps thoughtlessness on my part.

I cannot dwell on the matter. I am trying my best to go on, and to face the stern realities. Sara's letter to me was very beautiful, and showed her at her best. . . . It is now too late. Regrets are useless, but I cannot help bitterly bemoaning the fact that I did not return from Germany, and that my duty to my company forced me to Cape Town. I am sure that everything might have been straightened out. . . . In many ways I am now glad that I am faced with many difficult and terrible problems that keep me busy. . . . If it were not for this fact, I should certainly go mad. It is in the dark hours of the night when I awaken to the realisation of the pain that is in my heart, when life seems no longer possible.

Ernst did not alarm his family with the news that he was about to embark on a history-making air flight from Johannesburg to Berlin. His firm had cabled from New York that he was needed in Berlin and London as soon as possible, necessitating the cancellation of his business tour of Africa. Unwilling to give up the African leg of the trip, he chartered a small one-engine plane with open cockpits, piloted by a Captain R. R. Bentley, who had gained fame for several previous flights from England to South Africa. Although commercial passenger flights had long been common in Europe and America, they were still in the future in Africa. Taking off from Johannesburg on July 10, they flew at low altitudes over some of the continent's spectacular scenery—gorges, waterfalls, plains covered with wild game—stopping at several cities in Rhodesia, Tanganyika, Uganda, and the Belgian Congo before a longer stay in Nairobi, where Ernst gave a radio broadcast on July 25 about his flight. Newspaper publicity gathered momentum around the flying businessman as he proceeded to Cairo and finally Berlin, where he was celebrated as a pioneer and prophet of innovation in international business. From Berlin, he delivered an after-dinner speech to a National Foreign Trade Council convention in Baltimore, by transatlantic radio, another first. It was the pinnacle of his career.

The divorce action was formally filed on August 31, 1929. On September 5, Sara appeared in court with her attorney, and the divorce was routinely granted on grounds of extreme cruelty. Ernst, who had been traveling in Europe, learned of the final action only accidentally on September 14 in Paris from a woman he chanced to meet at a business lunch. She had read of it in the New York *Herald*. "Isn't life strange and tragic?" he wrote Irma. "I leave it to you to imagine how I felt to be told the news by a comparative stranger. Outwardly I am quite calm and no one could tell how I felt. Mentally and inwardly I am in the depths of hell and despair. Life has certainly crashed and I feel horribly dazed and stunned."

Sara returned to New York in September to the Gramercy Park Hotel, where she faced breaking the news to her friends, some of whom were indignant that they had been excluded from knowing of the divorce until it was over, and felt they should have been consulted. She had made up her mind not to discuss the reasons for her action, realizing that this would both increase sympathy for Ernst, whom some thought she had treated shabbily, and give rise to speculations that would be worse than the truth. But she stoically held to her course.

When Jack Wheelock visited her for the first time after her return from Reno, she made an uncharacteristically exuberant show of delight, tossing some small object in the air and shouting, "I'm a free woman, I can do anything I want." She believed she could now spend all her time writing and felt that she had simply been unsuitable for marriage. But, predictably, her euphoria did not last.

Ernst, now due to return to New York in early October, groped for some contact with Sara, and poured out his feelings to Jessie Rittenhouse:

> I write in the most terrible anguish, as I feel that I must talk to some one who knows and feels and understands. . . . Oh, my dear, dear Jessie, you can never realize, never imagine the terrible—the awful hurt. I know that *you* know, dear Jessie, that I love Sara today, more completely, more desperately, more tenderly than in all the time I've known her. Never for a moment did I cease to love her, to admire her—to respect her wonderful independence of spirit. I find it hard to believe that all this has happened in anything except an ill dream. Oh, that I could be as brave—or so indifferent—as Sara asked me to be! Do you remember the morning we first met a little over fourteen years ago? How clearly it is implanted on my memory! I loved Sara then—today I adore her—worship her! And I have always tried so hard to make her happy. To think I have failed—it is too awful! If only I had not taken that trip to South Africa. And Sara's terrible words in her last letter to me—"Your life is full to overflowing with your work"—what an awful, awful reproach.
>
> Jessie, my darling, both of us love Sara. For the sake of that love forgive me for writing you. It is only a cry from a tormented soul in the nethermost depths of hell.

Jessie, perhaps feeling that the letter was an oblique plea to approach Sara on his behalf, and ever the diplomat, offered her services as a go-between to ease the tension between them and persuade Sara to see him again. But Sara gently and firmly refused, pleading ill health: "If only I were not still weak from the grippe, I should try to see him now, if that is his wish, but I think it better, for both our sakes, to defer any talks together until later, but a letter from him would be welcome." She begged Jessie to influence him to slow his pace and watch his health, saying, "He is still dear to me and always will be."

It was Ernst's tragedy that, with all his faithfulness and adoration, and even his liberal respect for women's independence, he had never understood her interior life. Sara had married primarily because her upbringing required that a respectable woman have a husband. Ernst fulfilled this need and worshiped her as a respectable and devoted husband was supposed to do. But through the years her private inner life had grown more guarded, more isolated and completely alone, as if in secret rebellion against a marriage to which she had never given her inviolate self. Ernst, whose love took the form of indulging her "wonderful independence of spirit" as one might a precocious child one was half afraid of, never seems to have known how incomplete their relationship really was or to have correctly sensed her unspoken needs.

Sara had pushed Ernst toward success in business. From her father, she had an intuitive sense of how to capitalize on opportunities and often seemed to see Ernst's career in a clearer perspective than he could himself. Perhaps knowing how much she withheld from their marriage she wanted him to fill his life with the kind of independent success she herself had sought in her poetry; perhaps she wanted to be proud of him. It may seem perverse that she should charge him with neglecting her in the pursuit of an ambition that she herself encouraged. But she felt that he exerted no control over his multifarious affairs, letting himself be carried along on the mad current. She knew how to eliminate the irrelevant, to concentrate her energy and attention in order to produce something perfect, allowing a broad margin of time and silence. Their ways could not have been more opposite. If she had hoped to fall back on a kind of affectionate companionship, in lieu of love, even that had failed.

Marriage had plunged Sara into disastrous emotional conflicts she had not anticipated but had thereby revealed to her the double life she led. As an artist, she was in touch with her deeper feelings and was forced, in honesty, to follow their dictates. After fifteen years, she had paid her debt to convention and respectability as long as she was able. Divorce was an assertion of the smothered self, now more crippled than ever. But even as she dared to do it, she surrounded herself with elaborate precautions and secrecy, as if committing a guilty act.

In November 1929, Sara moved from the Gramercy Park Hotel back to a furnished apartment at the Cardinal, where she took a few of her personal things, including the Chinese embroidered hanging that Vachel had given her for a wedding present. She was glad her furniture was in storage, since it reminded her too much of her life with Ernst. She was somewhat uneasy about her financial future—although the stock market crash in October seems not to have alarmed her unduly—and decided that Ernst ought to set up a modest trust fund for her. It was most likely Jessie Rittenhouse who went to Ernst with Sara's expression of need; she knew he was anxious to prove how much he continued to care for her. But his first proposal was inadequate, she thought, and as he left again in November for another trip abroad she wrote to him complaining that his life insurance would only provide her $60 a month if anything happened to him. Something more had to be done. She felt his lawyer had influenced him to be niggardly, since his proposal was not "the generous one that you would wish to make it. . . . You know the expense that I am always under because of ill health," she reminded him. At Christmas from abroad, he had roses sent to her. And in wiring her thanks, she added frostily, "I hope the affair that is pending will be settled in the very near future. I shall greatly appreciate your arranging the matter now."

Sara was not able to insulate herself from all unpleasant repercussions of the divorce, although she tried. She was saddened, she wrote Jessie, when Ernst sent her "a beautiful box of flowers with a loving message" on their wedding anniversary, December 19. Vachel, who had been both disturbed and curious about the divorce, always having generously believed that their marriage was as solid as Sara represented it, visited her in New York in late November. On first hearing the news, he had simply written that he was "stunned. The best comment from us is no comment." Now he "wanted to know the ins and outs of this sad business," and she relaxed her self-imposed silence a little to give him an oblique explanation. She had not even wanted to see him, but found it impossible to refuse. As a result, he left, she felt, with a misunderstanding. "I was unwilling to state the case as it is (or was)," she wrote Jessie, "and I could see that he blamed me more or less and went off with an erroneous idea that I had probably done the thing because E's affections had wandered or something of the sort." Vachel knew and liked Ernst and would probably have found it hard to believe Sara's vague tale of mental cruelty and neglect. Her deeper reasons, in any case, were beyond discussing. "You are the only person," she told Jessie, "who knows the true inwardness of my troubles, except Margaret, and, in a measure, my sister and Jack Wheelock."

Ironically, Stafford Hatfield, after a silence of half a dozen years, wrote her again, sending a copy of a book he had just published, *The Conquest of Thought by Invention in the Mechanical State of the Future,* and spoke of an impending trip to America. But "I am proof against old loves," Sara told Jessie.

Sara made an effort to resume work again, but divorce had not opened any closed doors for her. Her thoughts still ran to her lost childhood, and, in casting about for an idea for another book of her own work, she proposed a collection of poems for children, combining previously published pieces with some new ones. In December and January, she wrote

"The Falling Star" (dedicating it privately to Margaret), "To Arcturus Returning," and "Night." The project occupied her sporadically for much of the coming year, as she combed through her notebooks for unpublished poems so the book would not be too weighted with work already familiar. She managed to find, and polish, seven more of these. But it would be more than a year before she recovered her faltering voice and began to write the deeply moving poems of resignation of her final period. In 1930, she still struggled to recover a wounded life that seemed to elude her efforts at regeneration.

Although—and perhaps because—Sara strove for heroic self-sufficiency, she grew increasingly more lonely, finding herself isolated in her apartment too much with no one to talk to, and no project demanding enough to fill her time. Margaret came to visit her almost every evening, walking the miles from Twelfth Street and Fifth Avenue to West Seventy-First Street, because she could not afford the car fare, the only person Sara could count on for companionship. Her life had been filled for so long with the struggle against her marriage that it seemed empty now. She begged Jack Wheelock to telephone her during his lunch hours—she yearned for someone to talk to during the long days—but he was too busy to call very often. Vachel visited her during another trip to New York in April 1930; and the Untermeyers, who to Sara's amazement had just adopted a fifteen-month-old child, had dinner with her. And on Harriet Monroe's suggestion she met Louis Bogan, whom she liked. But as she grew more lonely, Sara also grew more austere and inflexible in her relationships, as habits practiced since girlhood became more pronounced. If friends came to call and arrived even a few minutes early, she would have them wait in the lobby of her hotel. Aline Kilmer was once forced to wait uncomfortably holding her small daughter, who had been crippled by polio and was strapped to a board, until the exact moment of her appointment. Always maternal in her feeling for Margaret—she kept a large framed photograph of Margaret as a child on her mantel— she had become almost impossibly perfectionist in her expectations, so that Margaret lived in dread of disappointing her and of being punished by banishment if she disturbed Sara with some luckless remark. Once, when invited to Cromwell Hall for several days, where Sara's quarters had an extra room, Margaret was abruptly sent home to New York for saying something that apparently annoyed, although she never knew why.

Their relationship was put to the test again in the summer of 1930 when Sara arranged another long trip abroad, this time to Paris. They were to sail on the *Lafayette*, a French Line ship, on May 30. Macmillan had given Margaret an eight-week leave of absence, ending August 1, while Sara would stay on until the mood moved her to come home. She was footloose, trying to enjoy her freedom. She even suggested to Jessie, "I wish you and Clinton were free to come over and take a villa on the

Riviera or in southern Italy for the winter, and we could split expenses!"

But a repetition of the memorable summer of 1927 was not to be. She had hoped "to have my mind and heart blown clean," she wrote Harriet, by breaking free of the painful associations of the past two years, not returning until she felt on top of her life again. To their great distress, Margaret became ill with a severe intestinal ailment shortly after arrival. They tried to last it out, managing only one venture, on Sara's insistence, to Sylvia Beach's Shakespeare Book Shop, but the illness stubbornly hung on, and Sara, accustomed to being cared for rather than caring for others who were ill, became "too keyed up" and decided the only solution was to cancel the rest of the trip and return home. They sailed from France on July 5, 1930, aboard the *Carmania,* Margaret suffering not only her illness but also the distinct impression that she had let Sara down. Sara tried to practice stoical patience, but nursed the feeling that Margaret had "dashed" the joy of her summer. The intended therapy of the trip had failed, and she dismally faced the prospect of pulling her life together again. As a flight from grim reality into the Europe of her dreams of beauty, the trip might not have succeeded anyway, for past experience showed that the return was always a miserable letdown.

Near the end of July, Sara could no longer tolerate the city or the summer heat, and still fretting at her spoiled plans, gave up her apartment at the Cardinal, packed all her personal things in trunks, and moved herself to Brook Bend Tavern in Monterey, Massachusetts, where she stayed until mid-September. She had been restless and unsettled for an entire year after the divorce, unable to establish a residence or a new way of life. Associating her unhappiness with New York, she seemed to feel she could exorcise it only by a prolonged and pleasant trip away, or perhaps even a permanent move. She made tentative plans for another long winter season in Santa Barbara but felt too listless to carry through. After a week at the Alden Hotel on Central Park West in September, she finally decided to settle down in New York and make the best of it. She signed a lease for an unfurnished apartment at the Bolivar, 230 Central Park West, with attractive views of the park by day and a panorama of city lights at night. It had been her favorite kind of location ever since coming to New York years before. Ernst was predictably amenable to her using all of their furnishings, still in storage, although she dreaded the sadness of living with them again. And so after a flurry of cleaning and painting, she moved in around October 10. With an extra bedroom and bath, she could even offer visiting friends a place to stay, although she worried that the apartment was somewhat beyond her means.

At first it seemed good to settle into "something more or less like a home," after the "fizzling out" of the trip to France, and a "wash-out" of her summer generally. "I had 'over-prepared the event,'" she told Harriet Monroe, "to use Pound's phrase." But underneath the surface she knew that any move she might make was done with desperation. "I suppose no one in the world realizes the depression I am fighting—but there is no use to talk about it."

Her book of poems for children, *Stars To-Night,* illustrated with delicate ink drawings by Dorothy P. Lathrop, was published in October 1930 and was dedicated to Margaret Conklin. The twenty-five poems, most of which were reprinted from earlier volumes, reflected the refined and almost unearthly love of beauty in nature which she distilled from her past and associated with her childhood. The mood was hushed, the themes predominantly of stars, winter, twilight, and changing seasons. Sara did not feel that her work generally had an appeal to children. But this extract served its purpose. It was also the first book of her own work since *Dark of the Moon* in 1926 and would be the last published in her lifetime.

Margaret had finally recovered from her illness and resumed her daily visits, remaining the only friend who saw Sara regularly or cared for her needs. Sara always greeted her with an affectionate hug but never appeared to wonder how she got there or whether she were hungry, for Margaret, who often could not afford dinner, was obliged to watch Sara eat hers, sent up from the dining room, picking at it usually with little appetite. But there were long empty hours during the day when Sara had little or nothing to do. "I am often lonely," she wrote Elizabeth Lindsay. "There are not many people that I care for deeply, and they are scattered over the face of the planet. . . . It is strange to remember twenty years ago and to contrast to-day. Not too happy a proceeding." She had been oblivious to signs of the deepening financial depression until early 1931, when the drift of things suddenly began to seem ominous. "This city is full of poverty and one cannot take a short walk, even in the park, without seeing want and being besought for money. What a mess civilization has got itself into!" Her own financial affairs were soon to be affected, much to her alarm.

Sara had still not resumed the writing of poetry. In three years, her only output had been a series of poems about her unhappiness with Ernst, all of which she destroyed, including one apparently at his request, and three slight poems for children. In her desperate loneliness, she advertised for a companion and hired a French woman, a Mme. Lagasse, who knew a little about literature, to come to her apartment an hour a day during these months just to talk with her and help with such housekeeping as there was. Sara and Margaret called her "Madame, Your Cash," for she seemed always to have her hand stretched out for money.

Sara had an almost pathological inability to handle money openly, although she was skilled at managing it. Paying maids or delivery men or reimbursing Margaret for purchases or services she had performed was a torture she tried to avoid by leaving money discreetly in envelopes rather than giving it directly. She had always made Ernst take this responsibility during their marriage.

In late January and early February 1931, the time when she annually gave herself a winter holiday, she went south to the Biltmore House in Asheville, North Carolina, "more beautiful than most European palaces," she told Jessie, returning February 7. Vachel had tried to reach her in January during her absence. He had been invited to make phonograph recordings of his work at Columbia University and wanted Sara to join him. When in New York in late February, he telephoned again, but she pleaded illness in order to avoid seeing him, in her usual paradoxical way craving human contact but rejecting it as too much of a strain.

Vachel had written to Sara very seldom since his marriage, leaving his personal correspondence mainly to Elizabeth, but now he suddenly began scrawling long letters to Sara in an effort to stave off panic, as he had done during earlier crises in his life. At such times, he revived her image as the ideal poet of beauty and balance at whose feet he worshiped, who could save him from the complex disaster his professional life had become. "I remember everything," he said meaningfully in his first letter and then began begging for a chance to talk with her at length, as he wrote to her from Rochester and Springfield and from Charleston, South Carolina, on one of the endless recitation tours that were, he believed, destroying him. He pleaded for her help to get him back to writing "bran new tunes" again. "I have no strength left—after my tours, to form one. When we first met—that was *all* I had. I concentrated on them as I now do on audiences. Even at Rochester where I have recited seven times and where they are as letter-perfect in my work as any crowd could be—they said sententiously apologetically etc. and audibly—behind my back after the recital 'Mr. Lindsay is regrettably touchy about the Congo' etc. Not *one inch* of artistic curiosity about the new Ms. of which I read there. Twenty people yelled 'Congo' to me between every piece. You have in you the power to save me from the exhaustion of this running fire." Vachel, like Sara, wanted to return to the time before his bewildering troubles set in. What he expected from her was vague, except "maybe only half an hour a year" to go over his new poems with him and criticize them. Professor Greet at Columbia University would record his new work each year, he felt, helping to reestablish his reputation as a living artist.

But even as he reached out pathetically to Sara to save him, who could scarcely save herself, he realized grimly that he was trapped by financial responsibilities and really was "no more placed to do all this than when I worked in a factory three months in New York, twelve hours a day. I obey now (1.) My publisher (2.) My Lecture Manager (3.) The long string of bill collectors that Elizabeth has to shoo away from the door nearly every day of her life."

In a remarkable twenty-three-page letter, he unloaded his deepest frustrations: "Lest I tell all this to *everyone* with an indecent explosion I tell it to you, and to you only." It was partly another diatribe against audiences and the "tea-cup hell-cats" who entertained him after performances until he suffered that "dead eye and stuffed heart and quenched laughter." It was partly a rambling and half-mad reassertion of his "ideals" that centered on Springfield and his apotheosis of Lincoln as "the nearest to the Christ type the world has seen," with a weak threat to abandon his family and go walking. And it was partly a frenzied self-defense against the new literary and critical forces that seemed to be lined up with the enemy to destroy him. His pride had been deeply wounded by the critical treatment he had received in recent years, although it was difficult for him to talk about it.

> Now let the swine who love psychoanalysis do their worst.... I have been psychoanalyzed till there was not a shred of me, my books drawings or recitals left, worthy of respect. I abhor the preaching of free-love and the dirt of men like James Joyce. The world is *not* the parrot cage these people think. Certainly *my* world is *not*. I believe in faithfulness and clean love and high aspiration all the way to the cross. I do *not* believe the cross is a phallic symbol and the Jews can say it a million times without convincing me.... I believe in Christendom with all my heart and I am *not* going to have Frazier's [sic] Golden Bough argue it out of me. I believe in clean family life and I am not going to have Bertrand Russell argue it out of me. I believe in clean living and United States art. I do not consider men like Proust or any other Frenchmen the ultimate oracles of my life.... I do *not* believe cannibalism was merely a religious ceremony, the real beginning of the Lord's Supper, nor any other supper I ever ate. I do *not* believe my return to Springfield was a "Matriarchal Complex."

Sara did not realize that Vachel's appeal to her was a serious symptom of the emotional and mental breakdown that had gradually been approaching. During his few brief visits with her in recent years, he seemed "in fine health and spirits." She had long been familiar with his railing against audiences until, as he said, "I nearly crack." Elizabeth Lindsay had carefully hidden his frightening deterioration from everyone. For months, he had been given to unmanageable fits of rage, public rudeness, even threats against her life, as if she and the financial burden of supporting his family were responsible for his ruin as an artist. His brother-in-law and closest friend, Paul Wakefield, recommended that Vachel be institutionalized.7 Sara did not see the concealed depths within Elizabeth's remark to her, in a letter in spring of 1931, that "Vachel doesn't know me at all; and the few glimpses he has caught have been so utterly disconcerting to him, that it seemed wiser to adopt a kindly anonymity, and I do fear it has become a permanent gesture."

Vachel's slap at Proust was a conscious bit of defiance, for he knew that both Sara and Elizabeth were fond of Proust's work. It revealed Vachel's deep ambivalence, for in Sara he allowed himself to respect and even be guided by the spirit of international culture that otherwise he despised and feared. But Sara's internationalism was of the Henry James generation, from the older, safer pre-Freudian era, a time when Vachel's objection was more against manners, sophistication, and the lack of American democratic roots. The new postwar internationalism seemed like a nightmarish collapse of moral values, and it must have disturbed him to see Sara and his wife following the new writers with interest. Sara retained enough of Vachel's kind of Midwestern puritanism, however, to deplore Proust's "sickness of the soul, that is disgusting to the reader without being sufficiently revelatory to compensate the reader. . . . Anyway," she wrote Elizabeth Lindsay, "he knew us all."

Sara had always written to Elizabeth Lindsay simply as Vachel's wife, but now found her sensitive to literature, keenly intelligent, and well informed, and over and over wished wistfully that the Lindsays could live in New York instead of Illinois so she could have her for a friend. "I am tired to death of poetry and poets," she told Elizabeth. "I have been reading much more prose recently than since my girlhood and find some of it good." She liked "the raw novel by the young American Thomas Wolfe, 'Look Homeward Angel.' It is a great work in spite of faults." She had "great hopes of Mrs. Woolf with 'Mrs. Dalloway,' but she is becoming too satisfied with juggling technique." She thought that perhaps *Mrs. Dalloway* was "too painful to be repeated. As you grow older—or maybe you know it now—you will realize, as I have come to do, that it is the vague feelings of discontent and sorrow rather than the clearly defined ones, that are really tragic. One can do something about the one kind, but the other is too elusive. For this reason young people are usually annoyed with such books as 'Mrs. Dalloway' and the neurotic sufferings of typical Ibsen characters. Well, it all is more like modern states of mind than the clean-cut sorrows of the Greek heroines, any one of whom would have been satisfied by such a simple pleasure as getting her brother buried or her—but I see I can't make a point with the Greek women. They had a tough time on too many counts."

The renewed contact with Vachel not only had its dividends in Elizabeth but also brought both Sara and Vachel some relief from their problems—through his letters, which provided a safety valve for bottled-up frustrations, and in his visits to New York that spring, when they could talk as old friends who had suffered much pain in their personal lives. Sara told Jack Wheelock what "wonderful comfort she had just from Vachel's sitting there with his arm around her or holding her hand. Two unhappy people comforting each other." Whether her influence was a factor or not is impossible to tell, but by May Elizabeth wrote, "Vachel, about whom I was rather distressed for a while, is quite himself again."

Vachel did persuade Sara to let Professor William Greet make a recording of her reading her work in late March 1931, although "you know how afraid I am of reading aloud," she confessed to Jessie. She extracted a promise that the records would be destroyed if she did not approve them. On hearing them, she was mortified to find herself sounding loud, nasal, and Midwestern—or so she thought—and requested that they be destroyed immediately before anyone else could hear them. Professor Greet tried to change her mind, but she replied, "I am afraid that my decision is unshaken. It rests on vanity—that immutable quality in woman."[8]

In the spring of 1931, Sara finally faced up to the fact that something had to be done with her own life. She was jolted by her worsening financial outlook, for her assets and her income had begun to dwindle under the impact of the Great Depression. Rents had been cut or lost from St. Louis property in which she had a one-fourth interest, and the income from stocks and bonds, on which she depended, had declined. Her work continued in popularity, although royalties alone could not support her. She had been shrewdly aware since girlhood that the fragile pattern of her life—the physical weakness, the crises of health, the frequent escapes to quiet inns in the country, the sensitive shrinking from life's harshness—required a great deal of money. Realizing that her father's wealth had made possible the protected world of her childhood, she had added to her inheritance whatever she could muster and so was able to continue in precarious safety even after her divorce. She had, in effect, been able to extend the sheltered atmosphere of her childhood throughout her adult life. The threat to her financial security in 1931 was therefore a threat to life itself, for it was inconceivable that she should be able to live on any other terms.

It became painfully apparent that the Bolivar Hotel was beyond her means and that villas on the Riviera were to be relegated to the lost dreams of the past. She complained, with little actual truth, that she had given up her regular dinners from the hotel dining room and now prepared most of her meals herself for the first time in her life. Casting about for extra sources of income, she thought of writing reviews for the magazines, an activity she had always avoided out of a dread of controversy. She had declined an invitation to do reviews for the *New Republic* in 1928 for that reason. But there was the example of Louis Untermeyer, who had exploited reviewing to his profit for many years. Sara turned somewhat timidly to Harriet Monroe in March 1931: "Once long ago you said that if ever I cared to try my hand at an occasional criticism, you'd let me. I have been writing a bit of prose for self-discipline, and I find it a good thing for the spirits. I'd be glad to do any really interesting book—no very small fry. If you didn't care for the result, you could chuck it and my feelings would not be hurt." Harriet sent her *Under the Tree* by Elizabeth Madox Roberts, an author Sara liked. Her review, "A Child Sings," was published in *Poetry* in July 1931. It was an impressionistic response to a book that was a reissue rather than a new work, and Harriet indicated that it might have been more critical. Sara defended her treatment and hoped that she might be given a chance to do some more reviewing in the fall. She wrote to Elizabeth Lindsay of some "hack work" she was doing in addition to the review, although precisely what this was is unknown.

Formerly, she had been able to count on the publication of a new volume every few years, either her own work or an anthology, to keep her name before the public and the income from her writing periodically refreshed. But with the cessation of her own writing of poetry and the exhaustion of all the other ideas she could think of, she faced a total barrenness at a time when she needed most badly to produce something. She was "almost completely out of the writing game," she wrote Genevieve Taggard in May.9 But Jack Wheelock helped her find a new project after all. The year 1930 had been the centenary of Christina Rossetti's birth, and Sara had hoped that she might publish something appreciative about the poet who had been one of the most inportant influences on her own life and work. Wheelock urged her to pull her ideas together and write a study of Christina Rossetti's life. Sara discussed the possibility with Harold Latham, the chief editor at Macmillan, and by late spring of 1931, had developed a plan for arranging a selection of Rossetti's poems and supplying a biographical and critical introduction. She signed a contract on June 5 for *The Love Poems of Christina Rossetti*, with an understanding that the text would be ready for publication within a year. Sara always worked rapidly and expected to meet the deadline.

She had begun research for her project in the New York Public Library in the spring, entering her observations in a notebook. But she quickly realized that even an introductory essay would require a great deal more probing than she had anticipated. Christina Rossetti had died in 1894, and thirty-seven years later some who had known her were still living. In spite of some financial anxieties, Sara decided to make a trip to England in the summer of 1931 for the purpose of gathering biographical material and visiting the important sites first-hand. She was also restless to go abroad, for she still had the impulse to pull herself together by traveling to places that promised inner peace.

The undercurrent of Sara's fear for herself, however, was far more somber and threatening than anyone around her realized. Her worry over money was only the visible manifestation of an emotional crisis that pressed for resolution, for the way she had chosen to circumvent her problems had come to an impasse. The hope of recovering her lost life had failed; there was now no way ahead of her, seemingly, but ill health and the end. In March 1931, she turned again to poetry as a means of coming to terms with herself. Her silence had coincided with her struggle, and now creativity returned as she resigned herself to the despair she had fought most of her life. On March 8, 1931, she said goodbye to her life, which she portrayed as a child's world, in "In a Darkening Garden":

> Gather together, against the coming of night,
>     All that we played with here.

Among the "toys" is "the small flute, hollow and clear," perhaps a reference to her poetry; and "The apple that was not eaten, the grapes untasted—" the sensuous richness of life, of which she had been deprived.[10] The first draft of the poem is less ambiguous than the published version. All the childish things that preoccupy one's life are

> Hardly worth the bother, at last, to keep—
>     But they served for us;
> Put them away together
> Before we go to sleep.

With this self-renunciation, the doors of her productivity opened again, and she wrote half a dozen new lyrics in the next two months. The second of them, "To the Sea," returned to the imagery that had always been somewhat guarded and obscure, that of the sea, the source of passion and power in poetry. This, too, was laid to rest:

> Bitter and beautiful, sing no more;
> Scarf of the spindrift strewn on the shore,
> Burn no more in the noon-day light,
> Let there be night for me, let there be night.

Paraphrasing God's fiat in Genesis, "Let there be light," she reversed the creative act by invoking death, ambiguously suggesting both personal death and the end of her writing, the extinction of the light of the mind. And the imperative comes this time not from God but from her own will. She had walked the "restless beaches" with "The two that I loved," but now both she and they have changed: "I cannot face the unchanging sea."[11]

If there is any doubt that she was literally thinking of her own death, it is dispelled by an untitled poem she wrote on March 16, 1931, "I went before the night came down. . . ." Her room is left just as she had lived in it—lighted candles, a fire on the hearth, a meal on the table, books on the shelf—

> Everything as it always was
> Except that simple thing, myself.

This was followed rapidly by "Truce," signaling the end of the struggle, but with the preservation of pride:

> Pride, the lone pennon, ravelled by the storm-wind
> Stands in the sunset fires.[12]

And "Wisdom," a sonnet in which she returned to the one solace she had salvaged from the years when she first realized that her marriage was a disaster: "the last, essential me."

> If that is safe, then I am safe indeed,
> It is my citadel, my church, my home,
> My mother and my child, my constant friend;
> It is my music, making for my need
> A paean like the cymbals of the foam,
> Or silence, level, spacious, without end.[13]

Life was a history of failed relationships; the answer was to be totally self-sufficient, supplying all human needs from within oneself. In this, she went further than she had ever gone, for she did not even look out on the world with ironic amusement, but listened only to the silent music within. Totally withdrawn into the shell of herself, she wished only "to relinquish. . .to let go, without a cry or call."

On May 8, she wrote "Ashes," a literal reference to her death and the cremation of her body she desired:

> Laid in a quiet corner of the world
> There will be left no more of me some night
> Than the lone bat could carry in his flight. . . .
>
> Now without sorrow and without elation
> I can lay down my body, nor deplore
> How little, with her insufficient ration,
> Life has to feed us.

Her only regret was that "these hands," the creative hands of the artist, would have to go "in the same blank, ignominious way."[14]

She had for a long time viewed her life as a secret battle in which she, the mortally wounded, slowly bled to death as she strove in pride to lift some token of victory even in the extinction of herself. In the spring of 1931, the threat seemed to her to become literal and external as she began to fear that she could no longer support or take care of herself. Although she had no serious problems of health, she was now convinced that her heart had weakened and that a variety of unpleasant symptoms were caused by fluctuating blood pressure. Her poems suggest that she no longer doubted whether she would take her own life; the only question was how soon.

But, having exorcised her demons, she felt a certain measure of peace and looked forward happily to the trip to England. She sold a group of five poems for some welcome cash to *Harper's Bazaar*, to appear in the November issue. She was angered by the publication in May, she wrote Harriet Monroe, of a "wretched poem, not one line of which is mine," titled "Mother," that was appearing in newspapers around the country "in all of its maudlin sentimentality," signed with her name, although she was unable to do anything about it. She had been reading Virginia Woolf's *To the Lighthouse* and *A Room of One's Own* and had revised her opinion more favorably—"I am a mass of admiration," she wrote Elizabeth Lindsay. "I wish I could meet her in England, but I have grown so proud that I cannot bear to *seem* to want such things, and they rarely fall in one's lap. . . . I remember Vachel's words, 'They do not know my pride, Nor the storm of scorn I ride.' Virginia Woolf is a lady, and God knows the race is vanishing. I rather pride myself on being one, but I may not be one after all. I suppose one never knows oneself." It was the divorce that made her hesitate.

Sara sailed for England on June 13, accompanied by Louise Wardell, the nurse who had gone with her to Reno, eager to leave her worries behind her—as indeed she did for a few weeks. Her landlord at the Bolivar had lowered the rent, so she could afford to sign a lease for another year and would not come home to face another move. London seemed less affected by the Depression than was New York, and she visited galleries and the theatres, writing Vachel, "I haven't felt so happy for nearly—oh, well, since 1914. . . . I adore being out of New York. I have become a bit stale in that city." She did manage somehow to meet Virginia Woolf, casually, as if by accident, and so could preserve her pride, although it can be assumed that she calculated the effort carefully. She "found her as exquisite as I knew she would be." She was "charmed by her noble bearing and generosity," she told Harriet. Nothing else of their meeting is known.

Sara traced Christina Rossetti's life through all the locations in London where she had lived, from the site of her birthplace, now torn down, to her final dwelling on Torrington Square. Searching for materials in book shops, she discovered an unpublished letter from Christina to her brother Dante Gabriel and excitedly bought it. Undated, it could be placed, because of its address, sometime between 1867 and 1876, and it mentioned a public reading from her book *Goblin Market*. Sara later prepared a statement about the letter to distribute to the newspapers. It is less a news release than a capsule of the information and ideas she had been absorbing about the Rossetti family. Her characterization of Christina emphasizes her feminine pride: Dante Gabriel "was the only person from whom Christina ever took criticism—indeed he is the only person from whom she ever seemed to take anything. Her gentle stoicism masked an impassioned heart so effectually that even the two men who wished to marry her must have felt afraid of her unvarying self-command. And her sense of humor showed itself only in slightly terrifying, if very rare shafts of wit." Sara's study would be shaped by the fact that Christina Rossetti was a heroine to her, in whom she saw the conflict between inner passion and outer restraint, with its consequences for love and marriage, that was the story of her own life.

Sara's euphoria in London lasted only a few weeks. From the deep emotional depression of the spring, she had rebounded to heights of intense happiness only to collapse again at the end of July, an ominous indication of her increasing instability. Eunice Tietjens had written her, reviving an old and warm friendship, probably feeling obligated to say something about the divorce, for she had been responsible for introducing Ernst to Sara and helping to engineer their marriage. On July 28, Sara replied with a long, overwrought letter, unburdening her problems and anxieties. Later in the day she thought better of it and mailed Eunice a second letter asking that the first "be destroyed and its contents forgotten as soon as may be." She had evidently, because of Eunice's unique relationship with both her and Ernst, gone into the complex problem of her marriage and divorce honestly and in detail, for she had asked Eunice to show the letter to Harriet Monroe; it "contained an explanation that I have wanted to make. . .by word of mouth," but had been unable to. Sara doubtless regretted having broken her rule and put her intimate feelings into writing, perhaps to surface someday and reveal what she had taken such pains to keep buried. Six months later, she was still begging assurance that "that sorry testament was destroyed," although she was grateful for the warm and supportive response Eunice had given it.

Among other things, the letter had apparently dwelt on her ill health and the conviction that she suffered from "arterial trouble," which caused "frequent and *frightfully* severe headaches and so on. I have inherited it from both my father and my mother but it did not develop in them until far older than I. With serenity (but where is it in the world, especially now?) I may drag along even to old age." She was pathetically touched by this renewal of a valuable friendship. "I do long for my friends. I have none too many."

Sara was forced to return to New York at the end of August 1931 when her money ran short and she learned of further cuts in her income. "What a troubled world I have come back to!" she exclaimed to Harriet Monroe. "Where is the muddle going to end?" And to Eunice: "I am a lonely person, and I cling to the few others that I love." She had not made as much progress with the research on Christina Rossetti as she had hoped, perhaps feeling less enthusiasm for the project than she did at the outset. But it preoccupied her through the fall, as she watched the deteriorating state of the world around her with deep foreboding.

Ernst had probably been on her mind a great deal more than anyone knew. After her first refusal to see him following the divorce, she had relented, and twice—in January 1930 and January 1931—she had invited him to spend an evening "to have a good talk about the old days," if he wished, even offering her guest bedroom for a few nights. Perhaps because she had second thoughts, it had not worked out. Now, in early November 1931, she sent him a letter from her German translator, just as a matter of interest, using it as an excuse to write him again: "A year and a half ago you asked to come to see me, and at that time I thought the strain would outweigh any pleasure the visit might give us, but we must both have recovered our composure by now, and if you should care to come sometime, I should be glad to see you and talk over politics, world affairs, books and my project about Christina Rossetti and your many interests. The condition of my heart makes this quiet life necessary. I seldom leave this pleasant apartment—it is my one luxury."

Ernst accepted, and so they met again and had dinner that November for the first time since March 1929, when Ernst had left New York for the ill-fated trip abroad. "We had a good evening," Sara wrote Eunice, "both of us resolutely putting out of sight the hurt places. I thought he looked fairly well and by no means more worn by these years than was sure to be evident in us both." Ernst had lost his position with the Royal Baking Powder Company following the crash and had opened his own firm as a foreign trade consultant. Sara was still genuinely concerned about him. She had evaded any direct contact with his wild anguish following the divorce and had doubtless suffered a guilty fear that she had done irreparable damage to his life. This must have been the uppermost question in her mind as they finally met, and it was with relief that she found he had survived, perhaps better than she had. She was emotionally stirred and, according to Jack Wheelock, "found him more appealing than ever. . .because they were not living together. . .and he was a figure that appealed to her compassion." And there was his "unshakable devotion." Although she had tried coolly to steer the conversation to impersonal matters, Ernst's feeling for her would have found some form of indirect expression. They knew each other too well. Shortly after this meeting, Sara changed her will, leaving a substantial portion of her estate to him, rather than just a diamond ring, as her will of 1930 had provided.

On November 21, 1931 she wrote the highly ambiguous poem "Strange Victory," whose title she also chose for what would be her posthumous book of poems. Its apparent simplicity and strong feeling are offset by its being only a single incomplete sentence, a series of phrases with no main clause to complete their meaning. Neither is there any clue as to the identity of "you":

> To this, to this, after my hope was lost,
>   To this strange victory;
> To find you with the living, not the dead,

To find you glad of me;
To find you wounded even less than I,
   Moving as I across the stricken plain;
After the battle to have found your voice
   Lifted above the slain.[15]

The pronouns in Sara's poems are usually deliberately ambiguous to the reader but always clear in her own mind. She sometimes addressed herself as "you," although more often a particular unnamed person; never the reader or people generally, a form she doubtless considered naive. Her method was to work from very specific personal experience and then to conceal personal references so the poem would be open to impersonal interpretation. The person addressed in "Strange Victory" cannot possibly be herself. The only one who fits the circumstances hinted at in the poem is Ernst.

Sara's divorce had been an act of desperation in which she had been forced to accuse Ernst against her will, for the battle that bled her was was not against her husband but against the smothering forces of social convention within her own mind that had trapped her in marriage in the first place. Ridding herself of the marriage had not been enough to free her from the conflict. What made conflict so unbearable for her was her essential gentleness of nature, which would not permit her to win a victory at the cost of pain to anyone else. To overthrow the Victorian inhibitions planted deep within her by her mother was, in effect, to repudiate her mother, from whom she had wanted only love. Even as a woman approaching middle age she could not bring herself to do this, and so the suffering had to be directed on herself. The agony she endured in divorcing Ernst rose not only from her sense of guilt in rejecting the marriage vow and its obligations but also from the hurt she had inflicted on him. Her submissive instinct would have been to soothe the hurt with loving kindness, making up as best she could for having had to impose it, fearing his anger. She doubtless refused to see him for more than two years in order to prevent herself from giving in to the rush of compassion and guilt she would inevitably feel; and to find that she had come through this battle without having injured Ernst as she was afraid she would, finding him still "glad of me," was a "strange" and unexpected victory indeed.

Vachel had also visited her in mid-November 1931 while passing through New York on his way to Washington on his seasonal tour. Elizabeth Lindsay's cheerful letters to Sara had masked the increasingly desperate situation in the Lindsay household. After his spring tour and his exhausting emotional crisis, Vachel had sunk into lethargy, unable to work on any of the projects he had told Sara he desperately wanted to do. Elizabeth finally persuaded him to bury himself in the woods of northern Wisconsin for a rest and to escape the August heat of Spring-field. There he reread *Paradise Lost,* trying to resolve his own puzzlement over women, whose seductive beauty broke men's pride and will but who seemed to have heaven on their side. Writing Sara later in the fall, he enclosed a poem that summed up his view of Adam and Eve. It said in part,

> Though Adam preached till he stood blind
> Her whisper broke his sermons down.
> The angels gave the blind a song
> But gave his girl the future crown.

Eve was the "conquering lady"; Adam was king only by virtue of the fact that she was queen, not a real king but only a consort. It was the familiar impasse he had reached long ago when Sara first met him, an irresolvable conflict between his religious and his sexual impulses. Adam was a Puri-tan, he said, Eve a Cavalier.

Vachel's mental and emotional condition worsened on his return from Wisconsin. He swung wildly between paranoid hallucinations that his wife's father was plotting to kill him, along with accusations that she had destroyed his manhood, to tender and effusive appeals for her love. Over the past year, Elizabeth had gradually begun to earn extra money through part-time teaching, tutoring, and lecturing to women's clubs in order to take the pressure off of him, for she could see that his recitals were on the decline, "In the first place there is not so much," she told Sara, "and in the second, his nerves won't stand it." Everyone was apprehensive when he set off on his tour in November.

But Sara apparently saw nothing unusual in his behavior or state of mind when he visited her around November 15. They were two old friends, worn by the battle of life, who took comfort in each other. If anything, he probably seemed calmer than he had been in the spring.

She heard nothing further for three weeks, when the telephone rang on Saturday, December 5, with the news that he was dead. After returning to Springfield on November 30, almost in a daze, Vachel had moved rapidly toward a breakdown, and on the night of December 4 had swal-lowed a bottle of Lysol and died a few hours later in agonizing pain.

The news of Vachel's death was shattering. Sara telephoned John Hall Wheelock at once, but was so choked and hysterical he could not under-stand what she was saying and had to call her later when she had become coherent. Margaret Conklin, whom Elizabeth Lindsay had also called, went to Sara immediately. The next day Sara wrote the poem "In Memory of Vachel Lindsay," which was published in the *Saturday Review of Litera-ture* on December 12, 1931. Its opening line—" 'Deep in the ages,' you said, 'Deep in the ages' "—was taken from "The Chinese Nightingale," which he had written for her and considered his finest piece. In his poems, the beautiful Chinese spirit-princess, conjured out of the past, says

> Deep in the ages, long, long ago
> I was your sweetheart.[16]

The poem, she knew, was Vachel's half-disguised love fantasy centered on her. He insisted it always be placed first in his *Collected Poems,* a book that he also dedicated "To Sara Teasdale, Poet." Her poem thus returned a private acknowledgement of his love and expressed her feeling about the reason he wanted to die: he was now "Free of the fret, free of the weight of living."[17] It was a reason she shared.

His death "shook me to my roots," she wrote Eunice Tietjens a few weeks later. "I did not realize how constantly I should miss him. He was the last knight errant." It was all the more shocking for being unexpected and coming at a time when she seemed to be enjoying old friends more than she had done for several years. Jessie Rittenhouse, Vachel, and Ernst had all visited her within a few weeks, and then Harriet Monroe around February 1, 1932. But even the renewal of friendship had its sad ghosts: "A friendship of twenty years like hers and mine," she said of Harriet Monroe, "has so many graves in the literal as well as the figurative sense, strewn along the road." She had spent the previous Thanksgiving holiday weekend with the Untermeyers at their place in the Adirondacks, where again there was a painful past to be kept out of sight. Sara had written "Grace Before Sleep" there on Thanksgiving night, to commemorate the warmth and shared friendship of that day. But she thought of these few pleasant days as isolated moments in a threatening world:

> Each one of us has walked through storm
> And fled the wolves along the road.[18]

Vachel's death confirmed her profound fatalism. She wrote Louis Untermeyer in February 1932, "I think often of my happy days at your and Jean's house. They seemed to be given as the prelude to what was so soon to be a tragedy—Vachel's death. To me it was a tragedy, for he was one of the half dozen people who meant anything real to me. So far as he himself is concerned, I suppose it was a deep sleep for a man needing sleep. I do not quarrel with the fate that willed it, but my private sorrow in missing my friend is not lessened by these thoughts. He will be remembered with more acclaim by the next generation but one than by his own."

John Hall Wheelock believed that Vachel's suicide contributed to Sara's foreboding that she might take her own life. Its immediate effect was to make her supersensitive to any new threat to her health, as if death was now stalking her as well. On December 6, the day after his death, a benzoin inhalator that she was using to combat a chest cold exploded in her face, causing minor burns. She hired a nurse to take care of her, and she feared permanent disfigurement, although the accident turned out to be merely noisy and frightening, and not harmful. On December 26, another near-accident in a taxi had thrown her into a panic, although this time she suffered no injury. She hastily wrote the poem "Since Death Brushed Past Me":

> Since death brushed past me once more to-day,
> Let me say quickly what I must say.[19]

Her few friends were not aware for many months that after Vachel's death she lived almost constantly on the verge of panic, believing irrationally that a physical breakdown or accidental death was imminent.

During these troubled winter months, she wrote half a dozen new poems. Following the memorial poem for Vachel, there was the surprising lyric, "Last Prelude," written on December 19, 1931, the anniversary of her marriage, with its passionate depiction of a kind of ecstatic death in imagery of music:

> Or let me drown if need be
> Lost in the swirl of light. . . .
> Once more let heaven clutch me, plunge me under
> Miles on uncounted miles.[20]

Only a few days before, she had written her first love lyric in many years, an untitled poem she did not wish to publish, addressed to someone unnamed:

> Your face is beautiful beyond all other faces. . . .
> More to me now than anything I know.

The poem's imagery of sea, seashore, and storm indicate that she was thinking of one of the men she had considered herself in love with in her lifetime. Since she had never written of Vachel in this particular vein, it would almost certainly not be he, even if the fact of his recent death did not preclude the kind of feeling the poem expresses. Stafford Hatfield was too long out of the picture, even if there had been the possibility of seeing him again two years previously. The only remaining possibilities were Ernst and Jack Wheelock. Jack, however, was deeply involved in his work, finding it hard to see her often, and there is no hint of a renewal of her romantic feeling for him or even a stimulus for it. There is, on the other hand, her curious revival of affection for Ernst. From the beginning, the only men she found appealing were those who were unobtainable. Not only did this protect her from actual involvement, but it added the spice of adventure to the thought of a love relationship. In its private, guarded way, it was Sara's protest against the stifling proprieties her mother had imposed on her, which had arisen out of her mother's fear of sexual indiscretion. And so she found the most desirable state to be a suspension in the allure of the forbidden or the impossible—like the golden-haired lady in her youthful parable, provocative but untouchable, wishing to give herself, but unable. She had no intention, of course, of trying to restore her relationship with Ernst or of even letting him guess how she felt. Pride would prevent that, if nothing else. It was only one more self-defeating contradiction in her emotional history.

The poem "Since Death Brushed Past Me" is an attempt "to say quickly. . .before I am hurried away,"

> Take without shame the love I give you. . . .
> You are all I asked, my dear—
> My words are said, my way is clear.[21]

The person she addresses is "intrepid, noble, kind," words she would apply to Ernst, and the familiar tone suggests someone long and closely associated with her. But by December 30 she had begun to accept the impossibility of love again, writing "Advice to a Girl":

> No one worth possessing
> Can be quite possessed.[22]

And in February 1932, while taking her annual winter rest at the Mayflower Inn, she wrote "Return to a Country House," a "love sonnet," she told Eunice Tietjens, "reminiscent of E. B. F." It recalled the January night before the divorce, when the planet Venus cast a square of light on the bed,

> And in that light your dark and lovely head
> Lay for a while and seemed to be at rest.
> But that the light is gone, and that no more
> Even if it were here, would you be here,—
> That is one line in a long tragic play
> That has been acted many times before,
> And acted best when not a single tear
> Falls,—when the mind and not the heart holds sway.[23]

Stoical transcendence through detachment had been her hopeful refuge from the destructive power of Venus. But that was itself part of the tragedy.

As spring approached, Sara became increasingly uneasy at the June deadline with Macmillan for the Rossetti study, and finally began the actual writing of a draft. By early May 1932, she had produced about 6,000 words, and took herself off to the Mayflower Inn in Washington, Connecticut, to work on the book intensively. "Alas, it is only begun," she told Eunice Tietjens. The completed study was to be "six or seven times that length." She was suffering from a "sick headache" and was working "about nine or ten hours a day on the thing and am so keyed up with the strain that I am not worth much."

She might have felt more enthusiasm if she had not been taut with constant dread of financial insecurity, which had become a nightmarish obsession. "These days are rather like living in a prolonged hurricane," she wrote Louis Untermeyer, "I think we all look up in surprise to find that a roof is still over our heads." She had, in fact, written one of her last poems on that theme in April, "Even To-Day":

> What if the bridge men built goes down,
> What if the torrent sweeps the town.[24]

As long as the hills remain, she says, she can climb them and find a small, bare cottage and live out her days. She could no longer afford her two-bedroom apartment at the Bolivar, or anywhere on Central Park West, for that matter, and had to find a smaller and less expensive place to move when her lease expired at the end of September. She took time from her writing to begin searching forlornly in late May and June, first in Easthampton, where she would be near Mrs. Wheelock—but that, too, was beyond her means—and in New Jersey, which she found depressing. She invited Margaret to live with her, but Margaret wisely declined, feeling that the emotional strain would be too great. Sara finally discovered a suitable small apartment at One Fifth Avenue, on Washington Square, with a view down on Washington Mews, reminding her of London. She chose it, she said, because it was close to Macmillan and easier for Margaret to visit.

A further reason for discouragement with the Rossetti project, she wrote Eunice, was that "since the contract was signed, two or three biographies of her have come out, and part of my thunder is stolen. They are not all they might be—nor will mine be, for the matter of that." The Christina Rossetti she loved was the youthful author of the love poems, not the self-styled nun of later years. "She was a person of utmost probity —but a bit forbidding," Sara told Harriet Monroe. Christina's personality interested her, but the resolution of psychological conflict through religion she found incomprehensible. To her old St. Louis friend Vine Colby, she wrote, "C. [Christina] was so repressed a person that her life is as hard to write about as a bit of polished granite. If I had Virginia Woolf's gift I might make an interesting short study of her."[25]

Sara had not been able to see many of the persons she wished to, including Christina Rossetti's nieces, or to visit some of the places, on her trip to London in 1931. She had been given the name of a young Mr. Rosse, whom she wrote in the fall of 1931, who had a contact with one of the nieces and would introduce her if she came again and also owned several letters of the Rossetti family, which he would be willing to let her see. He had obligingly looked up information for her and sent her a photograph of one of the houses that had been razed. With this entrée, she was fired to return there in the summer of 1932 but could not see her way clear financially. Nevertheless, as early as March she was laying plans to go, even though she had then scarcely begun to write and Macmillan was expecting the manuscript in two months. In the back of her mind, she hoped to persuade them to give her an advance to cover expenses, once they understood the importance of the trip. After the burst of writing in early May, she was able to show her editor a draft of the early portion. She was encouraged by his response and seemed to pick up enthusiasm, feeling that the writing would go more rapidly. "I want to make her alive," she told Jessie—"the books that have come out about her in the last year since I signed my contract, are dry." At another favorable editorial conference on May 16, they decided to title it *Christina Rossetti: An Intimate Portrait.* By this time, the project, which had begun as an introduction to a selection of love poems, seems to have grown in scope to become another contribution to Rossetti biography. The 11,-000-word manuscript that she left unfinished at her death takes Christina only to her seventeenth year and her first mature poems. Macmillan did agree to give her an advance for the trip. She hoped to leave for London sometime in July.

Virtually all of her writing on the project seems to have been done in the two or three months before the final trip to England. Her method was to develop her study by accretion, and then to organize, rewrite, and polish as she went along, so that the earlier parts were virtually in final form long before later portions had even been outlined. She had begun her research by jotting notes in a little grey account book, now lost, and then, while in London in 1931, she had shifted to a bound leatherette notebook in which she grouped and classified her material according to subjects, mingling quotations, notes, even the first draft of her "Prefatory Note" and a sketch of the Rossetti children's early life. It is evident that she was searching for an organic design, which was to emerge only gradually as she discovered the "plot" of Christina Rossetti's life and the key to her character. She eventually added a table of contents to the notebook as the materials grew more complex, although the headings remained somewhat haphazard. One of them, significant to Sara, was "C. R.'s Illnesses."[26]

The work was apparently destined to go through many drafts before its completion, as Sara's perfectionism caused her constantly to return to what she had written to refine and correct. By July 1932 she had put together a first, heavily revised typescript of forty-six pages and had added to it the "Prefatory Note," a title page, and a dedication:

TO THE MEMORY OF
VACHEL LINDSAY
WHO LOVED THE POETRY
OF CHRISTINA ROSSETTI

The preface is dated "New York, July, 1932." After further revision, she then had the entire manuscript retyped neatly on 6-1/2 by 9-inch paper, which she could insert and carry in a loose-leaf notebook, as she was accustomed to doing when arranging a book of her poems for publication. This was probably done just before her departure for England in mid-July. This version was apparently intended to be final, although she continued inserting handwritten revisions, mostly stylistic. When she left it, the last ten pages were undergoing very extensive rewriting with several sheets of handwritten material ready for insertion, of interest because they reveal her increasingly firm grasp of the principles she believed shaped and governed Christina's character. Most of these late revisions and additions were probably made during the voyage and her stay in England.

When Sara penetrated the "forbidding" surface of Christina Rossetti, she found a personality, like her own, caught in a central life conflict: an inner warfare between the impulse of love, freedom, and sensuousness, and the repressive forces of social convention and religion. Christina's poetry, however, was her personal triumph over that conflict, for without a divided inner life there would not have been the motivation to write. This was a large theme that emerged and became clearer to her as she wrote. She planned to trace the origins of these aspects of Christina's personality in her family and the influence of her times. Sara wrote in the "Prefatory Note," "Her birth, coming as it did in 1830, was in the nick of time—a great change in thought and manners was about to occur. The boisterous England of the last of the four Georges was transformed in Christina Rossetti's lifetime into the formal country of Queen Victoria. Such changes are a strain on the individual called upon to undergo them. We cannot live through one of the crucial acts of the drama of civilization without paying for the privilege. Christina paid heavily, but that is our good fortune, for without conflicting impulses she would not have written poetry." In this, Sara echoed her attitude toward her own life, which had witnessed the catastrophic reversal of the Victorian experience. Sara's response was much like Christina's: "Her method of getting through the ordeal of life was to withdraw into herself and to make her art serve as her solace." Sara found her religion "a rigid doctrine, a somewhat narrow form of Christianity, but her own intensity lifted her into the realm of the great religious mystics. Her poems on love and death are finer even than her devotional poems."

Sara had sympathy for Christina's withdrawal even from love: "She need not be pitied because of what is called her limited experience and because she chose to remain unmarried. She was an impassioned woman, but not a passionate one. . . . With Dorothea in *Middlemarch*, She 'liked giving up.' . . . A person who knew Christina but who insists on remaining nameless, told me that the poet loved deeply a man who was married—a facet of her emotion that has never caught the light—but that she would not have his love at the cost of sorrow to his wife. I cannot feel that the incident is of much importance. . .she was singularly self-sufficing. . . ." To understand the "limpid and intensely personal work" of this poet, it was necessary to understand her life, for she "carved her life carefully as she would have carved a gem. . . . In the loneliness of her own arrogant heart she made a shifting and exquisite music."

The conditions of conflict and withdrawal and of finding solace in art were those which produced great lyric poetry. "A lyric poet is always a contemporary. He works in the changeless feelings of men and not in their changing thoughts that shift restlessly from decade to decade. Christina Rossetti was a lyric poet. She would write no differently today, if she happened to belong to our time. Of all the Victorians she is the least stamped by her period."

Sara traced the two sides of Christina's character to her parents. Her "restraint was inherited from her mother but her mind and spirit were a direct inheritance from her father, Gabriele Rossetti." She pictures Christina even as a child caught up in a "household surcharged with emotional excitement," yet shrinking from it. "Her life, one of the most perfect examples in literature of intensity in reticence, consistent, delicately and consciously moulded as a Tanagra figurine, kept its inner quiet inviolate to the end." The conflict was basic to the Rossetti family and found expression in the other children as well: Christina's brother Dante Gabriel was the personification of impetuous emotion; her sister Maria, of conventional and religious rigidity. Christina was, in effect, caught in the middle between these two extremes, adoring her brother but falling under the religious influence of her sister.

Nearly half of the work Sara completed deals with the background of the Rossetti family, and the remainder with the childhood of the Rossetti brothers and sisters, all of which she sketched with increasing attention to vivid pictorial detail and an amused sense of irony. As the writing progressed, she generalized less and went back over her work to modify expressions of opinion for greater objectivity. Her portrait of Christina shows a willful, imaginative child, whose world was that of the lively, precocious, and self-contained family, consistent with her view that it was precisely this enclosed family unit with its intense personalities that shaped Christina's life. She drew her entire sustenance from it and never needed anyone else.

She traced Christina's poetic development from early childhood to her teens, when, like her brothers and sisters, she found the direction of her life already set. At twelve, "Christina had learned that verse can be made to convey precisely what you want to say. But it was not until six years later that she ceased to be a mere versifier. Then the change that made her a poet came almost overnight. She learned the exquisite truth that a poem can convey what you never dreamed of saying." She reached her early maturity in the lyrics published in the short-lived little magazine of the Pre-Raphaelite Brotherhood: "In several of the poems in *The Germ* we come for the first time upon that juxtaposition of the prim and the luxuriant, the whimsical and the outright that is unalienably hers."

These were the last words of Sara's study, left unfinished just at the point of greatest literary interest. She apparently planned next to take up the problem of Christina's religious side, which she had already traced to the childhood influence of Maria, whose "fine sense of her own virtue" developed in Christina a feeling of inferiority. By nature, Christina resembled Dante Gabriel and "followed in his track from love of him and because, in spite of the vast difference that always marked the outward appearance of their lives, their impulses were fundamentally alike. Dante Gabriel's were allowed free rein; Christina's were held in check. She was originally as lawless and impulsive as he; they were both bowls of fire." The story Sara told was one she understood only too well. Boys were encouraged to be aggressive and free; girls were expected to be docile, restrained, and pious. She therefore felt a certain bias against Maria and had difficulty treating her sympathetically. In the draft of a page she intended to develop further, she wrote "Dante Gabriel was the liberating influence in Christina's life, and Maria was the restraining influence. As soon as Maria was confirmed she became relentlessly devout. . . . She had her father's devout nature without his speculative turn of mind. In the realm of religion her influence over Christina was supreme, but while Christina could share Maria's rigours, she was never blessed by an equal ecstasy. There was something almost Calvinistic in Christina's mind. It refused to be made happy by faith in God."

Sara's notes reveal that she took pains to soften her distaste for Maria Rossetti and to treat her more neutrally in the final draft. At first she had depicted Maria reacting against what she believed to be her sister's "laziness" and "dreaminess"—actually, of course, signs of poetic imagination. "A faintly priggish attitude on her part toward Christina is discernible for years. I am tempted to say that it lasted all her life." Another sketch showed Maria, who was not as pretty as Christina, either, to be ridiculous in her piety: "She went to church incessantly, even after she was a grown woman. She would not look at Blake's illustrations to the Book of Job because God was represented in them and this was contrary to the second commandment. The Egyptian Mummy Room at the British Museum was avoided all her life. She feared the embarrassment that would ensue if the last trumpet sounded during her visit and she was found in the company of the ancient kings rising for the judgment and clothed only in falling tatters." Maria's "strong will had something to do with changing Christina from an impulsive child into a repressed slightly sarcastic young person who brooded too much on her own imperfections." But such passages were either cut or heavily revised.

If Sara saw herself in Christina Rossetti, it is not hard to detect the shadowy presence of her own mother in the baneful Maria. Sara was peculiarly sensitive to the domination exercised by strong-minded, pious Victorian ladies, who, having turned against joy in their own lives, made other women under their influence sacrifice it also, usually in the name of a joyless religion. "Christina R.'s religion may have given her peace at times—never apparently for long—but it never gave her ecstasy. The raptures experienced by St. Teresa would have been considered unseemly by Christina." Christina Rossetti, like herself, had implanted within her the self-negation that was crippling to women of creative genius. Sara's study unavoidably struck deeper than she must have intended at the outset. But she was by no means ready to follow her interpretation where it was taking her. She had never been able to resolve the problem of her own life, and she appeared to be backing off from the implications of Maria's influence on Christina, probably to avoid any note of the controversial. It is doubtful that her study, if completed, would have fulfilled the promise that lay half-hidden between the lines.

Sara had also begun to gather ideas to support a critical discussion of Christina Rossetti's poetry. She turned to Yeats, whose speculative remarks on lyric poetry always seemed close to her own beliefs, and planned to quote from his *Reveries over Childhood and Youth*. "I was about to learn," he wrote, "that if a man is to write lyric poetry he must be shaped by nature and art to some one out of half a dozen traditional poses, and be lover or saint, sage or sensualist, or mere mocker of all life."[27] But Yeats had difficulty reconciling the artful "pose" and the individuality of the poet: "We should write out our own thoughts in as nearly as possible the language we thought them in, as though in a letter to an intimate friend. We should not disguise them in any way, for our lives give them force as the lives of people in plays give force to their words. . . . 'If I can be sincere and make my language natural, and without becoming discursive like a novelist, and so indiscreet and prosaic,' I said to myself, 'I shall, if good luck or bad luck make my life interesting, be a great poet; for it will be no longer a matter of literature at all.' "[28] But Yeats discovered himself operating within literary conventions even when practicing this kind of rigorous sincerity and furthermore suspected that his youthful sincerity of expression was often unoriginal and naive. Still, in finally accepting the necessity of artifice, he treated it as something to which the free spirit submitted with reluctance.

The literary notion of the free and natural as opposed to the formal and artificial was in the nineteenth century primarily a masculine concept, and was more prevalent in America than in England. Yeats in his early years had read Thoreau, whose ideal of "natural" or antiliterary expression was then close to his own. The romantic cult of the untrammeled male spirit emphasized sincerity, genuineness, and naturalness as against the supposed sophistication, manners, guile, traditionalism, and artificiality of feminine society. As a woman, Sara had the advantage of not being cast in this unrealistic masculine role, which was necessarily on the decline, with destructive effects on writers as diverse as Vachel Lindsay and Ernest Hemingway. She could readily find a comfortable place within literary convention and tradition, for she accepted it as naturally as the air she breathed and could therefore understand it far more subtly, and without Yeats's puzzlement, than if she had felt herself opposed. Far from threatening one's integrity, convention and restraint were, to her, necessary to civilized human life. Once this was accepted, one could discriminate between the good and the bad, the true and the false. There was no value in revolt and change for their own sake. It seemed nonsensical and irrelevant to praise a poem because of its newness of form or expression. She looked for the kind of mastery that began by accepting formal restraint and then managed it so skillfully that artifice seemed artless and the "pose" utterly sincere. Such poetry rose above the historical tradition that produced it to become timeless. Whatever differences there may have been, Yeats came closer to saying this than anyone else, and she was doubtless glad to have authoritative support for her critical estimation of Christina Rossetti's work, which exemplified her beliefs.

Sara's probing into the Rossetti childhood, her reading of Proust, her scrutiny of her own life, perhaps even the pervasive, indirect influence of Freudian ideas, all led her to think more deeply about the chain of cause and effect that created the pattern of a life, for she could see clearly how one's supposedly free acts created constantly narrowing limits for the future, imprisoning the will by degrees. She copied into her notebook a quotation from Paul Valéry's *Introduction to the Method of Leonardo da Vinci:* "All criticism is dominated by the outworn theory that the man is the cause of the work, as in the eyes of the law the criminal is the *cause* of the crime. Far rather are they both effects." She liked this idea so much she added in her own words, "We all know that the poetry of young people concerns matters about which they know nothing from experience—the revelation that is made is a forecast of their lives, not a record, and the forecast is infallibly correct." She applied this idea immediately to Dante Gabriel Rossetti, finding that the early version of "The Blessed Damozel," in *The Germ*, "was a forecast of all of his poetry, as well as of the pictures he painted." She doubtless planned to apply the idea to Christina's work as well.

Sara's observations on Christina Rossetti and other poets are always interesting for the light they throw on her own mind: "She had the Roman virtues. . .and she added to these an unremitting attempt to love her neighbor as herself." Sara admired "Roman virtues," but found Christina's religion grim. She suspected a strain of mental instability in the family, and even set up a category in her notebook for suicides touching them. She disagreed with the biographers who accepted the idea that Christina refused to marry Charles Cayley on religious grounds: "I feel that her disinclination to marry him sprang chiefly from her disinclination to marriage in general. She wished to be free to follow her own thoughts, to meditate in her own way. She was a born celibate in spite of her impassioned heart.... Nevertheless, if a man of great force and charm had chanced to love Christina, she would have forgotten her innate shrinking from marriage and would have married him forthwith.... It is said that many women marry to have a home of their own. This consideration weighed less than nothing with Christina.... She had 'no fancy for the housekeeping department,' as she says in one of her letters."

Comparisons with the two other great women poets of the nineteenth century—Elizabeth Barrett Browning and Emily Dickinson—were inevitable, although Sara had not developed her ideas beyond a few notes that indicate chiefly her distaste for Mrs. Browning: Christina's "music is to E. B. B. what a song by Shubert is to a street melody.... D. G. R. spoke of E. B. B.'s 'falsetto muscularity,' rebuking C. R. for sometimes imitating her." Sara seems not to have forgiven Mrs. Browning for disregarding Christina's work, but then "Mrs. B. was too full of her craze for politics & spiritualism (Napoleon III) to have much time for the current literature of her day." Sara noted Christina's approval of Emily Dickinson "in a measured way" and remarked that "Christina did not have Emily Dickinson's minute and exact knowledge of nature."

Sara's study of Christina Rossetti thus ends in fragments that promise much more than she had managed to achieve in the few months of writing she devoted to it in the late spring and early summer of 1932. Unquestionably, her enthusiasm increased as she began to explore the Rossetti family in greater depth and discovered her own relation to her material, although she found herself in the thick of problems she had not yet worked her way through.

Sara's plans for sailing were postponed week after week as she struggled with her financial problems and tried to figure how to get her four rooms of furniture into her new two-room apartment. She wrote Mr. Rosse on June 28, 1932, that she had decided to cancel the trip entirely: "What a d—— thing money is, or rather the lack of it."[29] But three days later she wrote him that she would definitely sail on the *Adriatic* on July 16, after all, arriving in Liverpool on July 25. Rosse would probably be unable to meet her. "Please don't, for the sake of seeing me, change an iota of your plans—" she told him, "I assure you I'm not worth any such sacrifice." She did "want desperately to meet Miss Rossetti" and planned to visit the family home at Hosmer Green in Buckinghamshire where Christina spent several years of her childhood. "I am by nature by no means energetic and I get tired before most people know they have started on a jaunt, so I am a hopelessly bad companion—if we do meet, no doubt you will find me a boring middle aged lady of a sort of Henry James tradition, and about thirty years behind my time. However, I love life as much as I ever did, which is a triumph due to my ancestors and not to me.[30]

For the first time in her life, Sara traveled completely alone, being unable to afford the expenses of a companion. But the voyage was uneventful, and England soothed her, as it always did, as she lay in bed in her familiar room at the American Women's Club on Grosvenor Street "listening to the beautiful quiet of this city" in the rain. She was anxious to avoid seeing Rosse, who had fortunately gone off to Iceland. She believed him to be effeminate and not "much of a reed to lean on anyway." Besides, she had written directly to Christina Rossetti's nieces herself, and they graciously received her at tea on July 28. She could afford to stay in England only three weeks, "a painfully short time to be in this adorable cold grey cozy darling city," she wrote Margaret, and not time enough to do anything but look for material for her book. She would not "try to lure Mrs. Woolf into my net" or travel much out of London, as she had done the year before when she visited the Henry James house at Rye and looked for tombs of her ancestors. Her old acquaintance Harriet Curtis wrote begging her to go to Germany with her, "but she is not what I want as a companion." She would have loved to live in London permanently, except for the winters, which she had been told were "detestable."

The brief stay seemed to go well. She fulfilled an old desire by visiting A. E. Housman and then Arthur Symons, who had praised her first small volume of poems in 1907 and who also had memories of Christina Rossetti. Symons was ill with bronchitis when she met him in early August, and to her dismay she shortly became ill, too, with a deep chest cold. As she frantically obtained medical attention and hired a nurse to care for her in her room at the American Women's Club, the "cold" turned out to be pneumonia in both lungs. She lay in bed profoundly depressed, desperate to return to New York, and watching the expenses mount as the month of August passed. Finally, in early September, fearing that she would never recover in the cool damp climate of London, she determined to sail home at any cost, although she was still too weak to walk or care for herself. A woman from New York whom she had met at the Club, a Mrs. Allison, made arrangements for the voyage, managed to get her aboard, and returned with her to America.

Margaret Conklin and Sara's sister Mamie, who had been filled with anxiety for more than a year over Sara's morbid despondency, met her at the pier with a wheelchair and two trained nurses on September 13, 1932. She returned to her apartment at the Bolivar, facing a move in scarcely two weeks when the lease expired. Since it proved impossible for Mamie and Margaret to pack her things while she remained there ill, she was moved to a furnished apartment at One Fifth Avenue on September 27, traveling in a taxi with a doctor and a nurse, Mamie following behind in another taxi with suitcases. Because of painting and minor remodeling, her own apartment was not ready until October 21, when she finally moved in, still too weak to leave her bed. The siege of pneumonia had ushered in a period of nightmarish horror that was not to end. "The illness seemed to me a becoming time to make my final exit," she wrote Eunice Tietjens. "But apparently that is to be delayed, and I am not too glad."

The work on her book had, of course, to be laid aside, and little if any attention was given to it again. She spent her time reading Virginia Woolf, Tolstoy, and Max Beerbohm, and on October 1 had written the last poem she was to enter in her notebook, "To M. [Margaret]":

> I shall find no better thing upon the earth
> Than the wilful, noble, faulty thing which is you.

It was an assurance that would enable her to "go, in some sort, a victor, down to my rest."[31]

Sara had borrowed money from Mamie to cover the unanticipated medical expenses and now began to dread being unable to meet the rent of even a two-room apartment. Although her financial affairs were actually not nearly as desperate as she imagined, she was seized with the fearful conviction that she was about to have the stroke and would be forced to live with Mamie and be at the mercy of her husband Joe Wheless, whom she could not abide. By the end of November, X-ray photographs taken in her apartment showed her lungs to be clear, and she became more and more restless, anxious to travel somewhere for the relief that travel always brought. Margaret and Jack Wheelock had both become concerned about her emotional state, for she seemed dangerously depressed. She was taking sleeping pills regularly and had hired a young English nurse, Rita Brown, to stay with her constantly. Several deaths during the fall— the poet Tom Jones and Jessie Rittenhouse's mother and husband—also deepened her despondency.

Still, she was able to appear remarkably "cheerful and amusing," for Aline Kilmer, visiting her in December, did not suspect the blackness that lay beneath the surface, although "She did say that she felt that her struggle to come through the pneumonia had not been worth while."[32] Sara apparently hoped that pneumonia would do for her what she was reluctant to do herself. In December, she began secretly accumulating a supply of sleeping pills. She was so convinced that her blood vessels were ready to rupture she claimed her doctor had warned her that a massive stroke was imminent, although he had not actually done so. Her blood pressure was somewhat elevated, but there was no medical basis for her hysterical fear. At some time in these weeks she went through her notebook methodically deciding which poems could be published after her death, writing on the flyleaf, "All poems that are not crossed out, can be published. Name of the book to be 'Strange Victory.' " Inside the cover of the notebook, she copied lines from "The Song of Enion" from Blake's *The Four Zoas*, which she had been reading probably because of the Rossettis' interest in him:

What is the price of Experience? do men buy it for a song?
Or wisdom for a dance in the street? No, it is bought with the price
Of all that a man hath, his house, his wife, his children.
Wisdom is sold in the desolate market where none come to buy,
And in the wither'd field where the farmer plows for bread in vain.

It echoed the thought she herself had come to, that the price of experience was life itself.

Then having at last come face to face with the death that had tantalized her for so long, she panicked and tried to escape from it. At the end of December 1932, she fled south to Winter Park, Florida to be with Jessie Rittenhouse, taking her nurse with her. Jessie was alarmed at her "dangerous state mentally" and discussed it with Sara's doctor and nurse, who felt that she ought to return north and seek psychiatric help.33 For two weeks Sara lay in a darkened room behind a drape where she could be alone and yet near Jessie and her visitors. Her anxiety did not quiet, however, and she decided to return to New York, with the same restlessness that had driven her away from there.

In mid-January 1933, back in her New York apartment, which had still not been completely decorated, many of her art objects still unpacked, she seemed quieter, although Sara's physician, Dr. Dana Atchley, watched her closely. On Friday, January 27, a blood vessel broke in her hand, and she became frantic with the idea that the long-awaited stroke was now ready to occur. Margaret privately telephoned Dr. Atchley, recommending that a psychiatrist be consulted, and he agreed. On Saturday, Sara summoned Mamie to her apartment and gave her power of attorney over her affairs in the event a stroke rendered her helpless and dependent. She evidently believed, with a kind of uncontrollable terror, that she could only sit and wait now for inevitable paraylsis and mental deterioration. Margaret Conklin spent the evening of Saturday, January 28, with her, reading aloud and listening to a recording of Beethoven's Fifth Symphony. Sara seemed tranquil, more concerned about Margaret's sprained ankle, which she had the nurse bind with elastic tape, than about herself. At the end of the music, she remarked, "Beethoven knew all the answers." Margaret said good night, knowing that Sara was quite ill, but feeling that she was more calm and natural that evening than she had been for many months.

Sometime in the early morning hours of Sunday, January 29, while her nurse was sleeping, Sara drew a bath, took a heavy dose of sleeping tablets, and lay down in the warm water. For some unexplained reason—

for she knew that Sara needed to be watched closely—Rita Brown did not look in on her until 9 AM, later than usual, and, not finding her in her room, discovered her body in the bathroom. She immediately telephoned Dr. Atchley. The water in the tub was still warm, and death had occurred only a short time before, suggesting that Sara might have timed her action in the hope that she would be discovered before it was too late—a last cry for help.

Dr. Atchley notified Margaret and Mamie, who came to the apartment bewildered and grief-stricken, to find the day a hubbub of newspaper reporters and medical officials. To their horror, Rita Brown chattered freely to the press about Sara's personal feelings and remarks she had made, telling them that Sara had discussed methods of suicide and had insisted on returning to the subject when she tried to change it. The *New York Times* printed the story prominently on the front page the next morning, and the St. Louis papers gave it a major headline. By this time, Sara's despondency following the pneumonia had become in the newspapers a "nervous breakdown." Mamie, desperately wanting to still the clamor and protect her sister's reputation, appealed to the medical examiner to minimize any news resulting from the autopsy. She clung pathetically to the hope that the facts would be sufficiently ambiguous to leave open the possibility of accidental death. When Margaret returned forlornly to Sara's apartment on Sunday evening to find an address book so she could write to Sara's relatives and friends, she found Rita Brown still there. A party was in full swing, and couples were dancing to jazz music on the Victrola where Sara had played Beethoven the night before. Margaret had the manager throw them out and seal the apartment until Sara's legal executors, the Morgan Guaranty Trust Company, could act officially the next day. Jewelry, clothing, and other items were later found to be missing.

The chief medical examiner, Dr. Charles Norris, issued a preliminary report on Monday, pending a chemical analysis, obligingly indicating that the cause of death was probably accidental due to "chronic unresolved pneumonia" and "submersion in tub."[34] The newspapers duly reported that Sara's death was "the result of accident and not suicide." But when completed, the investigation did show the presence of morphine and phenobarbitol drugs and the fact that submersion was not a factor after all.[35] This report, however, was never made public. Mamie and Sara's friends were greatly relieved and found comfort in accepting and promulgating Sara's belief that she was on the verge of terrible suffering and a prolonged death and so had acted bravely to circumvent it.

The funeral services were held at Grace Episcopal Church at Tenth and Broadway on Wednesday afternoon, February 1. John Hall Wheelock remembered that "she looked so strong and beautiful in death. . . . Her forehead was very wide, and she was completely peaceful, and I could hear the traffic roaring around the city, and felt that she'd really finally accomplished what she wanted." Her body was then cremated and the ashes buried in Bellefontaine Cemetery in St. Louis. Mamie had decided not to follow her request that her ashes be scattered at sea. The stone marker gives her name, as she asked in her will, as Sara Teasdale Filsinger.

Ironically, Ernst was in South Africa when the news reached him of Sara's death, as he had been three and a half years before when notified of the divorce. "Sara was a wonderful woman," he wrote Irma, "and it was a glorious thing to have had so many years with her." A year later, Ernst moved his business to Shanghai and spent most of his time thereafter in the Orient. "My life these years has been a most unhappy one," he wrote Jessie Rittenhouse, and he wondered at times whether the constant struggle was worth it. He died of a heart attack in Shanghai in May 1937 at the age of fifty-seven, perhaps as a result of the stress that Sara had always feared. Had he lived longer, he would have seen his business wiped out by war, a final frustration in a harried life. His ashes were returned to St. Louis and are buried in a family plot in Bellefontaine Cemetery not far from Sara's.

When Sara's will was probated in October 1933, her net assets were discovered to be $83,621, much more than her fear of poverty would have suggested. She had come through the depression relatively unscathed, through shrewd management. She left most of her personal effects and two-fifths of the income from her residual estate to Margaret Conklin, and the other three-fifths to Ernst, to revert to Margaret on his death; and then ultimately the entire residual estate to Wellesley College to establish an annual poetry prize. Mamie Wheless and Vachel Lindsay's daughter Susan each received $5,000. Her interest in St. Louis property was divided among Mamie and several nieces and nephews. She also left Wellesley College the choice of a hundred books from her library, and they now include those inscribed to her by Vachel Lindsay.

Margaret Conklin suffered profound shock at Sara's death and was unwell for months. No one had been as close to Sara in the last several years or had tried so valiantly to relieve her despondency. Their friendship had survived the fading of Sara's quest for a vicarious youth and Margaret's own outgrowing of her youthful heroine-worship. Appointed Sara's literary executor, as Sara had wished, Margaret faithfully edited *Strange Victory* from the twenty-two poems in her notebook that Sara wished to publish. The volume appeared in October 1933. Margaret Conklin, with John Hall Wheelock's assistance, also edited the *Collected*

*Poems of Sara Teasdale,* published in 1937, guided by notations Sara had left in copies of her books concerning poems she wished to include in such an edition. Margaret subsequently allowed the publication of one additional poem, "From a High Window," in the *Yale Review* in spring of 1950.

There were tributes in the magazines. Harriet Monroe saw her as the champion of a feminine point of view in poetry. Beginning with girlish daydreams, under the test of life "the true metal of the poet's character and style gained precision and hardness."[36] Louis Untermeyer, in the *Saturday Review of Literature,* wrote the kind of notice that was always Sara's despair, setting up so many negative criticisms to refute in her honor that his praise lost its emphasis, although he insisted melodramatically that her death "affects me so deeply, so privately, that it seems an indignity to write about it at all."[37] This was a scruple that did not last long, however, for a few years later in his memoirs he treated her patronizingly and with a touch of undeserved ridicule.

Reminiscing in later years, John Hall Wheelock said, "I did feel I was looking, in death, on the face of one of the great lyric poets of the English language. . . . The ordeal that she went through seemed to have done something to her. She rose to the occasion. Even when she was in anguish and panic she was writing those calm poems in *Strange Victory.* . . . She was a sane human being and she had a certain kind of strength that came out in the end. . . . You see her exchanging her gold for the brass of other people, making such tremendous efforts because she wanted so much to have people like her. That capacity for caring is very important in a poet. She cared supremely about her work, and that is what gives it its quality. She always had the instrument ready to do something worth while, because she had used it so much. A lot of her early work was like five-finger exercises, that were very useful, so that when the opportunity came and something great had her by the throat, as it were, she was able to cry out in a way that was not just crying, but a real Beethoven cry."

Wheelock was right in seeing that the will to assert herself as a woman and as a poet was greater, in the end, than the will to negate herself. For years she had observed the battle within herself closely, and when it drew to a fatal climax she took care to see that the best of her work was preserved, even while she stipulated that her ashes be scattered at sea so "that there may be neither trace nor remembrance." Too proud to allow everything to be taken from her, she could snatch triumph from a life of denial by turning her inner conflict into the calm perfection of her art. To the last, her favorite among her own poems was the faultless lyric written when she first realized fully that losing could yield a kind of victory greater for her than possession; for in writing beautifully of what had to be foregone and forgotten, she compelled herself to be remembered:

Let it be forgotten, as a flower is forgotten,
  Forgotten as a fire that once was singing gold,
Let it be forgotten for ever and ever,
  Time is a kind friend, he will make us old.

If anyone asks, say it was forgotten
  Long and long ago,
As a flower, as a fire, as a hushed footfall
  In a long forgotten snow.[38]

# Notes

## CHAPTER ONE: Sara Teasdale and the Feminine Tradition

1. New York, 1974. p. 78.
2. Preface to *The Answering Voice: Love Lyrics by Women*, New York, 1928, p. xv.
3. "Christina Rossetti," *The Century*, 46 (June 1893); quoted in Mary F. Sandars, *The Life of Christina Rossetti*, London, n.d., p. 111.
4. "Blue Squills," *Collected Poems*, New York, 1966, p. 115.
5. Urbana, Illinois, 1973, p. 322.
6. In Bullough, p. 323.

## CHAPTER TWO: The House of Dreams

1. "Notes on Sara Teasdale," Missouri Historical Society. All quotations ascribed to Williamina Parrish are from this document unless otherwise indicated.
2. *Private Collection*, New York, 1965, p. 53.
3. "Fear," in *Helen of Troy and Other Poems*, New York, 1911, p. 81.
4. This and all subsequent quotations from letters to John Myers O'Hara are courtesy of the Newberry Library, Chicago.
5. *The World at My Shoulder*, New York, 1938, pp. 28–29.
6. To Mrs. Henry J. Filsinger. All subsequent quotations from letters to Mr. and Mrs. Filsinger, Irma Filsinger Wetteroth, and Wanda Filsinger are courtesy of the late Mrs. Irma Wetteroth of St. Louis.

7. Henry A. Pochmann, *German Culture in America: 1600–1900*, Madison, Wisconsin, 1957, pp. 258, 260, 639n.
8. This and all subsequent quotations from letters of Sara Teasdale to Louis and Jean Untermeyer are courtesy of Lockwood Memorial Library, State University of New York at Buffalo.
9. New York, 1959, p. 18.
10. *H. L. Mencken; Iconoclast from Baltimore*, Chicago, 1971, pp. 67–68.
11. *The Education of Henry Adams*, New York, 1931, pp. 466–467.
12. Interview, New York, February 15, 1975. All quotations attributed to John Hall Wheelock are from this source unless otherwise indicated.
13. Travel Diary, Beinecke Library, Yale University. All quotations concerning the trip to Europe in 1905 are from this source unless otherwise indicated.
14. Williamina Parrish to Mrs. D. L. Parrish, Missouri Historical Society.
15. "The Treasure," *Flame and Shadow*, New York, 1920, p. 131; and Poetry Notebook, September 27, 1913. All quotations from the notebooks are courtesy of the Beinecke Library, Yale University.
16. "Madeira from the Sea," *Collected Poems*, p. 36.
17. This and all subsequent quotations from letters of William Marion Reedy to Sara Teasdale are courtesy of Margaret Haley Carpenter, Norfolk, Virginia.
18. *The Bang*, November 5, 1917, p. 4.
19. To Marion Cummings Stanley, February 19, 1909. This and all subsequent quotations from letters of Sara Teasdale to Marion Stanley are courtesy of Newberry Library, Chicago.
20. Missouri Historical Society.
21. George Tyler to Joseph Smith, 1901, quoted by Eva LeGallienne in *The*

*Mystic in the Theatre: Eleonora Duse,*
New York, 1966, p. 53.

22. *Eleonora Duse,* New York, 1927, reprinted 1969, p. 1.

23. LeGallienne, p. 18.

24. "To a Picture of Eleonora Duse in
'The Dead City,' " *Collected Poems,* p.
4.

25. Courtesy of Margaret Haley Carpenter.

26. "Guenevere," *Collected Poems,* p. 16.

27. "The House of Dreams," *Sonnets to
Duse and Other Poems,* Boston, 1907, p.
43.

## CHAPTER THREE: "If I Were Only Beautiful and a Genius"

1. "The Blind," *Helen of Troy and Other
Poems,* p. 33.

2. "The Princess in the Tower," *Ibid.,* p.
29.

3. "Lovely Chance," *Collected Poems,* p.
142.

4. *Studies in the Greek Poets,* New York,
n.d., v. 1, pp. 309, 310.

5. "Day's Ending (Tucson)," *Collected Poems,* p. 180.

6. "Song," *Ibid.,* p. 21.

7. New York, 1937, pp. 177–178.

8. *Ibid.,* p. 179.

9. *Ibid.*

10. *Ibid.,* pp. 179–180.

11. Courtesy of Margaret Haley Carpenter.

12. "On the Tower," *Helen of Troy and
Other Poems,* pp. 109–115.

13. "Youth and the Pilgrim," *Collected Poems,* p. 25.

## CHAPTER FOUR: "But Oh, the Girls Who Ask for Love..."

1. *My House of Life,* New York, 1934, p.
225.

2. Missouri Historical Society.

3. Rittenhouse, p. 228.

4. *Ibid.,* pp. 228–229.

5. "Coney Island," *Collected Poems,* p. 31.

6. "Union Square," *Collected Poems,* p.
31.

7. November 9, 1911. All quotations
from letters of Sara Teasdale to Jessie
Rittenhouse are courtesy of the Rollins College Library.

8. "I Shall Not Care," *Collected Poems,* p.
54.

9. "Sea Longing," *Collected Poems,* p. 73.

10. Missouri Historical Society.

11. "From the North," *Collected Poems,* p.
72.

12. New York Public Library.

13. Courtesy of Margaret Haley Carpenter.

14. New York Public Library.

15. *Smart Set,* v. 48 (April 1916), pp.
131–134. Reprinted in *Smart Set Anthology,* ed. Burton Rascoe and G.
Conklin, New York, 1934.

16. "By the Sea," *Helen of Troy and Other
Poems,* p. 91.

17. "Pierrot," *Collected Poems,* p. 27.

18. "The Inn of Earth," *Collected Poems,* p.
63.

19. "While I May," *Collected Poems,* p. 71.

20. Courtesy of Margaret Haley Carpenter.

21. Courtesy of Margaret Haley Carpenter.

22. "November," *Helen of Troy and Other
Poems* (1911), p. 57; *Love Songs*
(1917) p. 36; *Collected Poems,* p. 28.

23. Courtesy of Margaret Haley Carpenter.

24. *From Another World,* New York, 1939,
p. 32.

25. Courtesy of Margaret Haley Carpenter.

26. Courtesy of Margaret Haley Carpenter.

27. Courtesy of Margaret Haley Carpenter.

28. Courtesy of Margaret Haley Carpenter.

29. "A Cry," *Collected Poems,* p. 77.

30. "Over the Roofs, IV," *Collected Poems,*
p. 77.

31. *Private Collection,* pp. 52–53.
32. *From Another World,* p. 164.
33. Rittenhouse, p. 246.
34. "From the Sea," *Collected Poems,* p. 80. The poem, heavily revised after its composition on shipboard on May 25, 1912, is seventy-nine lines in its final published version.
35. Rittenhouse, pp. 246–247.
36. "Places," *Collected Poems,* p. 120.


CHAPTER FIVE: "Now at Last I Can Live!"


1. "The Old Maid," *Collected Poems,* p. 46.
2. "Sappho," *Collected Poems,* pp. 88–90.
3. Memorandum dated 1965, attached to Sara Teasdale's manuscript of *Rivers to the Sea,* University of Virginia Library.
4. Courtesy of Margaret Haley Carpenter.
5. University of Virginia Library, "Enough," *Collected Poems,* p. 56.
6. *Poems Old and New,* New York, 1956, p. 4.
7. University of Virginia Library.
8. In *Challenge,* New York, 1914, p. 7.
9. "Testament," *Rivers to the Sea,* New York, 1915, p. 118.
10. *From Another World,* New York, 1939, p. 57.
11. Courtesy of Margaret Haley Carpenter.
12. Houghton Library, Harvard University.
13. "Alchemy," *Collected Poems,* p. 57.
14. "The Fountain," *Collected Poems,* p. 68.
15. "Central Park," *Collected Poems,* p. 43.
16. All quotations from letters of Sara Teasdale to Harriet Monroe are courtesy of the Harriet Monroe Library of Modern Poetry, University of Chicago.
17. *A Poet's Life,* New York, 1938, pp. 323–324.
18. All quotations from letters of Sara Teasdale to Eunice Tietjens are courtesy of the Newberry Library, Chicago.
19. "The Star," *Rivers to the Sea,* p. 66. The two lines beginning "The star was romantic" were cut from the published version.
20. Courtesy of Margaret Haley Carpenter.
21. All quotations from letters of Vachel Lindsay to Sara Teasdale are courtesy of the Beinecke Library, Yale University.
22. Handwritten memorandum appended to Sara Teasdale's manuscript of *Rivers to the Sea,* dated by another hand, "5 March 1965." University of Virginia Library.
23. "Swans," *Collected Poems,* p. 46.
24. "The Kiss," *Collected Poems,* p. 45.
25. "At Night," *Collected Poems,* p. 47.
26. "After Parting," *Collected Poems,* p. 56.
27. "A November Night," *Collected Poems,* p. 110.
28. "The Mother of a Poet," *Collected Poems,* pp. 65–66.
29. Missouri Historical Society.
30. *Poetry,* 4 (April 1914), p. 26; also in Harriet Monroe, *A Poet's Life,* New York, pp. 337–338. Yeats's remarks are not verbatim, but were reconstructed by Miss Monroe immediately afterward from memory.
31. *The Little Review,* I, 2 (April 1914), pp. 12–15. "Frances Trevor" will be found listed in indexes to little magazines as a bona fide author.
32. August Forel, *The Sexual Question: A Scientific, Psychological, Hygienic and Sociological Study,* New York, 1925, pp. 330, 129, 332.
33. *The World at My Shoulder,* New York, 1938, p. 54.
34. All quotations from letters of Ernst Filsinger to Eunice Tietjens are courtesy of the Newberry Library.
35. "Sappho," *Collected Poems,* p. 91.
36. "I Hear Immanuel Singing," *Collected Poems,* New York, 1925, p. 370.
37. Tietjens, p. 54.
38. *Ibid.,* p. 55.

39. Quoted by Ernst Filsinger in a letter to Eunice Tietjens dated July 14, 1914.
40. Courtesy of Mrs. Irma Filsinger Wetteroth.
41. "Joy," *Collected Poems*, p. 51.

## CHAPTER SIX: "Caught in the Web of the Years"

1. "I Am Not Yours," *Collected Poems*, p. 70.
2. "New Year's Dawn—Broadway," *Rivers to the Sea*, p. 64.
3. "Come," *Collected Poems*, p. 48.
4. Courtesy of Margaret Haley Carpenter.
5. "Dreams," *Collected Poems*, p. 69.
6. "The India Wharf," *Collected Poems*, p. 54.
7. Courtesy of Margaret Haley Carpenter.
8. Courtesy of Margaret Haley Carpenter.
9. "The Broken Field," *Collected Poems*, p. 130.
10. All quotations from letters of Sara Teasdale to Amy Lowell, or from Amy Lowell to Sara Teasdale, are courtesy of the Houghton Library, Harvard University.
11. All quotations from letters of Sara Teasdale to Ernst Filsinger are courtesy of the Missouri Historical Society.
12. All quotations from letters of Sara Teasdale to Thomas Jones are courtesy of the Columbia University Library.
13. Quoted by Leon Edel from the preface to *Collected Poems* by A. M. F. Robinson, in *Literary Biography*, Bloomington, 1973, p. 56.
14. "Song Making," *Collected Poems*, p. 157.
15. "Wisdom." *Collected Poems*, p. 102.
16. "Barter," *Collected Poems*, p. 97.

17. "August Moonrise," *Collected Poems*, p. 119.
18. Courtesy of Margaret Haley Carpenter.
19. "Because," *Collected Poems*, p. 106.
20. "Doubt," *Collected Poems*, p. 108.
21. "The Wine," *Collected Poems*, p. 138.
22. *The Answering Voice*, New York, 1928, p. xv.
23. Courtesy of Margaret Haley Carpenter.
24. "Spray," *Collected Poems*, p. 147.
25. "To One Away," *Collected Poems*, p. 52.
26. "The Storm," *Collected Poems*, p. 155.
27. "Alone," *Collected Poems*, p. 157.
28. "The Nights Remember," *Collected Poems*, p. 134.
29. "Change," *Collected Poems*, p. 154.
30. "The Wind in the Hemlock," *Collected Poems*, p. 159.
31. *Poetry*, August 1918, p. 265.
32. Houghton Library, Harvard University.
33. "Only in Sleep," *Collected Poems*, p. 121.
34. "In a Cuban Garden," *Collected Poems*, p. 138.
35. "At Sea," *Collected Poems*, p. 151.
36. All quotations from letters of Sara Teasdale to Marguerite Wilkinson are courtesy of the Middlebury College Library.
37. "Dust," *Collected Poems*, p. 152.
38. "I Know the Stars," *Collected Poems*, p. 132.
39. "Understanding," *Collected Poems*, p. 133.
40. "Spring Torrents," *Collected Poems*, p. 132.
41. "It Is Not a Word," *Collected Poems*, p. 134.
42. "Let It Be Forgotten," *Collected Poems*, p. 135.
43. "Nightfall," *Collected Poems*, p. 133.
44. "On the Dunes," *Collected Poems*, p. 147.
45. "If Death Is Kind," *Collected Poems*, p. 148.
46. "The Long Hill," *Collected Poems*, p. 152.

47. "What Do I Care?" *Collected Poems*, p. 116.
48. "Oh You Are Coming," *Flame and Shadow*, New York, 1920, p. 33.
49. "The Sanctuary," *Collected Poems*, p. 151.
50. "Since There Is No Escape," *Flame and Shadow*, p. 67.
51. "Rhyme of November Stars," *Collected Poems*, p. 199.
52. "Compensation," *Collected Poems*, p. 125.
53. C. G. Jung, "On the Nature of the Psyche," *The Structure and Dynamics of the Psyche*, New York, 1960, p. 199.
54. "It Will Not Change," *Collected Poems*, p. 153.
55. "Gray Fog," *Collected Poems*, p. 141.
56. "White Fog," *Collected Poems*, p. 139.
57. "Sleepless Night," *Century*, 103 (March 1922), p. 711.

## CHAPTER SEVEN: "A Dream Lost Among Dreams"

1. "Leisure," *Collected Poems*, p. 181.
2. "The Solitary," *Collected Poems*, p. 179.
3. "The Crystal Gazer," *Collected Poems*, p. 179.
4. "Effigy of a Nun," *Collected Poems*, p. 172. Jean Starr Untermeyer, in *Private Collection*, pp. 59–62, gives an extended account of the episode and the text of her poem.
5. All quotations from letters of Sara Teasdale to John Gould Fletcher are courtesy of the University of Arkansas Library.
6. John Gould Fletcher, *Life Is My Song*, New York, 1937, p. 280.
7. *Ibid.*, pp. 281–283.
8. "The Mystery," *Collected Poems*, p. 127.
9. "Winter Sun (Lenox)," *Collected Poems*, p. 183.
10. Otto A. Rothert, *The Story of a Poet: The Life of Madison Cawein*, Louisville, 1921, p. 140.
11. "Never Again," *Collected Poems*, p. 189.
12. *Vanity Fair*, 19, 3 (November 1922), p. 69.
13. "It Is Not I," *Life*, 82 (November 1, 1923) p. 3.
14. "A Man Who Understood Women," *Life*, 81, (March 22, 1923).
15. "Wisdom," *Collected Poems*, p. 182.
16. "Land's End," *Collected Poems*, p. 169.
17. *Rainbow Gold*, New York, 1922, p. 6.
18. Horman Library, Wagner College, Staten Island, New York.
19. "The Old Enemy," *Collected Poems*, p. 182.
20. "Arcturus in Autumn," *Collected Poems*, p. 187.
21. "An End," *Collected Poems*, p. 187.
22. "Winter," *Collected Poems*, p. 188.
23. Marguerite Wilkinson, ed., *New Voices*, New York, 1936, pp. 199–201.
24. "Those Who Love," *Collected Poems*, p. 173.
25. Missouri Historical Society.
26. "Places," *Collected Poems*, p. 120.
27. "The Tune," *Collected Poems*, p. 190.
28. "I Could Snatch a Day," *Collected Poems*, p. 187.
29. "Autumn (Parc Monceau)," *Collected Poems*, p. 167.
30. "Fontainebleau," *Collected Poems*, p. 168.
31. Houghton Library, Harvard University.
32. "So This Was All," *Dark of the Moon*, p. 46.
33. Houghton Library, Harvard University.
34. Marcel Proust, *Remembrance of Things Past*, trans. C. K. Scott-Moncrieff, New York, 1927, v. 2, pp. 1119–1120.
35. Proust, pp. 1122–1123.
36. "On a March Day," *Collected Poems*, p. 192.
37. "Autumn on the Beaches," *Collected Poems*, p. 205.
38. "The Fountain," *Collected Poems*, p. 177.
39. Harriet Monroe Library of Modern Poetry, University of Chicago.

40. All quotations from letters of Elizabeth Lindsay to Sara Teasdale are courtesy of the Beinecke Library, Yale University.
41. "All That Was Mortal," *Collected Poems*, p. 212.

## CHAPTER EIGHT: "Let There Be Night"

1. Margaret Conklin to Anne Lundgren, July 2, 1927. Courtesy of Margaret Conklin.
2. "Age," *Collected Poems*, p. 206.
3. *The Answering Voice*, New York, 1928, pp. ix–xii.
4. "Age," *Collected Poems*, p. 206.
5. "The Kiss," *Collected Poems*, p. 28.
6. Case 30072, Second Judicial District Court of the State of Nevada, County of Washoe, August 31, 1929.
7. Eleanor Ruggles, *The West-Going Heart*, New York, 1959, pp. 414–415.
8. Columbia University Library.
9. New York Public Library.
10. "In a Darkening Garden," *Collected Poems*, p. 209.
11. "To the Sea," *Collected Poems*, p. 212.
12. "Truce," *Collected Poems*, p. 207.
13. "Wisdom," *Collected Poems*, p. 205.
14. "Ashes," *Collected Poems*, p. 210.
15. "Strange Victory," *Collected Poems*, p. 208.
16. Vachel Lindsay, *Collected Poems*, New York, 1925, p. 28.
17. "In Memory of Vachel Lindsay," *Collected Poems*, p. 210.
18. "Grace before Sleep," *Collected Poems*, p. 211.
19. "Since Death Brushed Past Me," *Collected Poems*, p. 213.
20. "Last Prelude," *Collected Poems*, p. 208.
21. "Since Death Brushed Past Me," *Collected Poems*, p. 213.

22. "Advice to a Girl," *Collected Poems*, p. 206.
23. "Return to a Country House," *Collected Poems*, p. 212.
24. "Even To-Day," *Collected Poems*, p. 207.
25. Missouri Historical Society.
26. All of the following quotations from the Rossetti Notebook and the two drafts of *Christina Rossetti: An Intimate Portrait* are from manuscripts in the Wellesley College Library and are printed with their permission.
27. *Autobiographies*, New York, 1927, p. 107. The passages quoted were marked by Sara Teasdale in her copy.
28. Yeats, p. 127.
29. Lockwood Memorial Library, State University of New York at Buffalo.
30. Berg Collection, New York Public Library.
31. "To M.," *Collected Poems*, p. 209.
32. Aline Kilmer to Jessie Rittenhouse. Rollins College Library.
33. Jessie Rittenhouse to Julia Altrocchi, February 14, 1938; quoted in Margaret Widdemer, *Jessie Rittenhouse: A Centenary Memoir-Anthology*, New York, 1969, p. 34.
34. Autopsy Report, Chief Medical Examiner, City of New York, January 30, 1933.
35. I am grateful to Dr. M. E. Aronson, Medical Examiner of the City of Philadelphia, for reviewing the final autopsy report for me. He points out that despite some ambiguities there are no natural or accidental reasons given for death, that the evidence is consistent with suicide by drugs, and that there was no on-scene investigation of details or proof of submersion and no detailed follow-up. Dr. Atchley has confirmed that Sara was not suffering from any critical problem of physical health.
36. *Poetry*, 42 (April 1933), p. 31.
37. *Saturday Review of Literature*, February 11, 1933, p. 426.
38. "Let It Be Forgotten," *Collected Poems*, p. 135.

# Index

Adams, Henry, 21–22
Aiken, Conrad, 168, 181, 219, 229
Akins, Zoë, 53–54, 84, 90, 99, 108, 123, 155
*The Answering Voice*, 156–57, 158–59, 161, 163, 167–68, 238, 243, 247, 249, 253
Atchley, Dr. Dana, 291, 292
Austin, Mary, 154

Baudelaire, Charles, 54, 63
Beach, Sylvia, 218, 264
Blake, William, 129, 291
Bogan, Louise, 263
Braithwaite, William Stanley, 151, 157, 158, 168, 200
Brontë, Emily, 2, 3, 4, 158
Brookes More Prize (1921), 207
Browning, Elizabeth Barrett, 1, 2, 4, 20, 288
Burton, Richard, 181
Bynner, Witter, 51, 66, 67, 165, 230

Cape, Jonathan, 219, 239
Cather, Willa, 67
Cawein, Madison, 64, 206
Charleston, S.C., 234
"The Chinese Nightingale," 127–28, 155
Chopin, Kate, 6
Christianity, 50, 52, 81, 204
*Collected Poems of Sara Teasdale*, 293–94
Columbia Poetry Prize, 173, 181
Conklin, Margaret, 239, 240–42, 245–48, 251, 252, 255, 256, 257, 263, 265, 277, 289, 290, 291, 292, 293
Cromwell Hall, 42, 50, 157, 164, 167, 176, 198, 204, 251, 253
Croy, Homer, 83
"The Crystal Cup," 32
Cullen, Countee, 230
Cummings, Marion. *See* Stanley, Marion Cummings
Curtis, Harriet, 238, 289

*Dark of the Moon*, 225, 233, 238, 239, 241, 242
de la Mare, Walter, 217
Dell, Floyd, 108
Dickinson, Emily, 1, 2, 3, 4, 20, 88, 288
Dreiser, Theodore, 162
Duncan, Isadora, 164
Duse, Eleonore, 24, 30, 33–34, 35, 222–23

Eastman, Max, 169, 179, 180
Eliot, T. S., 13, 16, 17, 21, 31, 152, 203, 214, 222, 235
Ernst, Lillie Rose, 21
Erskine, John, 222

Filsinger, Ernst, 124–25, 128; courtship, 135–41; background, 140–41, 142, 146, 153; career, "overwork," 161, 163, 173–74, 230–31,

232, 237, 240, 251; travels, 178–79, 185, 186, 221, 255, 259; divorce, 250, 252, 256–60; meets S. T. again, 274–76; death, 293
Firkins, Oscar, 153
*Flame and Shadow*, 195, 200, 203–4, 218, 219, 224
Fletcher, John Gould, 200, 201, 202, 219
Florida, 233–34
Forel, August, 123–24
Frost, Robert, 17, 146, 147, 152, 154, 201, 216

genteel tradition, 17
Gibson, Robert E. Lee, 55–56
Graves, Robert, 221

H. D., 180, 201
Hatfield, Stafford, 93, 95, 96, 97, 101, 102, 103, 152, 176, 182, 219–20, 236, 262
*Helen of Troy and Other Poems*, 64, 69, 73, 82, 90, 99
Hemingway, Ernest, 67, 247
Housman, A. E., 57, 69, 82, 216, 217, 289
Hovey, Richard, 19–20, 36
Hunt, Violet, 218

James, Henry, 67, 205, 235, 288, 289
Johns, Orrick, 54–55, 85, 86, 99
Jones, Thomas, 156, 290
Joyce, James, 11, 195, 218, 222, 235, 267
Jung, Carl G., 190

Kilmer, Aline, 165, 244, 263, 290

Lindsay, Elizabeth Connor, 228, 267, 268
Lindsay, Susan, 238, 293
Lindsay, Vachel, lit. relationship, 110, 115–19, 120–21; courtship, 125–26, 127–28, 129–32, 133–35, 139, 143, 150, 154; career, friendship, 140, 165, 195, 202–3, 226–28, 262, 263, 266–67, 268; breakdown, death, 276–78, 282
The Little Review, 122
Love Songs, 162, 167, 173
Lowell, Amy, 152–53, 165, 175, 179, 188–89, 194, 195, 223
*The Lyric Year* (1912), 99

MacLeod, Fiona, 18–19
Macmillan Co. (England), 218, 219
Markham, Edwin, 70, 90, 154, 194
Masefield, John, 155
Masters, Edgar Lee, 145, 147, 152, 181, 192, 201
Mencken, H. L., 75, 162
Mew, Charlotte, 218–19
Millay, Edna St. Vincent, 99, 102, 163, 202
Monroe, Harriet, 70, 102, 106, 107, 108, 110, 121, 124, 132, 151, 153, 155, 175, 179, 229, 269, 278, 294
Moore, Marianne, 16

302